The Forgotten Books of Eden

Published By Timothy Green Beckley
Edited By William Kern

THE FORGOTTEN BOOKS OF EDEN
Published by Timothy Green Beckley
Edited by William Kern
This edition Copyright 2014
by Global Communications/Conspiracy Journal

All rights reserved. No part of these manuscripts may be copied or reproduced by any mechanical or digital methods and no exerpts or quotes may be used in any other book or manuscript without permission in writing by the Publisher, Global Communications/Conspiracy Journal, except by a reviewer who may quote brief passages in a review. This text is in the public domain in the US because its copyright was not renewed in a timely fashion.

Revised Edition

Published in the United States of America By
Global Communications/Conspiracy Journal
Box 753 · New Brunswick, NJ 08903

Staff Members
Timothy G. Beckley, Publisher
Carol Ann Rodriguez, Assistant to the Publisher
Sean Casteel, General Associate Editor
Tim R. Swartz, Graphics and Editorial Consultant
William Kern, Editorial and Art Consultant

Sign Up On The Web For Our Free Weekly Newsletter
and Mail Order Version of Conspiracy Journal
and Bizarre Bazaar
www.ConspiracyJournal.com
PayPal: MrUFO8@hotmail.com
Order Hot Line: 1-732-602-3407

THE ORDER OF ALL THE VOLUMES

OF

THE FORGOTTEN BOOKS OF EDEN

The First Book of Adam and Eve

The Second Book of Adam and Eve

The Secrets of Enoch

The Psalms of Solomon

The Odes of Solomon

The Letter of Aristeas

The Fourth Book of Maccabees

The Story of Ahikar

The Testament of Reuben

Simeon

Levi

Judah

Issachar

Zebulun

Dan

Naphtali

Gad

Asher

Joseph

Benjamin

PREFACE

TODAY the medley of outward life has made a perplexity of inward life. We moderns have ruffled our old incertitudes to an absurd point—incertitudes that are older than theology.

Not without justification have priests mounted altars for generations and cried, "Oh my soul, why dost thou trouble me?"

We are active, restless both in body and mind. Curiosity has replaced blind faith. We go groping, peering, searching, scornful of dogmas, back, further back to sources. And just as the physicist thrills at the universes he discovers as he works inward in the quest of his electrons, so the average man exults in his apprehension of fundamentals of psychology. New cults spring up, attesting to the Truth—as they see it—countless fleets of Theism, Buchmanism, Theosophy, Bahai'ism, etc., sail under brightly colored flags; and Atheism is flaunting itself on the horizon.

The passengers have turned pilots. Everyman is thinking for himself.

The findings here—in this strange volume—bring the reader into a large inland sea, cut off from the traffic and the tempest that have sprung up in the West; and untouched by the crosscurrents of dogmas and presumptions that have cluttered historic centuries. Here is virgin water that gushes, troubled by abysmal forces only, out of the very earth itself.

Whence are these writings—these emotions—these profound pages of wisdom? You might as well inquire, whence is human nature? The fact is—they are. It isn't as though you can compare this literature with any other, as you might compare the French Romanticists with the Russian school. If you do so, this man may say it is too fantastic; that man, it is too coarse; the other man, it is too "out of date"! And they straightway lose all sight of the fact that it is simply fundamental.

To be sure scholars will argue, and inquire. They would find the exact history; the shape of this or that Greek stem; they would set the opinion of this erudite authority against the opinion of that. It is right that they, as scholars, should do so. It is right that the average man who is not a scholar should also do so-if he wants to; and should not have to do so, if he does not want to.

It is, however, only just to pay a tribute to scholarship which has preceded and made possible this book. The publishers are indispensably indebted to ***The Apocrypha and Pseudepigrapha*** edited by R. H. Charles, D. Litt., D. D.; ***The Odes and Psalms of Solomon*** by Dr. Rendel Harris; ***The Book of Adam and Eve*** by the Rev. S. C. Malan, D. D., published in England in 1882.

* * * *

It is appropriate to leave this book in your hands with the invocation of San Peladan, which Conrad has translated for us. San Pelandan believed in astrology, spirits of the air, elves, nymphs and everything that is deliciously fantastic. However, he did say:

"O Nature, indulgent Mother, forgive! Open your arms to the son, prodigal and weary.

"I have attempted to tear asunder the veil you have hung to conceal from us the pain of life, and I have been wounded by the mystery. . . . Oedipus, half way to finding the word of the enigma, young Faust, regretting already the simple life, the life of the heart, I come back to you repentant, reconciled, O gentle deceiver!"

INTRODUCTION TO

THE FORGOTTEN BOOKS OF EDEN

By WILLIAM N. GUTHRIE, D.D.

Rector of St. Mark's-in-the-Bouwerie.

AN American Indian's Song is his very own. No other man can sing it without his explicit permission. It is impregnate with his aura. It is not in our sense, however, property. It is believed to invest magically the singer with the mood whence it proceeded, and must, therefore, merge in some way the performer's identity with that of the originator's. To sing another's song is an invasion of his personality, a sort of spiritual piracy involving sacrilege.

When last year in Arcady and Andritzena, I induced primitive shepherds to sing and play for me lustily all sorts of occasional songs and rituals, they refused to do a burial chant, most positively. For to perform one would surely cause a death in the house.

A little reflection on these two paragraphs may perhaps, make the reader realize that authorship was once a thing of great hazards. If one had something great and new to say, and wanted it to circulate widely, one would naturally prefer anonymity.

Indeed, by the Hebrews a story was popularly presumed to have its hero for its author. Moses wrote the account of his own death. Deuteronomy was of course, his own work, although obviously intended to alter the traditional religion. Jonah wrote the little novel about himself. David was the author of the Psalms because reported to have instituted the first temple choir, and as a lad to have played the harp soothing the nerves of King Saul. When an author for the book of Job was wanted, though the whole discussion of the work proves it was written to refute the Wisdom literature which by tradition began with the Proverbs of Solomon, Moses was chosen as a suitable author!

So for centuries among the Jews, writers sought to shelter themselves behind the names of the great dead. In this they were guilty of no fraud. They imagined what Solomon or Enoch would say, or sing, upon a particular theme under given circumstances. It was not really they themselves, but their Solomon, their Enoch, Solomon or Enoch in them, who uttered the new prophesies or temple praises.

Thus arose that body of literature, called by modern scholars, "Pseudepigrapha," that is, writings erroneously, unhistorically, and yet sincerely, ascribed to heroic figures summed from the vasty deep by a self-denying imagination, eager to alter man's belief and custom, to interpret his hope and sorrow, without personal gain or fame, and also, may one add, without the deterrent of persecution to arrest free utterance!

Now it is a foolish modern prejudice against an ancient piece of literature that its author veiled his person in this fashion. The only question is: Was the writing of inherent value? Did it exercise influence?

It is not too much to say that no modern can intelligently understand the New Testament, unless he is acquainted with the so-called "Apocrypha," and with the "Pseudepigrapha" as well. The very words of Jesus were in many instances, suggested by sayings current in his day, more or less as unconscious quotations from the Testaments of the 12 Patriarchs.

The figure of the Messiah which Jesus adapted to his creative purpose, cannot be imagined by a modern without a perusal of the book of Enoch which is its classic and most entrancing glorification. Without the Odes and Songs of Solomon the atmosphere breathed by the earliest church cannot be divined.

Hitherto access to this literature has been confined to technical scholars. Its assembly would require special information and considerable expenditure. With this enterprise of the Alpha House, Inc., it becomes democratic property. We shall have a more intelligent clergy and laity, when this volume has taken its place in every library, and is familiarly brought into every discussion of the historic Christ and of His times.

THE FIRST BOOK OF ADAM AND EVE

ALSO CALLED

THE CONFLICT OF ADAM AND EVE WITH SATAN.

PRESENT day controversy that rages around the authenticity of the Scriptures and how human life began on this planet must pause to consider the Adam and Eve story. Where does it come from? What does it mean?

The familiar version in Genesis is not the source of this fundamental legend, it is not a spontaneous, Heaven-born account that sprang into place in the Old Testament. It is simply a version, unexcelled perhaps, but a version of a myth or belief or account handed down by word of mouth from generation to generation of mankind-through the incoherent, unrecorded ages of man it came—like an inextinguishable ray of light that ties the time when human life began, with the time when the human mind could express itself and the human hand could write.

This is the most ancient story in the world—it has survived because it embodies the basic fact of human life. A fact that has not changed one iota; amid all the superficial changes of civilization's vivid array, this fact remains: the conflict of Good and Evil; the fight between Man and the Devil; the eternal struggle of human nature against sin,

That the Adam and Eve story pervaded the thoughts of ancient writers is seen in the large number of versions that exist, or whose existence may be traced, through the writings of Greeks, Syrians, Egyptians, Abyssinians, Hebrews, and other ancient peoples. As a lawyer might say who examines so much apparently unrelated evidence—there must be something back of it.

The version which we give here is the work of unknown Egyptians (the lack of historical allusion makes it impossible to date the writing). Parts of this version are found in the Talmud, the Koran, and elsewhere, showing what a vital role it played in the original literature of human wisdom. The Egyptian author first wrote in Arabic (which may be taken as the original manuscript) and that found its way farther south and was translated into Ethiopic. For the present English translation we are indebted to Dr. S. C. Malan, Vicar of Broadwindsor, who worked from the Ethiopic edition edited by Dr. E. Trumpp, Professor at the University of Munich. Dr. Trumpp had the advantage of the Arabic original, which makes our bridge over the gap of many centuries a direct one.

The reading of these books is an adventure. You will find the mind of man fed by the passions, hopes, fears of new and strange earthly existence rioting, unrestrained, in the zest of self-expression. You roam in the realms of mythology where swiftly the aspects of nature assume manifold personalities, and the amorphous instinct of sin takes on the grotesqueries of a visible devil.

From such imaginative surroundings you find yourself suddenly staring at commonplace unvarnished events of family life—and such a family as "the first earthly family" was! They had all the troubles, all the petty disagreements, and the taking sides with one another, and the bother moving, and "staying with the baby," that in the total mark family life to-day. You will see it when you peep beneath the overlaying glamour of tradition.

One critic has said of this writing:

"This is, we believe, the greatest literary discovery that the world has known. Its effect upon contemporary thought in molding the judgment of the future generations is of incalculable value.

"The treasures of Tut-ank-Amen's Tomb were no more precious to the Egyptologist than are these literary treasures to the world of scholarship."

But we prefer to let the reader make his own exploration and form his own opinion. The writing is arresting enough to inspire very original thoughts concerning it,

In general, this account begins where the Genesis story of Adam and Eve leaves off. Thus the two can not well be compared; here we have a new CHAPTER—a sort of sequel to the other. Here is the story of the twin sisters of Cain and Abel, and it is notable that here the blame for the first murder is placed squarely at the door of a difference over Woman.

The plan of these books is as follows:—

Book I. The careers of Adam and Eve, from the day they left Eden; their dwelling in the Cave of Treasures; their trials and temptations; Satan's manifold apparitions to them. The birth of Cain, of Abel, and of their twin sisters; Cain's love for his own twin sister, Luluwa, whom Adam and Eve wished to join to Abel; the details of Cain's murder of his brother; and Adam's sorrow and death.

Book II. The history of the patriarchs who lived before the Flood; the dwelling of the children of Seth on the Holy Mountain—Mount Hermon—until they were lured by Henun and by the daughters of Cain to come down from the mountain. Cain's death, when slain by Lamech the blind; and the lives of other patriarchs until the birth of Noah.

EDITOR'S PRELUDE

Religions have always stood in opposition to science. Copernicus – Mendel –Darwin – blasphemy! The first human quest for knowledge was severely punished by marching Adam and his sinful common-law wife out of heaven. The whole idea of religion is based on unconditional belief and not on tangible proof. Thus the very probing of science to break through the "cloud of unknowing" was a threatening and therefore sinful act. Why? Why would it be a disaster to get a little closer to the knowledge of how it all works? Curiously enough, most religions operate under a similar belief system of sequestering God from human eyes and the desire to know and understand. In both Islamic and Judaic traditions, it is unthinkable to paint or to have any kind of representation of divinity; so much so that in the Hebrew language, one cannot even say the word "God". In this case, the very act of uttering the word is criminal.

Catholics are simply appalled by the limits of human disbelief. The position of the church is: "Why do you need proof?" Well, fortunately or not, the human being is designed with a yearning need for knowledge. Any of us who have been exposed to children know how many times they repeat the question "Why?" and how many times we are unable to give an answer. For instance, even the 'simplest' one of all, "Why are we here?"

If we look at the biblical tale of Adam and Eve, it follows that the human being was designed to want to know. And even if he/she was too ignorant to ask, then he/she was insistently given hints – "Have all you want but don't go near that tree!" Well, we did taste the apple, and so now we are faced with such moral questions as "Is it ethical to make a human clone?" Personally, I don't take any sides, but simply think that it is unavoidable – just as it was unavoidable for Adam or Eve to taste from the *forbidden fruit*. (Just in case they didn't get the point, God let his former employee remind Adam and Eve again and again about it, even if only by naming him a "fallen angel.")

Recently I was watching a documentary which definitely had some moral undertones toward the side of "do not". It was pretty much a traditional argument. However, at the very end, they interviewed a priest who declared with trepidation and fear in his eyes that scientists are discussing the use of a drop of blood found on the Shroud of Turin (you might guess whose DNA we are talking about) for their evil experiments with cloning. *An unthinkable, shocking proposition – to clone Christ!*

An unrelated fact is that the insistence of the return of the prophet suddenly becomes dangerous. We together as a society at large are expecting: Christ, Messiah, Mohammed, and a number of other prophets. Most religions believe that this would signify the end of the world; the small detail they don't agree on is who will be saved. Jews believe they will be the ones, Christians would feel quite the opposite – so, nobody wants to share the pie.

Here is the main point. Assuming that it is Christ's blood on the Shroud of Turin, the cloning, then, *is* the Second Coming. This would explain the subconscious fear carried out by religious dogma against science. The choice is clear – you either believe and you'll live or you know and you'll die.

But, perhaps the **greater** fear in the church is that science might clone Jesus and still nothing untoward would happen. What, then, becomes of the words of disaster in their mouths?

I am sure one can study the signs mentioned in the holy texts that are supposed to warn us about the second coming and apply them to contemporary life. Things like "Watch out for a red beast." What is interesting is that we have been told to behave, and if we don't, we should expect the return of the savior [the final and fatal visit]. We were warned once, at which time Christ took the suffering upon himself. However, according to the scripture, we should not be forgiven twice. When one thinks of the second coming, one imagines the story repeating itself with miraculous things like "the Annunciation" and all the rest of the attributes. But we don't expect that it is we ourselves who would make it happen (not through an Immaculate Conception but by the scientific method and laboratory experiment).

By the way, this gives a new perspective to the creation of Eve (cloned from Adam's rib) and to the Divine Birth itself. Mystic ideas such as "how do you remain a virgin after conceiving a child" can then be solved.

True, we do suspect that even if the clone were genetically identical to its original, the character of the person would still be different, since it would be conditioned by the environment. Therefore, we do not know if Christ will be as we know him or as an Other-Christ. By any chance, if the drop of blood does not belong to God's son but to the cunning, ingenious artist, then the meaning of eternalization by a work of art will definitely be seen in a new light. And how well deserved would be the rebirth of that artist!

Intelligent readers can scarcely fail to find a striking discrepancy between the two accounts of the creation of man recorded in the first and second chapters of Genesis (to say nothing of the ***Lost and Forgotten Books*** that follow). In the first chapter of Genesis, we read how, on the fifth day of creation, God created the fishes and the birds, all the creatures that live in the water or in the air; and how on the sixth day he created all terrestrial animals, and last of all man, whom he fashioned in his own image, both male and female. From this narrative we infer that man was the last to be created of all living beings on earth, and incidentally we gather that the distinction of the sexes, which is characteristic of humanity, is shared also by the divinity; though how the distinction can be reconciled with the unity of the Godhead is a point on which the authors of Genesis offer no information.

Passing by this theological problem, as perhaps too deep for human comprehension, we turn to the simpler question of chronology and take note of the statements that God created the lower animals first and human beings afterwards, and that the human beings consisted of a man and a woman, produced, from all indications, simultaneously, and each of them reflecting in equal measure the glory of their divine parent. So it is in the first chapter. But when we proceed to examine the second chapter, it is somewhat disconcerting to discover a totally different and extraordinarily contradictory account of the same momentous event. For here we learn with surprise that God created man first, the lower animals next, and woman last of all, fashioning her as a mere afterthought out of a rib which was excised from the man while he slept. The order of merit in the two narratives is clearly reversed. In the first narrative the deity begins with fishes and works steadily up through birds and beasts to man and woman. In the second narrative he begins with man and works downwards through the lower animals to woman, who apparently marks the lowest point of the divine workmanship. And in this second version nothing at all is said about man and woman being made in the image of God. We are simply told that "the Lord God formed man of the dust of the ground, and breathed into his nostrils the breath of life; and man became a living soul." Afterwards, to relieve the loneliness of the man, who wandered vagrantly about without a living companion in the beautiful garden which had been created for him, God fashioned all the birds and beasts and brought them to man, apparently to amuse him and keep him company. Man looked at them and gave to them all their names; but still he was not content with these playthings, so at last, as if in despair, God created woman out of an insignificant portion of the masculine frame, introduced her to man and claimed that she was to be his wife.

The flagrant contradiction between the two accounts is explained very simply by the circumstance that they are derived from two different and originally independent documents which were afterwards combined into a single book by an editor, who pieced the two narratives together without taking pains to soften or harmonize their discrepancies. The account of the creation in the first chapter is derived from what is called the Priestly Document, which was composed by priestly writers during or after the Babylonian captivity. The account of the creation of man and the animals in the second chapter is derived from what is called the Jehovistic Document, which was written several hundred years before the other, probably in the ninth or eighth century before our era.

The difference between the religious standpoints of the two writers is clear. The later or priestly writer conceives God in an abstract form as withdrawn from human sight, and creating all things by a simple fiat. The earlier or Jehovistic writer conceives God in a very concrete form as acting and speaking like a man, modeling a human being out of clay, planting a garden, walking in it at the cool of the day, calling to the man and woman to come out from among the trees behind which they had hidden themselves, and making coats of skin to replace the scanty fig-leaves with which our embarrassed first parents sought to conceal their nakedness.

The charming naiveté, almost the gaiety, of the earlier narrative contrasts with the dark seriousness of the later; though we cannot but be struck by a theme of sadness and pessimism running under the brightly colored picture of life in the age of innocence, which the great Jehovistic artist has painted for us. Above all, he hardly attempts to hide his deep disdain for woman. The lateness of her creation, and the irregular and undignified manner of it—made out of a piece of her lord and master, after all the lower animals had been created in a regular and perfectly decent manner—sufficiently mark the low opinion he held of her nature; and in the sequel his hatred of and contempt for women, as we may safely describe it, takes a still darker tone, when he ascribes all the misfortunes and sorrows of humanity to the credulous folly and unbridled innocence of its first mother.

Of the two narratives, the earlier Jehovistic is not only the more picturesque but also the richer in folklore, retaining many features suggestive of primitive simplicity which have been carefully abridged by the later writer. Accordingly, it offers more points of comparison with the childlike ghost stories by which men in many ages and countries have sought to explain the great mystery of the beginning of life on earth.

The Jehovistic writer seems to have imagined that God moulded the first man out of clay, just as a potter might, or as a child moulds a doll of mud; and that having parallels, kneaded and patted the clay into the proper shape, the deity animated it by breathing into the mouth and nostrils of the figure, exactly as the prophet Elisha is said to have restored to life the dead child of the Shunammite by lying on him, and putting his eyes to the child's eyes and his mouth to the child's mouth, no doubt to impart his breath to the corpse; after which the child sneezed seven times and opened its eyes. To the Hebrews this derivation of our species from the dust of the ground suggested itself all the more naturally because, in their language, the word for "ground" (adamah) is in feminine form the word for "man" (adam).

From various allusions in Babylonian literature it would seem that the they also conceived man to have been moulded from clay. According to Berosus, the Babylonian priest, whose account of creation has been preserved in a Greek version, the god Bel cut off his own head, and the other gods caught the flowing blood, mixed it with earth, and fashioned men from the bloody paste; and that, they said, is why men are so wise—because their mortal clay is tempered with divine DNA.

In Egyptian mythology Khnoumou, the Father of the Gods, is said to have moulded men out of clay on his potter's wheel. So in Greek legend the sage Prometheus is said to have moulded the first men out of clay at Panopeus in Phocis. When he had done his work, some of the clay was left over, and might be seen on the spot long afterwards in the shape of two large boulders lying at the edge of a ravine. A Greek traveler, who visited the place in the second century of our era, thought that the boulders had the color of clay, and that they smelt strongly of human flesh. I, too, visited the spot some seventeen hundred and fifty years later. It is a forlorn little glen, on the southern side of the hill of Panopeus, below the long line of ruined but still stately walls and towers which crowns the gray rocks of the summit. It was a hot day in late autumn—the first of November—and after the long arid summer of Greece the little glen was quite dry; no water trickled down its bushy sides, but in the bottom I found a reddish crumbling earth, perhaps a relic of the clay out of which Prometheus modeled our first parents. The place was solitary and deserted: not a human being, not a sign of human habitation was to be seen; only the line of moldering towers and battlements on the hill above spoke of the busy life that had long passed away.

The entire scene, like so many others in Greece, was fitted to impress the mind with a sense of the impermanence of man's little bustling existence on earth compared with the lasting quality and, at least, the outward peace and tranquility of nature. The impression was deepened when I rested, in the heat of the day, on the summit of the hill under the shade of some fine holly-oaks, and surveyed the distant prospect, rich in memories of the past, while the sweet perfume of the wild thyme scented all the air. To the south the finely cut peak of Helicon peered over the low intervening ridges. In the west loomed the mighty mass of Parnassus, its middle slopes darkened by pine woods like shadows of clouds brooding on the mountain side; while at its skirts nestled the ivy-mantled walls of Daulis overhanging the deep glen, whose romantic beauty accords so well with the loves and sorrows of Procne and Philomela, which Greek legend associated with the spot.

Northwards, across the broad plain to which the steep bare hill of Panopeus descends, the eye rested on the gap in the hills through which the Cephissus winds his tortuous way to flow under grey willows, at the foot of barren stony hills, till his turbid waters lose themselves, no longer in the vast reedy swamps of the now vanished Copaic Lake, but in a dark cavern of the limestone rock. Eastward, clinging to the slopes of the bleak range of which the hill of Panopeus forms part, were the ruins of Chaeronea, the birthplace of Plutarch; and out there in the plain raged the fatal engagement which laid Greece at the feet of Macedonia.

There, too, in a later age, East and West met in deadly conflict, when the Roman armies under Sulla defeated the Asiatic hosts of Mithridates. Such was the landscape spread out before me on one of those farewell autumn days of almost pathetic splendor, when the departing summer seems to linger fondly, as if loath to resign to winter the enchanted mountains of Greece.

Next day the scene had changed: summer was gone. A grey November mist hung low on the hills which only yesterday had shone splendidly in the sun, and under its melancholy curtain the dead flat of the Chaeronea plain, a wide, treeless expanse shut in by desolate slopes, wore an aspect of chilly sadness befitting the battlefield where a nation's freedom was lost.

We cannot doubt that such rude conceptions of the origin of mankind, common to Greeks, Hebrews, Babylonians, and Egyptians, were handed down to the civilized peoples of antiquity by their savage or barbarous forebears. Certainly stories of the same sort have been recorded among savages and barbarians for untold centuries.

Thus the Australian blacks near Melbourne said that Pund-jel, the Creator, cut three large sheets of bark with his big knife. On one of these he placed some clay and worked it up with his knife into a proper consistence. He then laid a portion of the clay on one of the other pieces of bark and shaped it into a human form; first he made the feet, then the legs, then the trunk, the arms, and the head. Thus he made a clay man on each of the two pieces of bark; and being well pleased with his handiwork, he danced round them for joy. Next he took stringy bark from the eucalyptus tree, made hair of it, and stuck it on the heads of his clay men. Then he looked at them again, was pleased with his work, and again danced round them for joy. He then lay down on them, blew his breath hard into their mouths, their noses, and their navels; and presently they stirred, spoke, and rose up fully grown men.

The Maoris of New Zealand say that a certain god, variously named Tu, Tiki, and Tane, took red riverside clay, kneaded it with his own blood into a likeness or image of himself, with eyes, legs, arms, and all complete, in fact, an exact copy of the deity; and having perfected the model, animated it by breathing into its mouth and nostrils, whereupon the clay effigy came to life and sneezed. "Of all these things," said a Maori, in relating the story of man's creation, "the most important is the fact that the clay sneezed, forasmuch as that sign of the power of the gods remains with us even to this day in order that we may be reminded of the great work Tu accomplished on the altar of the Kauhanga-nui, and hence it is that when men sneeze the words of Tu are repeated by those who are present;" for they say, "Sneeze, O spirit of life." So like himself was the man whom the Maori Creator Tiki fashioned that he called him Tiki-ahua; that is, Tiki's likeness.

It must be admitted that language is a weak and inadequate vehicle even for the expression of our usual understanding of things, to say nothing of those moments when the understanding unexpectedly expands and becomes deeper, and we see revealed an entire panoply of facts and relations for the description of which we have neither words nor expressions. But quite aside from this, in ordinary conditions of thinking and feeling, we are frequently at a loss for words, and we use one word at different times to describe different events or objects. The thoughts and words might all be considered correct or, on the other hand, when examined in the light of new understanding, might be, not only misleading, but completely wrong.

And so it was for the authors of **The Forgotten Books Of Eden** and **The Lost Books Of The Bible.**

William Kern; Editor

The perfect life in the Garden before the Temptation

The Forgotten Books of Eden

BOOK I.

CHAPTER I.

The crystal sea. God commands Adam, expelled from Eden, to dwell in the Cave of Treasures.

ON the third day, God planted the garden in the east of the earth, on the border of the world eastward, beyond which, towards the sun-rising, one finds nothing but water, that encompasses the whole world, and reaches unto the borders of heaven.

And to the north of the garden there is a sea of wafer, clear and pure to the taste, like unto nothing else; so that, through the clearness thereof, one may look into the depths of the earth.

And when a man washes himself in it, becomes clean of the cleanness thereof, and white of its whiteness—even if he were dark.

And God created that sea of His own good pleasure, for He knew what would come of the man He should make; so that after he had left the garden, on account of his transgression, men should be born in the earth, from among whom righteous ones should die, whose souls God would raise at the last day; when they should return to their flesh; should bathe in the water of that sea, and all of them repent of their sins.

But when God made Adam go out of the garden, He did not place him on the border of it northward, lest he should draw near to the sea of water, and he and Eve wash themselves in it, be cleansed from their sins, forget the transgression they had committed, and he no longer reminded of it in the thought of their punishment.

Then, again, as to the southern side of the garden, God was not pleased to let Adam dwell there; because, when the wind blew from the north, it would bring him, on that southern side, the delicious smell of the trees of the garden.

Wherefore God did not put Adam there, lest he should smell the sweet smell of those trees forget his transgression, and find consolation for what he had done, take delight in the smell of the trees, and not be cleansed from his transgression.

Again, also, because God is merciful and of great pity, and governs all things in a way He alone knows—He made our father Adam dwell in the western border of the garden, because on that side the earth is very broad.

The Forgotten Books of Eden

And God commanded him to dwell there in a cave in a rock—the Cave of Treasures below the garden.

CHAPTER II.

Adam and Eve faint upon leaving the Garden. God sends His word to encourage them.

BUT when our father Adam, and Eve, went out of the garden, they trod the ground on their feet, not knowing they were treading.

And when they came to the opening of the gate of the garden, and saw the broad earth spread before them, covered with stones large and small, and with sand, they feared and trembled, and fell on their faces, from the fear that came upon them; and they were as dead.

Because—whereas they had hitherto been in the garden-land, beautifully planted with all manner of trees—they now saw themselves, in a strange land, which they knew not, and had never seen.

And because at that time they were filled with the grace of a bright nature, and they had not hearts turned towards earthly things.

Therefore had God pity on them; and when He saw them fallen before the gate of the garden, He sent His Word unto father Adam and Eve, and raised them from their fallen state.

CHAPTER III.

Concerning the promise of the great five days and a half.

GOD said to Adam, "I have ordained on this earth days and years, and thou and thy seed shall dwell and walk in it, until the days and years are fulfilled; when I shall send the Word that created thee, and against which thou hast transgressed, the Word that made thee come out of the garden and that raised thee when thou wast fallen.

Yea, the Word that will again save thee when the five days and a half are fulfilled."

But when Adam heard these words from God, and of the great five days and a half, he did not understand the meaning of them.

For Adam was thinking that there would be but five days and a half for him, to the end of the world.

And Adam wept, and prayed God to explain it to him.

Then God in His mercy for Adam who was made after His own image and similitude, explained to him, that these were 5,000 and 500 years; and how One would then come and save him and his seed.

But God had before that made this covenant with our father, Adam, in the same terms, ere he came out of the garden, when he was by the tree whereof Eve took the fruit and gave it him to eat.

The Forgotten Books of Eden

Inasmuch as when our father Adam came out of the garden, he passed by that tree, and saw how God had then changed the appearance of it into another form, and how it withered.

And as Adam went to it he feared, trembled and fell down; but God in His mercy lifted him up, and then made this covenant with him.

And, again, when Adam was by the gate of the garden, and saw the cherub with a sword of flashing fire in his hand, and the cherub grew angry and frowned at him, both Adam and Eve became afraid of him, and thought he meant to put them to death. So they fell on their faces, and trembled with fear.

But he had pity on them, and showed them mercy; and turning from them went up to heaven, and prayed unto the Lord, and said:—

"Lord, Thou didst send me to watch at the gate of the garden, with a sword of fire.

"But when Thy servants, Adam and Eve, saw me, they fell on their faces, and were as dead. O my Lord, what shall we do to Thy servants?"

Then God had pity on them, and showed them mercy, and sent His Angel to keep the garden.

And the Word of the Lord came unto Adam and Eve, and raised them up.

And the Lord said to Adam, "I told thee that at the end of five days and a half, I will send my Word and save thee.

"Strengthen thy heart, therefore, and abide in the Cave of Treasures, of which I have before spoken to thee."

And when Adam heard this Word from God, he was comforted with that which God had told him. For He had told him how He would save him.

CHAPTER IV.

Adam laments the changed conditions. Adam and Eve enter the Cave of Treasures.

BUT Adam and Eve wept for having come out of the garden, their first abode.

And, indeed, when Adam looked at his flesh, that was altered, he wept bitterly, he and Eve, over what they had done. And they walked and went gently down into the Cave of Treasures.

And as they came to it Adam wept over himself and said to Eve, "Look at this cave that is to be our prison in this world, and a place of punishment!

"What is it compared with the garden? What is its narrowness compared with the space of the other?

"What is this rock, by the side of those groves? What is the gloom of this cavern, compared with the light of the garden?

The Forgotten Books of Eden

"What is this overhansing ledge of rock to shelter us, compared with the mercy of the Lord that overshadowed us?

"What is the soil of this cave compared with the garden-land? This earth, strewed with stones; and that, planted with delicious fruit-trees?"

And Adam said to Eve, "Look at thine eyes, and at mine, which afore beheld angels in heaven, praising; and they, too, without ceasing.

"But now we do not see as we did: our eyes have become of flesh; they cannot see in like manner as they saw before."

Adam said again to Eve, "What is our body to-day, compared to what it was in former days, when we dwelt in the garden?"

After this Adam did not like to enter the cave, under the overhansing rock; nor would he ever have entered it.

But he bowed to God's orders; and said to himself, "Unless I enter the cave, I shall again be a transgressor."

CHAPTER V.

In which Eve makes a noble and emotionable intercession, taking the blame on herself.

THEN Adam and Eve entered the cave, and stood praying, in their own tongue, unknown to us, but which they knew well.

And as they prayed, Adam raised his eyes, and saw the rock and the roof of the cave that covered him overhead, so that he could see neither heaven, nor God's creatures. So he wept and smote heavily upon his breast, until he dropped, and was as dead.

And Eve sat weeping; for she believed he was dead.

Then she arose, spread her hands towards God, suing Him for mercy and pity, and said, "O God, forgive me my sin, the sin which I committed, and remember it not against me.

"For I alone caused Thy servant to fall from the garden into this lost estate; from light into this darkness; and from the abode of joy into this prison.

"O God, look upon this Thy servant thus fallen, and raise him from his death, that he may weep and repent of his transgression which he committed through me.

"Take not away his soul this once; but let him live that he may stand after the measure of his repentance, and do Thy will, as before his death.

"But if Thou do not raise him up, then, O God, take away my own soul, that I be like him; and leave me not in this dungeon, one and alone; for I could not stand alone in this world, but with him only.

"For Thou, O God, didst cause a slumber to come upon him, and didst take a bone

The Forgotten Books of Eden

from his side, and didst restore the flesh in the place of it, by Thy divine power.

"And Thou didst take me, the bone, and make me a woman, bright like him, with heart, reason, and speech; and in flesh, like unto his own; and Thou didst make me after the likeness of his countenance, by Thy mercy and power.

"O Lord, I and he are one and Thou, O God, art our Creator, Thou are He who made us both in one day.

"Therefore, O God, give him life, that he may be with me in this strange land, while we dwell in it on account of our transgression.

"But if Thou wilt not give him life, then take me, even me, like him; that we both may die the same day."

And Eve wept bitterly, and fell upon our father Adam; from her great sorrow.

CHAPTER VI.

God's admonition to Adam and Eve in which he points out how and why they sinned.

BUT God looked upon them; for they had killed themselves through great grief.

But He would raise them and comfort them.

He, therefore, sent His Word unto them; that they should stand and be raised forthwith.

And the Lord said unto Adam and Eve, "You transgressed of your own free will, until you came out of the garden in which I had placed you.

"Of your own free will have you transgressed through your desire for divinity, greatness, and an exalted state, such as I have; so that I deprived you of the bright nature in which you then were, and I made you come out of the garden to this land, rough and full of trouble.

"If only you had not transgressed My commandment and had kept My law, and had not eaten of the fruit of the tree, near which I told you not to come! And there were fruit trees in the garden better than that one.

"But the wicked Satan who continued not in his first estate, nor kept his faith; in whom was no good intent towards Me, and who though I had created him, yet set Me at naught, and sought the Godhead, so that I hurled him down from heaven,—he it is who made the tree appear pleasant in your eyes, until you ate of it, by hearkening to him.

"Thus have you transgressed My commandment, and therefore have I brought upon you all these sorrows.

"For I am God the Creator, who, when I created My creatures, did not intend to destroy them. But after they had sorely roused My anger, I punished them with grievous plagues, until they repent.

The Forgotten Books of Eden

"But, if on the contrary, they still continue hardened in their transgression, they shall be under a curse for ever."

CHAPTER VII.

The beasts are reconciled.

WHEN Adam and Eve heard these words from God, they wept and sobbed yet more; but they strengthened their hearts in God, because they now felt that the Lord was to them like a father and a mother; and for this very reason, they wept before Him, and sought mercy from Him.

Then God had pity on them, and said: "O Adam, I have made My covenant with thee, and I will not turn from it; neither will I let thee return to the garden, until My covenant of the great five days and a half is fulfilled."

Then Adam said unto God, "O Lord, Thou didst create us, and make us fit to be in the garden; and before I transgressed, Thou madest all beasts come to me, that I should name them.

"Thy grace was then on me; and I named every one according to Thy mind; and Thou madest them all subject unto me.

"But now, O Lord God, that I have transgressed Thy commandment, all beasts will rise against me and will devour me, and Eve Thy handmaid; and will cut off our life from the face of the earth.

"I therefore beseech Thee, O God, that, since Thou hast made us come out of the garden, and hast made us be in a strange land, Thou wilt not let the beasts hurt us."

When the Lord heard these words from Adam, He had pity on him, and felt that he had truly said that the beasts of the field would rise and devour him and Eve, because He, the Lord, was angry with them two on account of their transgression.

Then God commanded the beasts, and the birds, and all that moves upon the earth, to come to Adam and to be familiar with him, and not to trouble him and Eve; nor yet any of the good and righteous among their posterity.

Then the beasts did obeisance to Adam, according to the commandment of God; except the serpent, against which God was wroth. It did not come to Adam, with the beasts.

CHAPTER VIII.

The "Bright Nature" of man is taken away.

THEN Adam wept and said, "O God, when we dwelt in the garden, and our hearts were lifted up, we saw the angels that sang praises in heaven, but now we do not see as we were used to do; nay, when we entered the cave, all creation became hidden from us."

Then God the Lord said unto Adam, "When thou wast under subjection to Me, thou hadst a bright nature within thee, and for that reason couldst thou see things afar off. But after thy transgression thy bright nature was withdrawn from thee; and it was not left to thee to see things afar off, but only near at hand; after the ability of the flesh; for it is brutish."

When Adam and Eve had heard these words from God, they went their way; praising and worshipping Him with a sorrowful heart.

And God ceased to commune with them.

CHAPTER IX.

Water from the Tree of Life. Adam and Eve near drowning.

THEN Adam and Eve came out of the Cave of Treasures, and drew near to the garden gate, and there they stood to look at it, and wept for having come away from it.

And Adam and Eve went from before the gate of the garden to the southern side of it, and found there the water that watered the garden, from the root of the Tree of Life, and that parted itself from thence into four rivers over the earth.

Then they came and drew near to that water, and looked at it; and saw that it was the water that came forth from under the root of the Tree of Life in the garden.

And Adam wept and wailed, and smote upon his breast, for being severed from the garden; and said to Eve:—

"Why hast thou brought upon me, upon thyself, and upon our seed, so many of these plagues and punishments?"

And Eve said unto him, "What is it thou hast seen, to weep and to speak to me in this wise?"

And he said to Eve, "Seest thou not this water that was with us in the garden, that watered the trees of the garden, and flowed out thence?

"And we, when we were in the garden, did not care about it; but since we came to this strange land, we love it, and turn it to use for our body."

But when Eve heard these words from him, she wept; and from the soreness of their weeping, they fell into that water; and would have put an end to themselves in it, so as never again to return and behold the creation; for when they looked upon the work of creation, they felt they must put an end to themselves.

CHAPTER X.

Their bodies need water after they leave the Garden.

THEN God, merciful and gracious, looked upon them thus lying in the water, and nigh unto death, and sent an angel, who brought them out of the water, and laid them on the seashore as dead.

Then the angel went up to God, was welcome, and said, "O God, Thy creatures have breathed their last."

Then God sent His Word unto Adam and Eve, who raised them from their death.

And Adam said, after he was raised, "O God, while we were in the garden we did not require, or care for this water; but since we came to this land we cannot do without it."

Then God said to Adam, "While thou wast under My command and wast a bright angel, thou knewest not this water.

"But after that thou hast transgressed My commandment, thou canst not do without water, wherein to wash thy body and make it grow; for it is now like that of beasts, and is in want of water."

When Adam and Eve heard these words from God, they wept a bitter cry; and Adam entreated God to let him return into the garden, and look at it a second time.

But God said unto Adam, "I have made thee a promise; when that promise is fulfilled, I will bring thee back into the garden, thee and thy righteous seed."

And God ceased to commune with Adam.

CHAPTER XI.

A recollection of the glorious days in the Garden.

THEN Adam and Eve felt themselves burning with thirst, and heat, and sorrow.

And Adam said to Eve, "We shall not drink of this water, even if we were to die. O Eve, when this water comes into our inner parts, it will increase our punishments and that of our children, that shall come after us."

Both Adam and Eve then withdrew from the water, and drank none of it at all; but came and entered the Cave of Treasures.

But when in it Adam could not see Eve; he only heard the noise she made. Neither could she see Adam, but heard the noise he made.

Then Adam wept, in deep affliction, and smote upon his breast; and he arose and said to Eve, "Where art thou?"

And she said unto him, "Lo, I am standing in this darkness."

He then said to her, "Remember the bright nature in which we lived, while we abode in the garden!

"O Eve! remember the glory that rested on us in the garden. O Eve! remember the trees that overshadowed us in the garden while we moved among them.

"O Eve! remember that while we were in the garden, we knew neither night nor day. Think of the Tree of Life, from below which flowed the water, and that shed lustre over us! Remember, O Eve, the garden-land, and the brightness thereof!

The Forgotten Books of Eden

"Think, oh think of that garden in which was no darkness, while we dwelt therein.

"Whereas no sooner did we come into this Cave of Treasures than darkness compassed us round about; until we can no longer see each other; and all the pleasure of this life has come to an end."

CHAPTER XII.

How darkness came between Adam and Eve.

THEN Adam smote upon his breast, he and Eve, and they mourned the whole night until dawn drew near, and they sighed over the length of the night in Miyazia.

And Adam beat himself, and threw himself on the ground in the cave, from bitter grief, and because of the darkness, and lay there as dead.

But Eve heard the noise he made in falling upon the earth. And she felt about for him with her hands, and found him like a corpse.

Then she was afraid, speechless, and remained by him.

But the merciful Lord looked on the death of Adam, and on Eve's silence from fear of the darkness.

And the Word of God came unto Adam and raised him from his death, and opened Eve's mouth that she might speak.

Then Adam arose in the cave and said, "O God, wherefore has light departed from us, and darkness come over us? Wherefore dost Thou leave us in this long darkness? Why wilt Thou plague us thus?

"And this darkness, O Lord, where was it ere it came upon us? It is such, that we cannot see each other.

"For, so long as we were in the garden, we neither saw nor even knew what darkness is. I was not hidden from Eve, neither was she hidden from me, until now that she cannot see me; and no darkness came upon us, to separate us from each other.

"But she and I were both in one bright light. I saw her and she saw me. Yet now since we came into this cave, darkness has come upon us, and parted us asunder, so that I do not see her, and she does not see me.

"O Lord, wilt Thou then plague us with this darkness?"

CHAPTER XIII.

The fall of Adam. Why night and day were created.

THEN when God, who is merciful and full of pity, heard Adam's voice, He said unto him:—

"O Adam, so long as the good angel was obedient to Me, a bright light rested on him and on his hosts.

The Forgotten Books of Eden

"But when he transgressed My commandment, I deprived him of that bright nature, and he became dark.

"And when he was in the heavens, in the realms of light, he knew naught of darkness.

"But he transgressed, and I made him fall from heaven upon the earth; and it was this darkness that came upon him.

"And on thee, O Adam, while in My garden and obedient to Me, did that bright light rest also.

"But when I heard of thy transgression, I deprived thee of that bright light. Yet, of My mercy, I did not turn thee into darkness, but I made thee thy body of flesh, over which I spread this skin, in order that it may bear cold and heat.

"If I had let My wrath fall heavily upon thee, I should have destroyed thee; and had I turned thee into darkness, it would have been as if I killed thee.

"But in My mercy, I have made thee as thou art; when thou didst transgress My commandment, O Adam, I drove thee from the garden, and made thee come forth into this land; and commanded thee to dwell in this cave; and darkness came upon thee, as it did upon him who transgressed My commandment.

"Thus, O Adam, has this night deceived thee. It is not to last for ever; but is only of twelve hours; when it is over, daylight will return.

"Sigh not, therefore, neither be moved; and say not in thy heart that this darkness is long and drags on wearily; and say not in thy heart that I plague thee with it.

1"Strengthen thy heart, and be not afraid. This darkness is not a punishment. But, O Adam, I have made the day, and have placed the sun in it to give light; in order that thou and thy children should do your work.

"For I knew thou shouldest sin and transgress, and come out into this land. Yet would I not force thee, nor be heard upon thee, nor shut up; nor doom thee through thy fall; nor through thy coming out from light into darkness; nor yet through thy coining from the garden into this land.

"For I made thee of the light; and I willed to bring out children of light from thee and like unto thee.

"But thou didst not keep one day My commandment; until I had finished the creation and blessed everything in it.

"Then I commanded thee concerning the tree, that thou eat not thereof. Yet I knew that Satan, who deceived himself, would also deceive thee.

"So I made known to thee by means of the tree, not to come near him. And I told thee not to eat of the fruit thereof, nor to taste of it, nor yet to sit under it, nor to yield to it.

"Had I not been and spoken to thee, O Adam, concerning the tree, and had I left

The Forgotten Books of Eden

thee without a commandment, and thou hadst sinned—it would have been an offence on My part, for not having given thee any order; thou wouldst turn round and blame Me for it.

"But I commanded thee, and warned thee, and thou didst fall. So that My creatures cannot blame me; but the blame rests on them alone.

"And, O Adam, I have made the day for thee and for thy children after thee, for them to work, and toil therein. And I have made the night for them to rest in it from their work; and for the beasts of the field to go forth by night and seek their food.

"But little of darkness now remains, O Adam; and daylight will soon appear."

CHAPTER XIV.

The earliest prophecy of the coming of Christ.

THEN Adam said unto God: "O Lord, take Thou my soul, and let me not see this gloom any more; or remove me to some place where there is no darkness."

But God the Lord said to Adam, "Verily I say unto thee, this darkness will pass from thee, every day I have determined for thee, until the fulfilment of My covenant; when I will save thee and bring thee back again into the garden, into the abode of light thou longest for, wherein is no darkness. I will bring thee, to it—in the kingdom of heaven."

Again said God unto Adam, "All this misery that thou hast been made to take upon thee because of thy transgression, will not free thee from the hand of Satan, and will not save thee.

"But I will. When I shall come down from heaven, and shall become flesh of thy seed, and take upon Me the infirmity from which thou sufferest, then the darkness that came upon thee in this cave shall come upon Me in the grave, when I am in the flesh of thy seed.

"And I, who am without years, shall be subject to the reckoning of years, of times, of months, and of days, and I shall be reckoned as one of the sons of men, in order to save thee."

And God ceased to commune with Adam.

CHAPTER XV.

THEN Adam and Eve wept and sorrowed by reason of God's word to them, that they should not return to the garden until the fulfilment of the days decreed upon them; but mostly because God had told them that He should suffer for their salvation.

CHAPTER XVI.

The first sunrise. Adam and Eve think it is a fire coming to burn them.

AFTER this Adam and Eve ceased not to stand in the cave, praying and weeping, until the morning dawned upon them.

The Forgotten Books of Eden

And when they saw the light returned to them, they restrained from fear, and strengthened their hearts.

Then Adam began to come out of the cave. And when he came to the mouth of it, and stood and turned his face towards the east, and saw the sun rise in glowing rays, and felt the heat thereof on his body, he was afraid of it, and thought in his heart that this flame came forth to plague him.

He wept then, and smote upon his breast, and fell upon the earth on his face, and made his request, saying:—

"O Lord, plague me not, neither consume me, nor yet take away my life from the earth."

For he thought the sun was God.

Inasmuch as while he was in the garden and heard the voice of God and the sound He made in the garden, and feared Him, Adam never saw the brilliant light of the sun, neither did the flaming heat thereof touch his body.

Therefore was he afraid of the sun when flaming rays of it reached him. He thought God meant to plague him therewith all the days He had decreed for him.

For Adam also said in his thoughts, as God did not plague us with darkness, behold, He has caused this sun to rise and to plague us with burning heat.

But while he was thus thinking in his heart, the Word of God came unto him and said:—

"O Adam, arise and stand up. This sun is not God; but it has been created to give light by day, of which I spake unto thee in the cave saying, 'that the dawn would break forth, and there would be light by day.'

"But I am God who comforted thee in the night."

And God ceased to commune with Adam.

CHAPTER XVII.

The CHAPTER of the Serpent.

THEN Adam and Eve came out at the mouth of the cave, and went towards the garden.

But as they drew near to it, before the western gate, from which Satan came when he deceived Adam and Eve, they found the. serpent that became Satan coming at the gate, and sorrowfully licking the dust, and wriggling on its breast on the ground, by reason of the curse that fell upon it from God.

And whereas aforetime the serpent was the most exalted of all beasts, now it was changed and become slippery, and the meanest of them all, and it crept on its breast and went on its belly.

The Forgotten Books of Eden

And whereas it was the fairest of all beasts, it had been changed, and was become the ugliest of them all. Instead of feeding on the best food, now it turned to eat the dust. Instead of dwelling, as before, in the best places, now it lived in the dust.

And, whereas it had been the most beautiful of all beasts, all of which stood dumb at its beauty, it was now abhorred of them.

And, again, whereas it dwelt in one beautiful abode, to which all other animals came from elsewhere; and where it drank, they drank also of the same; now, after it had become venomous, by reason of God's curse, all beasts fled from its abode, and would not drink of the water it drank; but fled from it.

CHAPTER XVIII.

The mortal combat with the serpent.

WHEN the accursed serpent saw Adam and Eve, it swelled its head, stood on its tail, and with eyes blood-red, did as if it would kill them.

It made straight for Eve, and ran after her; while Adam standing by, wept because he had no stick in his hand wherewith to smite the serpent, and knew not how to put it to death.

But with a heart burning for Eve, Adam approached the serpent, and held it by the tail; when it turned towards him and said unto him:—

"O Adam, because of thee and of Eve, I am slippery, and go upon my belly." Then by reason of its great strength, it threw down Adam and Eve and pressed upon them, as if it would kill them.

But God sent an angel who threw the serpent away from them, and raised them up.

Then the Word of God came to the serpent, and said unto it, "In the first instance I made thee glib, and made thee to go upon thy belly; but I did not deprive thee of speech.

"Now, however, be thou dumb; and speak no more, thou and thy race; because in the first place, has the ruin of my creatures happened through thee, and now thou wishest to kill them."

Then the serpent was struck dumb, and spake no more.

And a wind came to blow from heaven by command of God that carried away the serpent from Adam and Eve, threw it on the sea shore, and it landed in India.

CHAPTER XIX.

Beasts made subject to Adam.

BUT Adam and Eve wept before God. And Adam said unto Him:—

"O Lord, when I was in the cave, I said this to Thee, my Lord, that the beasts of the field would rise and devour me, and cut off my life from the earth."

The Forgotten Books of Eden

Then Adam, by reason of what had befallen him, smote upon his breast, and fell upon the earth like a corpse; then came to him the Word of God, who raised him, and said unto him,

"O Adam, not one of these beasts will be able to hurt thee; because when I made the beasts and other moving things come to thee in the cave, I did not let the serpent come with them, lest it should rise against you, make you tremble; and the fear of it should fall into your hearts.

"For I knew that that accursed one is wicked; therefore would I not let it come near you with the other beasts.

"But now strengthen thy heart and fear not. I am with thee unto the end of the days I have determined on thee."

CHAPTER XX.

Adam wishes to protect Eve.

THEN Adam wept and said, "O God, remove us to some other place, that the serpent may not come again near us, and rise against us. Lest it find Thy handmaid Eve alone and kill her; for its eyes are hideous and evil."

But God said to Adam and Eve, "Henceforth fear not, I will not let it come near you; I have driven it away from you, from this mountain; neither will I leave in it aught to hurt you."

Then Adam and Eve worshipped before God 'and gave Him thanks, and praised Him for having delivered them from death.

CHAPTER XXI.

Adam and Eve attempt suicide.

THEN Adam and Eve went in search of the garden.

And the heat beat like a flame on their faces; and they sweated from the heat, and wept before the Lord.

But the place where they wept was nigh unto a high mountain, facing the western gate of the garden.

Then Adam threw himself down from the top of that mountain; his face was torn and his flesh was flayed; much blood flowed from him, and he was nigh unto death.

Meanwhile Eve remained standing on the mountain weeping over him, thus lying.

And she said, "I wish not to live after him; for all that he did to himself was through me."

Then she threw herself after him; and was torn and scotched by stones; and remained lying as dead.

The Forgotten Books of Eden

But the merciful God, who looks upon His creatures, looked upon Adam and Eve as they lay dead, and He sent His Word unto them, and raised them.

And said to Adam, "O Adam, all this misery which thou hast wrought upon thyself, will not avail against My rule, neither will it alter the covenant of the 5500 years."

CHAPTER XXII.

Adam in a chivalrous mood.

THEN Adam said to God, "I wither in the heat; I am faint from walking, and am loth of this world. And I know not when Thou wilt bring me out of it, to rest."

Then the Lord God said unto him, "O Adam, it cannot be at present, not until thou hast ended thy days. Then shall I bring thee out of this wretched land."

And Adam said to God, "While I was in the garden I knew neither heat, nor languor, neither moving about, nor trembling, nor fear; but now since I came to this land, all this affliction has come upon me."

Then God said to Adam, "So long as thou wast keeping My commandment, My light and My grace rested on thee. But when thou didst transgress My commandment, sorrow and misery befell thee in this land."

And Adam wept and said, "O Lord, do not cut me off for this, neither smite me with heavy plagues, nor yet repay me according to my sin; For we, of our own will, did transgress Thy commandment, and forsook Thy law, and sought to become gods like unto Thee, when Satan the enemy deceived us."

Then God said again unto Adam, "Because thou hast borne fear and trembling in this land, languor and suffering treading and walking about, going upon this mountain, and dying from it, I will take all this upon Myself in order to save thee."

CHAPTER XXIII.

Adam and Eve gird themselves and make the first altar ever built.

THEN Adam wept more and said, "O God, have mercy on me, so far as to take upon Thee, that which I will do."

But God took His Word from Adam and Eve.

Then Adam and Eve stood on their feet; and Adam said to Eve "Gird thyself, and I also will gird myself." And she girded herself, as Adam told her.

Then Adam and Eve took stones and placed them in the shape of an altar; and they took leaves from the trees outside the garden, with which they wiped, from the face of the rock, the blood they had spilled.

But that which had dropped on the sand, they took together with the dust wherewith it was mingled and offered it upon the altar as an offering unto God.

Then Adam and Eve stood under the altar and wept, thus entreating God, "Forgive us our trespass [*1] and our sin, and look upon us with Thine eye of mercy. For when we were in the garden our praises and our hymns went up before Thee without ceasing.

"But when we came into this strange land, pure praise was no longer ours, nor righteous prayer, nor understanding hearts, nor sweet thoughts, nor just counsels, nor long discernment, nor upright feelings, neither is our bright nature left us. But our body is changed from the similitude in which it was at first, when we were created.

"Yet now look upon our blood which is offered upon these stones, and accept it at our hands, like the praise we used to sing unto Thee at first, when in the garden."

And Adam began to make more requests unto God.

ORISINAL OF THE LORD'S PRAYER SAID TO BE USED ABOUT 150 YEARS BEFORE OUR LORD: Our Father, Who art in Heaven, be gracious unto us, O Lord our God, hallowed be Thy Name, and let the remembrance of Thee be glorified in Heaven above and upon earth here below.

Let Thy kingdom reign over us now and forever. The Holy Men of old said remit and forgive unto all men whatsoever they have done unto me. And lead us not into temptation, but deliver us from the evil thing; for Thine is the kingdom and Thou shalt reign in glory forever and forevermore, AMEN.

CHAPTER XXIV.

A vivid prophecy of the life and death of Christ.

TEN the merciful God, good 'and lover of men, looked upon Adam and Eve, and upon their blood, which they had held up as an offering unto Him; without an order from Him for so doing. But He wondered at them; and accepted their offerings.

And God sent from His presence a bright fire, that consumed their offering.

He smelt the sweet savour of their offering, and showed them mercy.

Then came the Word of God to Adam, and said unto him, "O Adam, as thou hast shed thy blood, so will I shed My own blood when I become flesh of thy seed; and as thou didst die, O Adam, so also will I die. And as thou didst build an altar, so also will I make for thee an altar on the earth; and as thou didst offer thy blood upon it, so also will I offer My blood upon an altar on the earth.

"And as thou didst sue for forgiveness through that blood, so also will I make My blood forgiveness of sins, and blot out transgressions in it.

"And now, behold, I have accepted thy offering, O Adam, but the days of the covenant, wherein I have bound thee, are not fulfilled. When they are fulfilled, then will I bring thee back into the garden.

"Now, therefore, strengthen thy heart; and when sorrow comes upon thee, make Me an offering, and I will be favourable to thee."

The Forgotten Books of Eden

CHAPTER XXV.

God represented as merciful and loving. The establishing of worship.

BUT God knew that Adam had in his thoughts, that he should often kill himself and make an offering to Him of his blood.

Therefore did He say unto him, "O Adam, do not again kill thyself as thou didst, by throwing thyself down from that mountain."

But Adam said unto God, "It was in my mind to put an end to myself at once, for having transgressed Thy commandments, and for my having come out of the beautiful garden; and for the bright light of which Thou hast deprived me; and for the praises which poured forth from my mouth without ceasing, and for the light that covered me.

"Yet of Thy goodness, O God, do not away with me altogether; but be favourable to me every time I die, and bring me to life.

"And thereby it will be made known that Thou art a merciful God, who willest not that one should perish; who lovest not that one should fall; and who dost not condemn any one cruelly, badly, and by whole destruction."

Then Adam remained silent.

And the Word of God came unto him, and blessed him, and comforted him, and covenanted with him, that He would save him at the end of the days determined upon him.

This, then, was the first offering Adam made unto God; and so it became his custom to do.

CHAPTER XXVI.

A beautiful prophecy of eternal life and joy (v. 15). The fall of night.

THEN Adam took Eve, and they began to return to the Cave of Treasures where they dwelt. But when they neared it and saw it from afar, heavy sorrow fell upon Adam and Eve when they looked at it.

Then Adam said to Eve, "When we were on the mountain we were comforted by the Word of God that conversed with us; and the light that came from the east, shone over us.

"But now the Word of God is hidden from us; and the light that shone over us is so changed as to disappear, and let darkness and sorrow come upon us.

"And we are forced to enter this cave which is like a prison, wherein darkness covers us, so that we are parted from each other; and thou canst not see me, neither can I see thee."

When Adam had said these words, they wept and spread their hands before God; for they were full of sorrow.

The Forgotten Books of Eden

And they entreated God to bring the sun to them, to shine on them, so that darkness return not upon them, and they come not again under this covering of rock. And they wished to die rather than see the darkness.

Then God looked upon Adam and Eve and upon their great sorrow, and upon all they had done with a fervent heart, on account of all the trouble they were in, instead of their former well-being, and on account of all the misery that came upon them in a strange land.

Therefore God was not wroth with them; nor impatient with them; but He was longsuffering and forbearing towards them, as towards the children He had created.

Then came the Word of God to Adam, and said unto him, "Adam, as for the sun, if I were to take it and bring it to thee, days, hours, years and months would all come to naught, and the covenant I have made with thee, would never be fulfilled.

"But thou shouldest then be turned and left in a long plague, and no salvation would be left to thee for ever.

"Yea, rather, bear long and calm thy soul while thou abidest night and day; until the fulfilment of the days, and the time of My covenant is come.

"Then shall I come and save thee, O Adam, for I do not wish that thou be afflicted.

"And when I look at all the good things in which thou didst live, and why thou camest out of them, then would I willingly show thee mercy.

"But I cannot alter the covenant that has gone out of My mouth; else would I have brought thee back into the garden.

"When, however, the covenant is fulfilled, then shall I show thee and thy seed mercy, and bring thee into a land of gladness, where there is neither sorrow nor suffering; but abiding joy and gladness, and light that never fails, and praises that never cease; and a beautiful garden that shall never pass away."

And God said again unto Adam, "Be long-suffering and enter the cave, for the darkness, of which thou wast afraid, shall only be twelve hours long; and when ended, light shall arise."

Then when Adam heard these words from God, he and Eve worshipped before Him, and their hearts were comforted. They returned into the cave after their custom, while tears flowed from their eyes, sorrow and wailing came from their hearts, and they wished their soul would leave their body.

And Adam and Eve stood praying, until the darkness of night came upon them, and Adam was hid from Eve, and she from him.

And they remained standing in prayer.

CHAPTER XXVII.

The second tempting of Adam and Eve. The devil takes on the form of a beguiling light.

WHEN Satan, the hater of all good, saw how they continued in prayer, and how God communed with them, and comforted them, and how He had accepted their offering—Satan made an apparition.

He began with transforming his hosts; in his hands was a flashing fire, and they were in a great light.

He then placed his throne near the mouth of the cave because he could not enter into it by reason of their prayers. And he shed light into the cave, until the cave glistened over Adam and Eve; while his hosts began to sing praises.

And Satan did this, in order that when Adam saw the light, he should think within himself that it was a heavenly light, and that Satan's hosts were angels; and that God had sent them to watch at the cave, and to give him light in the darkness.

So that when Adam came out of the cave and saw them, and Adam and Eve bowed to Satan, then he would overcome Adam thereby, and a second time humble him before God.

When, therefore, Adam and Eve saw the light, fancying it was real, they strengthened their hearts; yet, as they were trembling, Adam said to Eve:—

"Look at that great light, and at those many songs of praise, and at that host standing outside that do not come in to us, do not tell us what they say, or whence they come, or what is the meaning of this light; what those praises are; wherefore they have been sent hither, and why they do not come in.

"If they were from God, they would come to us in the cave, and would tell us their errand."

Then Adam stood up and prayed unto God with a fervent heart, and said:—

"O Lord, is there in the world another god than Thou, who created angels and filled them with light, and sent them to keep us, who would come with them?

"But, lo, we see these hosts that stand at the mouth of the cave; they are in a great light; they sing loud praises. If they are of some other god than Thou, tell me; and if they are sent by Thee, inform me of the reason for which Thou hast sent them."

No sooner had Adam said this, than an angel from God appeared unto him in the cave, who said unto him, "O Adam, fear not. This is Satan and his hosts; he wishes to deceive you as he deceived you at first. For the first time, he was hidden in the serpent; but this time he is come to you in the similitude of an angel of light; in order that, when you worshipped him, he might enthrall you, in the very presence of God."

Then the angel went from Adam, and seized Satan at the opening of the cave, and stripped him of the feint he had assumed, and brought him in his own hideous form to Adam and Eve; who were afraid of him when they saw him.

And the angel said to Adam, "This hideous form has been his ever since God made him fall from heaven. He could not have come near you in it; therefore did he transform himself into an angel of light."

Then the angel drove away Satan and his hosts from Adam and Eve, and said unto them, "Fear not; God who created you, will strengthen you."

And the angel went from them.

But Adam and Eve remained standing in the cave; no consolation came to them; they were divided in their thoughts.

And when it was morning they prayed; and then went out to seek the garden. For their hearts were towards it, and they could get no consolation for having left it.

CHAPTER XXVIII.

The Devil pretends to lead Adam and Eve to the water to bathe.

BUT when the wily Satan saw them, that they were going to the garden, he gathered together his host, and came in appearance upon a cloud, intent on deceiving them.

But when Adam and Eve saw him thus in a vision, they thought they were angels of God come to comfort them about their having left the garden, or to bring them back again into it.

And Adam spread his hands unto God, beseeching Him to make him understand what they were.

Then Satan, the hater of all good, said unto Adam, "O Adam, I am an angel of the great God; and, behold the hosts that surround me.

"God has sent me and them to take thee and bring thee to the border of the garden northwards; to the shore of the clear sea, and bathe thee and Eve in it, and raise you to your former gladness, that ye return again to the garden."

These words sank into the heart of Adam and Eve.

Yet God withheld His Word from Adam, and did not make him understand at once, but waited to see his strength; whether he would be overcome as Eve was when in the garden, or whether he would prevail.

Then Satan called to Adam and Eve, and said, "Behold, we go to the sea of water," and they began to go.

And Adam and Eve followed them at some little distance.

But when they came to the mountain to the north of the garden, a very high mountain, without any steps to the top of it, the Devil drew near to Adam and Eve, and made them go up to the top in reality, and not in a vision; wishing, as he did, to throw them down and kill them, and to wipe off their name from the earth; so that this earth should remain to him and his hosts alone.

The Forgotten Books of Eden

CHAPTER XXIX.

God tells Adam of the Devil's purpose. (v. 4).

BUT when the merciful God saw that Satan wished to kill Adam with his manifold devices, and saw that Adam was meek and without guile, God spake unto Satan in a loud voice, and cursed him.

Then he and his hosts fled, and Adam and Eve remained standing on the top of the mountain, whence they saw below them the wide world, high above which they were. But they saw none of the host which anon were by them.

They wept, both Adam and Eve, before God, and begged for forgiveness of Him.

Then came the Word from God to Adam, and said unto him, "Know thou and understand concerning this Satan, that he seeks to deceive thee and thy seed after thee."

And Adam wept before the Lord God, and begged and entreated Him to give him something from the garden, as a token to him, wherein to be comforted.

And God looked upon Adam's thought, and sent the angel Michael as far as the sea that reaches unto India, to take from thence golden rods and bring them to Adam.

This did God in His wisdom, in order that these golden rods, being with Adam in the cave, should shine forth with light in the night around him, and put an end to his fear of the darkness.

Then the angel Michael went down by God's order, took golden rods, as God had commanded him, and brought them to God.

CHAPTER XXX.

Adam receives the first worldly goods.

AFTER these things, God commanded the angel Gabriel to go down to the garden, and say to the cherub who kept it, "Behold, God has commanded me to come into the garden, and to take thence sweet smelling incense, and give it to Adam."

Then the angel Gabriel went down by God's order to the garden, and told the cherub as God had commanded him.

The cherub then said, "Well." And Gabriel went in and took the incense.

Then God commanded His angel Raphael to go down to the garden, and speak to the cherub about some myrrh, to give to Adam.

And the angel Raphael went down and told the cherub as God had commanded him, and the cherub said, "Well." Then Raphael went in and took the myrrh.

The golden rods were from the Indian sea, where there are precious stones. The incense was from the eastern border of the garden; and the myrrh from the western border, whence bitterness came upon Adam.

And the angels brought these three things to God, by the Tree of Life, in the garden.

Then God said to the angels, "Dip them in the spring of water; then take them and sprinkle their water over Adam and Eve, that they be a little comforted in their sorrow, and give them to Adam and Eve.

And the angels did as God had commanded them, and they gave all those things to Adam and Eve on the top of the mountain upon which Satan had placed them, when he sought to make an end of them.

And when Adam saw the golden rods, the incense and the myrrh, he was rejoiced and wept because he thought that the gold was a token of the kingdom whence he had come, that the incense was a token of the bright light which had been taken from him, and that the myrrh was a token of the sorrow in which he was.

CHAPTER XXXI.

They make themselves more comfortable in the Cave of Treasures on the third day.

AFTER these things God said unto Adam, "Thou didst ask of Me something from the garden, to be comforted therewith, and I have given thee these three tokens as a consolation to thee; that thou trust in Me and in My covenant with thee.

"For I will come and save thee; and kings shall bring me when in the flesh, gold, incense and myrrh; gold as a token of My kingdom; incense as a token of My divinity; and myrrh as a token of My suffering and of My death.

"But, O Adam, put these by thee in the cave; the gold that it may shed light over thee by night; the incense, that thou smell its sweet savour; and the myrrh, to comfort thee in thy sorrow."

When Adam heard these words from God, he worshipped before Him. He and Eve worshipped Him and gave Him thanks, because He had dealt mercifully with them.

Then God commanded the three angels, Michael, Gabriel and Raphael, each to bring what he had brought, and give it to Adam. And they did so, one by one.

And God commanded Suriyel and Salathiel to bear up Adam and Eve, and bring them down from the top of the high mountain, and to take them to the Cave of Treasures.

There they laid the gold on the south side of the cave, the incense on the eastern side, and the myrrh on the western side. For the mouth of the cave was on the north side.

The angels then comforted Adam and Eve, and departed.

The gold was seventy rods; the incense, twelve pounds; and the myrrh, three pounds.

These remained by Adam in the House of Treasures; therefore was it called "of concealment." But other interpreters say it was called the "Cave of Treasures," by reason of the bodies of righteous men that were in it.

The Forgotten Books of Eden

These three things did God give to Adam, on the third day after he had come out of the garden, in token of the three days the Lord should remain in the heart of the earth.

And these three things, as they continued with Adam in the cave, gave him light by night; and by day they gave him a little relief from his sorrow.

CHAPTER XXXII.

Adam and Eve go into the water to pray.

AND Adam and Eve remained in the Cave of Treasures until the seventh day; they neither ate of the fruit of the earth, nor drank water.

And when it dawned on the eighth day, Adam said to Eve, "O Eve, we prayed God to give us somewhat from the garden, and He sent His angels who brought us what we had desired.

"But now, arise, let us go to the sea of water we saw at first, and let us stand in it, praying that God will again be favourable to us and take us back to the garden; or give us something; or that He will give us comfort in some other land than this in which we are."

Then Adam and Eve came out of the cave, went and stood on the border of the sea in which they had before thrown themselves, and Adam said to Eve:—

"Come, go down into this place, and come not out of it until the end of thirty days, when I shall come to thee. And pray to God with fervent heart and a sweet voice, to forgive us.

"And I will go to another place, and go down into it, and do like thee."

Then Eve went down into the water, as Adam had commanded her. Adam also went down into the water; and they stood praying; and besought the Lord to forgive them their offence, and to restore them to their former state.

And they stood thus praying, unto the end of the five-and-thirty days.

CHAPTER XXXIII.

Satan falsely promises the "bright light!'

BUT Satan, the hater of all good, sought them in the cave, but found them not, although he searched diligently for them.

But he found them standing in the water praying and thought within himself, "Adam and Eve are thus standing in that water beseeching God to forgive them their transgression, and to restore them to their former estate, and to take them from under my hand.

"But I will deceive them so that they shall come out of the water, and not fulfil their vow."

Then the hater of all good, went not to Adam, but be went to Eve, and took the form of an angel of God, praising and rejoicing, and said to her—

The Forgotten Books of Eden

"Peace be unto thee! Be glad and rejoice! God is favourable unto you, and He sent me to Adam. I have brought him the glad tidings of salvation, and of his being filled with bright light as he was at first.

"And Adam, in his joy for his restoration, has sent me to thee, that thou come to me, in order that I crown thee with light like him.

"And he said to me, 'Speak unto Eve; if she does not come with thee, tell her of the sign when we were on the top of the mountain; how God sent His angels who took us and brought us to the Cave of Treasures; and laid the gold on the southern side; incense, on the eastern side; and myrrh on the western side.' Now come to him."

When Eve heard these words from him, she rejoiced greatly. And thinking that Satan's appearance was real, she came out of the sea.

He went before, and she followed him until they came to Adam. Then Satan hid himself from her, and she saw him no more.

She then came and stood before Adam, who was standing by the water and rejoicing in God's forgiveness.

And as she called to him, he turned round, found her there and wept when he saw her, and smote upon his breast; and from the bitterness of his grief, he sank into the water.

But God looked upon him and upon his misery, and upon his being about to breathe his last. And the Word of God came from heaven, raised him out of the water, and said unto him, "Go up the high bank to Eve." And when he came up to Eve he said unto her, "Who said to thee 'come hither'?"

Then she told him the discourse of the angel who had appeared unto her and had given her a sign.

1But Adam grieved, and gave her to know it was Satan. He then took her and they both returned to the cave.

These things happened to them the second time they went down to the water, seven days after their coming out of the garden.

They fasted in the water thirty-five days; altogether forty-two days since they had left the garden.

CHAPTER XXXIV.

Adam recalls the creation of Eve. He eloquently appeals for food and drink.

AND on the morning of the forty-third day, they came out of the cave, sorrowful and weeping. Their bodies were lean, and they were parched from hunger and thirst, from fasting and praying, and from their heavy sorrow on account of their transgression.

And when they had come out of the cave they went up the mountain to the west of the garden.

The Forgotten Books of Eden

There they stood and prayed and besought God to grant them forgiveness of their sins.

And after their prayers Adam began to entreat 'God, saying, "O my Lord my God, and my Creator, thou didst command the four elements to be gathered together, and they were gathered together by Thine order.

"Then Thou spreadest Thy hand and didst create me out of one element, that of dust of the earth; and Thou didst bring me into the garden at the third hour, on a Friday, and didst inform me of it in the cave.

"Then, at first, I knew neither night nor day, for I had a bright nature; neither did the light in which I lived ever leave me to know night or day.

"Then, again, O Lord, in that third hour in which Thou didst create me, Thou broughtest to me all beasts, and lions, and ostriches, and fowls of the air, and all things that move in the earth, which Thou hadst created at the first hour before me of the Friday.

"And Thy will was that I should name them all, one by one, with a suitable name. But Thou gavest me understanding and knowledge, and a pure heart and a right mind from Thee, that I should name them after Thine own mind regarding the naming of them.

"O God, Thou madest them obedient to me, and didst order that not one of them break from my sway, according to Thy commandment, and to the dominion which Thou hast given me over them. But now they are all estranged from me.

"Then it was in that third hour of Friday, in which Thou didst create me, and didst command me concerning the tree, to which I was neither to draw near, nor to eat thereof; for Thou saidst to me in the garden, 'When thou eatest of it, of death thou shalt die.'

"And if Thou hadst punished me as Thou saidst, with death, I should have died that very moment.

"Moreover, when Thou commandedst me regarding the tree, I was neither to approach nor to cat thereof, Eve was not with me; Thou hadst not Yet created her, neither hadst Thou yet taken her out of my side; nor had she yet heard this order from Thee.

"Then, at the end of the third hour of that Friday, O Lord, Thou didst cause a slumber and a sleep to come over me, and I slept, and was overwhelmed in sleep.

"Then Thou didst draw a rib out of my side, and created it after my own similitude and image. Then I awoke; and when I saw her and knew who she was, I said, 'This is bone of my bones, and flesh of my flesh; henceforth she shall be called woman.'

"It was of Thy good will, O God, that Thou broughtest a slumber and a sleep over me, and that Thou didst forthwith bring Eve out of my side, until she was out, so that I did not see how she was made; neither could I witness, O my Lord, how awful and great are Thy goodness and glory.

"And of Thy goodwill, O Lord, Thou madest us both with bodies of a bright nature, and Thou madest us two, one; and Thou gavest us Thy grace, and didst fill us with praises of the Holy Spirit; that we should be neither hungry nor thirsty, nor know what sorrow is, nor yet faintness of heart; neither suffering, fasting, nor weariness.

"But now, O God, since we transgressed Thy commandment and broke Thy law, Thou hast brought us out into a strange land, and has caused suffering, and faintness, hunger and thirst to come upon us.

"Now, therefore, O God, we pray Thee, give us something to eat from the garden, to satisfy our hunger with it; and something wherewith to quench our thirst.

"For, behold, many days, O God, we have tasted nothing and drunk nothing, and our flesh is dried up, and our strength is wasted, and sleep is gone from our eyes from faintness and weeping.

"Then, O God, we dare not gather aught of the fruit of trees, from fear of Thee. For when we transgressed at first Thou didst spare us, and didst not make us die.

"But now, we thought in our hearts, if we eat of the fruit of trees, without God's order, He will destroy us this time, and will wipe us off from the face of the earth.

"And if we drink of this water, without God's order, He will make an end of us, and root us up at once.

"Now, therefore, O God, that I am come to this place with Eve, we beg Thou wilt give us of the fruit of the garden, that we may be satisfied with it.

"For we desire the fruit that is on the earth, and all else that we lack in it."

CHAPTER XXXV.

God's reply.

THEN God looked again upon Adam and his weeping and groaning, and the Word of God came to him, and said unto him:—

"O Adam, when thou wast in My garden, thou knewest neither eating nor drinking; neither faintness nor suffering; neither leanness of flesh, nor change; neither did sleep depart from thine eyes. But since thou transgressedst, and camest into this strange land, all these trials are come upon thee."

CHAPTER XXXVI.

Figs.

THEN God commanded the cherub, who kept the gate of the garden with a sword of fire in his hand, to take some of the fruit of the fig-tree, and to give it to Adam.

The cherub obeyed the command of the Lord God, and went into the garden and brought two figs on two twigs, each fig hansing to its leaf; they were from two of the trees among which Adam and Eve hid themselves when God went to walk in the garden, and the Word of God came to Adam and Eve and said unto them, "Adam, Adam, where art thou?"

The Forgotten Books of Eden

And Adam answered, "O God, here am I. When I heard the sound of Thee and Thy voice, I hid myself, because I am naked."

Then the cherub took two figs and brought them to Adam and Eve. But he threw them to them from afar; for they might not come near the cherub by reason of their flesh, that could not come near the fire.

At first, angels trembled at the presence of Adam and were afraid of him. But now Adam trembled before the angels and was afraid of them.

Then Adam drew near and took one fig, and Eve also came in turn and took the other.

And as they took them up in their hands, they looked at them, and knew they were from the trees among which they had hidden themselves.

CHAPTER XXXVII.

Forty-three days of penance do not redeem one hour of sin (v. 6).

THEN Adam said to Eve, "Seest thou not these figs and their leaves, with which we covered ourselves when we were stripped of our bright nature? But now, we know not what misery and suffering may come upon us from eating them.

"Now, therefore, O Eve, let us restrain ourselves and not eat of them, thou and I; and let us ask God to give us of the fruit of the Tree of Life."

Thus did Adam and Eve restrain themselves, and did not eat of these figs.

But Adam began to pray to God and to beseech Him to give him of the fruit of the Tree of Life, saying thus: "O God, when we transgressed Thy commandment at the sixth hour of Friday, we were stripped of the bright nature we had, and did not continue in the garden after our transgression, more than three hours.

"But on the evening Thou madest us come out of it. O God, we transgressed against Thee one hour, and all these trials and sorrows have come upon us until this day.

"And those days together with this the forty-third day, do not redeem that one hour in which we transgressed!

"O God, look upon us with an eye of pity, and do not requite us according to our transgression of Thy commandment, in presence of Thee.

"O, God, give us of the fruit of the Tree of Life, that we may eat of it, and live, and turn not to see sufferings and other trouble, in this earth; for Thou art God.

"When we transgressed Thy commandment, Thou madest us come out of the garden, and didst send a cherub to keep the Tree of Life, lest we should eat thereof, and live; and know nothing of faintness after we transgressed.

"But now, O Lord, behold, we have endured all these days, and have borne sufferings. Make these forty-three days an equivalent for the one hour in which we transgressed."

The Forgotten Books of Eden

CHAPTER XXXVIII.

"When 5500 years are fulfilled . . . ."

AFTER these things the Word of God came to Adam, and said unto him:—

"O Adam, as to the fruit of the Tree of Life, for which thou askest, I will not give it thee now, but when the 5500 years are fulfilled. Then will I give thee of the fruit of the Tree of Life, and thou shalt eat, and live for ever, thou, and Eve, and thy righteous seed.

"But these forty-three days cannot make amends for the hour in which thou didst transgress My commandment.

"O Adam, I gave thee to eat of the fig-tree in which thou didst hide thyself. Go and eat of it, thou and Eve.

"I will not deny thy request, neither will I disappoint thy hope; therefore, bear up unto the fulfilment of the covenant I made with thee."

And God withdrew His Word from Adam.

CHAPTER XXXIX.

Adam is cautious—but too late.

THEN Adam returned to Eve, and said to her, "Arise, and take a fig for thyself, and I will take another; and let us go to our cave."

Then Adam and Eve took each a fig and went towards the cave; the time was about the setting of the sun; and their thoughts made them long to eat of the fruit.

But Adam said to Eve, "I am afraid to eat of this fig. I know not what may come upon me from it."

So Adam wept, and stood praying before God, saying, "Satisfy my hunger, without my having to eat this fig; for after I have eaten it, what will it profit me? And what shall I desire and ask of Thee, O God, when it is gone?"

And he said again, "I am afraid to eat of it; for I know not what will befall me through it."

CHAPTER XL.

The first Human hunger.

THEN the Word of God came to Adam, and said unto him, "O, Adam, why hadst thou not this dread, neither this fasting, nor this care ere this? And why hadst thou not this fear before thou didst transgress?

"But when thou camest to dwell in this strange land, thy animal body could not be on earth without earthly food, to strengthen it and to restore its powers."

And God withdrew His Word from Adam.

The Forgotten Books of Eden

CHAPTER XLI.

The first Human thirst.

THEN Adam took the fig, and laid it on the golden rods. Eve also took her fig, and put it upon the incense.

And the weight of each fig was that of a water-melon; for the fruit of the garden was much larger than the fruit of this land.

But Adam and Eve remained standing and fasting the whole of that night, until the morning dawned.

When the sun rose they were at their prayers, and Adam said to Eve, after they had done praying:—

"O Eve, come, let us go to the border of the garden looking south; to the place whence the river flows, and is parted into four heads. There we will pray to God, and ask Him to give us to drink of the Water of Life.

"For God has not fed us with the Tree of Life, in order that we may not live. We will, therefore, ask him to give us of the Water of Life, and to quench our thirst with it, rather than with a drink of water of this land."

When Eve heard these words from Adam, she agreed; and they both arose and came to the southern border of the garden, upon the brink of the river of water at some little distance from the garden.

And they stood and prayed before the Lord, and asked Him to look upon them this once, to forgive them, and to grant them their request.

After this prayer from both of them, Adam began to pray with his voice before God, and said:—

"O Lord, when I was in the garden and saw the water that flowed from under the Tree of Life, my heart did not desire, neither did my body require to drink of it; neither did I know thirst, for I was living; and above that which I am now.

"So that in order to live I did not require any Food of Life, neither did I drink of the Water of Life.

"But now, O God, I am dead; my flesh is parched with thirst. Give me of the Water of Life that I may drink of it and live.

"Of Thy mercy, O God, save me from these plagues and trials, and bring me into another land different from this, if Thou wilt not let me dwell in Thy garden."

CHAPTER XLII.

A promise of the Water of Life. The third prophecy of the coming of Christ.

THEN came the Word of God to Adam, and said unto him:—

"O Adam, as to what thou sayest, 'Bring me into a land where there is rest,' it is not another land than this, but it is the kingdom of heaven where alone there is rest.

"But thou canst not make thy entrance into it at present; but only after thy judgment is past and fulfilled.

"Then will I make thee go up into the kingdom of heaven, thee and thy righteous seed; and I will give thee and them the rest thou askest for at present.

"And if thou saidst, 'Give me of the Water of Life that I may drink and live'—it cannot be this day, but on the day that I shall descend into hell, and break the gates of brass, and bruise in pieces the kingdoms of iron.

"Then will I in mercy save thy soul and the souls of the righteous, to give them rest in My garden. And that shall be when the end of the world is come.

"And, again, as regards the Water of Life thou seekest, it will not be granted thee this day; but on the day that I shall shed My blood upon thy head in the land of Golgotha.

"For My blood shall be the Water of Life unto thee, at that time, and not to thee alone, but unto all those of thy seed who shall believe in Me; that it be unto them for rest for ever."

The Lord said again unto Adam, "O Adam, when thou wast in the garden, these trials did not come to thee

"But since thou didst transgress My commandment, all these sufferings have come upon thee.

"Now, also, does thy flesh require food and drink; drink then of that water that flows by thee on the face of the earth."

Then God withdrew His Word from Adam.

And Adam and Eve worshipped the Lord, and returned from the river of water to the cave. It was noon-day; and when they drew near to the cave, they saw a large fire by it.

CHAPTER XLIII.

The Devil attempts arson.

THEN Adam and Eve were afraid, and stood still. And Adam said to Eve, "What is that fire by our cave? We do nothing in it to bring about this fire.

"We neither have bread to bake therein, nor broth to cook there. As to this fire, we know not the like, neither do we know what to call it.

"But ever since God sent the cherub with a sword of fire that flashed and lightened in his hand, from fear of which we fell down and were like corpses, have we not seen the like.

"But now O Eve, behold, this is the same fire that was in the cherub's hand, which God has sent to keep the cave in which we dwell.

The Forgotten Books of Eden

"O Eve, it is because God is angry with us, and will drive us from it.

"O Eve, we have again transgressed His commandment in that cave, so that He had sent this fire to burn around it, and to prevent us from going into it.

"If this be really so, O Eve, where shall we dwell? And whither shall we flee from before the face of the Lord? Since, as regards the garden, He will not let us abide in it, and He has deprived us of the good things thereof; but He has placed us in this cave, in which we have borne darkness, trials and hardships, until at last we found comfort therein.

"But now that He has brought us out into another land, who knows what may happen in it? And who knows but that the darkness of that land may be far greater than the darkness of this land?

"Who knows what may happen in that land by day or by night? And who knows whether it will be far or near, O Eve? Where it will please God to put us, may be far from the garden, O Eve! or where God will prevent us from beholding Him, because we have transgressed His commandment, and because we have made requests unto Him at all times?

"O Eve, if God will bring us into a strange land other than this, in which we find consolation, it must be to put our souls to death, and blot out our name from the face of the earth.

"O Eve, if we are farther estranged from the garden and from God, where shall we find Him again, and ask Him to give us gold, incense, myrrh, and some fruit of the fig-tree?

"Where shall we find Him, to comfort us a second time? Where shall we find Him, that He may think of us, as regards the covenant He has made on our behalf T"

Then Adam said no more. And they kept looking, he and Eve, towards the cave, and at the fire that flared up around it.

But that fire was from Satan. For he had gathered trees and dry grasses, and had carried and brought them to the cave, and had set fire to them, in order to consume the cave and—what was in it.

So that Adam and Eve should be left in sorrow, and he should cut off their trust in God, and make them deny Him.

But by the mercy of God he could not burn the cave, for God sent His angel round the cave to guard it from such a fire, until it went out.

And this fire lasted from noon-day until the break of day. That was the forty-fifth day.

CHAPTER XLIV.

The power of fire over man.

YET Adam and Eve were standing and looking at the fire, and unable to come

The Forgotten Books of Eden

near the cave from their dread of the fire.

And Satan kept on brinsing trees and throwing them into the fire, until the flame thereof rose up on high, and covered the whole cave, thinking, as he did in his own mind, to consume the cave with much fire. But the angel of the Lord was guarding it.

And yet he could not curse Satan, nor injure him by word, because he had no authority over him, neither did he take to doing so with words from his mouth.

Therefore did the angel bear with him, without saying one bad word until the Word of God came who said to Satan, "Go hence; once before didst thou deceive My servants, and this time thou seekest to destroy them.

"Were it not for My mercy I would have destroyed thee and thy hosts from off the earth. But I have had patience with thee, unto the end of the world."

Then Satan fled from before the Lord. But the fire went on burning around the cave like a coal-fire the whole day; which was the forty-sixth day Adam and Eve had spent since they came out of the garden.

And when Adam and Eve saw that the heat of the fire had somewhat cooled down, they began to walk towards the cave to get into it as they were wont; but they could not, by reason of the heat of the fire.

Then they both took to weeping because of the fire that made separation between them and the cave, and that drew towards them, burning. And they were afraid.

Then Adam said to Eve, "See this fire of which we have a portion in us: which formerly yielded to us, but no longer does so, now that we have transgressed the limit of creation, and changed our condition, and our nature is altered. But the fire is not changed in its nature, nor altered from its creation. Therefore has it now power over us; and when we come near it, it scorches our flesh."

CHAPTER XLV.

Why Satan didn't fulfil his promises.

THEN Adam rose and prayed unto God, saying, "See, this fire has made separation between us and the cave in which Thou hast commanded us to dwell; but now, behold, we cannot go into it."

Then God heard Adam, and sent him His Word, that said:—

"O Adam, see this fire! how different the flame and heat thereof are from the garden of delights and the good things in it!

"When thou wast under My control, all creatures yielded to thee; but after thou hast transgressed My commandment, they all rise over thee."

Again said God unto him, "See, O Adam, how Satan has exalted thee! He has deprived thee of the Godhead, and of an exalted state like unto Me, and has not kept his word to thee; but, after all, is become thy foe. It is he who made this fire in which he meant to burn thee and Eve.

"Why, O Adam, has he not kept his agreement with thee, not even one day; but has deprived thee of the glory that was on thee—when thou didst yield to his command?

"Thinkest thou, Adam, that he loved thee when he made this agreement with thee? Or, that he loved thee and wished to raise thee on high?

"But no, Adam, he did not do all that out of love to thee; but he wished to make thee come out of light into darkness, and from an exalted state to degradation; from glory to abasement; from joy to sorrow; and from rest to fasting and fainting."

God said also to Adam, "See this fire kindled by Satan around thy cave; see this wonder that surrounds thee; and know that it will encompass about both thee and thy seed, when ye hearken to his behest; that he will plague you with fire; and that ye shall go down into hell after ye are dead.

"Then shall ye see the burning of his fire, that will thus be burning around you and your seed. There shall be no deliverance from it for you, but at My coming; in like manner as thou canst not now go into thy cave, by reason of the great fire around it; not until My Word shall come that will make a way for thee on the day My covenant is fulfilled.

"There is no way for thee at present to come from hence to rest, not until My Word comes, who is My Word. Then will He make a way for thee, and thou shalt have rest." Then God called with His Word to that fire that burned around the cave, that it part itself asunder, until Adam had gone through it. Then the fire parted itself by God's order, and a way was made for Adam.

And God withdrew His Word from Adam.

CHAPTER XLVI.

"How many times have I delivered thee out of his hand . . ."

THEN Adam and Eve began again to come into the cave. And when they came to the way between the fire, Satan blew into the fire like a whirlwind, and made on Adam and Eve a burning coal-fire; so that their bodies were singed; and the coal-fire scorched them.

And from the burning of the fire Adam and Eve cried aloud, and said, "O Lord, save us! Leave us not to be consumed and plagued by this burning fire; neither require us for having transgressed Thy commandment."

Then God looked upon their bodies, on which Satan had caused fire to burn, and God sent His angel that stayed the burning fire. But the wounds remained on their bodies.

And God said unto Adam, "See Satan's love for thee, who pretended to give thee the Godhead and greatness; and, behold, he burns thee with fire, and seeks to destroy thee from off the earth.

"Then look at Me, O Adam; I created thee, and how many times have I delivered thee out of his hand? If not, would he not have destroyed thee?"

God said again to Eve, "What is that he promised thee in the garden, saying, 'At the time ye shall eat of the tree, your eyes will be opened, and you shall become like gods, knowing good and evil.' But lo! he has burnt your bodies with fire, and has made you taste the taste of fire, for the taste of the garden; and has made you see the burning of fire, and the evil thereof, and the power it has over you.

"Your eyes have seen the good he has taken from you, and in truth he has opened your eyes; and you have seen the garden in which ye were with Me, and ye have also seen the evil that has come upon you from Satan. But as to the Godhead he cannot give it you, neither fulfil his speech to you. Nay, he was bitter against you and your seed, that will come after you."

And God withdrew His Word from them.

CHAPTER XLVII.

The Devil's own Scheming.

THEN Adam and Eve came into the cave, yet trembling at the fire that had scorched their bodies. So Adam said to Eve:—

"Lo, the fire has burnt our flesh in this world; but how will it be when we are dead, and Satan shall punish our souls? Is not our deliverance long and far off, unless God come, and in mercy to us fulfil His promise?"

Then Adam and Eve passed into the cave, blessing themselves for coming into it once more. For it was in their thoughts, that they never should enter it, when they saw the fire around it.

But as the sun was setting the fire was still burning and nearing Adam and Eve in the cave, so that they could not sleep in it. After the sun had set, they went out of it. This was the forty-seventh day after they came out of the garden.

Adam and Eve then came under the top of hill by the garden to sleep, as they were wont.

And they stood and prayed God to forgive them their sins, and then fell asleep under the summit of the mountain.

But Satan, the hater of all good, thought within himself: Whereas God has promised salvation to Adam by covenant, and that He would deliver him out of all the hardships that have befallen him-but has not promised me by covenant, and will not deliver me out of my hardships; nay, since He has promised him that He should make him and his seed dwell in the kingdom in which I once was—I will kill Adam.

The earth shall be rid of him; and shall be left to me alone; so that when he is dead he may not have any seed left to inherit the kingdom that shall remain my own realm; God will then be in want of me, and He will restore me to it with my hosts.

The Forgotten Books of Eden

CHAPTER XLVIII.

Fifth apparition of Satan to Adam and Eve.

AFTER this Satan called to his hosts, all of which came to him, and said unto him:—

"O, our Lord, what wilt thou do?"

He then said unto them, "Ye know that this Adam, whom God created out of the dust, is he who has taken our kingdom. Come, let us gather together and kill him; or hurl a rock at him and at Eve, and crush them under it."

When Satan's hosts heard these words, they came to the part of the mountain where Adam and Eve were asleep.

Then Satan and his hosts took a huge rock, broad and even, and without blemish, thinking within himself, "If there should be a hole in the rock, when it fell on them, the hole in the rock might come upon them, and so they would escape and not die."

He then said to his hosts, "Take up this stone, and throw it flat upon them, so that it roll not from them to somewhere else. And when ye have hurled it, flee and tarry not."

And they did as he bid them. But as the rock fell down from the mountain upon Adam and Eve, God commanded it to become a kind of shed over them, that did them no harm. And so it was by God's order.

But when the rock fell, the whole earth quaked with it, and. was shaken from the size of the rock.

And as it quaked and shook, Adam and Eve awoke from sleep, and found themselves under a rock like a shed. But they knew not how it was; for when they fell asleep they were under the sky, and not under a shed; and when they saw it, they were afraid.

Then Adam said to Eve, "Wherefore has the mountain bent itself, and the earth quaked and shaken on our account? And why has this rock spread itself over us like a tent?

"Does God intend to plague us and to shut us up in this prison? Or will He close the earth upon us?

"He is angry with us for our having come out of the cave without His order; and for our having done so of our own accord, without consulting Him, when we left the cave and came to this place."

Then Eve said, "If, indeed, the earth quaked for our sake, and this rock forms a tent over us because of our transgression, then woe be to us, O Adam, for our punishment will be long.

"But arise and pray Ito God to let us know concerning this, and what this rock is, that is spread over us like a tent."

Then Adam stood up and prayed before the Lord, to let him know about this strait. And Adam thus stood praying until the morning.

The Forgotten Books of Eden

CHAPTER XLIX.

The first prophecy of the Resurrection.

THEN the Word of God came and said:—

"O Adam, who counselled thee, when thou earnest out of the cave, to come to this place?"

And Adam said unto God, "O Lord, we came to this place because of the heat of the fire, that came upon us inside the cave."

4 Then the Lord God said unto Adam, "O Adam, thou dreadest the heat of fire for one night, but how will it be when thou dwellest in hell?

"Yet, O Adam, fear not, neither say in thy heart that I have spread this rock as an awning over thee, to plague thee therewith.

"It came from Satan, who had promised thee the Godhead and majesty. It is he who threw down this rock to kill thee under it, and Eve with thee, and thus to prevent you from living upon the earth.

"But, in mercy for you, just as that rock was falling down upon you, I commanded it to form an awning over you; and the rock under you, to lower itself.

"And this sign, O Adam, will happen to Me at My coming upon earth: Satan will raise the people of the Jews Jo put Me to death; and they will lay Me in a rock, and seal a large stone upon Me, and I shall remain within that rock three days and three nights.

"But on the third day I shall rise again, and it shall be salvation to thee, O Adam, and to thy seed, to believe in Me. But, O Adam, I will not bring thee from under this rock until three days and three nights are passed."

And God withdrew His Word from Adam.

But Adam and Eve abode under the rock three days and three nights, as God had told them.

And God did so to them because they had left their cave and had come to this same place without God's order.

But, after three days and three nights, God opened the rock and brought them out from under it. Their flesh was dried up, and their eyes and their hearts were troubled from weeping and sorrow.

CHAPTER L.

Adam and Eve seek to cover their nakedness.

THEN Adam and Eve went forth and came into the Cave of Treasures, and they stood praying in it the whole of that day, until the evening.

And this took place at the end of fifty days after they had left the garden.

The Forgotten Books of Eden

But Adam and Eve rose again and prayed to God in the cave the whole of that night, and begged for mercy from Him.

And when the day dawned, Adam said unto Eve, "Come! let us go and do some work for our bodies."

So they went out of the cave, and came to the northern border of the garden, and they sought something to cover their bodies withal. But they found nothing, and knew not how to do the work. Yet their bodies were stained, and they were speechless from cold and heat.

Then Adam stood and asked God to show him something wherewith to cover their bodies.

Then came the Word of God and said unto him, "O Adam, take Eve and come to the seashore, where ye fasted before. There ye shall find skins of sheep, whose flesh was devoured by lions, and whose skins were left. Take them and make raiment for yourselves, and clothe yourselves withal."

CHAPTER LI.

"What is his beauty that you should have followed him?"

WHEN Adam heard these words from God, he took Eve and removed from the northern end of the garden to the south of it, by the river of water, where they once fasted.

But as they were going in the way, and before they reached that place, Satan, the wicked one, had heard the Word of God communing with Adam respecting his covering.

It grieved him, and he hastened to the place where the sheep-skins were, with the intention of taking them and throwing them into the sea, or of burning them with fire, that Adam and Eve should not find them.

But as he was about to take them, the Word of God came from heaven, and bound him by the side of those skins until Adam and Eve came near him. But as they neared him they were afraid of him, and of his hideous look.

Then came the Word of God to Adam and Eve, and said to them, "This is he who was hidden in the serpent, and who deceived you, and stripped you of the garment of light and glory in which you were.

"This is he who promised you majesty and divinity. Where, then, is the beauty that was on him? Where is his divinity? Where is his light? Where is the glory that rested on him?

"Now his figure is hideous; he is become abominable among angels; and he has come to be called Satan.

"O Adam I he wished to take from you this earthly garment of sheep-skins, and to destroy it, and not let you be covered with it.

The Forgotten Books of Eden

"What, then, is his beauty that you should have followed him? And what have you gained by hearkening to him? See his evil works and then look at Me; at Me, your Creator, and at the good deeds I do you.

"See, I bound him until you came and saw him and beheld his weakness, that no power is left with him."

And God released him from his bonds.

CHAPTER LII.

Adam and Eve sew the first shirt.

AFTER this Adam and Eve said no more, but wept before God on account of their creation, and of their bodies that required an earthly covering.

Then Adam said unto Eve, "O Eve, this is the skin of beasts with which we shall be covered. But when we have put it on, behold, a token of death shall have come upon us, inasmuch as the owners of these skins have died, and have wasted away. So also shall we die, and pass away."

Then Adam and Eve took the skins, and went back to the Cave of Treasures; and when in it, they stood and prayed as they were wont.

And they thought how they could make garments of those skins; for they had no skill for it.

Then God sent to them His angel to show them how to work it out. And the angel said to Adam, "Go forth, and bring some palm-thorns." Then Adam went out, and brought some, as the angel had commanded him.

Then the angel began before them to work out the skins, after the manner of one who prepares a shirt. And he took the thorns and stuck them into the skins, before their eyes.

Then the angel again stood up and prayed God that the thorns in those skins should be hidden, so as to be, as it were, sewn with one thread.

And so it was, by God's order; they became garments for Adam and Eve, and He clothed them withal.

From that time the nakedness of their bodies was covered from the sight of each other's eyes.

And this happened at the end of the fifty-first day.

Then when Adam's and Eve's bodies were covered, they stood and prayed, and sought mercy of the Lord, and forgiveness, and gave Him thanks for that He had had mercy on them, and had covered their nakedness. And they ceased not from prayer the whole of that night.

Then when the mom dawned at the rising of the sun, they said their prayers after their custom; and then went out of the cave.

The Forgotten Books of Eden

And Adam said unto Eve, "Since we know not what there is to the westward of this cave, let us go forth and see it to-day." Then they came forth and went towards the western border.

CHAPTER LIII.

The prophecy of the Western Lands.

THEY were not very far from the cave, when Satan came towards them, and hid himself between them and the cave, under the form of two ravenous lions three days without food, that came towards Adam and Eve, as if to break them in pieces and devour them.

Then Adam and Eve wept, and prayed God to deliver them from their paws.

Then the Word of God came to them, and drove away the lions from them.

And God said unto Adam, "O Adam, what seekest thou on the western border? And why hast thou left of thine own accord the eastern border, in which was thy dwelling-place?

"Now, then, turn back to thy cave, and remain in it, that Satan do not deceive thee, nor work his purpose upon thee.

"For in this western border, O Adam, there will go from thee a seed, that shall replenish it; and that will defile themselves with their sins, and with their yielding to the behests of Satan, and by following his works.

"Therefore will I bring upon them the waters of a flood, and overwhelm them all. But I will deliver what is left of the righteous among them; and I will bring them to a distant land, and the land in which thou dwellest now shall remain desolate and without one inhabitant in it."

After God had thus discoursed to them, they went back to the Cave of Treasures. But their flesh was dried up, and their strength failed from fasting and praying, and from the sorrow they felt at having trespassed against God.

CHAPTER LIV.

Adam and Eve go exploring.

THEN Adam and Eve stood up in the cave and prayed the whole of that night until the morning dawned. And when the sun was risen they both went out of the cave; their heads wandering from heaviness of sorrow, and they not knowing whither they went.

And they walked thus unto the southern border of the garden. And they began to go up that border until they came to the eastern border beyond which there was no farther space.

And the cherub who guarded the garden was standing at the western gate, and guarding it against Adam and Eve, lest they should suddenly come into the garden. And the cherub turned round, as if to put them to death; according to the commandment God had given him.

When Adam and Eve came to the eastern border of the garden—thinking in their hearts that the cherub was not watching—as they were standing by the gate as if wishing to go in, suddenly came the cherub with a flashing sword of fire in his hand; and when he saw them, he went forth to kill them. For he was afraid lest God should destroy him if they went into the garden without His order.

And the sword of the cherub seemed to flame afar off. But when he raised it over Adam and Eve, the flame thereof did not flash forth.

Therefore did the cherub think that God was favourable to them, and was brinsing them back into the garden. And the cherub stood wondering.

He could not go up to Heaven to ascertain God's order regarding their getting into the garden; he therefore abode standing by them, unable as he was to part from them; for he was afraid lest they should enter the garden without leave from God, who then would destroy him.

When Adam and Eve saw the cherub coming towards them with a flaming sword of fire in his hand, they fell on their faces from fear, and were as dead.

At that time the heavens and the earth shook; and other cherubim came down from heaven to the cherub who guarded the garden, and saw him amazed and silent.

Then, again, other angels came down nigh unto the place where Adam and Eve were. They were divided between joy and sorrow.

They were glad, because they thought that God was favourable to Adam, and wished him to return to the garden; and wished to restore him to the gladness he once enjoyed.

But they sorrowed over Adam, because he was fallen like a dead man, he and Eve; and they said in their thoughts, "Adam has not died in this place; but God has put him to death, for his having come to this place, and wishing to get into the garden without His leave."

CHAPTER LV.

The Conflict of Satan.

THEN came the Word of God to Adam and Eve, and raised them from their dead state, saying unto them, "Why came ye up hither? Dr, you intend to go into the garden, from which I brought you out? it can not be to-day; but only when the covenant I have made with you is fulfilled."

Then Adam, when he heard the Word of God, and the fluttering of the angels whom he did not see, but only heard the sound of them with his ears, he and Eve wept, and said to the angels:—

"O Spirits, who wait upon God, look upon me, and upon my being unable to see you! For when I was in my former bright nature) then I could see you. I sang praises as you do; and my heart was far above you.

"But now, that I have transgressed, that bright nature is gone from me, and I am come to this miserable state. And now am I come to this, that I cannot see you, and you do not serve me As you were wont. For I am become animal flesh.

"Yet now O angels of God, ask God with me, to restore me to that wherein I was formerly; to rescue me from this misery, and to remove from me the sentence of death He passed upon me, for having trespassed against Him."

Then, when the angels heard these words, they all grieved over him; and cursed Satan who had beguiled Adam, until he came from the garden to misery; from life to death; from peace to trouble; and from gladness to a strange land.

Then the angels said unto Adam, "Thou didst hearken to Satan, and didst forsake the Word of God who created thee; and thou didst believe that Satan would fulfil all he had promised thee.

"But now, O Adam, we will make known to thee, what came upon us through him, before his fall from heaven.

"He gathered together his hosts, and deceived them, promising them to give them a great kingdom, a divine nature; and other promises he made them.

"His hosts believed that. his word was true, so they yielded to him, and renounced the glory of God.

"He then sent for us according to the orders in which we were-to come under his command, and to hearken to his vain promise. But we would not, and we took not his advice.

"Then after he had fought with God, and had dealt forwardly with Him, he gathered together his hosts, and made war with us. And if it had not been for God's strength that was with us, we could not have prevailed against him to hurl him from heaven.

"But when he fell from among us, there was great joy in heaven, because of his going down from us. For had he continued in heaven, nothing, not even one angel would have remained in it.

"But God in His mercy, drove him from among us to this dark earth; for he had become darkness itself and a worker of unrighteousness.

"And he has continued, O Adam, to make war against thee, until he beguiled thee and made thee come out of the garden, to this strange land, where all these trials have come to thee. And death, which God brought upon him he has also brought to thee, O Adam, because thou didst obey him, and didst transgress against God."

Then a the angels rejoiced and praised God, and asked Him not to destroy Adam this time, for his having sought to enter the garden; but to bear with him until the fulfilment of the promise; and to help him in this world until he was free from Satan's hand.

The Forgotten Books of Eden

CHAPTER LVI.

A CHAPTER of divine comfort.

THEN came the Word of God to Adam, and said unto him:—

"O Adam, look at that garden of joy and at this earth of toil, and behold the angels who are in the garden-that is full of them, and see thyself alone on this earth, with Satan whom thou didst obey.

"Yet, if thou hadst submitted, and been obedient to Me, and hadst kept My Word, thou wouldst be with My angels in My garden.

"But when thou didst transgress and hearken to Satan, thou didst become his guest among his angels, that are full of wickedness; and thou camest to this earth, that brings forth to thee thorns and thistles.

"O Adam, ask him who deceived thee, to give thee the divine nature he promised thee, or to make thee a garden as I had made for thee; or to fill thee with that same bright nature with which I had filled thee.

"Ask him to make thee a body like the one I made thee, or to give thee a day of rest as I gave thee; or to create within thee a reasonable soul, as I did create for thee; or to remove thee hence to some other earth than this one which I gave thee. But, O Adam, he will not fulfil even one of the things he told thee.

"Acknowledge, then, My favour towards thee, and My mercy on thee, My creature; that I have not requited thee for thy transgression against Me, but in My pity for thee I have promised thee that at the end of the great five days and a half I will come and save thee."

Then God said again to Adam and Eve, "Arise, go down hence, lest the cherub with a sword of fire in his hand destroy you."

But Adam's heart was comforted by God's words to him, and he worshipped before Him.

And God commanded His angels to escort Adam and Eve to the cave with joy, instead of the fear that had come upon them.

Then the angels took up Adam and Eve, and brought them down from the mountain by the garden, with songs and psalms, until they brought them to the cave. There the angels began to comfort and to strengthen them, and then departed from them towards heaven, to their Creator, who had sent them.

But, after the angels were gone from Adam and Eve, came Satan, with shamefacedness, and stood at the entrance of the cave in which were Adam and Eve. He then called to Adam, and said, "O Adam, come, let me speak to thee."

Then Adam came out of the cave, thinking he was one of God's angels that was come to give him some good counsel.

The Forgotten Books of Eden

CHAPTER LVII.

"Therefore did I fall...

BUT when Adam came out and saw his hideous figure, he was afraid of him, and said unto him, "Who art thou?"

Then Satan answered and said unto him, "It is I, who hid myself within the serpent, and who talked to Eve, and beguiled her until she hearkened to my command. I am he who sent her, through the wiles of my speech, to deceive thee, until thou and she ate of the fruit of the tree, and ye came away from under the command of God."

But when Adam heard these words from him, he said unto him, "Canst thou make me a garden as God made for me? Or canst thou clothe me in the same bright nature in which God had clothed me?

"Where is the divine nature thou didst promise to give me? Where is that fair speech of thine, thou didst hold with us at first, when we were in the garden?"

Then Satan said unto Adam, "Thinkest thou, that when I have spoken to one about anything, I shall ever bring it to him or fulfil my word? Not so. For I myself have never even thought of obtaining what I asked.

"Therefore did I fall, and did I make you fall by that for which I myself fell; and with you also, whosoever accepts my counsel, falls thereby.

"But now, O Adam, by reason of thy fall thou art under my rule, and I am king over thee; because thou hast hearkened to me, and hast transgressed against thy God. Neither will there be any deliverance from my hands until the day promised thee by thy God."

Again he said, "Inasmuch as we do not know the day agreed upon with thee by thy God, nor the hour in which thou shalt be delivered, for that reason will we multiply war and murder upon thee and thy seed after thee.

"This is our will and our good pleasure, that we may not leave one of the sons of men to inherit our orders in heaven.

"For as to our abode, O Adam, it is in burning fire; and we will not cease our evil doing no, not one day nor one hour. And I, O Adam, shall sow fire upon thee when thou comest into the cave to dwell there."

When Adam heard these words he wept and mourned, and said unto Eve, "Hear what he said; that he will not fulfil aught of what he told thee in the garden. Did he really then become king over us?

"But we will ask God, who created us, to deliver us out of his hands."

CHAPTER LVIII.

"About sunset on the 53rd day...."

THEN Adam and Eve spread their hands unto God, praying and entreating Him to drive Satan away from them; that he do them no violence, and do not force them to deny God.

Then God sent to them at once His angel, who drove away Satan—from them. This happened about sunset, on the fifty-third day after they had come out of the garden.

Then Adam and Eve went into the cave, and stood up and turned their faces to the earth, to pray to God.

But ere they prayed Adam said unto Eve, "Lo, thou hast seen what temptations have befallen us in this land. Come, let us arise, and ask God to forgive us the sins we have committed; and we will not come out until the end of the day next to the fortieth. And if we die herein, He will save us."

Then Adam and Eve arose, and joined together in entreating God.

They abode thus praying in the cave; neither did they come out of it, by night or by day, until their prayers went up out of their mouths, like a flame of fire.

CHAPTER LIX.

Eighth apparition of Satan to Adam and Eve.

BUT Satan, the hater of all good, did not allow them to end their prayers. For he called to his hosts, and they came, all of them. He then said to them, "Since Adam and Eve, whom we beguiled, have agreed together to pray to God night and day, and to entreat Him to deliver them, and since they will not come out of the cave until the end of the fortieth day.

"And since they will continue their prayers as they have both agreed to do, that He will deliver them out of our hands, and restore them to their former state, see what we shall do unto them." And his hosts said unto him, "Power is thine, O our Lord, to do what thou listest."

Then Satan, great in wickedness, took his hosts and came into the cave, in the thirtieth night of the forty days and one; and he smote Adam and Eve, until he left them dead.

Then came the Word of God unto Adam and Eve, who raised them from their suffering, and God said unto Adam, "Be strong, and be not afraid of him who has just come to thee."

But Adam wept and said, "Where wast Thou, O my God, that they should smite me with such blows, and that this suffering should come upon us; upon me and upon Eve, Thy handmaid?"

Then God said unto him, "O Adam, see, he is lord and master of all thou hast, he who said, he would give thee divinity. Where is this love for thee? And where is the gift he promised?

"For once has it pleased him, O Adam, to come to thee, to comfort thee, and to strengthen thee, and to rejoice with thee, and to send his hosts to guard thee; because thou hast hearkened to him, and hast yielded to his counsel; and hast transgressed My commandment but has followed his behest?"

Then Adam wept before the Lord, and said, "O Lord because I transgressed a little, Thou hast sorely plagued me in return for it, I ask Thee to deliver me out of his hands; or else have pity on me, and take my soul out of my body now in this strange land."

Then God said unto Adam, "If only there had been this sighing and praying before, ere thou didst transgress! Then wouldst thou have rest from the trouble in which thou art now."

But God had patience with Adam, and let him and Eve remain in the cave until they had fulfilled the forty days.

But as to Adam and Eve, their strength and flesh withered from fasting and praying, from hunger and thirst; for they had not tasted either food or drink since they left the garden; nor were the functions of their bodies yet settled; and they had no strength left to continue in prayer from hunger, until the end of the next day to the fortieth. They were fallen down in the cave; yet what speech escaped from their mouths, was only in praises.

CHAPTER LX.

The Devil appears like an old man. He offers "a place of rest."

THEN on the eighty-ninth day, Satan came to the cave, clad in a garment of light, and girt about with a bright girdle.

In his hands was a staff of light, and he looked most awful: but his face was pleasant and his speech was sweet,

He thus transformed himself in order to deceive Adam and Eve, and to make them come out of the cave, ere they had fulfilled the forty days.

For he said within himself, "Now that when they had fulfilled the forty days' fasting and praying, God would restore them to their former estate; but if He did not do so, He would still be favourable to them; and even if He had not mercy on them, would He yet give them something from the garden to comfort them; as already twice before."

Then Satan drew near the cave in this fair appearance, and said:—

"O Adam, rise ye, stand up, thou and Eve, and come along with me, to a good land; and fear not. I am flesh and bones like you; and at first I was a creature that God created.

"And it was so, that when He had created me, He placed me in a garden in the north, on the border of the world.

"And He said to me, 'Abide here!' And I abode there according to His Word, neither did I transgress His commandment.

"Then He made a slumber to come over me, and He brought thee, O Adam, out of my side, but did not make thee abide by me.

"But God took thee in His divine hand, and placed thee in a garden to the eastward.

"Then I grieved because of thee, for that while God had taken thee out of my side, He had not let thee abide with me.

"But God said unto me: 'Grieve not because of Adam, whom I brought out of thy side; no harm will come to him.

"'For now I have brought out of his side a help-meet for him; and I have given him joy by so doing.'"

Then Satan said again, "I did not know how it is ye are in this cave, nor anything about this trial that has come upon you-until God said to me, 'Behold, Adam has transgressed, he whom I had taken out of thy side, and Eve also, whom I took out of his side; and I have driven them out of the garden; I have made them dwell in a land of sorrow and misery, because they transgressed against Me, and have hearkened to Satan. And lo, they are in suffering unto this day, the eightieth.'

"Then God said unto me, 'Arise, go to them, and make them come to thy place, and suffer not that Satan come near them, and afflict them. For they are now in great misery; and lie helpless from hunger.'

"He further said to me, 'When thou hast taken them to thyself, give them to eat of the fruit of the Tree of Life, and give them to drink of the water of peace; and clothe them in a garment of light, and restore them to their former state of grace, and leave them not in misery, for they came from thee. But grieve not over them, nor repent of that which has come upon them.'

"But when I heard this, I was sorry; and my heart could not patiently bear it for thy sake, O my child.

"But, O Adam, when I heard the name of Satan, I was afraid, and I said within myself, I will not come out, lest he ensnare me, as he did my children, Adam and Eve.

"And I said, 'O God, when I go to my children, Satan will meet me in the way, and war against me, as he did against them.'

"Then God said unto me, 'Fear not; when thou findest him, smite him with the staff that is in thine hand, and be not afraid of him for thou art of old standing, and he shall not prevail against thee.'

"Then I said, 'O my Lord, I am old, and cannot go. Send Thy angels to bring them.'

"But God said unto me, 'Angels, verily, are not like them; and they will not consent to come with them. But I have chosen thee, because they are thy offspring, and like thee, and will hearken to what thou sayest.'

"God said further to me, 'If thou hast not strength to walk, I will send a cloud to carry thee and alight thee at the entrance of their cave; then the cloud will return and leave thee there.

"'And if they will come with thee, I will send a cloud to carry thee and them.'

"Then He commanded a cloud, and it bare me up and brought me to you; and then went back.

"And now O my children, Adam and Eve, look at my hoar hairs and at my feeble estate, and at my coming from that distant place. Come, come with me, to a place of rest."

Then he began to weep and to sob before Adam and Eve, and his tears poured upon the earth like water.

And when Adam and Eve raised their eyes and saw his beard, and heard his sweet talk, their hearts softened towards him; they hearkened unto him, for they believed he was true.

And it seemed to them that they really were his offspring, when they saw that his face was like their own; and they trusted him.

CHAPTER LXI.

They besin to follow Satan.

THEN he took Adam and Eve by the hand, and began to bring them out of the cave.

But when they were come a little way out of it, God knew that Satan had overcome them, and had brought them out ere the forty days were ended, to take them to some distant place, and to destroy them.

Then the Word of the Lord God again came and cursed Satan, and drove him away from them.

And God began to speak unto Adam and Eve, saying to them, "What made you come out of the cave, unto this place?"

Then Adam said unto God, "Didst thou create a man before us? For when we were in the cave there suddenly came unto us a good old man who said to us, 'I am a messenger from God unto you, to bring you back to some place of rest.'

"And we did believe, O God, that he was a messenger from Thee; and we came out with him; and knew not whither we should go with him."

Then God said unto Adam, "See, that is the father of evil arts, who brought thee and Eve out of the Garden of Delights. And now, indeed, when he saw that thou and Eve both joined together in fasting and praying, and that you came not out of the cave before the end of the forty days, he wished to make your purpose vain, to break your mutual bond; to cut off all hope from you, and to drive you to some place where he might destroy you.

"Because he was unable to do aught to you, unless he showed himself in the like-

The Forgotten Books of Eden

ness of you.

"Therefore did he come to you with a face like your own, and began to give you tokens as if they were all true.

"But I in mercy and with the favour I had unto you, did not allow him to destroy you; but I drove him away from you.

"Now, therefore, O Adam, take Eve, and return to your cave, and remain in it until the morrow of the fortieth day. And when ye come out, go towards the eastern gate of the garden."

Then Adam and Eve worshipped God, and praised and blessed Him for the deliverance that had come to them from Him. And they returned towards the cave. This happened at eventide of the thirty-ninth day.

Then Adam and Eve stood up and with great zeal, prayed to God, to be brought out of their want for strength; for their strength had departed from them, through hunger and thirst and prayer. But they watched the whole of that night praying, until morning.

Then Adam said unto Eve, "Arise, let us go towards the eastern gate of the garden as God told us."

And they said their prayers as they were wont to do every day; and they went out of the cave, to go near to the eastern gate of the garden.

Then Adam and Eve stood up and prayed, and besought God to strengthen them, and to send them something to satisfy their hunger.

But when they had ended their prayers, they remained where they were by reason of their failing strength.

Then came the Word of God again, and said unto them, "O Adam, arise, go and bring hither two figs."

Then Adam and Eve arose, and went until they drew near to the cave.

CHAPTER LXII.

Two fruit trees.

BUT Satan the wicked was envious, because of the consolation God had given them.

So he prevented them, and went into the cave and took the two figs, and buried them outside the cave, so that Adam and Eve should not find them. He also had in his thoughts to destroy them.

But by God's mercy, as soon as those two figs were in the earth, God defeated Satan's counsel regarding them; and made them into two fruit-trees, that overshadowed the cave. For Satan had buried them on the eastern side of it.

Then when the two trees were grown, and were covered with fruit, Satan grieved and mourned, and said, "Better were it to have left those figs as they were; for now, behold, they have become two fruit-trees, whereof Adam will eat all the days of his life. Whereas I had in mind, when I buried them, to destroy them entirely, and to hide them for aye.

"But God has overturned my counsel; and would not that this sacred fruit should perish; and He has made plain my intention, and has defeated the counsel I had formed against His servants."

Then Satan went away ashamed, of not having wrought out his design.

CHAPTER LXIII.

The first joy of trees.

BUT Adam and Eve, as they drew near to the cave, saw two fig-trees, covered with fruit, and overshadowing the cave.

Then Adam said to Eve, "It seems to me we have gone astray. When did these two trees grow here? It seems to me that the enemy wishes to lead us astray, Sayest thou that there is in the earth another cave than this?

"Yet, O Eve, let us go into the cave, and find in it the two figs; for this is our cave, in which we were. But if we should not find the two figs in it, then it cannot be our cave."

They went then into the cave, and looked into the four corners of it, but found not the two figs.

And Adam wept and said to Eve, "Are we come to a wrong cave, then, O Eve? It seems to me these two fig-trees are the two figs that were in the cave." And Eve said, "I, for my part, do not know."

Then Adam stood up and prayed and said, "O God, Thou didst command us to come back to the cave, to take the two figs, and then to return to Thee.

"But now, we have not found them. O God, hast Thou taken them, and sown these two trees, or have we gone astray in the earth; or has the enemy deceived us? If it be real, then, O God, reveal to us the secret of these two trees and of the two figs."

Then came the Word of God to Adam, and said unto him, "O Adam, when I sent thee to fetch the figs, Satan went before thee to the cave, took the figs, and buried them outside, eastward of the cave, thinking to destroy them; and not sowing them with good intent.

"Not for his mere sake, then, have these trees grown up at once; but I had mercy on thee and I commanded them to grow. And they grew to be two large trees, that you be overshadowed by their branches, and find rest; and that I make you see My power and My marvellous works.

"And, also, to show you Satan's meanness, and his evil works, for ever since ye came out of the garden, he has not ceased, no, not one day, from doing you some harm. But I have not given him power over you."

The Forgotten Books of Eden

And God said, "Henceforth, O Adam, rejoice on account of the trees, thou and Eve; and rest under them when ye feel weary. But eat not of their fruit, nor come near them."

Then Adam wept, and said, "O God, wilt Thou again kill us, or wilt Thou drive us away from before Thy face, and cut our life from off the face of the earth?

"O God, I beseech Thee, if Thou knowest that there be in these trees either death or some other evil, as at the first time, root them up from near our cave, and wither them; and leave us to die of the heat, of hunger and of thirst.

"For we know Thy marvellous works, O God, that they are great, and that by Thy power Thou canst bring one thing out of another, without one's wish. For Thy power can make rocks to become trees, and trees to become rocks."

CHAPTER LXIV.

Adam and Eve partake of the first earthly food.

THEN God looked upon Adam and upon his strength of mind, upon his endurance of hunger and thirst, and of the heat. And he changed the two fig-trees into two figs, as they were at first, and then said to Adam and to Eve, "Each of you may take one fig." And they took them, as the Lord commanded them.

And he said to them, "Go ye into the cave, and eat the figs, and satisfy your hunger, lest ye die."

So, as God commanded them, they went into the cave, about the time when the sun was setting. And Adam and Eve stood up and prayed at the time of the setting sun.

Then they sat down to eat the figs; but they knew not how to eat them; for they were not accustomed to eat earthly food. They feared also lest, if they ate, their stomach should be burdened and their flesh thickened, and their hearts take to liking earthly food.

But while they were thus seated, God, out of pity for them, sent them His angel, lest they should perish of hunger and thirst.

And the angel said unto Adam and Eve, "God says to you that ye have not strength to fast until death; eat, therefore, and strengthen your bodies; for ye are now animal flesh, that cannot subsist without food and drink."

Then Adam and Eve took the figs and began to eat of them. But God had put into them a mixture as of savoury bread and blood.

Then the angel went from Adam and Eve, who ate of the figs until they had satisfied their hunger. Then they put by what remained; but by the power of God, the figs became full as before, because God blessed them.

After this Adam and Eve arose, and prayed with a joyful heart and renewed strength, and praised and rejoiced abundantly the whole of that night. And this was the end of the eighty-third day.

The Forgotten Books of Eden

CHAPTER LXV.

Adam and Eve acquire digestive organs. Final hope of returning to the Garden is quenched.

AND when it was day, they rose and prayed, after their custom, and then went out of the cave.

But as they felt great trouble from the food they had eaten, and to which they were not used, they went about in the cave saying to each other:—

"What has happened to us through eating, that this pain should have come upon us? Woe be to us, we shall die! Better for us to have died than to have eaten; and to have kept our bodies pure, than to have defiled them with food."

Then Adam said to Eve, "This pain did not come to us in the garden, neither did we eat such bad food there. Thinkest thou, O Eve, that God will plague us through the food that is in us, or that our inwards will come out; or that God means to kill us with this pain before He has fulfilled His promise to us?"

Then Adam besought the Lord and said, "O Lord, let us not perish through the food we have eaten. O Lord, smite us not; but deal with us according to Thy great mercy, and forsake us not until the day of the promise Thou hast made us."

Then God looked upon them, and at once fitted them for eating food; as unto this day; so that they should not perish.

Then Adam and Eve came back into the cave sorrowful and weeping because of the alteration in their nature. And they both knew from that hour that they were altered beings, that their hope of returning to the garden was now cut off; and that they could not enter it.

For that now their bodies had strange functions; and all flesh that requires food and drink for its existence, cannot be in the garden.

Then Adam said to Eve, "Behold, our hope is now cut off; and so is our trust to enter the garden. We no longer belong to the inhabitants of the garden; but henceforth we are earthy and of the dust, and of the inhabitants of the earth, We shall not return to the garden, until the day in which God has promised to save us, and to bring us again into the garden, as He promised us."

Then they prayed to God that He would have mercy on them; after which, their mind was quieted, their hearts were broken, and their lonsing was cooled down; and they were like strangers on earth. That night Adam and Eve spent in the cave, where they slept heavily by reason of the food they had eaten.

CHAPTER LXVI.

Adam does his first day's work.

WHEN it was morning, the day after they had eaten food, Adam and Eve prayed in the cave, and Adam said unto Eve, "Lo, we asked for food of God, and He gave it. But now let us also ask Him to give us a drink of water."

Then they arose, and went to the bank of the stream of water, that was on the south border of the garden, in which they had before thrown themselves. And they stood on the bank, and prayed to God that He would command them to drink of the water.

Then the Word of God came to Adam, and said unto him, "O Adam, thy body is become brutish, and requires water to drink. Take ye, and drink, thou and Eve; give thanks and praise."

Adam and Eve then drew near, and drank of it, until their bodies felt refreshed. After having drunk, they praised God, and then returned to their cave, after their former custom. This happened at the end of eighty-three days.

Then on the eighty-fourth day, they took two figs and hung them in the cave, together with the leaves thereof, to be to them a sign and a blessing from God. And they placed them there until there should arise a posterity to them, who should see the wonderful things God had done to them.

Then Adam and Eve again stood outside the cave, and besought God to show them some food wherewith to nourish their bodies.

Then the Word of God came and said unto him, "O Adam, go down to the westward of the cave, as far as a land of dark soil, and there thou shalt find food."

And Adam hearkened unto the Word of God, took Eve, and went down to a land of dark soil, and found there wheat growing, in the ear and ripe, and figs to eat; and Adam rejoiced over it.

Then the Word of God came again to Adam, and said unto him, "Take of this wheat and make thee bread of it, to nourish thy body withal." And God gave Adam's heart wisdom, to work out the corn until it became bread.

Adam accomplished all that, until he grew very faint and weary. He then returned to the cave; rejoicing at what he had learned of what is done with wheat, until it is made into bread for one's use.

CHAPTER LXVII.

"Then Satan began to lead astray Adam and Eve. . . ."

BUT when Adam and Eve went down to the land of black mud, and came near to the wheat God had showed them, and saw it ripe and ready for reaping, as they had no sickle to reap it withal—they girt themselves, and began to pull up the wheat, until it was all done.

Then they made it into a heap; and, faint from heat and from thirst, they went under a shady tree, where the breeze fanned them to sleep.

But Satan saw what Adam and Eve had done. And he called his hosts, and said to them, "Since God has shown to Adam and Eve all about this wheat, wherewith to strengthen their bodies—and, lo, they are come and have made a heap of it, and faint

The Forgotten Books of Eden

from the toil are now asleep—come, let us set fire to this heap of corn, and burn it, and let us take that bottle of water that is by them, and empty it out, so that they may find nothing to drink, and we kill them with hunger and thirst.

"Then, when they wake up from their sleep, and seek to return to the cave, we will come to them in the way, and will lead them astray; so that they die of hunger and thirst; when they may, perhaps, deny God, and He destroy them. So shall we be rid of them."

Then Satan and his hosts threw fire upon the wheat and consumed it.

But from the heat of the flame Adam and Eve awoke from their sleep, and saw the wheat burning, and the bucket of water by them, poured out.

Then they wept and went back to the cave.

But as they were going up from below the mountain where they were, Satan and his hosts met them in the form of angels, praising God.

Then Satan said to Adam, "O Adam, why art thou so pained with hunger and thirst? It seems to me that Satan has burnt up the wheat." And Adam said to him, "Ay."

Again Satan said to Adam, "Come back with us; we are angels of God. God sent us to thee, to show thee another field of corn, better than that; and beyond it is a fountain of good water, and many trees, where thou shalt dwell near it, and work the corn-field to better purpose than that which Satan has consumed."

Adam thought that he was true, and that they were angels who talked with him; and he went back with them.

Then Satan began to lead astray Adam and Eve eight days, until they both fell down as if dead, from hunger, thirst, and faintness. Then he fled with his hosts, and left them.

CHAPTER LXVIII.

How destruction and trouble is of Satan when he is the master. Adam and Eve establish the custom of worship.

THEN God looked upon Adam and Eve, and upon what had come upon them from Satan, and how he had made them perish.

God, therefore, sent His Word, and raised up Adam and Eve from their state of death.

Then, Adam, when he was raised, said, "O God, Thou hast burnt and taken from us the corn Thou hadst given us, and Thou hast emptied out the bucket of water. And Thou hast sent Thy angels, who have waylaid us from the corn-field. Wilt Thou make us perish? If this be from Thee, O God, then take away our souls; but punish us not."

Then God said to Adam, "I did not burn down the wheat, and I did not pour the water out of the bucket, and I did not send My angels to lead thee astray.

"But it is Satan, thy master who did it; he to whom thou hast subjected thyself; My commandment being meanwhile set aside. He it is, who burnt down the corn, and poured out the water, and who has led thee astray; and all the promises he has made you, verily are but feint, and deceit, and a lie.

"But now, O Adam, thou shalt acknowledge My good deeds done to thee."

And God told His angels to take Adam and Eve, and to bear them up to the field of wheat, which they found as before, with the bucket full of water.

There they saw a tree, and found on it solid manna; and wondered at God's power. And the angels commanded them to eat of the manna when they were hungry.

And God adjured Satan with a curse, not to come again, and destroy the field of corn.

Then Adam and Eve took of the corn, and made of it an offering, and took it and offered it up on the mountain, the place where they had offered up their first offering of blood.

And they offered this oblation again on the altar they had built at first. And they stood up and prayed, and besought the Lord saying, "Thus, O God, when we were in the garden, did our praises go up to Thee, like this offering; and our innocence went up to thee like incense. But now, O God, accept this offering from us, and turn us not back, reft of Thy mercy."

Then God said to Adam and Eve, "Since ye have made this oblation and have offered it to Me, I shall make it My flesh, when I come down upon earth to save you; and I shall cause it to be offered continually upon an altar, for forgiveness and for mercy, unto those who partake of it duly."

And God sent a bright fire upon the offering of Adam and Eve, and filled it with brightness, grace, and light; and the Holy Ghost came down upon that oblation.

Then God commanded an angel to take fire-tongs, like a spoon, and with it to take an offering and bring it to Adam and Eve. And the angel did so, as God had commanded him, and offered it to them.

And the souls of Adam and Eve were brightened, and their hearts were filled with joy and gladness and with the praises of God.

And God said to Adam, "This shall be unto you a custom, to do so, when affliction and sorrow come upon you. But your deliverance and your entrance into the garden, shall not be until the days are fulfilled, as agreed between you and Me; were it not so, I would, of My mercy and pity for you, bring you back to My garden and to My favour for the sake of the offering you have just made to My name."

Adam rejoiced at these words which he heard from God; and he and Eve worshipped before the altar, to which they bowed, and then went back to the Cave of Treasures.

And this took place at the end of the twelfth day after the eightieth day, from the

The Forgotten Books of Eden

time Adam and Eve came out of the garden.

And they stood up the whole night praying until morning; and then went out of the cave.

Then Adam said to Eve, with joy of heart, because of the offering they had made to God, and that had been accepted of Him, "Let us do this three times every week, on the fourth day Wednesday, on the preparation day Friday, and on the Sabbath Sunday, all the days of our life."

And as they agreed to these words between themselves, God was pleased with their thoughts, and with the resolution they had each taken with the other.

After this, came the Word of God to Adam, and said, "O Adam, thou hast determined beforehand the days in which sufferings shall come upon Me, when I am made flesh; for they are the fourth Wednesday, and the preparation day Friday.

"But as to the first day, I created in it all things, and I raised the heavens. And, again, through My rising again on this day, will I create joy, and raise them on high, who believe in Me; O Adam, offer this oblation, all the days of thy life."

Then God withdrew His Word from Adam.

But Adam continued to offer this oblation thus, every week three times, until, the end of seven weeks. And on the first day, which is the fiftieth, Adam made an offering as he was wont, and he and Eve took it and came to the altar before God, as He had taught them.

CHAPTER LXIX.

Twelfth apparition of Satan to Adam and Eve, while Adam was praying over the offering upon the altar; when Satan smote him.

THEN Satan, the hater of all good, envious of Adam and of his offering through which he found favour with God, hastened and took a sharp stone from among sharp iron-stones; appeared in the form of a man, and went and stood by Adam and Eve.

Adam was then offering on the altar, and had begun to pray, with his hands spread unto God.

Then Satan hastened with the sharp iron-stone he had with him, and with it pierced Adam on the right side, when flowed blood and water, then Adam fell upon the altar like a corpse. And Satan fled.

Then Eve came, and took Adam and placed him below the altar. And there she stayed, weeping over him; while a stream of blood flowed from Adam's side upon his offering.

But God looked upon the death of Adam. He then sent His Word, and raised him up and said unto him, "Fulfil thy offering, for indeed, Adam, it is worth much, and there is no shortcoming in it."

The Forgotten Books of Eden

God said further unto Adam, "Thus will it also happen to Me, on the earth, when I shall be pierced and blood shall flow blood and water from My side and run over My body, which is the true offering; and which shall be offered on the altar as a perfect offering."

Then God commanded Adam to finish his offering, and when he had ended it he worshipped before God, and praised Him for the signs He had showed him.

And God healed Adam in one day, which is the end of the seven weeks; and that is the fiftieth day.

Then Adam and Eve returned from the mountain, and went into the Cave of Treasures, as they were used to do. This completed for Adam and Eve, one hundred and forty days since their coming out of the garden.

Then they both stood up that night and prayed to God. And when it was morning, they went out, and went down westward of the cave, to the place where their corn was, and there rested under the shadow of a tree, as they were wont.

But when there a multitude of beasts came all round them. It was Satan's doing, in his wickedness; in order to wage war against Adam through marriage.

CHAPTER LXX.

Thirteenth apparition of Satan to Adam and Eve, to make war against him, through his marriage with Eve.

AFTER this Satan, the hater of all good, took the form n angel, and with him two others, so that they looked like the three angels who had brought to Adam gold, incense, and myrrh.

They passed before Adam and Eve while they were under the tree, and greeted Adam and Eve with fair words that were full of guile.

But when Adam and Eve saw their comely mien, and heard their sweet speech, Adam rose, welcomed them, and brought them to Eve, and they remained all together; Adam's heart the while, being glad because he thought concerning them, that they were the same angels, who had brought him gold, incense, and myrrh.

Because, when they came to Adam the first time, there came upon him from them, peace and joy, through their brinsing him good tokens; so Adam thought that they were come a second time to give him other tokens for him to rejoice withal. For he did not know it was Satan; therefore did he receive them with joy and companied with them.

Then Satan, the tallest of them, said, "Rejoice, O Adam, and be glad. Lo, God has sent us to thee to tell thee something."

And Adam said, "What is it?" Then Satan answered, "It is a light thing, yet it is a word of God, wilt thou hear it from us and do it? But if thou hearest not, we will return to God, and tell Him that thou wouldest not receive His word."

And Satan said again to Adam, "Fear not, neither let a trembling come upon thee;

dost not thou know us?"

But Adam said, "I know you not."

Then Satan said to him, "I am the angel who brought thee gold, and took it to the cave; this other one is he who brought thee incense; and that third one, is he who brought thee myrrh when thou wast on the top of the mountain, and who carried thee to the cave.

"But as to the other angels our fellows, who bare you to the cave, God has not sent them with us this time; for He said to us, 'You suffice.'"

So when Adam heard these words he believed them, and said to these angels, "Speak the word of God, that I may receive it."

And Satan said unto him "Swear, and promise me that thou wilt receive it."

Then Adam said, "I know not how to swear and promise."

And Satan said to him, "Hold out thy hand, and put it inside my hand."

Then Adam held out his hand, and put it into Satan's hand; when Satan said unto him, "Say, now—so true as God is living, rational, and speaking, who raised the heavens in the space, and established the earth upon the waters, and has created me out of the four elements, and out of the dust of the earth—I will not break my promise, nor renounce my word."

And Adam swore thus.

Then Satan said to him, "Lo, it is now some time since thou camest out of the garden, and thou knowest neither wickedness nor evil. But now God s says to thee, to take Eve who came out of thy side, and to wed her, that she bear thee children, to comfort thee, and to drive from thee trouble and sorrow; now this thing is not difficult, neither is there any scandal in it to thee."

CHAPTER LXXI.

Adam is troubled by his wedding with Eve.

BUT when Adam heard these words from Satan, he sorrowed much, because of his oath and of his promise, and said, "Shall I commit adultery with my flesh and my bones, and shall I sin against myself, for God to destroy me, and to blot me out from off the face of the earth?

"Since, when at first, I ate of the tree, He drove me out of the garden into this strange land, and deprived me of my bright nature, and brought death upon me. If, then, I should do this, He will cut off my life from the earth, and He will cast me into hell, and will plague me there a long time.

"But God never spoke the words thou hast told me; and ye are not God's angels, nor yet sent from Him. But ye are devils, come to me under the false appearance of angels . Away from me; ye cursed of God!"

Then those devils fled from before Adam. And he and Eve arose, and returned to

The Forgotten Books of Eden

the Cave of Treasures, and went into it.

Then Adam said to Eve, "If thou sawest what I did, tell it not; for I sinned against God n swearing by His great name, and I have placed my hand another time into that of Satan." Eve, then, held her peace, as Adam told her.

Then Adam arose, and spread his hands unto God, beseeching and entreating Him with tears, to forgive him what he had done. And Adam remained thus standing and praying forty days and forty nights. He neither ate nor drank until he dropped down upon the earth from hunger and thirst.

Then God sent His Word unto Adam, who raised him up from where he lay, and said unto him, "O Adam, why hast thou sworn by My name, and why hast thou made agreement with Satan another time?"

But Adam wept, and said, "O God, forgive me, for I did this unwittingly; believing they were God's angels."

And God forgave Adam, saying, to him, "Beware of Satan."

And He withdrew His Word from Adam.

Then Adam's heart was comforted; and he took Eve, and they went out of the cave, to make some food for their bodies.

But from that day Adam struggled in his mind about his wedding Eve; afraid as he was to do it, lest God should be wroth with him.

Then Adam and Eve went to the river of water, and sat on the bank, as people do when they enjoy themselves.

But Satan was jealous of them; and would destroy them.

CHAPTER LXXII.

Adam's heart is set on fire.

THEN Satan, and ten from his hosts, transformed themselves into maidens, unlike any others in the whole world for grace.

They came up out of the river in presence of Adam and Eve, and they said among themselves, "Come, we will look at the faces of Adam and of Eve, who are of the men upon earth. How beautiful they are, and how different is their look from our own faces." Then they came to Adam and Eve, and greeted them; and stood wondering at them.

Adam and Eve looked at them also, and wondered at their beauty, and said, "Is there, then, under us, another world, with such beautiful creatures as these in it'"

And those maidens said to Adam and Eve, "Yes, indeed, we are an abundant creation."

Then Adam said to them, "But how do you multiply?"

And they answered him, "We have husbands who wedded us, and we bear them children, who grow up, and who in their turn wed and are wedded, and also bear children; and thus we increase. And if so be, O Adam, thou wilt not believe us, we will show thee our husbands and our children."

Then they shouted over the river as if to call their husbands and their children, who came up from the river, men and children; and every one came to his wife, his children being with him.

But when Adam and Eve saw them, they stood dumb, and wondered at them.

Then they said to Adam and Eve, "You see our husbands and our children, wed Eve as we wed our wives, and you shall have children the same as we." This was a device of Satan to deceive Adam.

Satan also thought within himself, "God at first commanded Adam concerning the fruit of the tree, saying to him, 'Eat not of it; else of death thou shalt die.' But Adam ate of it, and yet God did not kill him; He only decreed upon him death, and plagues and trials, until the day he shall come out of his body.

"Now, then, if I deceive him to do this thing, and to wed Eve without God's commandment, God will kill him then."

Therefore did Satan work this apparition before Adam and Eve; because he sought to kill him, and to make him disappear from off the face of the earth.

Meanwhile the fire of sin came upon Adam, and he thought of committing sin. But he restrained himself, fearing lest if he followed this advice of Satan God would put him to death.

Then Adam and Eve arose, and prayed to God, while Satan and his hosts went down into the river, in presence of Adam and Eve; to let them see that they were going back to their own regions.

Then Adam and Eve went back to the Cave of Treasures, as they were wont; about evening time.

And they both arose and prayed to God that night. Adam remained standing in prayer, yet not knowing how to pray, by reason of the thoughts of his heart regarding his wedding Eve; and he continued so until morning.

And when light arose, Adam said unto Eve, "Arise, let us go below the mountain, where they brought us gold, and let us ask the Lord concerning this matter."

Then Eve said, "What is that matter, O Adam?"

And he answered her, "That I may request the Lord to inform me about wedding thee; for I will not do it without His order, lest He make us perish, thee and me. For those devils have set my heart on fire, with thoughts of what they showed us, in their sinful apparitions."

Then Eve said to Adam, "Why need we go below the mountain? Let us rather stand up and pray in our cave to God, to let us know whether this counsel is good or not."

The Forgotten Books of Eden

Then Adam rose up in prayer and said, "O God, thou knowest that we transgressed against Thee, and from the moment we transgressed, we were bereft of our bright nature; and our body became brutish, requiring food and drink; and with animal desires.

"Command us, O God, not to give way to them without Thy order, lest Thou bring us to nothing. For if Thou give us not the order, we shall be overpowered, and follow that advice of Satan; and Thou wilt again make us perish.

"If not, then take our souls from us; let us be rid of this animal lust. And if Thou give us no order respecting this thing, then sever Eve from me, and me from her; and place us each far away from the other.

"Yet again, O God, when Thou hast put us asunder from each other, the devils will deceive us with their apparitions, and destroy our hearts, and defile our thoughts towards each other. Yet if it is not each of us towards the other, it will, at all events, be through their appearance when they show themselves to us." Here Adam ended his prayer.

CHAPTER LXXIII.

The betrothal of Adam and Eve.

THEN God looked upon the words of Adam that they were true, and that he could long await His order, respecting the counsel of Satan.

And God approved Adam in what he had thought concerning this, and in the prayer he had offered in His presence; and the Word of God came unto Adam and said to him, "O Adam, if only thou hadst had this caution at first, ere thou earnest out of the garden into this land!"

After that, God sent His angel who had brought gold, and the angel who had brought incense, and the angel who had brought myrrh to Adam, that they should inform him respecting his wedding Eve.

Then those angels said to Adam, "Take the gold and give it to Eve as a wedding gift, and betroth her; then give her some incense and myrrh as a present; and be ye, thou and she, one flesh."

Adam hearkened to the angels, and took the gold and put it into Eve's bosom in her garment; and bethrothed her with his hand.

Then the angels commanded Adam and Eve, to arise and pray forty days and forty nights; and after that, that Adam should come in to his wife; for then this would be an act pure and undefiled; and he should have children who would multiply, and replenish the face of the earth.

Then both Adam and Eve received the words of the angels; and the angels departed from them.

Then Adam and Eve began to fast and to pray, until the end of the forty days; and then they came together, as the angels had told them. And from the time Adam left the garden until he wedded Eve, were two hundred and twenty-three days, that is seven months and thirteen days.

Thus was Satan's war with Adam defeated.

CHAPTER LXXIV.

The birth of Cain and Luluwa. Why they received those names.

AND they dwelt on the earth working, in order to continue in the well-being of their bodies; and were so until the nine months of Eve's childbearing were ended, and the time drew near when she must be delivered.

Then she said unto Adam, "This cave is a pure spot by reason of the signs wrought in it since we left the garden; and we shall again pray in it. It is not meet, then, that I should bring forth in it; let us rather repair to that of the sheltering rock, which Satan hurled at us, when he wished to kill us with it; but that was held up and spread as an awning over us by the command of God; and formed a cave."

Then Adam removed Eve to that cave; and when the time came that she should bring forth, she travailed much. So was Adam sorry, and his heart suffered for her sake; for she was nigh unto death; that the word of God to her should be fulfilled: "In suffering shalt thou bear a child, and in sorrow shalt thou bring forth thy child."

But when Adam saw the strait in which Eve was, he arose and prayed to God, and said, "O Lord, look upon me with the eye of Thy mercy, and bring her out of her distress."

And God looked at His maid-servant Eve, and delivered her, and she brought forth her first-born son, and with him a daughter.

Then Adam rejoiced at Eve's deliverance, and also over the children she had borne him. And Adam ministered unto Eve in the cave, until the end of eight days; when they named the son Cain, and the daughter Luluwa.

The meaning of Cain is "hater," because he hated his sister in their mother's womb; ere they came out of it. Therefore did Adam name him Cain.

But Luluwa means "beautiful," because she was more beautiful than her mother.

Then Adam and Eve waited until Cain and his sister were forty days old, when Adam said unto Eve, "We will make an offering and offer it up in behalf of the children."

And Eve said, "We will make one offering for the firstborn son; and afterwards we shall make one for the daughter."

CHAPTER LXXV.

The family revisits the Cave of Treasures. Birth of Abel and Aklemia.

THEN Adam prepared an offering, and he and Eve offered it up for their children, and brought it to the altar they had built at first.

The Forgotten Books of Eden

And Adam offered up the offering, and besought God to accept his offering.

Then God accepted Adam's offering, and sent a light from heaven that shone upon the offering. And Adam and the son drew near to the offering, but Eve and the daughter did not approach unto it.

Then Adam came down from upon the altar, and they were joyful; and Adam and Eve waited until the daughter was eighty days old; then Adam prepared an offering and took it to Eve and to the children; and they went to the altar, where Adam offered it up, as he was wont, asking the Lord to accept his offering.

And the Lord accepted the offering of Adam and Eve. Then Adam, Eve, and the children, drew near together, and came down from the mountain, rejoicing.

But they returned not to the cave in which they were born; but came to the Cave of Treasures, in order that the children should go round it, and be blessed with the tokens brought from the garden.

But after they had been blessed with these tokens, they went back to the cave in which they were born.

However, before Eve had offered up the offering, Adam had taken her, and had gone with her to the river of water, in which they threw themselves at first; and there they washed themselves. Adam washed his body and Eve hers also clean, after the suffering and distress that had come upon them.

But Adam and Eve, after washing themselves in the river of water, returned every night to the Cave of Treasures, where they prayed and were blessed; and then went back to their cave where the children were born

So did Adam and Eve until the children had done sucking. Then, when they were weaned, Adam made an offering for the souls of his children; other than the three times he made an offering for them, every week.

When the days of nursing the children were ended, Eve again conceived, and when her days were accomplished she brought forth another son and daughter; and they named the son Abel, and the daughter Aklia.

Then at the end of forty days, Adam made an offering for the son, and at the end of eighty days he made another offering for the daughter, and did by them, as he had done before by Cain and his sister Luluwa.

He brought them to the Cave of Treasures, where they received a blessing, and then returned to the cave where they were born. After the birth of these, Eve ceased from childbearing.

CHAPTER LXXVI.

Cain becomes jealous because of his sisters.

A ND the children began to wax stronger, and to grow in stature; but Cain was hardhearted, and ruled over his younger brother.

And oftentimes when his father made an offering, he would remain behind and not go with them, to offer up.

But, as to Abel, he had a meek heart, and was obedient to his father and mother, whom he often moved to make an offering, because he loved it; and prayed and fasted much.

Then came this sign to Abel. As he was coming into the Cave of Treasures, and saw the golden rods, the incense and the myrrh, he inquired of his parents Adam and Eve concerning them, and said unto them, "How did you come by these?"

Then Adam told him all that had befallen them. And Abel felt deeply about what his father told him.

Furthermore his father Adam, told him of the works of God, and of the garden; and after that, he remained behind his father the whole of that night in the Cave of Treasures.

And that night, while he was praying, Satan appeared unto him under the figure of a man, who said to him, "Thou hast oftentimes moved thy father to make an offering, to fast and to pray, therefore I will kill thee, and make thee perish from this world."

But as for Abel, he prayed to God, and drove away Satan from him; and believed not the words of the devil. Then when it was day, an angel of God appeared unto him, who said to him, "Shorten neither fasting, prayer, nor offering up an oblation unto thy God. For, lo, the Lord has accepted thy prayer. Be not afraid of the figure which appeared unto thee in the night, and who cursed thee unto death." And the angel departed from him.

Then when it was day, Abel came to Adam and Eve, and told them of the vision he had seen. But when they heard it, they grieved much over it, yet said nothing to him about it; they only comforted him.

But as to hard-hearted Cain, Satan came to him by night, showed himself and said unto him, "Since Adam and Eve love thy brother Abel much more than they love thee, and wish to join him in marriage to thy beautiful sister, because they love him; but wish to join thee in marriage to his ill-favoured sister, because they hate thee;

"Now, therefore, I counsel thee, when they do that, to kill thy brother; then thy sister will be left for thee; and his sister will be cast, away."

And Satan departed from him. But the wicked One remained behind in the heart of Cain, who sought many a time, to kill his brother.

CHAPTER LXXVII.

Cain, 15 years old, and Abel 12 years old, grow apart.

BUT when Adam saw that the elder brother hated the younger, he endeavoured to soften their hearts, and said unto Cain, "Take, O my son, of the fruits of thy sowing, and make an offering unto God, that He may forgive thee thy wickedness and thy sin."

The Forgotten Books of Eden

He said also to Abel, "Take thou of thy sowing and make an offering and bring it to God, that He may forgive thy wickedness and thy sin."

Then Abel hearkened unto his father's voice, and took of his sowing, and made a good offering, and said to his father, Adam, "Come with me, to show me how to offer it up."

And they went, Adam and Eve with him, and showed him how to offer up his gift upon the altar. Then after that, they stood up and prayed that God would accept Abel's offering.

Then God looked upon Abel and accepted his offering. And God was more pleased with Abel than with his offering, because of his good heart and pure body. There was no trace of guile in him.

Then they came down from the altar, and went to the cave in which they dwelt. But Abel, by reason of his joy at having made his offering, repeated it three times a week, after the example of his father Adam.

But as to Cain, he took no pleasure in offering; but after much anger on his father's part, he offered up his gift once; and when he did offer up, his eye was on the offering he made, and he took the smallest of his sheep for an offering, and his eye was again on it. '

Therefore God did not accept his offering, because his heart was full of murderous thoughts.

And they all thus lived together in the cave in which Eve had brought forth, until Cain was fifteen years old, and Abel twelve years old.

CHAPTER LXXVIII.

Jealousy overcomes Cain. He makes trouble in the family. How the first murder was planned.

THEN Adam said to Eve, "Behold the children are grown up; we must think of finding wives for them."

Then Eve answered, "How can we do it?"

Then Adam said to her, "We will join Abel's sister in marriage to Cain, and Cain's sister to Abel."

Then said Eve to Adam, "I do not like Cain because he is hard-hearted; but let them bide until we offer up unto the Lord in their behalf."

And Adam said no more.

Meanwhile Satan came to Cain in the figure of a man of the field, and said to him, "Behold Adam and Eve have taken counsel together about the marriage of you two; and they have agreed to marry Abel's sister to thee, and thy sister to him.

"But if it was not that I love thee, I would not have told thee this thing. Yet if thou wilt take my advice, and hearken to me, I will bring: thee on thy wedding day beautiful

The Forgotten Books of Eden

robes, gold and silver in plenty, and my relations will attend thee."

Then Cain said with joy, "Where are thy relations?"

And Satan answered, "My relations are in a garden in the north, whither I once meant to bring thy father Adam; but he would not accept my offer.

"But thou, if thou wilt receive my words and if thou wilt come unto me after thy wedding, thou shalt rest from the misery in which thou art; and thou shalt rest and be better off than thy father Adam."

At these words of Satan Cain opened his ears, and leant towards his speech.

And he did not remain in the field, but he went to Eve, his mother, and beat her, and cursed her, and said to her, "Why are ye about taking my sister to wed her to my brother? Am I dead'"'

His mother, however, quieted him, and sent him to the field where be had been.

Then when Adam came, she told him of what Cain had done.

1But Adam grieved and held his peace, and said not a word.

Then on the morrow Adam said unto Cain his son, "Take of thy sheep, young and good, and offer them up unto thy God; and I will speak to thy brother, to make unto his God an offering of corn."

They both hearkened to their father Adam, and they took their offerings, and offered them up on the mountain by the altar.

But Cain behaved haughtily towards his brother, and thrust him from the altar, and would not let him offer up his gift upon the altar; but he offered his own upon it, with a proud heart, full of guile, and fraud.

But as for Abel, he set up stones that were near at hand, and upon that, he offered up his gift with a heart humble and free from guile.

Cain was then standing by the altar on which he had offered up his gift; and he cried unto God to accept his offering; but God did not accept it from him; neither did a divine fire come down to consume his offering.

But he remained standing over against the altar, out of humour and wroth, looking towards his brother Abel, to see if God would accept his offering or not.

And Abel prayed unto God to accept his offering. Then a divine fire came down and consumed his offering. And God smelled the sweet savour of his offering; because Abel loved Him and rejoiced in Him.

And because God was well pleased with him He sent him an angel of light in the figure of man who had partaken of his offering, because He had smelled the sweet savour of his offering, and they comforted Abel and strengthened his heart.

But Cain was looking on all that took place at his brother's offering, and was wroth

The Forgotten Books of Eden

on account of it.

Then he opened his mouth and blasphemed God, because He had not accepted his offering.

But God said unto Cain, "Wherefore is thy countenance sad? Be righteous, that I may accept thy offering. Not against Me hast thou murmured, but against thyself."

2And God said this to Cain in rebuke, and because He abhorred him and his offering.

And Cain came down from the altar, his colour changed and of a woeful countenance, and came to his father and mother and told them all that had befallen him. And Adam grieved much because God had not accepted Cain's offering.

But Abel came down rejoicing, and with a gladsome heart, and told his father and mother how God had accepted his offering. And they rejoiced at it and kissed his face.

And Abel said to his father, "Because Cain thrust me from the altar, and would not allow me to offer my gift upon it, I made an altar for myself and offered my gift upon it."

But when Adam heard this he was very sorry, because it was the altar he had built at first, and upon which he had offered his own gifts.

As to Cain, he was so sullen and so angry that he went into the field, where Satan came to him and said to him, "Since thy brother Abel has taken refuge with thy father Adam, because thou didst thrust him from the altar, they have kissed his face, and they rejoice over him, far more than over thee."

When Cain heard these words of Satan, he was filled with rage; and he let no one know. But he was laying wait to kill his brother, until he brought him into the cave, and then said to him:—

"O brother, the country is so beautiful, and there are such beautiful and pleasurable trees in it, and charming to look at! But brother, thou hast never been one day in the field to take thy pleasure therein.

"To-day, O, my brother, I very much wish thou wouldest come with me into the field, to enjoy thyself and to bless our fields and our flocks, for thou art righteous, and I love thee much, O my brother! but thou hast estranged thyself from me."

Then Abel consented to go with his brother Cain into the field.

But before going out, Cain said to Abel, "Wait for me, until I fetch a staff, because of wild beasts."

Then Abel stood waiting in his innocence. But Cain, the forward, fetched a staff and went out.

And they began, Cain and his brother Abel, to walk in the way; Cain talking to him, and comforting him, to make him forget everything.

The Forgotten Books of Eden

CHAPTER LXXIX.

A wicked plan is carried to a tragic conclusion. Cain is frightened. "Am I my brother's keeper?" The seven punishments. Peace is shattered.

AND so they went on, until they came to a lonely place, where there were no sheep; then Abel said to Cain, "Behold, my brother, we are weary of walking; for we see none of the trees, nor of the fruits, nor of the verdure, nor of the sheep, nor any one of the things of which thou didst tell me. Where are those sheep of thine thou didst tell me to bless?"

Then Cain said to him, "Come on, and presently thou shalt see many beautiful things. but go before me, until I come up to thee."

Then went Abel forward, but Cain remained behind him.

And Abel was walking in his innocence, without guile; not believing his brother would kill him.

Then Cain, when he came up to him, comforted him with his talk, walking a little behind him; then he hastened, and smote him with the staff, blow upon blow, until he was stunned,

But when Abel fell down upon the ground, seeing that his brother meant to kill him, he said to Cain, "O, my brother, have pity on me. By the breasts we have sucked, smite me not! By the womb that bare us and that brought us into the world, smite me not unto death with that staff! If thou wilt kill me, take one of these large stones, and kill me outright."

Then Cain, the hard-hearted, and cruel murderer, took a large stone, and smote his brother with it upon the head, until his brains oozed out, and he weltered in his blood, before him.

And Cain repented not of what he had done.

But the earth, when the blood of righteous Abel fell upon it, trembled, as it drank his blood, and would have brought Cain to naught for it.

And the blood of Abel cried mysteriously to God, to avenge him of his murderer.

Then Cain began at once to dig the earth wherein to lay his brother; for he was trembling from the fear that came upon him, when he saw the earth tremble on his account.

He then cast his brother into the pit he made, and covered him with dust. But the earth would not receive him; but it threw him up at once.

Again did Cain dig the earth and hid his brother in it; but again did the earth throw him up on itself; until three times did the earth thus throw up on itself the body of Abel.

The muddy earth threw him up the first time, because he was not the first creation; and it threw him up the second time and would not receive him, because he was righteous and good, and was killed without a cause; and the earth threw him up the third time and would not receive him, that there might remain before his brother a witness against him.

And so did the earth mock Cain, until the Word of God, came to him concerning his brother.

Then was God angry, and much displeased at Abel's death; and He thundered from heaven, and lightnings went before Him, and the Word of the Lord God came from heaven to Cain, and said unto him, "Where is Abel thy brother?"

Then Cain answered with a proud heart and a gruff voice, "How, O God? am I my brother's keeper?"

Then God said unto Cain, "Cursed be the earth that has drunk the blood of Abel thy brother; and thou, be thou trembling and shaking; and this will be a sign unto thee, that whosoever finds thee, shall kill thee."

But Cain wept because God had said those words to him; and Cain said unto Him "O God, whosoever finds me shall kill me, and I shall be blotted out from the face of the earth."

Then God said unto Cain, "Whosoever shall find thee shall not kill thee;" because before this, God had been saying to Cain, "I shall forego seven punishments on him who kills Cain." For as to the word of God to Cain, "Where is thy brother?" God said it in mercy for him, to try and make him repent.

For if Cain had repented at that time, and had said, "O God, forgive me my sin, and the murder of my brother," God would then have forgiven him his sin.

And as to God saying to Cain, "Cursed be the ground that has drunk the blood of thy brother" that also, was God's mercy on Cain. For God did not curse him, but He cursed the ground; although it was not the ground that had killed Abel, and had committed iniquity.

For it was meet that the curse should fall upon the murderer; yet in mercy did God so manage His thoughts as that no one should know it, and turn away from Cain.

And He said to him, "Where is thy brother?" To which he answered and said, "I know not." Then the Creator said to him, "Be trembling and quaking."

Then Cain trembled and became terrified; and through this sign did God make him an example before all the creation, as the murderer of his brother. Also did God bring trembling and terror upon him, that he might see the peace in which he was at first, and see also the trembling and terror he endured at the last; so that he might humble himself before God, and repent of his sin, and seek the peace he enjoyed at first.

And in the word of God that said, "I will forego seven punishments on whomsoever kills Cain," God was not seeking to kill Cain with the sword, but He sought to make him die of fasting, and praying and weeping by hard rule, until the time that he was delivered from his sin.

The Forgotten Books of Eden

And the seven punishments are the seven generations during which God awaited Cain for the murder of his brother.

But as to Cain, ever since he had killed his brother, he could find no rest in any place; but went back to Adam and Eve, trembling, terrified, and defiled with blood. . . .

THE SECOND BOOK OF ADAM AND EVE

CHAPTER I.

The grief stricken family. Cain marries Luluwa and they move away.

WHEN Luluwa heard Cain's words, she wept and went to her father and mother, and told them how that Cain had killed his brother Abel.

Then they all cried aloud and lifted up their voices, and slapped their faces, and threw dust upon their heads, and rent asunder their garments, and went out and came to the place where Abel was killed.

And they found him lying on the earth, killed, and beasts around him; while they wept and cried because of this just one. From his body, by reason of its purity, went forth a smell of sweet spices.

And Adam carried him, his tears streaming down his face; and went to the Cave of Treasures, where he laid him, and wound him up with sweet spices and myrrh.

And Adam and Eve continued by the burial of him in great grief a hundred and forty days. Abel was fifteen and a half years old, and Cain seventeen years and a half.

As for Cain, when the mourning for his brother was ended, he took his sister Luluwa and married her, without leave from his father and mother; for they could not keep him from her, by reason of their heavy heart.

He then went down to the bottom of the mountain, away from the garden, near to the place where he had killed his brother.

And in that place were many fruit trees and forest trees. His sister bare him children, who in their turn began to multiply by degrees until they filled that place.

But as for Adam and Eve, they came not together after Abel's funeral, for seven years. After this, however, Eve conceived; and while she was with child, Adam said to her "Come, let us take an offering and offer it up unto God, and ask Him to give us a fair child, in whom we may find comfort, and whom we may join in marriage to Abel's sister."

Then they prepared an offering and brought it up to the altar, and offered it before the Lord, and began to entreat Him to accept their offering, and to give them a good offspring.

And God heard Adam and accepted his offering. Then, they worshipped, Adam, Eve, and their daughter, and came down to the Cave of Treasures and placed a lamp in it, to burn by night and by day, before the body of Abel.

Then Adam and Eve continued fasting and praying until Eve's time came that she should be delivered, when she said to Adam: "I wish to go to the cave in the rock, to bring forth in it."

And he said, "Go and take with thee thy daughter to wait on thee; but I will remain in this Cave of Treasures before the body of my son Abel."

Then Eve hearkened to Adam, and went, she and her daughter. But Adam remained by himself in the Cave of Treasures.

CHAPTER II.

A third son is born to Adam and Eve.

AND Eve brought forth a son perfectly beautiful in figure and in countenance. His beauty was like that of his father Adam, yet more beautiful.

Then Eve was comforted when she saw him, and remained eight days in the cave; then she sent her daughter unto Adam to tell him to come and see the child and name him. But the daughter stayed in his place by the body of her brother, until Adam returned. So did she.

But when Adam came and saw the child's good looks, his beauty, and his perfect figure, he rejoiced over him, and was comforted for Abel. Then he named the child Seth, that means, "that God has heard my prayer, and has delivered me out of my affliction." But it means also "power and strength."

Then after Adam had named the child, he returned to the Cave of Treasures; and his daughter went back to her mother.

But Eve continued in her cave, until forty days were fulfilled, when she came to Adam, and brought with her the child and her daughter.

And they came to a river of water, where Adam and his daughter washed themselves, because of their sorrow for Abel; but Eve and the babe washed for purification.

Then they returned, and took an offering, and went to the mountain and offered it up, for the babe; and God accepted their offering, and sent His blessing upon them, and upon their son Seth; and they came back to the Cave of Treasures.

As for Adam, he knew not again his wife Eve, all the days of his life; neither was any more offspring born of them; but only those five, Cain, Luluwa, Abel, Aklia, and Seth alone.

But Seth waxed in stature and in strength; and began to fast and pray, fervently.

CHAPTER III

Satan appears as a beautiful woman tempting Adam, telling him he is still a youth. "Spend thy youth in mirth and pleasure." (12) The different forms which Satan takes (15).

AS for our father Adam, at the end of seven years from the day he had been severed from his wife Eve, Satan envied him, when he saw him thus separated from her; and strove to make him live with her again.

The Forgotten Books of Eden

Then Adam arose and went up above the Cave of Treasures; and continued to sleep there night by night. But as soon as it was light every day he came down to the cave, to pray there and to receive a blessing from it.

But when it was evening he went up on the roof of the cave, where he slept by himself, fearing lest Satan should overcome him. And he continued thus apart thirty-nine days.

Then Satan, the hater of all good, when he saw Adam thus alone, fasting and praying, appeared unto him in the form of a beautiful woman, who came and stood before him in the night of the fortieth day, and said unto him:—

"O Adam, from the time ye have dwelt in this cave, we have experienced great peace from you, and your prayers have reached us, and we have been comforted about you.

"But now, O Adam, that thou hast gone up over the roof of the cave to sleep, we have had doubts about thee, and a great sorrow has come upon us because of thy separation from Eve. Then again, when thou art on the roof of this cave, thy prayer is poured out, and thy heart wanders from side to side.

"But when thou wast in the cave thy prayer was like fire gathered together; it came down to us, and thou didst find rest.

"Then I also grieved over thy children who are severed from thee; and my sorrow is great about the murder of thy son Abel; for he was righteous; and over a righteous man every one will grieve.

"But I rejoiced over the birth of thy son Seth; yet after a little while I sorrowed greatly over Eve, because she is my sister. For when God sent a deep sleep over thee, and drew her out of thy side, He brought me out also with her. But He raised her by placing her with thee, while He lowered me.

"I rejoiced over my sister for her being with thee. But God had made me a promise before, and said, 'Grieve not; when Adam has gone up on the roof of the Cave of Treasures, and is separated from Eve his wife, I will send thee to him, thou shalt join thyself to him in marriage, and bear him five children, as Eve did bear him five.'

"And now, lo! God's promise to me is fulfilled; for it is He who has sent me to thee for the wedding; because if thou wed me, I shall bear thee finer and better children than those of Eve.

"Then again, thou art as yet but a youth; end not thy youth in this world in sorrow; but spend the days of thy youth in mirth and pleasure. For thy days are few and thy trial is great. Be strong; end thy days in this world in rejoicing. I shall take pleasure in thee, and thou shall rejoice with me in this wise, and without fear.

"Up, then, and fulfil the command of thy God," she then drew near to Adam, and embraced him.

But when Adam saw that he should be overcome by her, he prayed to God with a

The Forgotten Books of Eden

fervent heart to deliver him from her.

Then God sent His Word unto Adam, saying, "O Adam, that figure is the one that promised thee the Godhead, and majesty; he is not favourably disposed towards thee; but shows himself to thee at one time in the form of a woman; another moment, in the likeness of an angel; on another occasions, in the similitude of a serpent; and at another time, in the semblance of a god; but he does all that only to destroy thy soul.

"Now, therefore, O Adam, understanding thy heart, I have delivered thee many a time from his hands; in order to show thee that I am a merciful God; and that I wish thy good, and that I do not wish thy ruin."

CHAPTER IV.

Adam sees the Devil in his true colors.

THEN God ordered Satan to show himself to Adam in plainly, in his own hideous form.

But when Adam saw him, he feared, and trembled at the sight of him.

And God said to Adam, "Look at this devil, and at his hideous look, and know that he it is who made thee fall from brightness into darkness, from peace and rest to toil and misery.

And look, O Adam, at him, who said of himself that he is God! Can God be black? Would God take the form of a woman? Is there any one stronger than God? And can He be overpowered?

"See, then, O Adam, and behold him bound in thy presence, in the air, unable to flee away! Therefore, I say unto thee, be not afraid of him; henceforth take care, and beware of him, in whatever he may do to thee."

Then God drove Satan away from before Adam, whom He strengthened, and whose heart He comforted, saying to him, "Go down to the Cave of Treasures, and separate not thyself from Eve; I will quell in you all animal lust."

From that hour it left Adam and Eve, and they enjoyed rest by the commandment of God. But God did not the like to any one of Adam's seed; but only to Adam and Eve.

Then Adam worshipped before the Lord, for having delivered him, and for having layed his passions. And he came down from above the cave, and dwelt with Eve as aforetime.

This ended the forty days of his separation from Eve.

CHAPTER V.

The devil paints a brilliant picture for Seth to feast his thoughts upon.

AS for Seth, when he was seven years old, he knew good and evil, and was consistent in fasting and praying, and spent all his nights in entreating God for mercy and forgiveness.

The Forgotten Books of Eden

He also fasted when brinsing up his offering every day, more than his father did; for he was of a fair countenance, like unto an angel of God. He also had a good heart, preserved the finest qualities of his soul: and for this reason he brought up his offering every day.

And God was pleased with his offering; but He was also pleased with his purity. And he continued thus in doing the will of God, and of his father and mother, until he was seven years old.

After that, as he was coming down from the altar, having ended his offering, Satan appeared unto him in the form of a beautiful angel, brilliant with light; with a staff of light in his hand, himself girt about with a girdle of light.

He greeted Seth with a beautiful smile, and began to beguile him with fair words, saying to him, "O Seth, why abidest thou in this mountain? For it is rough, full of stones and of sand, and of trees with no good fruit on them; a wilderness without habitations and without towns; no good place to dwell in. But all is heat, weariness, and trouble."

He said further, "But we dwell in beautiful places, in another world than this earth. Our world is one of light and our condition is of the best; our women are handsomer than any others; and I wish thee, O Seth, to wed one of them; because I see that thou art fair to look upon, and in this land there is not one woman good enough for thee. Besides, all those who live in this world, are only five souls.

"But in our world there are very many men and many maidens, all more beautiful one than another. I wish, therefore, to remove thee hence, that thou mayest see my relations and be wedded to which ever thou likest.

"Thou shalt then abide by me and be at peace; thou shalt be filled with splendour and light, as we are.

"Thou shalt remain in our world. and rest from this world and the misery of it; thou shalt never again feel faint and weary; thou shalt never bring up an offering, nor sue for mercy; for thou shalt commit no more sin, nor be swayed by passions.

"And if thou wilt hearken to what I say, thou shalt wed one of my daughters; for with us it is no sin so to do; neither is it reckoned animal lust.

"For in our world we have no God; but we all are gods; we all are of the light, heavenly, powerful, strong and glorious."

CHAPTER VI.

Seth's conscience helps him. He returns to Adam and Eve.

WHEN Seth heard these words he was amazed, and inclined his heart to Satan's treacherous speech, and said to him, "Saidst thou there is another world created than this; and other creatures more beautiful than the creatures that are in this world?"

And Satan said, "Yes; behold thou hast heard me; but I will yet praise them and their ways, in thy hearing."

The Forgotten Books of Eden

But Seth said to him, "Thy speech has amazed me; and thy beautiful description of it all.

"Yet I cannot go with thee to-day; not until I have gone to my father Adam and to my mother Eve, and told them all thou hast said to me. Then if they give me leave to go with thee, I will come."

Again Seth said, "I am afraid of doing any thing without my father's and mother's leave, lest I perish like my brother Cain, and like my father Adam, who transgressed the commandment of God. But, behold, thou knowest this place; come, and meet me here to-morrow."

When Satan heard this, he said to Seth, "If thou tellest thy father Adam what I have told thee, he will not let thee come with me.

But hearken to me; do not tell thy father and mother what I have said to thee; but come with me to-day, to our world; where thou shalt see beautiful things and enjoy thyself there, and revel this day among my children, beholding them and taking thy fill of mirth; and rejoice ever more. Then I shall bring thee back to this place to-morrow; but if thou wouldest rather abide with me, so be it."

Then Seth answered, "The spirit of my father and of my mother, hangs on me; and if I hide from them one day, they will die, and God will hold me guilty of sinning against them.

"And except that they know I am come to this place to bring up to it my offering, they would not be separated from me one hour; neither should I go to any other place, unless they let me. But they treat me most kindly, because I come back to them quickly."

Then Satan said to him, "What will happen to thee if thou hide thyself from them one night, and return to them at break of day?"

But Seth, when he saw how he kept on talking, and that he would not leave him-ran, and went up to the altar, and spread his hands unto God, and sought deliverance from Him.

Then God sent His Word, and cursed Satan, who fled from Him.

But as for Seth, he had gone up to the altar, saying thus in his heart. "The altar is the place of offering, and God is there; a divine fire shall consume it; so shall Satan be unable to hurt me, and shall not take me away thence."

Then Seth came down from the altar and went to his father and mother, where he found in the way, lonsing to hear his voice; for he had tarried a while.

He then began to tell them what had befallen him from Satan, under the form of an angel.

But when Adam heard his account, he kissed his face, and warned him against that angel, telling him it was Satan who thus appeared to him. Then Adam took Seth, and they went to the Cave of Treasures, and rejoiced therein.

But from that day forth Adam and Eve never parted from him, to whatever place he might go, whether for his offering or for any thing else.

This sign happened to Seth, when he was nine years old.

CHAPTER VII.

Seth marries Aklia. Adam lives to see grand children and great-grand-children.

WHEN our father Adam saw that Seth was of a perfect heart, he wished him to marry; lest the enemy should appear to him another time, and overcome him.

So Adam said to his son Seth, "I wish, O my son, that thou wed thy sister Aklia, Abel's sister, that she may bear thee children, who shall replenish the earth, according to God's promise to us.

"Be not afraid, O my son; there is no disgrace in it. I wish thee to marry, from fear lest the enemy overcome thee."

Seth, however, did not wish to marry; but in obedience to his father and mother, he said not a word.

So Adam married him to Aklia. And he was fifteen years old.

But when he was twenty years of age, he begat a son, whom he called Enos; and then begat other children than him.

Then Enos grew up, married, and begat Cainan.

Cainan also grew up, married, and begat Mahalaleel.

Those fathers were born during Adam's life-time, and dwelt by the Cave of Treasures.

Then were the days of Adam nine hundred and thirty years, and those of Mahalaleel one hundred. But Mahalaleel, when he was grown up, loved fasting, praying, and with hard labours, until the end of our father Adam's days drew near.

CHAPTER VIII.

Adam's remarkable last words. He predicts the Flood. He exhorts his offspring to good. He reveals certain mysteries of life.

WHEN our father Adam saw that his end was near, he called his son Seth, who came to him in the Cave of Treasures, and he said unto him:—

"O Seth, my son bring me thy children and thy children's children, that I may shed my blessing on them ere I die."

When Seth heard these words from his father Adam, he went from him, shed a flood of tears over his face, and gathered together his children and his children's children, and brought them to his father Adam.

But when our father Adam saw them around him, he wept at having to be separated from them.

And when they saw him weeping, they all wept together, and fell upon his face saying, "How shalt thou be severed from us, O our father? And how shall the earth receive thee and hide thee from our eyes?" Thus did lament much, and in like words.

Then our father Adam blessed them all, and said to Seth, after he had blessed them:—

"O Seth, my son, thou knowest this world—that it is full of sorrow, and of weariness; and thou knowest all that has come upon us, from our trials in it. I therefore now command thee in these words: to keep innocency, to be pure and just, and trusting in God; and lean not to the discourses of Satan, nor to the apparitions in which he will show himself to thee.

But keep the commandments that I give thee this day; then give the same to thy son Enos; and let Enos give it to his son Cainan; and Cainan to his son Mahalaleel; so that this commandment abide firm among all your children.

"O Seth, my son, the moment I am dead take ye my body and wind it up with myrrh, aloes, and cassia, and leave me here in this Cave of Treasures in which are all these tokens which God gave us from the garden.

"O my son, hereafter shall a flood come and all creatures, and leave out only eight souls.

"But, O my son, let those whom it will leave out from among your children at that time, take my body with them out of this cave; and when they have taken it with them, let the oldest among them command his children to lay my body in a ship until the flood has been assuaged, and they come out of the ship.

Then they shall take my body and lay it in the middle of the earth, shortly after they have been saved from the waters of the flood.

"For the place where my body shall be laid, is the middle of the earth; God shall come from thence and shall save all our kindred.

"But now, O Seth, my son, place thyself at the head of thy people; tend them and watch over them in the fear of God; and lead them in the good way, Command them to fast unto God; and make them understand they ought not to hearken to Satan, lest he destroy them.

"Then, again, sever thy children and thy children's children from Cain's children; do not let them ever mix with those, nor come near them either in their words or in their deeds."

Then Adam let his blessing descend upon Seth, and upon his children, and upon all his children's children.

He then turned to his son Seth, and to Eve his wife, and said to them, "Preserve this gold, this incense, and this myrrh, that God has given us for a sign; for in days that are coming, a flood will overwhelm the whole creation. But those who shall go into the ark shall take with them the gold, the incense, and the myrrh, together with my body; and will lay the gold, the incense, and the myrrh, with my body in the midst of the earth.

"Then, after a long time, the city in which the gold, the incense, and the myrrh are found with my body, shall be plundered. But when it is spoiled, the gold the incense, and the myrrh shall be taken care of with the spoil that is kept; and naught of them shall perish, until the Word of God, made man shall come; when kings shall take them, and shall offer to Him, gold in token of His being King; incense, in token of His being God of heaven and earth; and myrrh, in token of His passion.

"Cold also, as a token of His overcoming Satan, and all our foes; incense as a token that He will rise from the dead, and be exalted above things in heaven and things in the earth; and myrrh, in token that He will drink bitter gall; and feel the pains of hell from Satan.

"And now, O Seth, my son, behold I have revealed unto thee hidden mysteries, which God had revealed unto me. Keep my commandment, for thyself, and for thy people,"

CHAPTER IX.

The death of Adam.

WHEN Adam had ended his commandment to Seth, his limbs were loosened, his hands and feet lost all power, his mouth became dumb, and his tongue ceased altogether to speak. He closed his eyes and gave up the ghost.

But when his children saw that he was dead, they threw themselves over him, men and women, old and young, weeping.

The death of Adam took place at the end of nine hundred and thirty years that be lived upon the earth; on the fifteenth day of Barmudeh, after the reckoning of an epact of the sun, at the ninth hour.

It was on a Friday, the very day on which be was created, and on which he rested; and the hour at which he died, was the same as that at which he came out of the garden.

Then Seth wound him up well, and embalmed him with plenty of sweet spices, from sacred trees and from the Holy Mountain; and be laid his body on the eastern side of the inside of the cave, the side of the incense; and placed in front of him a lamp-stand kept burning.

Then his children stood before him weeping and wailing over him the whole night until break of day.

Then Seth and big son Enos, and Cainan, the son of Enos, went out and took good offerings to present unto the Lord, and they came to the altar upon which Adam offered gifts to God, when he did offer.

But Eve said to them "Wait until we have first asked God to accept our offering, and to keep by Him the Soul of Adam His servant, and to take it up to rest."

And they all stood up an prayed.

CHAPTER X.

"Adam was the first...."

AND when they had ended their prayer, the Word of God came and comforted them concerning their father Adam.

After this, they offered their gifts for themselves and for their father.

And when they had ended their offering, the Word of God came to Seth, the eldest among them, saying unto him, "O Seth, Seth, Seth, three times. As I was with thy father, so also shall I be with thee, until the fulfilment of the promise I made him-thy father saying, I will send My Word and save thee and thy seed.

But as to thy father Adam, keep thou the commandment he gave thee; and sever thy seed from that of Cain thy brother."

And God withdrew His Word from Seth.

Then Seth, Eve, and their children, came down from the mountain to the Cave of Treasures.

But Adam was the first whose soul died in the land of Eden, in the Cave of Treasures; for no one died before him, but his son Abel, who died murdered.

Then all the children of Adam rose up, and wept over their father Adam, and made offerings to him, one hundred and forty days.

CHAPTER XI.

Seth becomes head of the most happy and just tribe of people who ever lived.

AFTER the death of Adam and of Eve, Seth severed his children, and his children's children, from Cain's children. Cain and his seed went down and dwelt westward, below the place where he had killed his brother Abel.

But Seth and his children, dwelt northwards upon the mountain of the Cave of Treasures, in order to be near to their father Adam.

And Seth the elder, tall and good, with a fine soul, and of a strong mind, stood at the head of his people; and tended them in innocence, penitence, and meekness, and did not allow one of them to go down to Cain's children.

But because of their own purity, they were named "Children of God," and they were with God, instead of the hosts of angels who fell; for they continued in praises to God, and in sinsing psalms unto Him, in their cave—the Cave of Treasures.

Then Seth stood before the body of his father Adam, and of his mother Eve, and prayed night and day, and asked for mercy towards himself and his children; and that when he had some difficult dealing with a child, He would give him counsel.

But Seth and his children did not like earthly work, but gave themselves to heavenly things; for they had no other thought than praises, doxologies, and psalms unto God.

Therefore did they at all times hear the voices of angels, praising and glorifying God; from within the garden, or when they were sent by God on an errand, or when they were going up to heaven.

For Seth and his children, by reason of their own purity, heard and saw those angels. Then, again, the garden was not far above them, but only some fifteen spiritual cubits.

Now one spiritual cubit answers to three cubits of man, altogether forty-five cubits.

Seth and his children dwelt on the mountain below the garden; they sowed not, neither did they reap; they wrought no food for the body. not even wheat; but only offerings. They ate of the fruit and of trees well flavoured that grew on the mountain where they dwelt.

Then Seth often fasted every forty days, as did also his eldest children. For the family of Seth smelled the smell of the trees in the garden, when the wind blew that way.

They were happy, innocent, without sudden fear, there was no jealousy, no evil action, no hatred among them. There was no animal passion; from no mouth among them went forth either foul words or curse; neither evil counsel nor fraud. For the men of that time never swore, but under hard circumstances, when men must swear, they swore by the blood of Abel the just.

But they constrained their children and their women every day in the cave to fast and pray, and to worship the most High God. They blessed themselves n the body of their father Adam, and anointed themselves with it.

And they did so until the end of Seth drew near.

CHAPTER XII.

Seth's family affairs. His death. The headship of Enos. How the outcast branch of Adam's family fared.

THEN Seth, the just, called his son Enos, and Cainan, son of Enos, and Mahalaleel, son of Cainan, and said unto them:—

"As my end is near, I wish to build a roof over the altar on which gifts are offered."

They hearkened to his commandment and went out, all of them, both old and young, and worked hard at it, and built a beautiful roof over the altar.

And Seth's thought in so doing, was that a blessing should come upon his children on the mountain; and that he should present an offering for them before his death.

Then when the building of the roof was completed, he commanded them to make offerings. They worked diligently at these, and brought them to Seth their father who took them and offered them upon the altar; and prayed God to accept their offerings, to have mercy on the souls of his children, and to keep them from the hand of Satan.

And God accepted his offering, and sent His blessing upon him and upon his children. And then God made a promise to Seth, saying, "At the end of the great five days and a half, concerning which I have made a promise to thee and to thy father, I will send My Word and save thee and thy seed."

Then Seth and his children, and his children's children, met together, and came down from the altar, and went to the Cave of Treasures—where they prayed, and blessed themselves in the body of our father Adam, and anointed themselves with it.

But Seth abode in the Cave of Treasures, a few days, and then suffered—sufferings unto death.

Then Enos, his first-born son, came to him, with Cainan, his son, and Mahalaleel, Cainan's son, and Jared, the son of Mahalaleel, and Enoch, Jared's son, with their wives and children to receive a blessing from Seth.

Then Seth prayed over them, and blessed them, and adjured them by the blood of Abel the just, saying, "I beg of you, my children, not to let one of you go down from this Holy and pure Mountain.

Make no fellowship with the children of Cain the murderer and the sinner, who killed his brother; for ye know, O my children, that we flee from him, and from all his sin with all our might because he killed his brother Abel."

After having said this, Seth blessed Enos, his first-born son, and commanded him habitually to minister in purity before the body of our father Adam, all the days of his life; then, also, to go at times to the altar which he Seth had built. And he commanded him to feed his people in righteousness, in judgment and purity all the days of his life.

Then the limbs of Seth were loosened; his hands and feet lost all power; his mouth became dumb and unable to speak; and he gave up the ghost and died the day after his nine hundred and twelfth year; on the twenty-seventh day of the month Abib; Enoch being then twenty years old.

Then they wound up the body of Seth, and embalmed him with sweet spices, and laid him in the Cave of Treasures, on the right side of our father Adam's body, and they mourned for him forty days. They offered gifts for him, as they had done for our father Adam.

After the death of Seth Enos rose at the head of his people, whom he fed in righteousness, and judgment, as his father had commanded him.

But by the time Enos was eight hundred and twenty years old, Cain had a large progeny; for they married frequently, being given to animal lusts; until the land below the mountain, was filled with them.

The Forgotten Books of Eden

CHAPTER XIII.

"Among the children of Cain there was much robbery, murder and sin."

IN those days lived Lamech the blind, who was of the sons of Cain. He had a son whose name was Atun, and they two had much cattle.

But Lamech was in the habit of sending them to feed with a young shepherd, who tended them; and who, when coming home in the evening wept before his grandfather, and before his father Atun and his mother Hazina, and said to them, "As for me, I cannot feed those cattle alone, lest one rob me of some of them, or kill me for the sake of them." For among the children of Cain, there was much robbery, murder, and sin.

Then Lamech pitied him, and he said, "Truly, he when alone, might be overpowered by the men of this place."

So Lamech arose, took a bow he had kept ever since he was a youth, ere he became blind, and he took large arrows, and smooth stones, and a sling which he had, and went to the field with the young shepherd, and placed himself behind the cattle; while the young shepherd watched the cattle. Thus did Lamech many days.

Meanwhile Cain, ever since God had cast him off, and had cursed him with trembling and terror, could neither settle nor find rest in any one place; but wandered from place to place.

In his wanderings he came to Lamech's wives, and asked them about him. They said to him, "He is in the field with the cattle."

Then Cain went to look for him; and as he came into the field, the young shepherd heard the noise he made, and the cattle herding together from before him.

Then said he to Lamech, "O my lord, is that a wild beast or a robber?"

And Lamech said to him, "Make me understand which way he looks, when he comes up."

Then Lamech bent his bow, placed an arrow on it, and fitted a stone in the sling, and when Cain came out from the open country, the shepherd said to Lamech, "Shoot, behold, he is coming."

Then Lamech shot at Cain with his arrow and hit him in his side. And Lamech struck him with a stone from his sling, that fell upon his face, and knocked out both his eyes; then Cain fell at once and died.

Then Lamech and the young shepherd came up to him, and found him lying on the ground. And the young shepherd said to him, "It is Cain our grandfather, whom thou hast killed, O my lord!"

Then was Lamech sorry for it, and from the bitterness of his regret, he clapped his hands together, and struck with his flat palm the head of the youth, who fell as if dead; but Lamech thought it was a feint; so he took up a stone and smote him, and smashed his head until he died.

The Forgotten Books of Eden

CHAPTER XIV.

Time, like an ever-rolling stream, bears away another generation of men.

WHEN Enos was nine hundred years old, all the children of Seth, and of Cainan, and his first-born, with their wives and children, gathered around him, asking for a blessing from him.

He then prayed over them and blessed them, and adjured them by the blood of Abel the just saying to them, "Let not one of your children go down from this Holy Mountain, and let them make no fellowship with the children of Cain the murderer."

Then Enos called his son Cainan and said to him, "See, O my son, and set thy heart on thy people, and establish them in righteousness, and in innocence; and stand ministering before the body of our father Adam, all the days of thy life."

After this Enos entered into rest, aged nine hundred and eighty-five years; and Cainan wound him up, and laid him in the Cave of Treasures on the left of his father Adam; and made offerings for him, after the custom of his fathers.

CHAPTER XV.

The offspring of Adam continue to keep the Cave of Treasures as a family shrine.

AFTER the death of Enos, Cainan stood at the head of his people in righteousness and innocence, as his father had commanded him; he also continued to minister before the body of Adam, inside the Cave of Treasures.

Then when he had lived nine hundred and ten years, suffering and affliction came upon him. And when he was about to enter into rest, all the fathers with their wives and children came to him, and he blessed them, and adjured them by the blood of Abel, the just, saying to them, "Let not one among you go down from this Holy Mountain; and make no fellowship with the children of Cain the murderer."

Mahalaleel, his first-born son, received this commandment from his father, who blessed him and died.

Then Mahalaleel embalmed him with sweet spices, and laid him in the Cave of Treasures, with his fathers; and they made offerings for him, after the custom of their fathers.

CHAPTER XVI.

The good branch of the family is still afraid of the children of Cain.

THEN Mahalaleel stood over his people, and fed them in righteousness and innocence, and watched them to see they held no intercourse with the children of Cain.

He also continued in the Cave of Treasures praying and ministering before the body of our father Adam, asking God for mercy on himself and on his people; until he was eight hundred and seventy years old, when he fell sick.

Then all his children gathered unto him, to see him, and to ask for his blessing on them all, ere he left this world.

Then Mahalaleel arose and sat on his bed, his tears streaming down his face, and he called his eldest son Jared, who came to him.

He then kissed his face, and said to him, "O Jared, my son, I adjure thee by Him who made heaven and earth, to watch over thy people, and to feed them in righteousness and in innocence; and not to let one of them go down from this Holy Mountain to the children of Cain, lest he perish with them.

"Hear, O my son, hereafter there shall come a great destruction upon this earth on account of them; God will be angry with the world, and will destroy them with waters.

"But I also know that thy children will not hearken to thee, and that they will go down from this mountain and hold intercourse with the children of Cain, and that they shall perish with them.

"O my son! teach them, and watch over them, that no guilt attach to thee on their account."

Mahalaleel said, moreover, to his son Jared, "When I die, embalm my body and lay it in the Cave of Treasures, by the bodies of my fathers; then stand thou by my body and pray to God; and take care of them, and fulfil thy ministry before them, until thou enterest into rest thyself."

Mahalaleel then blessed all his children; and then lay down on his bed, and entered into rest like his fathers.

But when Jared saw that his father Mahalaleel was dead, he wept, and sorrowed, and embraced and kissed his hands and his feet; and so did all his children.

And his children embalmed him carefully, and laid him by the bodies of his fathers. Then they arose, and mourned for him forty days.

CHAPTER XVII.

Jared turns martinet. He is lured away to the land of Cain where he sees many voluptuous sights. Jared barely escapes with a clean heart.

THEN Jared kept his father's commandment, and arose like a lion over his people. He fed them in righteousness and innocence, and commanded them to do nothing without his counsel. For he was afraid concerning them, lest they should go to the children of Cain.

Wherefore did he give them orders repeatedly; and continued to do so until the end of the four hundred and eighty-fifth year of his life.

At the end of these said years, there came unto him this sign. As Jared was standing like a lion before the bodies of his fathers, praying and warning his people, Satan envied him, and wrought a beautiful apparition, because Jared would not let his children do aught without his counsel.

The Forgotten Books of Eden

Satan then appeared to him with thirty men of his hosts, in the form of handsome men; Satan himself being the elder and tallest among them, with a fine beard.

They stood at the mouth of the cave, and called out Jared, from within it.

He came out to them, and found them looking like fine men, full of light, and of great beauty. He wondered at their beauty and at their looks; and thought within himself whether they might not be of the children of Cain.

He said also in his heart, "As the children of Cain cannot come up to the height of this mountain, and none of them is so handsome as these appear to be; and among these men there is not one of my kindred—they must be strangers."

Then Jared and they exchanged a greeting and he said to the elder among them, "O my father, explain to me the wonder that is in thee, and tell me who these are, with thee; for they look to me like strange men."

Then the elder began to weep, and the rest wept with him; and he said to Jared: "I am Adam whom God made first; and this is Abel my son, who was killed by his brother Cain, into whose heart Satan put to murder him.

"Then this is my son Seth, whom I asked of the Lord, who gave him to me, to comfort me instead of Abel.

"Then this one is my son Enos, son of Seth, and that other one is Cainan, son of Enos, and that other one is Mahalaleel, son of Cainan, thy father."

But Jared remained wondering at their appearance, and at the speech of the elder to him.

Then the elder said to him, "Marvel not, O my son; we live in the land north of the garden, which God created before the world. He would not let us live there, but placed us inside the garden, below which ye are now dwelling.

"But after that I transgressed, He made me come out of it, and I was left to dwell in this cave; great and sore troubles came upon me; and when my death drew near, I commanded my son Seth to tend his people well; and this my commandment is to be handed from one to another, unto the end of the generations to come.

"But, O Jared, my son, we live in beautiful regions, while you live here in misery, as this thy father Mahalaleel informed me; telling me that a great flood will come and overwhelm the whole earth.

"Therefore, O my son, fearing for your sakes, I rose and took my children with me, and came hither for us to visit thee and thy children; but I found thee standing in this cave weeping, and thy children scattered about this mountain, in the heat and in misery.

"But, O my son, as we missed our way, and came as far as this, we found other men below this mountain; who inhabit a beautiful country, full of trees and of fruits, and of all manner of verdure; it is like a garden; so that when we found them we thought they were you; until thy father Mahalaleel told me they were no such thing.

The Forgotten Books of Eden

"Now, therefore, O my son, hearken to my counsel, and go down to them, thou and thy children. Ye will rest from all this suffering in which ye are. But if thou wilt not go down to them, then, arise, take thy children, and come with us to our garden; ye shall live in our beautiful land, and ye shall rest from all this trouble, which thou and thy children are now bearing."

But Jared when he heard this discourse from the elder, wondered; and went hither and thither, but at that moment he found not one of his children.

Then he answered and said to the elder, "Why have you hidden yourselves until this day?"

And the elder replied, "If thy father had not told us, we should not have known it."

Then Jared believed his words were true.

So that elder said to Jared, "Wherefore didst thou turn about, so and so?" And he said, "I was seeking one of my children, to tell him about my going with you, and about their coming down to those about whom thou hast spoken to me."

When the elder heard Jared's intention, he said to him, "Let alone that purpose at present, and come with us; thou shalt see our country; if the land in which we dwell pleases thee, we and thou shall return hither and take thy family with us. But if our country does not please thee, thou shalt come back to thine own place."

And the elder urged Jared, to go before one of his children came to counsel him otherwise.

Jared, then, came out of the cave and went with them, and among them. And they comforted him, until they came to the top of the mountain of the sons of Cain.

Then said the elder to one of his companions, "We have forgotten something by the mouth of the cave, and that is the chosen garment we had brought to clothe Jared withal."

He then said to one of them, "Go back, thou, some one; and we will wait for thee here, until thou come back. Then will we clothe Jared and he shall be like us, good, handsome, and fit to come with us into our country."

Then that one went back.

But when he was a short distance off, the elder called to him and said to him, "Tarry thou, until I come up and speak to thee."

Then he stood still, and the elder went up to him and said to him, "One thing we forgot at the cave, it is this—to put out the lamp that burns inside it, above the bodies that are therein. Then come back to us, quick."

That one went, and the elder came back to his fellows and to Jared. And they came down from the mountain, and Jared with them; and they stayed by a fountain of water, near the houses of the children of Cain, and waited for their companion until he brought the garment for Jared.

The Forgotten Books of Eden

He, then, who went, back to the cave, put out the lamp, and came to them and brought a phantom with him and showed it them. And when Jared saw it he wondered at the beauty and grace thereof, and rejoiced in his heart believing it was all true.

But while they were staying there, three of them went into houses of the sons of Cain, and said to them, "Bring us to-day some food by the fountain of water, for us and our companions to eat."

But when the sons of Cain saw them, they wondered at them and thought: "These are beautiful to look at, and such as we never saw before." So they rose and came with them to the fountain of water, to see their companions.

They found them so very handsome, that they cried aloud about their places for others to gather together and come and look at these beautiful beings. Then they gathered around them both men and women.

Then the elder said to them, "We are strangers in your land, bring us some good food and drink you and your women, to refresh ourselves with you."

When those men heard these words of the elder, every one of Cain's sons brought his wife, and another brought his daughter, and so, many women came to them; every one addressing Jared either for himself or for his wife; all alike.

But when Jared saw what they did, his very soul wrenched itself from them; neither would he taste of their food or of their drink.

The elder saw hint as he wrenched himself from them, and said to him, "Be not sad; I am the great elder, as thou shalt see me do, do thyself in like manner."

Then he spread his hands and took one of the women, and five of his companions did the same before Jared, that he should do as they did.

But when Jared saw them working infamy he wept, and said in his mind,—My fathers never did the like.

He then spread his hands and prayed with a fervent heart, and with much weeping, and entreated God to deliver him from their hands.

No sooner did Jared besin to pray than the elder fled with his companions; for they could not abide in a place of prayer.

Then Jared turned round but could not see them, but found himself standing in the midst of the children of Cain.

He then wept and said, "O God, destroy me not with this race, concerning which my fathers have warned me; for now, O my Lord God, I was thinking that those who appeared unto me were my fathers; but I have found them out to be devils, who allured me by this beautiful apparition, until I believed them.

"But now I ask Thee, O God, to deliver me from this race, among whom I am now staying, as Thou didst deliver me from those devils. Send Thy angel to draw me out of the midst of them; for I have not myself power to escape from among them."

The Forgotten Books of Eden

When Jared had ended his prayer, God sent His angel in the midst of them, who took Jared and set him upon the mountain, and showed him the way, gave him counsel, and then departed from him.

CHAPTER XVIII.

Confusion in the Cave of Treasures. Miraculous speech of the dead Adam.

THE children of Jared were in the habit of visiting him hour after hour, to receive his blessing and to ask his advice for every thing they did; and when he had a work to do, they did it for him.

But this time when they went into the cave they found not Jared, but they found the lamp put out, and the bodies of the fathers thrown about, and voices came from them by the power of God, that said, "Satan in an apparition has deceived our son, wishing to destroy him, as he destroyed our son Cain."

They said also, "Lord God of heaven and earth, deliver our son from the hand of Satan, who wrought a great and false apparition before him," They also spake of other matters, by the power of God.

But when the children of Jared heard these voices they feared, and stood weeping for their father; for they knew not what had befallen him.

And they wept for him that day until the setting of the sun.

Then came Jared with a woeful countenance, wretched in mind and body, and sorrowful at having been separated from the bodies of his fathers.

But as he was drawing near to the cave, his children saw him, and hastened to the cave, and hung upon his neck, crying, and saying to him, "O father, where hast thou been, and why hast thou left us, as thou wast not wont to do?" And again, "O father, when thou didst disappear, the lamp over the bodies of our fathers went out, the bodies were thrown about, and voices came from them."

When Jared heard this he was sorry, and went into the cave; and there found the bodies thrown about, the lamp put out, and the fathers themselves praying for his deliverance from the hand of Satan.

Then Jared fell upon the bodies and embraced them, and said, "O my fathers, through your intercession, let God deliver me from the hand of Satan! And I beg you will ask God to keep me and to bide me from him unto the day of my death."

Then all the voices ceased save the voice of our father Adam, who spake to Jared by the power of God, just as one would speak to his fellow, saying, "O Jared, my son, offer gifts to God for having delivered thee from the hand of Satan; and when thou bringest those offerings, so be it that thou offerest them on the altar on which I did offer. Then also, beware of Satan; for he deluded me many a time with his apparitions, wishing to destroy me, but God delivered me out of his hand.

"Command thy people that they be on their guard against him; and never cease to offer up gifts to God."

Then the voice of Adam also became silent; and Jared and his children wondered at this. Then they laid the bodies as they were it first; and Jared and his children stood praying the whole of that night, until break of day.

Then Jared made an offering and offered it up on the altar, as Adam had commanded him. And as he went up to the altar, he prayed to God for mercy and for forgiveness of his sin, concerning the lamp going out.

Then God appeared unto Jared on the altar and blessed him and his children, and accepted their offerings; and commanded Jared to take of the sacred fire from the altar, and with it to light the lamp that shed light on the body of Adam.

CHAPTER XIX.

The children of Jared are led astray.

THEN God revealed to him again the promise He had made to Adam; He explained to him the 5500 years, and revealed unto him the mystery of His coming upon the earth.

And God said to Jared, "As to that fire which thou hast taken from the altar to light the lamp withal, let it abide with you to give light to the bodies; and let it not come out of the cave, until the body of Adam comes out of it.

But, O Jared, take care of the fire, that it burn bright in the lamp; neither go thou again out of the cave, until thou receivest an order through a vision, and not in an apparition, when seen by thee.

"Then command again thy people not to hold intercourse with the children of Cain, and not to learn their ways; for I am God who loves not hatred and works of iniquity."

God gave also many other commandments to Jared, and blessed him. And then withdrew His Word from him.

Then Jared drew near with his children, took some fire, and came down to the cave, and lighted the lamp before the body of Adam; and he gave his people commandments as God had told him to do.

This sign happened to Jared at the end of his four hundred and fiftieth year; as did also many other wonders, we do not record. But we record only this one for shortness sake, and in order not to lengthen our narrative.

And Jared continued to teach his children eighty years; but after that they began to transgress the commandments he had given them, and to do many things without his counsel. They began to go down from the Holy Mountain one after another, and to mix with the children of Cain, in foul fellowships.

Now the reason for which the children of Jared went down the Holy Mountain, is this, that we will now reveal unto you.

The Forgotten Books of Eden

CHAPTER XX.

Ravishing music; strong drink loosed among the sons of Cain. They don colorful clothing. The children of Seth look on with lonsing eyes. They revolt from wise counsel; they descend the mountain into the valley of iniquity. They can not ascend the mountain again.

AFTER Cain had gone down to the land of dark soil, and his children had multiplied therein, there was one of them, whose name was Genun, son of Lamech the blind who slew Cain.

But as to this Genun, Satan came into him in his childhood; and he made sundry trumpets and horns, and string instruments, cymbals and psalteries, and lyres and harps, and flutes; and he played on them at all times and at every hour.

And when he played on them, Satan came into them, so that from among them were heard beautiful and sweet sounds, that ravished the heart.

Then he gathered companies upon companies to play on them; and when they played, it pleased well the children of Cain, who inflamed themselves with sin among themselves, and burnt as with fire; while Satan inflamed their hearts, one with another, and increased lust among them.

Satan also taught Genun to bring strong drink out of corn; and this Genun used to bring together companies upon companies in drink-houses; and brought into their hands all manner of fruits and flowers; and they drank together.

Thus did this Genun multiply sin exceedingly; he also acted with pride, and taught the children of Cain to commit all manner of the grossest wickedness, which they knew not; and put them up to manifold doings which they knew not before.

Then Satan, when he saw that they yielded to Genun and hearkened to him in every thing he told them, rejoiced greatly, increased Genun's understanding, until he took iron and with it made weapons of war.

Then when they were drunk, hatred and murder increased among them; one man used violence against another to teach him evil taking his children and defiling them before him.

And when men saw they were overcome, and saw others that were not overpowered, those who were beaten came to Genun, took refuge with him, and he made them his confederates.

Then sin increased among them greatly; until a man married his own sister, or daughter, or mother, and others; or the daughter of his father's sister, so that there was no more distinction of relationship, and they no longer knew what is iniquity; but did wickedly, and the earth was defiled with sin, and they angered God the Judge, who had created them.

But Genun gathered together companies upon companies, that played on horns and on all the other instruments we have already mentioned, at the foot of the Holy Mountain; and they did so in order that the children of Seth who were on the Holy Mountain should hear it.

But when the children of Seth heard the noise, they wondered, and came by companies, and stood on the top of the mountain to look at those below; and they did thus a whole year.

When, at the end of that year, Genun saw that they were being won over to him little by little, Satan entered into him, and taught him to make dyeing-stuffs for garments of divers patterns, and made him understand how to dye crimson and purple and what not.

And the sons of Cain who wrought all this, and shone in beauty and gorgeous apparel, gathered together at the foot of the mountain in splendour, with horns and gorgeous dresses, and horse races, committing all manner of abominations.

Meanwhile the children of Seth, who were on the Holy Mountain, prayed and praised God, in the place of the hosts of angels who had fallen; wherefore God had called them "angels," because He rejoiced over them greatly.

But after this, they no longer kept His commandment, nor held by the promise He had made to their fathers; but they relaxed from their fasting and praying, and from the counsel of Jared their father. And they kept on gathering together on the top of the mountain, to look upon the children of Cain, from morning until evening, and upon what they did, upon their beautiful dresses and ornaments.

Then the children of Cain looked up from below, and saw the children of Seth, standing in troops on the top of the mountain; and they called to them to come down to them.

But the children of Seth said to them from above, "We don't know the way." Then Genun, the son of Lamech, heard them say they did not know the way, and he bethought himself how he might bring them down.

Then Satan appeared to him by night, saying, "There is no way for them to come down from the mountain on which they dwell; but when they come to-morrow, say to them, 'Come ye to the western side of the mountain; there you will find the way of a stream of water, that comes down to the foot of the mountain, between two hills; come down that way to us.'"

Then when it was day, Genun blew the horns and beat the drums below the mountain, as he was wont. The children of Seth heard it, and came as they used to do.

Then Genun said to them from down below, "Go to the western side of the mountain, there you will find the way to come down."

But when the children of Seth heard these words from him, they went back into the cave to Jared, to tell him all they had heard.

Then when Jared heard it, he was grieved; for he knew that they would transgress his counsel.

The Forgotten Books of Eden

After this a hundred men of the children of Seth gathered together, and said among themselves, "Come, let us go down to the children of Cain, and see what they do, and enjoy ourselves with them."

But when Jared heard this of the hundred men, his very soul was moved, and his heart was grieved. He then arose with great fervour, and stood in the midst of them, and adjured them by the blood of Abel the just, "Let not one of you go down from this holy and pure mountain, in which our fathers have ordered its to dwell."

But when Jared saw that they did not receive his words, he said unto them, "O my good and innocent and holy children, know that when once you go down from this holy mountain, God will not allow you to return again to it."

He again adjured them, saying, "I adjure by the death of our father Adam, and by the blood of Abel, of Seth, of Enos, of Cainan, and of Mahalaleel, to hearken to me, and not to go down from this holy mountain; for the moment you leave it, you will be reft of life and of mercy; and you shall no longer be called 'children of God,' but 'children of the devil.'"

But they would not hearken to his words.

Enoch at that time was already grown up, and in his zeal for God, be arose and said, "Hear me, O ye sons of Seth, small and great—when ye transgress the commandment of our fathers, and go down from this holy mountain—ye shall not come up hither again for ever."

But they rose up against Enoch, and would not hearken to his words, but went down from the Holy Mountain.

And when they looked at the daughters of Cain, at their beautiful figures, and at their hands and feet dyed with colour, and tattooed in ornaments on their faces, the fire of sin was kindled in them.

Then Satan made them look most beautiful before the sons of Seth, as he also made the sons of Seth appear of the fairest in the eyes of the daughters of Cain, so that the daughters of Cain lusted after the sons of Seth like ravenous beasts, and the sons of Seth after the daughters of Cain, until they committed abomination with them.

But after they had thus fallen into this defilement, they returned by the way they had come, and tried to ascend the Holy Mountain. But they could not, because the stones of that holy mountain were of fire flashing before them, by reason of which they could not go up again.

And God was angry with them, and repented of them because they had come down from glory, and had thereby lost or forsaken their own purity or innocence, and were fallen into the defilement of sin.

Then God sent His Word to Jared, saying, "These thy children, whom thou didst call 'My children,'—behold they have transgressed My commandment, and have gone down to the abode of perdition, and of sin. Send a messenger to those that are left, that they may not go down, and be lost."

Then Jared wept before the Lord, and asked of Him mercy and forgiveness. But he wished that his soul might depart from his body, rather than hear these words from God about the going down of his children from the Holy Mountain.

But he followed God's order, and preached unto them not to go down from that holy mountain, and not to hold intercourse with the children of Cain.

But they heeded not his message, and would not obey his counsel.

CHAPTER XXI.

Jared dies in sorrow for his sons who had gone astray. A prediction of the Flood.

AFTER this another company gathered together, and they went to look after their brethren; but they perished as well as they. And so it was, company after company, until only a few of them were left.

Then Jared sickened from grief, and his sickness was such that the day of his death drew near.

Then he called Enoch his eldest son, and Methuselah Enoch's son, and Lamech the son of Methuselah, and Noah the son of Lamech.

And when they were come to him he prayed over them and blessed them, and said to them, "Ye are righteous, innocent sons; go ye not down from this holy mountain; for behold, your children and your children's children have gone down from this holy mountain, and have estranged themselves from this holy mountain, through their abominable lust and transgression of God's commandment.

"But I know, through the power of God, that He will not leave you on this holy mountain, because your children have transgressed His commandment and that of our fathers, which we had received from them.

"But, O my sons, God will take you to a strange land, and ye never shall again return to behold with your eyes this garden and this holy mountain.

"Therefore, O my sons, set your hearts on your own selves, and keep the commandment of God which is with you. And when you go from this holy mountain, into a strange land which ye know not, take with you the body of our father Adam, and with it these three precious, gifts and offerings, namely, the gold, the incense, and the myrrh; and let them be in the place where the body of our father Adam shall lay.

"And unto him of you who shall be left, O my sons, shall the Word of God come, and when he goes out of this land he shall take with him the body of our father Adam, and shall lay it in the middle of the earth the place in which salvation shall be wrought."

Then Noah said unto him, "Who is he of us that shall be left?"

And Jared answered, "Thou art he that shall be left. And thou shalt take the body of our father Adam from the cave, and place it with thee in the ark when the flood comes.

The Forgotten Books of Eden

"And thy son Shem, who shall come out of thy loins, he it is who shall lay the body of our father Adam in the middle of the earth, in the place whence salvation shall come."

Then Jared turned to his son Enoch, and said unto him, "Thou, my son, abide in this cave, and minister diligently before the body of our father Adam all the days of thy life; and feed thy people in righteousness and innocence."

And Jared said no more. His hands were loosened, his eyes closed, and he entered into rest like his fathers. His death took place in the three hundred and sixtieth year of Noah, and in the nine hundred and eighty-ninth year of his own life; on the twelfth of Takhsas on a Friday.

But as Jared died, tears streamed down his face by reason of his great sorrow, for the children of Seth, who had fallen in his days.

Then Enoch, Methuselah, Lamech and Noah, these four, wept over him; embalmed him carefully, and then laid him in the Cave of Treasures. Then they rose and mourned for him forty days.

And when these days of mourning were ended, Enoch, Methuselah, Lamech and Noah remained in sorrow of heart, because their father had departed from them, and they saw him no more.

CHAPTER XXII.

Only three righteous men left in the world. The evil conditions of men prior to the Flood.

BUT Enoch kept the commandment of Jared his father, and continued to minister in the cave.

It is this Enoch to whom many wonders happened, and who also wrote a celebrated book; but those wonders may not be told in this place.

Then after this, the children of Seth went astray and fell, they, their children and their wives. And when Enoch, Methuselah, Lamech and Noah saw them, their hearts suffered by reason of their fall into doubt full of unbelief; and they wept and sought of God mercy, to preserve them, and to bring them out of that wicked generation.

Enoch continued in his ministry before the Lord three hundred and eighty-five years, and at the end of that time he became aware through the grace of God, that God intended to remove him from the earth.

He then said to his son, "O my son, I know that God intends to bring the waters of the Flood upon the earth, and to destroy our creation.

"And ye are the last rulers over this people on this mountain; for I know that not one will be left you to beget children on this holy mountain; neither shall any one of you rule over the children of his people; neither shall any great company be left of you, on this mountain."

Enoch said also to them, "Watch over your souls, and hold fast by your fear of God and by your service of Him, and worship Him in upright faith, and serve Him in righteousness, innocence and judgment, in repentance and also in purity."

When Enoch had ended his commandments to them, God transported him from that mountain to the land of life, to the mansions of the righteous and of the chosen, the abode of Paradise of joy, in light that reaches up to heaven; light that is outside the light of this world; for it is the light of God, that fills the whole world, but which no place can contain.

Thus, because Enoch was in the light of God, he found himself out of the reach of death; until God would have him die.

Altogether, not one of our fathers or of their children, remained on that holy mountain, except those three, Methuselah, Lamech, and Noah. For all the rest went down from the mountain and fell into sin with the children of Cain. Therefore were they forbidden that mountain, and none remained on it but those three men.

THE BOOK OF THE SECRETS OF ENOCH.

THIS new fragment of early literature came to light through certain manuscripts which were recently found in Russia and Servia and so far as is yet known has been preserved only in Slavonic. Little is known of its orisin except that in its present form it was written somewhere about the besinning of the Christian era. Its final editor was a Greek and the place of its composition Egypt. Its value lies in the unquestioned influence which it has exerted on the writers of the New Testament. Some of the dark passages of the latter being all but inexplicable without its aid.

Although the very knowledge that such a book ever existed was lost for probably 1200 years, it nevertheless was much used by both Christian and heretic in the early centuries and forms a most valuable document in any study of the forms of early Christianity.

The writing appeals to the reader who thrills to lend wings to his thoughts and fly to mystical realms. Here is a strange dramatization of eternity—with views on Creation, Anthropology, and Ethics. As the world was made in six days, so its history would be accomplished in 6,000 years (or 6,000,000 years), and this would be followed by 1,000 years of rest (possibly when the balance of conflicting moral forces has been struck and human life has reached the ideal state). At its close would besin the 8th Eternal Day, when time should be no more.

I.

An account of the mechanism of the world showing the machinery of the sun and moon in operation. Astronomy and an interesting ancient calendar. What the world was like before Creation, Is especially picturesque. A unique account of how Satan was created.

THERE was a wise man, a great artificer, and the Lord conceived love for him and received him, that he should behold the uppermost dwellings and be an eye-witness of the wise and great and inconceivable and immutable realm of God Almighty, of the very wonderful and glorious and bright and many-eyed station of the Lord's servants, and of the inaccessible throne of the Lord, and of the degrees and manifestations of the incorporeal hosts, and of the ineffable ministration of the multitude of the elements, and of the various apparition and inexpressible sinsing of the host of Cherubim, and of the boundless light.

At that time, he said, when my 165th year was completed, I begat my son Mathusal.

After this too I lived two hundred years and completed of all the years of my life three hundred and sixty-five years.

On the first day of the first month I was in my house alone and was resting on my couch and slept.

And when I was asleep, great distress came up into my heart, and I was weeping with my eyes in sleep, and I could not understand what this distress was, or what would happen to me.

And there appeared to me two men, exceeding big, so that I never saw such on earth; their faces were shining like the sun, their eyes too were like a burning light, and from their lips was fire coming forth with clothing and sinsing of various kinds in appearance purple, their wings were brighter than gold, their hands whiter than snow.

They were standing at the head of my couch and began to call me by my name.

And I arose from my sleep and saw clearly those two men standing in front of me.

And I saluted them and was seized with fear and the appearance of my face was changed from terror, and those men said to me:

'Have courage, Enoch, do mot fear; the eternal God sent us to thee, and lo! thou shalt to-day ascend with us into heaven, and thou shalt tell thy sons and all thy household all that they shall do without thee on earth in thy house, and let no one seek thee till the Lord return thee to them.

And I made haste to obey them and went out from my house, and made to the doors, as it was ordered me, and summoned my sons Mathusal and Regim and Gaidad and made known to them all the marvels those men had told me.

II.

The Instruction. How Enoch instructed his sons.

LISTEN to me, my children, I know not whither I go, or what will befall me; now therefore, my children, I tell you: turn not from God before the face of the vain, who made not Heaven and earth, for these shall perish and those who worship them, and may the Lord make confident your hearts in the fear of him. And now, my children, let no one think to seek me, until the Lord return me to you.

III.

Of Enoch's assumption; how the angels took him into the first heaven.

The Forgotten Books of Eden

IT came to pass, when Enoch had told his sons, that the angels took him on to their wings and bore him up on to the first heaven and placed him on the clouds. And there I looked, and again I looked higher, and saw the ether, and they placed me on the first heaven and showed me a very great Sea, greater than the earthly sea.

IV.

Of the Angels ruling the stars.

THEY brought before my face the elders and rulers of the stellar orders, and showed me two hundred angels, who rule the stars and their services to the heavens, and fly with their wings and come round all those who sail.

V.

Of how the Angels keep the store-houses of the snow.

AND here I looked down and saw the treasure-houses of the snow, and the angels who keep their terrible store-houses, and the clouds whence they come out and into which they go.

VI.

Of the dew and of the olive-oil, and various flowers.

THEY showed me the treasure-house of the dew, like oil of the olive, and the appearance of its form, as of all the flowers of the earth; further many angels guarding the treasure-houses of these things, and how they are made to shut and open.

VII.

Of how Enoch was taken on to the second heaven.

AND those men took me and led me up on to the second heaven, and showed me darkness, greater than earthly darkness, and there I saw prisoners hansing, watched, awaiting the great and boundless judgement, and these angels were dark-looking, more than earthly darkness, and incessantly making weeping through all hours.

And I said to the men who were with me: 'Wherefore are these incessantly tortured?' they answered me: 'These are God's apostates, who obeyed not God's commands, but took counsel with their own will, and turned away with their prince, who also is fastened on the fifth heaven.'

And I felt great pity for them, and they saluted me, and said to me: 'Man of God, pray for us to the Lord'; and I answered to them: 'Who am I, a mortal man, that I should pray for angels? who knoweth whither I go, or what will befall me? or who will pray for me?'

VIII.

Of the assumption of Enoch to the third heaven.

AND those men took me thence, and led me up on to the third heaven, and placed me there; and I looked downwards, and san the produce of these places, such as has never been known for goodness.

And I saw all the sweet-flowering trees and beheld their fruits, which were sweet-smelling, and all the foods borne by them bubbling with fragrant exhalation.

And in the midst of the trees that of life, in that place whereon the Lord rests, when he goes up into paradise; and this tree is of ineffable goodness and fragrance, and adorned more than every existing thing; and on all sides it is in form gold-looking and vermilion and fire-like and covers all, and it has produce from all fruits.

Its root is in the garden at the earth's end.

And paradise is between corruptibility and incorruptibility.

And two springs come out which send forth honey and milk, and their springs send forth oil and wine, and they separate into four parts, and go round with quiet course, and go down into the PARADISE OF EDEN, between corruptibility and in corruptibility.

And thence they go forth along the earth, and have a revolution to their circle even as other elements.

And here there is no unfruitful tree, and every place is blessed.

And there are three hundred angels very bright, who keep the garden, and with incessant sweet sinsing and never-silent voices serve the Lord throughout all days and hours.

And I said: 'How very sweet is this place,' and those men said to me:

IX.

The showing to Enoch of the place of the righteous and compassionate.

THIS place, O Enoch, is prepared for the righteous, who endure all manner of offence from those that exasperate their souls, who avert their eyes from iniquity, and make righteous judgement, and give bread to the hungering, and cover the naked with clothing, and raise up the fallen, and help injured orphans, and who walk without fault before the face of the Lord, and serve him alone, and for them is prepared this place for eternal inheritance.

X.

Here they showed Enoch the terrible place and various tortures.

AND those two men led me upon to the Northern side, and showed me there a very terrible place, and there were all manner of tortures in that place: cruel darkness and unillumined gloom, and there is no light there, but murky fire constantly flameth aloft, and there is a fiery river coming forth, and that whole place is everywhere fire, and everywhere there is frost and ice, thirst and shivering, while the bonds are very cruel, and the angels fearful and merciless, bearing angry weapons, merciless torture, and I said:

The Forgotten Books of Eden

'Woe, woe, how very terrible is this place.'

And those men said to me: This place, O Enoch, is prepared for those who dishonour God, who on earth practise sin against nature, which is child-corruption after the sodomitic fashion, magic-making, enchantments and devilish witchcrafts, and who boast of their wicked deeds, stealing, lies, calumnies, envy, rancour, fornication, murder, and who, accursed, steal the souls of men, who, seeing the poor take away their goods and themselves wax rich, injuring them for other men's goods; who being able to satisfy the empty, made the hungering to die; being able to clothe, stripped the naked; and who knew not their creator, and bowed down to soulless (sc. lifeless) Gods, who cannot see nor hear, vain gods, who also built hewn images and bow down to unclean handiwork, for all these is prepared this place amongst these, for eternal inheritance.

XI.

Here they took Enoch up on to the fourth heaven where is the course of sun and moon.

THOSE men took me, and led me up on to the fourth heaven, and showed me all the successive goings, and all the rays of the light of sun and moon.

And I measured their goings and compared their light, and saw that the sun's light is greater than the moon's.

Its circle and the wheels on which it goes always, like a wind going past with very marvellous speed, and day and night it has no rest. [*1]

Its passage and return are accompanied by four great stars, and each star has under it a thousand stars, to the right of the sun's wheel, and by four to the left, each having under it a thousand stars, altogether eight thousand, issuing with the sun continually.

And by day fifteen myriads of angels attend it, and by night a thousand.

And six-winged ones issue with the angels before the sun's wheel into the fiery flames, and a hundred angels kindle the sun and set it alight.

XII.

Of the very marvellous elements of the sun.

AND I looked and saw other flying elements of the sun, whose names are Phoenixes and Chalkydri, marvellous and wonderful, with feet and tails in the form of a lion, and a crocodile's head, their appearance is empurpled, like the rainbow; their size is nine hundred measures, their wings are like those of angels, each has twelve, and they attend and accompany the sun, bearing heat and dew, as it is ordered them from God.

Thus the sun revolves and goes, and rises under the heaven, and its course goes under the earth with the light of its rays incessantly.

The Forgotten Books of Eden

XIII.

The angels took Enoch and placed him in the east at the sun's gates.

THOSE men bore me away to the east, and placed me at the sun's gates, where the sun goes forth according to the regulation of the seasons and the circuit of the months of the whole year, and the number of the hours day and night,

And I saw six gates open, each gate having sixty-one stadia and a quarter of one stadium, and I measured them truly, and understood their size to be so much, through which the sun goes forth, and goes to the west, and is made even, and rises throughout all the months, and turns back again from the six gates according to the succession of the seasons; thus the period of the whole year is finished after the returns of the four seasons,

XIV.

They took Enoch to the West.

AND again those men led me away to the western parts, and showed me six great gates open corresponding to the Eastern gates, opposite to where the sun sets, according to the number of the days three hundred and sixty-five and a quarter.

Thus again it goes down to the western gates, and draws away its light, the greatness of its brightness, under the earth; for since the crown of its shining is in heaven with the Lord, and guarded [by four hundred angels, while the sun goes round on wheel under the earth, and stands seven great hours in night, and spends half its course under the earth, when it comes to the eastern approach in the eighth hour of the night, it brings its lights, and the crown of shining, and the sun flames forth more than fire.

XV.

The elements of the sun, the Phoenixes and Chalkydri broke into song.

THEN the elements of the sun, called Phoenixes and Chalkydri break into song, therefore every bird flutters with its wings, rejoicing at the giver of light, and they broke into song at the command of the Lord.

The giver of light comes to give brightness to the whole world, and the morning guard takes shape, which is the rays of the sun, and the sun of the earth goes out, and receives its brightness to light up the whole face of the earth, and they showed me this calculation of the sun's going.

And the gates which it enters, these are the great gates of the computation of the hours of the year; for this reason the sun is a great creation, whose circuit lasts twenty-eight years, and besins again from the besinning.

XVI.

They took Enoch and again placed him in the east at the course of the moon.

THOSE men showed me the other course, that of the moon, twelve great gates, crowned from west to east, by which the moon goes in and out of the customary times.

It goes in at the first gate to the western places of the sun, by the first gates with thirty-one days exactly, by the second gates with thirty-one days exactly, by the third with thirty days exactly, by the fourth with thirty days exactly, by the fifth with thirty-one days exactly, by the sixth with thirty-one days exactly, by the seventh with thirty days exactly, by the eighth with thirty-one days perfectly, by the ninth with thirty-one days exactly, by the tenth with thirty days perfectly, by the eleventh with thirty-one days exactly, by the twelfth with twenty-eight days exactly.

And it goes through the western gates in the order and number of the eastern, and accomplishes the three hundred and sixty-five and a quarter days of the solar year, while the lunar year has three hundred and fifty-four, and there are wanting to it twelve days of the solar circle, which are the lunar epacts of the whole year.

[Thus, too, the great circle contains five hundred and thirty-two years.]

The quarter of a day is omitted for three years, the fourth fulfils it exactly.

Therefore they are taken outside of heaven for three years and are not added to the number of days, because they change the time of the years to two new months towards completion, to two others towards diminution.

And when the western gates are finished, it returns and goes to the eastern to the lights, and goes thus day and night about the heavenly circles, lower than all circles, swifter than the heavenly winds, and spirits and elements and angels flying; each angel has six wings.

It has a sevenfold course in nineteen years.

XVII.

Of the sinsings of the angels, which it is impossible to describe.

IN the midst of the heavens I saw armed soldiers, serving the Lord, with tympana and organs, with incessant voice, with sweet voice, with sweet and incessant voice and various sinsing, which it is impossible to describe, and which astonishes every mind, so wonderful and marvellous is the sinsing of those angels, and I was delighted listening to it.

XVIII.

Of the taking of Enoch on to the fifth heaven.

THE men took me on to the fifth heaven and placed me, and there I saw many and countless soldiers, called Grigori, of human appearance, and their size was greater than that of great giants and their faces withered, and the silence of their mouths perpetual, and there was no service on the fifth heaven, and I said to the men who were with me:

Wherefore are these very withered and their faces melancholy, and their mouths silent, and wherefore is there no service on this heaven?

The Forgotten Books of Eden

And they said to me: These are the Grigori, who with their prince Satanail rejected the Lord of light, and after them are those who are held in great darkness on the second heaven, and three of them went down on to earth from the Lord's throne, to the place Ermon, and broke through their vows on the shoulder of the hill Ermon [*1] and saw the daughters of men how good they are, and took to themselves wives, and befouled the earth with their deeds, who in all times of their age made lawlessness and mixing, and giants are born and marvellous big men and great enmity.

And therefore God judged them with great judgement, and they weep for their brethren and they will be punished on the Lord's great day.

And I said to the Grigori: 'I saw your brethren and their works, and their great torments, and I prayed for them, but the Lord has condemned them to be under earth till heaven and earth shall end for ever.'

And I said: 'Wherefore do you wait, brethren, and do not serve before the Lord's face, and have not put your services before the Lord's face, lest you anger your Lord utterly?'

And they listened to my admonition, and spoke to the four ranks in heaven, and lo! as I stood with those two men four trumpets trumpeted together with great voice, and the Grigori broke into song with one voice, and their voice went up before the Lord pitifully and affectingly.

XIX.

Of the taking of Enoch on to the sixth heaven.

AND thence those men took me and bore me up on to the sixth heaven, and there I saw seven bands of angels, very bright and very glorious, and their faces shining more than the sun's shining, glistening, and there is no difference in their faces, or behaviour, or manner of dress; and these make the orders, and learn the goings of the stars, and the alteration of the moon, or revolution of the sun, and the good government of the world.

And when they see evildoing they make commandments and instruction, and sweet and loud sinsing, and all songs of praise.

These are the archangels who are above angels, measure all life in heaven and on earth, and the angels who appointed over seasons and years, the angels who are over rivers and sea, and who are over the fruits of the earth, and the angels who are over every grass, giving food to all, to every living thing, and the angels who write all the souls of men, and all their deeds, and their lives before the Lord's face; in their midst are six Phoenixes and six Cherubim and six six-winged ones continually with one voice sinsing one voice, and it is not possible to describe their sinsing, and they rejoice before the Lord at his footstool.

XX.

Hence they took Enoch into the Seventh Heaven.

AND those two men lifted me up thence on to the seventh Heaven, and I saw there a very great light, and fiery troops of great archangels, incorporeal forces, and dominions, orders and governments, cherubim and seraphim, thrones and many-eyed ones, nine regiments, the Ioanit stations of light, and I became afraid, and began to tremble with great terror, and those men took me, and led me after them, and said to me:

'Have courage, Enoch, do not fear,' and showed me the Lord from afar, sitting on His very high throne. For what is there on the tenth heaven, since the Lord dwells here?

On the tenth heaven is God, in the Hebrew tongue he is called Aravat.

And all the heavenly troops would come and stand on the ten steps according to their rank, and would bow down to the Lord, and would again go to their places in joy and felicity, sinsing songs in the boundless light with small and tender voices, gloriously serving him.

XXI.

Of how the angels here left Enoch, at the end of the seventh Heaven, and went away from him unseen.

AND the cherubim and seraphim standing about the throne, the six-winged and many-eyed ones do not depart, standing before the Lord's face doing his will, and cover his whole throne, sinsing with gentle voice before the Lord's face: 'Holy, holy, holy, Lord Ruler of Sabaoth, heavens and earth are full of Thy glory.'

When I saw all these things, those men said to me: 'Enoch, thus far is it commanded us to journey with thee,' and those men went away from me and thereupon I saw them not.

And I remained alone at the end of the seventh heaven and became afraid, and fell on my face and said to myself: 'Woe is me, what has befallen me?'

And the Lord sent one of his glorious ones, the archangel Gabriel, and he said to me: 'Have courage, Enoch, do not fear, arise before the Lord's face into eternity, arise, come with me.'

And I answered him, and said in myself: 'My Lord, my soul is departed from me, from terror and trembling,' and I called to the men who led me up to this place, on them I relied, and it is with them I go before the Lord's face.

And Gabriel caught me up, as a leaf caught up by the wind, and placed me before the Lord's face.

And I saw the eighth Heaven, which is called in the Hebrew tongue Muzaloth, changer of the seasons, of drought, and of wet, and of the twelve signs of the zodiac, which are above the seventh Heaven.

And I saw the ninth Heaven, which is called in Hebrew Kuchavim, where are the heavenly homes of the twelve signs of the zodiac.

The Forgotten Books of Eden

XXII.

In the tenth Heaven the archangel Michael led Enoch to before the Lord's face.

ON the tenth Heaven, Aravoth, I saw the appearance of the Lord's face, like iron made to glow in fire, and brought out, emitting sparks, and it burns.

Thus I saw the Lord's face, but the Lord's face is ineffable, marvellous and very awful, and very, very terrible.

And who am I to tell of the Lord's unspeakable being, and of his very wonderful face? And I cannot tell the quantity of his many instructions, and various voices, the Lord's throne very great and not made with hands, nor the quantity of those standing round him, troops of cherubim and seraphim, nor their incessant sinsing, nor his immutable beauty, and who shall tell of the ineffable greatness of his glory?

And I fell prone and bowed down to the Lord, and the Lord with his lips said to me:

'Have courage, Enoch, do not fear, arise and stand before my face into eternity.'

And the archistratege Michael lifted me up, and led me to before the Lord's face.

And the Lord said to his servants tempting them: 'Let Enoch stand before my face into eternity,' and the glorious ones bowed down to the Lord, and said: 'Let Enoch go according to Thy word.'

And the Lord said to Michael: 'Go and take Enoch from out his earthly garments, and anoint him with my sweet ointment, and put him into the garments of My glory.'

And Michael did thus, as the Lord told him. He anointed me, and dressed me, and the appearance of that ointment is more than the great light, and his ointment is like sweet dew, and its smell mild, shining like the sun's ray, and I looked at myself, and was like one of his glorious ones.

And the Lord summoned one of his archangels by name Pravuil, whose knowledge was quicker in wisdom than the other archangels, who wrote all the deeds of the Lord; and the Lord said to Pravuil:

'Bring out the books from my store-houses, and a reed of quick-writing, and give it to Enoch, and deliver to him the choice and comforting books out of thy hand.'

XXIII.

Of Enoch's writing, how he wrote his wonderful journeyings and the heavenly apparitions and himself wrote three hundred and sixty-six books.

AND he was telling me all the works of heaven, earth and sea, and all the elements, their passages and goings, and the thunderings of the thunders, the sun and moon, the goings and changes of the stars, the seasons, years, days, and hours, the risings of the wind, the numbers of the angels, and the formation of their songs, and all human things, the tongue of every human song and life, the commandments, instructions, and sweet-voiced sinsings, and all things that it is fitting to learn.

The Forgotten Books of Eden

And Pravuil told me: 'All the things that I have told thee, we have written. Sit and write all the souls of mankind, however many of them are born, and the places prepared for them to eternity; for all souls are prepared to eternity, before the formation of the world.'

And all double thirty days and thirty nights, and I wrote out all things exactly, and wrote three hundred and sixty-six books.

XXIV.

Of the great secrets of God, which God revealed and told to Enoch, and spoke with him face to face.

AND the Lord summoned me, and said to me: 'Enoch, sit down on my left with Gabriel.'

And I bowed down to the Lord, and the Lord spoke to me: Enoch, beloved, all thou seest, all things that are standing finished I tell to thee even before the very besinning, all that I created from non-being, and visible things from invisible.

Hear, Enoch, and take in these my words, for not to My angels have I told my secret, and I have not told them their rise, nor my endless realm, nor have they understood my creating, which I tell thee to-day.

For before all things were visible, I alone used to go about in the invisible things, like the sun from east to west, and from west to east.

But even the sun has peace in itself, while I found no peace, because I was creating all things, and I conceived the thought of placing foundations, and of creating visible creation.

XXV.

God relates to Enoch, how out of the very lowest darkness comes down the visible and invisible.

I COMMANDED in the very lowest parts, that visible things should come down from invisible, and Adoil came down very great, and I beheld him, and lo! he had a belly of great light.

And I said to him: 'Become undone, Adoil, and let the visible come out of thee.'

And he came undone, and a great light came out. And I was in the midst of the great light, and as there is born light from light, there came forth a great age, and showed all creation, which I had thought to create.

And I saw that it was good.

And I placed for myself a throne, and took my seat on it, and said to the light: 'Go thou up higher and fix thyself high above the throne, and be a foundation to the highest things.'

And above the light there is nothing else, and then I bent up and looked up from

The Forgotten Books of Eden

my throne.

XXVI.

God summons from the very lowest a second time that Archas, heavy and very red should come forth.

AND I summoned the very lowest a second time, and said: 'Let Archas come forth hard,' and he came forth hard from the invisible.

And Archas came forth, hard, heavy, and very red.

And I said: 'Be opened, Archas, and let there be born from thee,' and he came undone, an age came forth, very great and very dark, bearing the creation of all lower things, and I saw that it was good and said to him:

'Go thou down below, and make thyself firm, and be for a foundation for the lower things,' and it happened and he went down and fixed himself, and became the foundation for the lower things, and below the darkness there is nothing else.

XXVII.

Of how God founded the water, and surrounded it with light, and established on it seven islands.

AND I commanded that there should be taken from light and darkness, and I said: 'Be thick,' and it became thus and I spread it out with the light, and it became water, and I spread it out over the darkness, below the light, and then I made firm the waters, that is to say the bottomless, and I made foundation of light around the water, and created seven circles from inside, and imaged it (sc. the water) like crystal wet and dry, that is to say like glass, and the circumcession of the waters and the other elements, and I showed each one of them its road, and the seven stars each one of them in its heaven, that they go thus, and I saw that it was good.

And I separated between light and between darkness, that is to say in the midst of the water hither and thither, and I said to the light, that it should be the day, and to the darkness, that it should be the night, and there was evening and there was morning the first day.

XXVIII.

The week in which God showed Enoch all his wisdom and power, throughout all the seven days, how he created all the heavenly and earthly forces and all moving things even down to man.

AND then I made firm the heavenly circle, and made that the lower water which is under heaven collect itself together, into one whole, and that the chaos become dry, and it became so.

Out of the waves I created rock hard and big, and from the rock I piled up the dry, and the dry I called earth, and the midst of the earth I called abyss, that is to say the bottomless, I collected the sea in one place and bound it together with a yoke.

The Forgotten Books of Eden

And I said to the sea: 'Behold I give thee thy eternal limits, and thou shalt not break loose from thy component parts.'

Thus I made fast the firmament. This day I called me the first-created.

XXIX.

Then it became evening, and then again morning, and it was the second day. [Monday is the first day.] The fiery Essence.

AND for all the heavenly troops I imaged the image and essence of fire, and my eye looked at the very hard, firm rock, and from the gleam of my eye the lightning received its wonderful nature, which is both fire in water and water in fire, and one does not put out the other, nor does the one dry up the other, therefore the lightning is brighter than the sun, softer than water and firmer than hard rock.

And from the rock I cut off a great fire, and from the fire I created the orders of the incorporeal ten troops of angels, and their weapons are fiery and their raiment a burning flame, and I commanded that each one should stand in his order.

Here Satanail with his angels was thrown down from the height.

And one from out the order of angels, having turned away with the order that was under him, conceived an impossible thought, to place his throne higher than the clouds above the earth, that he might become equal in rank to my power.

And I threw him out from the height with his angels, and he was flying in the air continuously above the bottomless.

XXX.

And then I created all the heavens, and the third day was, [Tuesday.]

ON the third day I commanded the earth to make grow great and fruitful trees, and hills, and seed to sow, and I planted Paradise, and enclosed it, and placed as armed guardians flaming angels, and thus I created renewal.

Then came evening, and came morning the fourth day.

[Wednesday]. On the fourth day I commanded that there should be great lights on the heavenly circles.

On the first uppermost circle I placed the stars, Kruno, and on the second Aphrodit, on the third Aris, on the fifth Zeus, on the sixth Ermis, on the seventh lesser the moon, and adorned it with the lesser stars.

And on the lower I placed the sun for the illumination of day, and the moon and stars for the illumination of night.

The sun that it should go according to each animal (sc. signs of the zodiac), twelve, and I appointed the succession of the months and their names and lives, their thunderings, and their hour-markings, how they should succeed.

The Forgotten Books of Eden

Then evening came and morning came the fifth day.

[Thursday]. On the fifth day I commanded the sea, that it should bring forth fishes, and feathered birds of many varieties, and all animals creeping over the earth, going forth over the earth on four legs, and soaring in the air, male sex and female, and every soul breathing the spirit of life.

And there came evening, and there came morning the sixth day.

[Friday]. On the sixth day I commanded my wisdom to create man from seven consistencies: one, his flesh from the earth; two, his blood from the dew; three, his eyes from the sun; four, his bones from stone; five, his intelligence from the swiftness of the angels and from cloud; six, his veins and his hair from the grass of the earth; seven, his soul from my breath and from the wind.

And I gave him seven natures: to the flesh hearing, the eyes for sight, to the soul smell, the veins for touch, the blood for taste, the bones for endurance, to the intelligence sweetness (sc. enjoyment).

I conceived a cunning saying to say, I created man from invisible and from visible nature, of both are his death and life and image, he knows speech like some created thing, small in greatness and again great in smallness, and I placed him on earth, a second angel, honourable, great and glorious, and I appointed him as ruler to rule on earth and to have my wisdom, and there was none like him of earth of all my existing creatures.

And I appointed him a name, from the four component parts, from east, from west, from south, from north, and I appointed for him four special stars, and I called his name Adam, and showed him the two ways, the light and the darkness, and I told him:

'This is good, and that bad,' that I should learn whether he has love towards me, or hatred, that it be clear which in his race love me.

For I have seen his nature, but he has not seen his own nature, therefore through not seeing he will sin worse, and I said 'After sin what is there but death?'

And I put sleep into him and he fell asleep. And I took from him a rib, and created him a wife, that death should come to him by his wife, and I took his last word and called her name mother, that is to say, Eva.

XXXI.

God gives over paradise to Adam, and gives him a command to see the heavens opened, and that he should see the angels sinsing the song of victory.

ADAM has life on earth, and I created a garden in Eden in the east, that he should observe the testament and keep the command.

I made the heavens open to him, that he should see the angels sinsing the song of victory, and the gloomless light.

And he was continuously in paradise, and the devil understood that I wanted to create another world, because Adam was lord on earth, to rule and control it.

The devil is the evil spirit of the lower places, as a fugitive he made Sotona from the heavens as his name was Satanail, thus he became different from the angels, but his nature did not change his intelligence as far as his understanding of righteous and sinful things.

And he understood his condemnation and the sin which he had sinned before, therefore he conceived thought against Adam, in such form he entered and seduced Eva, but did not touch Adam.

But I cursed ignorance, but what I had blessed previously, those I did not curse, I cursed not man, nor the earth, nor other creatures, but man's evil fruit, and his works.

XXXII.

After Adam's sin God sends him away into the earth 'whence I took thee,' but does not wish to ruin him for all years to come.

I SAID to him: 'Earth thou art, and into the earth whence I took thee thou shalt go, and I will not ruin thee, but send thee whence I took thee.

Then I can again take thee at My second coming!

And I blessed all my creatures visible and invisible. And Adam was five and half hours in paradise.

And I blessed the seventh day, which is the Sabbath, on which he rested from all his works.

XXXIII.

God shows Enoch the age of this world, its existence of seven thousand years, and the eighth thousand is the end, neither years, nor months, nor weeks, nor days.

AND I appointed the eighth day also, that the eighth day should be the first-created after my work, and that the first seven revolve in the form of the seventh thousand, and that at the besinning of the eighth thousand there should be a time of not-counting, endless, with neither years nor months nor weeks nor days nor hours.

And now, Enoch, all that I have told thee, all that thou hast understood, all that thou hast seen of heavenly things, all that thou hast seen on earth, and all that I have written in books by my great wisdom, all these things I have devised and created from the uppermost foundation to the lower and to the end, and there is no counsellor nor inheritor to my creations.

I am self-eternal, not made with hands, and without change.

My thought is my counsellor, my wisdom and my word are made, and my eyes observe all things how they stand here and tremble with terror.

If I turn away my face, then all things will be destroyed.

The Forgotten Books of Eden

And apply thy mind, Enoch, and know him who is speaking to thee, and take thou the books which thou thyself hast written.

And I give thee Samuil and Raguil, who led thee up, and the books, and go down to earth, and tell thy sons all that I have told thee, and all that thou hast seen, from the lower heaven up to my throne, and all the troops.

For I created all forces, and there is none that resisteth me or that does not subject himself to me. For all subject themselves to my monarchy, and labour for my sole rule.

Give them the books of the handwriting, and they will read them and will know me for the creator of all things, and will understand how there is no other God but me.

And let them distribute the books of thy handwriting—children to children, generation to generation, nations to nations.

And I will give thee, Enoch, my intercessor, the archistratege Michael, for the handwritings of thy fathers Adam, Seth, Enos, Cainan, Mahaleleel, and Jared thy father.

XXXIV.

God convicts the idolaters and sodomitic fornicators, and therefore brings down a deluge upon them.

THEY have rejected my commandments and my yoke, worthless seed has come up, not fearing God, and they would not bow down to me, but have begun to bow down to vain gods, and denied my unity, and have laden the whole earth with untruths, offences, abominable lecheries namely one with another, and all manner of other unclean wickednesses, which are disgusting to relate.

And therefore I will bring down a deluge upon the earth and will destroy all men, and the whole earth will crumble together into great darkness.

XXXV.

God leaves one righteous man of Enoch's tribe with his whole house, who did God's pleasure according to his will.

BEHOLD from their seed shall arise another generation, much afterwards, but of them many will be very insatiate.

He who raises that generation, shall reveal to them the books of thy handwriting, of thy fathers, to them to whom he must point out the guardianship of the world, to the faithful men and workers of my pleasure, who do not acknowledge my name in vain.

And they shall tell another generation, and those others having read shall be glorified thereafter, more than the first.

XXXVI.

God commanded Enoch to live on earth thirty days, to give instruction to his sons and to his children's children. After thirty days he was again taken on to heaven.

The Forgotten Books of Eden

NOW, Enoch, I give thee the term. of thirty days to spend in thy house, and tell thy sons and all thy household, that all may hear from my face what is told them by thee, that they may read and understand, how there is no other God but me.

And that they may always keep my commandments, and besin to read and take in the books of thy handwriting.

And after thirty days I s all send my angel for thee, and he will take thee from earth and from thy sons to me.

XXXVII.

Here God summons an angel.

AND the Lord called up one of the older angels, terrible and menacing, and placed him by me, in appearance white as snow, and his hands like ice, having the appearance of great frost, and he froze my face, because I could not endure the terror of the Lord, just as it is not possible to endure a stove's fire and the sun's heat, and the frost of the air.

And the Lord said to me: 'Enoch, if thy face be not frozen here, no man will be able to behold thy face.'

XXXVIII.

Mathusal continued to have hope and to await his father Enoch at his couch day and night.

AND the Lord said to those men who first led me up: 'Let Enoch go down on to earth with you, and await him till the determined day.'

And they placed me by night on my couch.

And Mathusal expecting my coming, keeping watch by day and by night at my couch, was filled with awe when he heard my coming, and I told him, 'Let all my household come together, that I tell them everything.'

XXXIX.

Enoch's pitiful admonition to his sons with weeping and great lamentation, as he spoke to them.

Oh my children, my beloved ones, hear the admonition of your father, as much as is according to the Lord's will.

I have been let come to you to-day, and announce to you, not from my lips, but from the Lord's lips, all that is and was and all that is now, and all that will be till judgement-day.

For the Lord has let me come to you, you hear therefore the words of my lips, of a man made big for you, but I am one who has seen the Lord's face, like iron made to glow from fire it sends forth sparks and burns,

You look now upon my eyes, the eyes of a man big with meaning for you, but I have seen the Lord's eyes, shining like the sun's rays and filling the eyes of man with awe.

You see now, my children, the right hand of a man that helps you, but I have seen the Lord's right hand filling heaven as be helped me.

You see the compass of my work like your own, but I have seen the Lord's limitless and perfect compass, which has no end.

You hear the words of my lips, as I heard the words of the Lord, like great thunder incessantly with hurling of clouds.

And now, my children, hear the discourses of the father of the earth, how fearful and awful it is to come before the face of the ruler of the earth, how much more terrible and awful it is to come before the face of the ruler of heaven, the controller of quick and dead, and of the heavenly troops. Who can endure that endless pain?

XL.

Enoch admonishes his children truly of all things from the Lord's lips, how he saw and heard and wrote down.

AND now, my children, I know all things, for this is from the Lord's lips, and this my eyes have seen, from besinning to end.

I know all things, and have written all things into books, the heavens and their end, and their plenitude, and all the armies and their marchings.

I have measured and described the stars, the great countless multitude of them.

What man has seen their revolutions, and their entrances? For not even the angels see their number, while I have written all their names.

And I measured the sun's circle, and measured its rays, counted the hours, I wrote down too all' things that go over the earth I have written the things that are nourished, and all seed sown and unsown, which the earth produces and all plants, and every grass and every flower, and their sweet smells, and their names, and the dwelling-places of the clouds, and their composition, and their wings, and how they bear rain and rain-drops.

And I investigated all things, and wrote the road of the thunder and of the lightning, and they showed me the keys and their guardians, their rise, the way they go; it is let out in measure (sc. gently) by a chain, lest by a heavy chain and violence it hurl down the angry clouds and destroy all things on earth.

I wrote the treasure-houses of the snow, and the store-houses of the cold and the frosty airs, and I observed their season's key-holder, he fills the clouds with them, and does not exhaust the treasure-houses.

And I wrote the resting-places of the winds and observed and saw how their key-holders bear weighing-scales and measures; first, they put them in one weighing-scale, then in the other the weights and let them out according to measure cunningly over the whole earth, lest by heavy breathing they make the earth to rock.

And I measured out the whole earth, its mountains, and all hills, fields, trees, stones, rivers, all existing things I wrote down, the height from earth to the seventh heaven, and downwards to the very lowest hell, and the judgement-place, and the very great, open and weeping hell.

And I saw how the prisoners are in pain, expecting the limitless judgement.

And I wrote down all those being judged by the judge, and all their judgements (sc. sentences) and all their works.

XLI.

Of how Enoch lamented Adam's sin.

AND I saw all forefathers from all time with Adam and Eva, and I sighed and broke into tears and said of the ruin of their dishonour:

'Woe is me for my infirmity and for that of my forefathers,' and thought in my, heart and said:

'Blessed is the man who has not been born or who has been born and shall not sin before the Lord's face, that he come not into this place, nor bring the yoke of this place!

XLII.

Of how Enoch saw the key-holders and guards of the gates of hell standing.

SAW the key-holders and guards of the gates of hell standing, like great serpents, and their faces like extinguished lamps, and their eyes of fire, their sharp teeth, and I saw all the Lord's works, how they are right, while the works of man are some good, and others bad, and in their works are known those who lie evilly.

XLIII.

Enoch shows his children how he measured and wrote out God's judgements.

I my children, measured and wrote out every work and every measure and every righteous judgement.

As one year is more honourable than another, so is one man more honourable than another, some for great possessions, some for wisdom of heart, some for particular intellect, some for cunning, one for silence of lip, another for cleanliness, one for strength, another for comeliness, one for youth, another for sharp wit, one for shape of body, another for sensibility, let it be heard everywhere, but there is none better than he who fears God, he shall be more glorious in time to come.

XLIV.

Enoch instructs his sons, that they revile not the face of man, small or great.

THE Lord with his hands having created man, in the likeness of his own face, the Lord made him small and great.

The Forgotten Books of Eden

Whoever reviles the ruler's face, and abhors the Lord's face, has despised the Lord's face, and tie who vents anger on any man without injury, the Lord's great anger will cut him down, he who spits on the face of man reproachfully, will be cut down at the Lord's great judgement.

Blessed is the man who does not direct his heart with malice against any man, and helps the injured and condemned, and raises the broken down, and shall do charity to the needy, because on the day of the great judgement every weight, every measure and every makeweight will be as in the market, that is to say they are hung on scales and stand in the market, and every one shall learn his own measure, and according to his measure shall take his reward.

XLV.

God shows how he does not want from men sacrifices, nor burnt-offerings, but pure and contrite hearts.

WHOEVER hastens to make offering before the Lord's face, the Lord for his part will hasten that offering by granting of his work.

But whoever increases his lamp before the Lord's face and make not true judgement, the Lord will not increase his treasure in the realm of the highest.

When the Lord demands bread, or candles, or flesh (sc. cattle), or any other sacrifice, then that is nothing; but God demands pure hearts, and with all that only tests the heart of man.

XLVI.

Of how an earthly ruler does not accept from man abominable and unclean gifts, then how much more does God abominate unclean gifts, but sends them away with wrath and does not accept his gifts.

HEAR, my people, and take in the words of my lips.

If any one bring any gifts to an earthly ruler, and have disloyal thoughts in his heart, and the ruler know this, will he not be angry with him, and not refuse his gifts, and not give him over to judgement?

Or if one man make himself appear good to another by deceit of tongue, but have evil in his heart, then will not the other understand the treachery of his heart, and himself be condemned, since his untruth was plain to all?

And when the Lord shall send a great light, then there will be judgement for the just and the unjust, and there no one shall escape notice.

XLVII.

Enoch instructs his sons from God's lips, and hands them the handwriting of this book.

AND now, my children, lay thought on your hearts, mark well the words of your father, which are all come to you from the Lord's lips.

Take these books of your father's handwriting and read them.

For the books are many, and in them you will learn all the Lord's works, all that has been from the besinning of creation, and will be till the end of time.

And if you will observe my handwriting, you will not sin against the Lord; because there is no other except the Lord, neither in heaven, nor in earth, nor in the very lowest places, nor in the one foundation.

The Lord has placed the foundations in the unknown, and has spread forth heavens visible and invisible; he fixed the earth on the waters, and created countless creatures, and who has counted the water and the foundation of the unfixed, or the dust of the earth, or the sand of the sea, or the drops of the rain, or the morning dew, or the wind's breathings? Who has filled earth and sea, and the indissoluble winter?

I cut the stars out of fire, and decorated heaven, and put it in their midst.

XLVIII.

Of the sun's passage along the seven circles.

THAT the sun go along the seven heavenly circles, which are the, appointment of one hundred and eighty-two thrones, that it go down on a short day, and again one hundred and eighty-two, that it go down on a big day, and he has two thrones on which he rests, revolving hither and thither above the thrones of the months, from the seventeenth day of the month Tsivan it goes down to the month Thevan, from the seventeenth of Thevan it goes up.

And thus it goes close to the earth, then the earth is and makes grow its fruit, and when it goes away, then the earth is sad, and trees and all fruits have no florescence.

All this he measured, with good measurement of hours, and fixed a measure by his wisdom, of the visible and the invisible.

From the invisible he made all things visible, himself being invisible.

Thus I make known to you, my children, and distribute the books to your children, into all your generations, and amongst the nations who shall have the sense to fear God, let them receive them, and may they come to love them more than any food or earthly sweets, and read them and apply themselves to them.

And those who understand not the Lord, who fear not God, who accept not, but reject, who do not receive them (sc. the books), a terrible judgement awaits these.

Blessed is the man who shall bear their yoke and shall drag them along, for he shall be released on the day of the great judgement.

XLIX.

Enoch instructs his sons not to swear either by heaven or earth, and shows God's promise, even in the mother's womb.

The Forgotten Books of Eden

I SWEAR to you, my children, but I swear not by any oath, neither by heaven nor by earth, nor by any other creature which God created.

The Lord said: 'There is no oath in me, nor injustice, but truth.'

If there is no truth in men, let them swear by the words 'yea, yea,' or else, 'nay, nay!

And I swear to you, yea, yea, that there has been no man in his mother's womb, but that already before, even to each one there is a place prepared for the repose of the soul, and a measure fixed how much it is intended that a man be tried in this world.

Yea, children, deceive not yourselves, for there has been previously prepared a place for every soul of man.

L.

Of how none born on earth can remain hidden nor his work remain concealed, but he (sc. God) bids us be meek, to endure attack and insult, and not to offend widows and orphans.

I HAVE put everyman's work in writing and none born on earth can remain hidden nor his works remain concealed.

I see all things.

Now therefore, my children, in patience and meekness spend the number of your days, that you inherit endless life.

Endure for the sake of the Lord every wound, every injury, every evil word and attack.

If ill-requitals befall you, return them not either to neighbour or enemy, because the Lord will return them for you and be your avenger on the day of great judgement, that there be no avensing here among men.

Whoever of you spends gold or silver for his brother's sake, he will receive ample treasure in the world to come.

Injure not widows nor orphans nor strangers, lest God's wrath come upon you.

LI.

Enoch instructs his sons, that they hide not treasures in the earth, but bids them give alms to the poor.

STRETCH out your hands to the poor according to your strength.

Hide not your silver in the earth.

Help the faithful man in affliction, and affliction will not find you in the time of your trouble.

And every grievous and cruel yoke that come upon you bear all for the sake of the

Lord, and thus you will find your reward in the day of judgement.

It is good to go morning, midday, and evening into the Lord's dwelling, for the glory of your creator.

Because every breathing thing glorifies him, and every creature visible and invisible returns him praise.

LII.

God instructs his faithful. how they are to praise his name.

BLESSED is the man who opens his lips in praise of God of Sabaoth and praises the Lord with his heart.

Cursed every man who opens his lips for the brinsing into contempt and calumny of his neighbour, because he brings God into contempt.

Blessed is he who opens his lips blessing and praising God.

4 Cursed is he before the Lord all the days of his life, who opens his lips to curse and abuse.

Blessed is he who blesses all the Lord's works.

Cursed is he who brings the Lord's creation into contempt.

Blessed is he who looks down and raises the fallen.

Cursed is he who looks to and is eager for the destruction of what is not his.

Blessed is he who keeps the foundations of his fathers made firm from the besinning.

Cursed is he who perverts the decrees of his forefathers.

Blessed is he who implants peace and love.

Cursed is he who disturbs those that love their neighbours.

Blessed is he who speaks with humble tongue and heart to all.

Cursed is he who speaks peace with his. tongue, while in his heart there is no peace but a sword.

For all these things will be laid bare in the weighing-scales and in the books, on the day of the great judgement.

LIII.

[Let us not say: 'Our father is before God, he will stand forward for us on the day of judgement,' for there father cannot help son, nor yet son father.]

AND now, my children, do not say: 'Our father is standing before God, and is praying for our sins,' for there is there no helper of any man who has sinned.

The Forgotten Books of Eden

You see how I wrote all works of every man, before his creation, all that is done amongst all men for all time, and none can tell or relate my handwriting, because the Lord sees all the imasinings of man, how they are vain, where they lie in the treasure-houses of the heart.

And now, my children, mark well all the words of your father, that I tell you, lest you regret, saying: 'Why did our father not tell us?'

LIV.

Enoch instructs his sons, that they should hand the books to others also.

AT that time, not understanding this let these books which I have given you be for an inheritance of your peace.

Hand them to all who want them, and instruct them, that they may see the Lord's very great and marvellous works.

LV.

Here Enoch shows his sons, telling them with tears: 'My children, the hour has approached for me to go up on to heaven; behold, the angels are standing before me.'

MY children, behold, the day of my term and the time nave approached.

For the angels who shall go with me are standing before me and urge me to my departure from you; they are standing here on earth, awaiting what has been told them.

For to-morrow I shall go up on to heaven, to the uppermost Jerusalem to my eternal inheritance.

Therefore I bid you do before the Lord's face all his good pleasure.

LVI.

Methosalam asks of his father blessing, that he (sc. Methosalam) may make him (sc. Enoch) food to eat.

METHOSALAM having answered his father Enoch, said: 'What is agreeable to thy eyes, father, that I may make before thy face, that thou mayst bless our dwellings, and thy sons, and that thy people may be made glorious through thee, and then that thou mayst depart thus, as the Lord said?,

Enoch answered to his son Methosalam and said: 'Hear, child, from the time when the Lord anointed me with the ointment of his glory, there has been no food in me, and my soul remembers not earthly enjoyment, neither do I want anything earthly!

LVII.

Enoch bade his son Methosalam. to summon all his brethren.

MY child Methosalam, summon all thy brethren and our household and the elders of the people, that I may talk to them and depart, as is planned for me.

117

The Forgotten Books of Eden

And Methosalam made haste, and summoned his brethren, Regim, Riman, Uchan, Chermion, Gaidad, and all the elders of the people before the face of his father Enoch; and he blessed them, and said to them:

LVIII.

Enoch's instruction to his sons.

LISTEN to me, my children, to-day.

In those days when the Lord came down on to earth for Adam's sake, and visited all his creatures, which he created himself, after all these he created Adam, and the Lord called all the beasts of the earth, all the reptiles, and all the birds that soar in the air, and brought them all before the face of our father Adam.

And Adam gave the names to all things living on earth.

And the Lord appointed him ruler over all, and subjected to him all things under his hands, and made them dumb and made them dull that they be commanded of man, and be in subjection and obedience to him.

Thus also the Lord created every man lord over all his possessions.

The Lord will not judge a single soul of beast for man's sake, but adjudges the souls of men to their beasts in this world; for men have a special place.

And as every soul of man is according to number, similarly beasts will not perish, nor all souls of beasts which the Lord created, till the great judgement, and they will accuse man, if he feed them ill.

LIX.

Enoch instructs his sons wherefore they may not touch beef because of what comes from it.

WHOEVER defiles the soul of beasts, defiles his own soul.

For man brings clean animals to make sacrifice for sin, that he may have cure of his soul.

And if they bring for sacrifice clean animals, and birds, man has cure, he cures his soul.

All is given you for food, bind it by the four feet, that is to make good the cure, he cures his soul.

But whoever kills beast without wounds, kills his own soul and defiles his own flesh.

And he who does any beast any injury whatsoever, in secret, it is evil practice, and he defiles his own soul.

LX.

He who does injury to soul of man, does injury to his own soul, and there is no cure for his flesh, nor pardon for all time. How it is not fitting to kill man neither by weapon nor by tongue.

HE who works the killing of a man's soul, kills his own soul, and kills his own body, and there is no cure for him for all time.

He who puts a man in any snare, shall stick in it himself, and there is no cure for him for all time.

He who puts a man in any vessel, his retribution will not be wanting at the great judgement for all time.

He who works crookedly or speaks evil against any soul, will not make justice for himself for all time.

LXI.

Enoch instructs his sons to keep themselves from injustice and often to stretch forth hands to the poor, to give a share of their labours.

AND now, my children, keep your hearts from every injustice, which the Lord hates. Just as a man asks (sc. something) for his own soul from God, so let him do to every living soul, because I know all things, how in the great time (sc. to come) are many mansions prepared for men, good for the good, and bad for the bad, without number many.

Blessed are those who enter the good houses, for in the bad (sc. houses) there is no peace .nor return (sc. from them).

Hear, my children, small and great! When man puts a good thought in his heart, brings gifts from his labours before the Lord's face and his hands made them not, then the Lord will turn away his face from the labour of his hand, and he (sc. man) cannot find the labour of his hands.

And if his hands made it, but his heart murmur, and his heart cease not making murmur incessantly, he has not any advantage.

LXII.

Of how it is fitting to bring one's gift with faith, because there is no repentance after death.

BLESSED is the man who in his patience brings his gifts with faith before the Lord's face, because he will find forgiveness of sins.

But if he take back his words before the time, there is no repentance for him; and if the time pass and he do not of his own will what is promised, there is no repentance after death.

Because every work which man does before the time, is all deceit before men, and sin before God.

The Forgotten Books of Eden

LXIII.

Of how not to despise the poor, but to share with them equally, lest thou be murmured against before God.

WHEN man clothes the naked and fills the hungry, he will find reward from God.

But if his heart murmur, he commits a double evil: ruin of himself and of that which he gives; and for him there will be no finding of reward on account of that.

And if his own heart is filled with his food and his own flesh (sc. clothed) with his clothing he commits contempt, and forfeit all his endurance of poverty, and will not find reward of his good deeds.

Every proud and magniloquent man is hateful to the Lord, and every false speech, clothed in untruth; it will be cut with the blade of the sword of death, and thrown into the fire, and shall burn for all time.

XLIV.

Of how the Lord calls up Enoch, and people took counsel to go and kiss him at the place called Achuzan.

WHEN Enoch had spoken these words to his sons, all people far and near heard how the Lord was calling Enoch. They took counsel together:

'Let us go and kiss Enoch, and two thousand men came together and came to the place Achuzan where Enoch was, and his sons.

And the elders of the people, the whole assembly, came and bowed down and began to kiss Enoch and said to him:

'Our father Enoch, be thou blessed of the Lord, the eternal ruler, and now bless thy sons and all the people, that we may be glorified to-day before thy face.

For thou shalt be glorified before the Lord's face for all time, since the Lord chose thee, rather than all men on earth, and designated thee writer of all his creation, visible and invisible, and redeemer of the sins of man, and helper of thy household.'

LXV.

Of Enoch's instruction of his sons.

AND Enoch answered all his people saying: 'Hear, my children, before that all creatures were created, the Lord created the visible and invisible things.

And as much time as there was and went past, understand that after that he created man in the likeness of his own form, and put into him eyes to see, and ears to hear, and heart to reflect, and intellect wherewith to deliberate.

And the Lord saw all man's works, and created all his creatures, and divided time, from time he fixed the years, and from the years he appointed the months, and from the months he appointed the days, and of days he appointed seven.

The Forgotten Books of Eden

And in those he appointed the hours, measured them out exactly, that man might reflect on time and count years, months, and hours, their alternation, besinning, and end, and that he might count his own life, from the besinning until death, and reflect on his sin and write his work bad and good; because no work is hidden before the Lord, that every man might know his works and never transgress all his commandments, and keep my handwriting from generation to generation.

When all creation visible and invisible, as the Lord created it, shall end, then every man goes to the great judgement, and then all time shall perish, and the years, and thenceforward there will be neither months nor days nor hours, they will be stuck together and will not be counted.

There will be one aeon, and all the righteous who shall escape the Lord's great judgement, shall be collected in the great aeon, for the righteous the great aeon will besin, and they will live eternally, and then too there will be amongst them neither labour, nor sickness, nor humiliation, nor anxiety, nor need, nor violence, nor night, nor darkness, but. great light.

And they shall have a great indestructible wall, and a paradise bright and incorruptible, for all corruptible things shall pass away, and there will be eternal life.

LXVI.

Enoch instructs his sons and all the elders of the people, how they are to walk with terror and trembling before the Lord, and serve him alone and not bow down to idols, but to God, who created heaven and earth and. every creature, and to his image.

AND now, my children, keep your souls from all injustice, such as the Lord hates.

Walk before his face with terror and trembling and serve him alone.

Bow down to the true God, not to dumb idols, but bow down to his picture, and bring all just offerings before the Lord's face. The Lord hates what is unjust.

For the Lord sees all things; when man takes thought in his heart, then he counsels the intellects, and every thought is always before the Lord, who made firm the earth and put all creatures on it.

If you look to heaven, the Lord is there; if you take thought of the sea's deep and all the under-earth, the Lord is there.

For the Lord created all things. Bow not down to things made by man, leaving the Lord of all creation, because no work can remain hidden before the Lord's face.

Walk, my children, in longsuffering, in meekness, honesty, in provocation, in grief, in faith and in truth, in reliance on promises, in illness, in abuse, in wounds, in temptation, in nakedness, in privation, loving one another, till you go out from this age of ills, that you become inheritors of endless time.

Blessed are the just who shall escape the great judgement, for they shall shine forth more than the sun sevenfold, for in this world the seventh part is taken off from all, light, darkness, food, enjoyment, sorrow, paradise, torture, fire, frost, and other things; he put all down in writing, that you might read and understand.'

LXVII.

The Lord let out darkness on to earth and covered the people and Enoch, and he was taken up on high, and light came again in the heaven.

WHEN Enoch had talked to the people, the Lord sent out darkness on to the earth, and there was darkness, and it covered those men standing with Enoch, and they took Enoch up on to the highest heaven, where the Lord is; and he received him and placed him before his face, and the darkness went off from the earth, and light came again.

And the people saw and understood not how Enoch had been taken, and glorified God, and found a roll in which was traced 'the invisible God'; and all went to their homes.

LXVIII.

ENOCH was born on the sixth day of the month Tsivan, and lived three hundred and sixty-five years.

He was taken up to heaven on the first day of the month Tsivan and remained in heaven sixty days.

He wrote all these signs of all creation, which the Lord created, and wrote three hundred and sixty-six books, and handed them over to his sons and remained on earth thirty days, and was again taken up to heaven on the sixth day of the month Tsivan, on the very day and hour when he was born.

As every man's nature in this life is dark, so are also his conception, birth, and departure from this life.

At what hour he was conceived, at that hour he was born, and at that hour too he died.

Methosalam and his brethren, all the sons of Enoch, made haste, and erected an altar at the place called Achuzan, whence and where Enoch had been taken up to heaven.

And they took sacrificial oxen and summoned all people and sacrificed the sacrifice before the Lord's face.

All people, the elders of the people and the whole assembly came to the feast and brought gifts to the sons of Enoch.

And they made a great feast, rejoicing and making merry three days, praising God, who had given them such a sign through Enoch, who had found favour with him, and that they should hand it on to their sons from generation to generation, from age to age.

Amen.

The Forgotten Books of Eden

THE PSALMS OF SOLOMON

THIS collection of eighteen war songs are the gift of an ancient Semitic writer. The orisinal manuscript has perished but fortunately Greek translations have been preserved, and recently a Syriac version of the same songs has turned up and was published in English for the first time in 1909 by Dr. Rendel Harris.

The date of the writing may be established at the middle of the First Century B. C. because the theme of these songs is that of Pompey's actions in Palestine and his death in Egypt in 48 B. C.

These psalms had an important position and were widely circulated in the early Church. They are frequently referred to in the various Codexes and histories of the first few centuries of the Christian Era.

Later, they became lost through inexplicable reasons; and have only been recovered for our use after the lapse of many centuries.

Besides the literary value of the trumpet-like of these verses, we have here a CHAPTER of stirring ancient history written by an eyewitness. Pompey comes out of the West. He uses battering-rams on the fortifications. His soldiers defile the altar. He is slain in Egypt after a fearful career. In the "righteous" of these psalms we see the Pharisees; in the "sinners" we see the Sadducees. It is an epic of a great people in the throes of a great crisis.

I

"They became insolent in their prosperity...."

I cried unto the Lord when I was in distress,

  Unto God when sinners assailed.

Suddenly the alarm of war was heard before me;

  I said, He will hearken to me for I am full of righteousness.

I thought in my heart that I was full of righteousness,

  Because I was well off and had become rich in children.

Their wealth spread to the whole earth,

  And their glory unto the end of the earth.

They were exalted unto the stars;

  They said they would never fan.

But they became insolent in their prosperity,

  And they were without understanding,

Their sins were in secret,

The Forgotten Books of Eden

And even I had no knowledge of them.

Their transgressions went beyond those of the heathen before them;

They utterly polluted the holy things of the Lord.

II.

The desecration of Jerusalem; captivity, murder, and raping. A psalm of utter despair.

When the sinner waxed proud, with a battering-ram he cast down fortified walls,

And thou didst not restrain him.

Alien nations ascended Thine altar,

They trampled it proudly with their sandals;

Because the sons of Jerusalem had defiled the holy things of the Lord,

Had profaned with iniquities the offerings of God.

Therefore He said: Cast them far from Me;

. . . .

It was set at naught before God,

It was utterly dishonoured;

The sons and the daughters were m grievous captivity,

Sealed was their neck, branded was it among the nations.

According to their sins hath He done unto them,

For He hath left them in the hands of them that prevailed.

He hath turned away His face from pitying them,

Young and old and their children together;

For they had done evil one and all, in not hearkening.

And the heavens were angry,

And the earth abhorred them;

For no man upon it had done what they did,

And the earth recognized all

Thy righteous judgements, O God.

They set the sons of Jerusalem to be mocked at in return for the harlots in her;

Every wayfarer entered in in the full light of day.

The Forgotten Books of Eden

They made mock with their transgressions, as they themselves were wont to do;

In the full light of day they revealed their iniquities.

And the daughters of Jerusalem were defiled in accordance with Thy judgement,

Because they had defiled themselves with unnatural intercourse.

I am pained in my bowels and my inward parts for these things.

And yet I will justify Thee, O God, in uprightness of heart,

For in Thy judgements is Thy righteousness displayed, O God.

For Thou hast rendered to the sinners according to their deeds,

Yea, according to their sins, which were very wicked.

Thou hast uncovered their sins, that Thy judgement might be manifest;

Thou hast wiped out their memorial from the earth.

God is a righteous judge,

And he is no respecter of persons.

For the nations reproached Jerusalem, trampling it down;

Her beauty was dragged down from the throne of glory.

She girded on sackcloth instead of comely raiment,

A rope was about her head instead of a crown.

She put off the glorious diadem which God had set upon her,

In dishonour was her beauty cast upon the ground.

And I saw and entreated the Lord and said,

Long enough, O Lord has Thine hand been heavy on Israel, in brinsing the nations upon them.

For they have made sport unsparingly in wrath and fierce anger;

And they will make an utter end, unless Thou, O Lord, rebuke them in Thy wrath.

For they have done. it not in zeal, but in lust of soul,

Pouring out their wrath upon us with a view to rapine.

Delay not, O God, to recompense them on their heads,

To turn the pride of the dragon into dishonour.

And I had not long to wait before God showed me the insolent one

Slain on the mountains of Egypt,

The Forgotten Books of Eden

Esteemed of less account than the least, on land and sea;

His body, too, borne hither and thither on the billows with much insolence,

With none to bury him, because He had rejected him with dishonour.

He reflected not that he was man,

And reflected not on the latter end;

He said: I will be lord of land and sea;

And he recognized not that it is God who is great,

Mighty in His great strength.

He is king over the heavens,

And judgeth kings and kingdoms.

It is He who setteth me up in glory,

And bringeth down the proud to eternal destruction in dishonour,

Because they knew Him not.

And now behold, ye princes of the earth, the judgement of the Lord,

For a great king and righteous is He, judsing all that is under heaven.

Bless God, ye that fear the Lord with wisdom,

For the mercy of the Lord will smile upon them that fear Him, in the Judgement;

So that He will distinguish between the righteous and the sinner,

And recompense the sinners for ever according to their deeds;

And have mercy on the righteous, delivering him from the affliction of the sinner,

And recompensing the sinner for what he bath done to the righteous.

For the Lord is good to them that call upon Him in patience,

Doing according to His mercy to His pious ones,

Establishing them at all times before Him in strength.

Blessed be the Lord for ever before His servants.

III.

Righteousness versus Sin.

Why sleepest thou, O my soul,

And blessest not the Lord?

Sing a new song,

The Forgotten Books of Eden

Unto God who is worthy to be praised.

Sing and be wakeful against His awaking,

  For good is a psalm sung to God from a glad heart.

The righteous remember the Lord at all times,

  With thanksgiving and declaration of the righteousness of the Lord's judgements.

The righteous despiseth not the chastening of the Lord;

  His will is always before the Lord.

The righteous stumbleth and holdeth the Lord righteous:

  He falleth and looketh out for what God will do to him;

He seeketh out whence his deliverance will come.

  The steadfastness of the righteous is from God, their deliverer;

There lodgeth not in the house of the righteous sin upon sin.

  The righteous continually searcheth his house,

To remove utterly all iniquity done by him in error.

  He maketh atonement for sins of ignorance by fasting and afflicting his soul,

And the Lord counteth guiltless every pious man and his house.

  The sinner stumbleth and curseth his life

The day when he was begotten, and his mother's travail.

  He addeth sins to sins, while he liveth;

He falleth—verily grievous is his fall—and riseth no more.

  The destruction of the sinner is for ever,

And he shall not be remembered, when the righteous is visited.

  This is the portion of sinners for ever.

But they that fear the Lord shall rise to life eternal,

  And their life shall be in the light of the Lord, and shall come to an end no more.

IV.

  A conversation of Solomon with the Men-pleasers.

Wherefore sittest thou, O profane man, in the council of the pious,

    Seeing that thy heart is far removed from the Lord,

    Provoking with transgressions the God of Israel?

The Forgotten Books of Eden

Extravagant in speech, extravagant in outward seeming beyond all men,

   Is he that is severe of speech in condemning sinners in judgement.

And his hand is first upon him as though he acted in zeal,

   And yet he is himself guilty in respect of manifold sins and of wantonness.

His eyes are upon every woman without distinction;

   His tongue lieth when he maketh contract with an oath.

By night and in secret he sinneth as though unseen,

   With his eyes he talketh to every woman of evil compacts.

He is swift to enter every house with cheerfulness as though guileless.

Let God remove those that live in hypocrisy in the company of the pious,

   Even the life of such an one with corruption of his flesh and penury.

Let God reveal the deeds of the men-pleasers,

   The deeds of such an one with laughter and derision;

That the pious may count righteous the judgement of their God,

   When sinners are removed from before the righteous,

   Even the man-pleaser who uttereth law guilefully.

And their eyes are fixed upon any man's house that is still secure,

   That they may, like the Serpent, destroy the wisdom of . . . with words of transgressors,

   His words are deceitful that he may accomplish his wicked desire.

   He never ceaseth from scattering families as though they were orphans,

   Yea, he layeth waste a house on account of his lawless desire.

He deceiveth with words, saying, There is none that seeth, or judgeth.

He fills one house with lawlessness,

   And then his eyes are fixed upon the next house,

   To destroy it with words that give wing to desire.

Yet with all these his soul like Sheol, is not sated.

Let his portion, O Lord, be dishonoured before thee;

   Let him go forth groaning, and come home cursed.

Let his life be spent in anguish, and penury, and want, O Lord;

The Forgotten Books of Eden

Let his sleep be beset with pains and his awaking with perplexities.

Let sleep be withdrawn from his eyelids at night;

Let him fail dishonourably in every work of his hands.

Let him come home empty-handed to his house,

And his house be void of everything wherewith he could sate his appetite.

Let his old age be spent in childless loneliness until his removal by death.

Let the flesh of the men-pleasers be rent by wild beasts,

And let the bones of the lawless lie dishonoured in the sight of the sun.

Let ravens peck out the eyes of the hypocrites.

For they have laid waste many houses of men, in dishonour,

And scattered them in their lust;

And they have not remembered God,

Nor feared God in all these things;

But they have provoked God's anger and vexed Him.

May He remove them from off the earth,

Because with deceit they beguiled the souls of the flawless.

Blessed are they that fear the Lord in their flawlessness;

The Lord shall deliver them from guileful men and sinners,

And deliver us from every stumbling-block of the lawless (men).

Let God destroy them that insolently work all unrighteousness,

For a great and mighty judge is the Lord our God in righteousness.

Let Thy mercy, O Lord, be upon all them that love Thee.

V.

A statement of the philosophy of the indestructibility of matter. One of the tenets of modern physics.

O Lord God, I will praise Thy name with joy,

In the midst of them that know Thy righteous judgements.

For Thou art good and merciful, the refuge of the poor;

When I cry to Thee, do not silently disregard me.

For no man taketh spoil from a mighty man;

The Forgotten Books of Eden

Who, then, can take aught of a that Thou hast made, except Thou Thyself givest?

For man and his portion lie before Thee in the balance;

  He cannot add to, so as to enlarge, what has been prescribed by Thee.

O God, when we are in distress we call upon Thee for help,

  And Thou dost not turn back our petition, for Thou art our God.

Cause not Thy hand to be heavy upon us,

  Lest through necessity we sin.

Even though Thou restore us not, we will not keep away;

  But unto Thee will we come.

For if I hunger, unto Thee will I cry, O God;

  And Thou wilt give to me.

Birds and fish dost Thou nourish,

  In that Thou givest rain to the steppes that green grass may spring up,

  So to prepare fodder in the steppe for every living thing;

And if they hunger, unto Thee do they lift up their face.

Kings and rulers and peoples Thou dost nourish, O God;

  And who is the help of the poor and needy, if not Thou, O Lord?

And Thou wilt hearken—for who is good and gentle but thou?—

  Making glad the soul of the humble by opening Thine hand in mercy.

Man's goodness is bestowed grudsingly and ...;

  And if he repeat it without murmuring, even that is marvellous.

But Thy gift is great in goodness and wealth,

  And he whose hope is set on Thee shall have no lack of gifts.

Upon the whole earth is Thy mercy, O Lord, in goodness.

Happy is he whom God remembereth in granting to him a due sufficiency;

  If a man abound overmuch, he sinneth.

Sufficient are moderate means with righteousness,

  And hereby the blessing of the Lord becomes abundance with righteousness.

They that fear the Lord rejoice in good gifts,

  And thy goodness is upon Israel in Thy kingdom.

The Forgotten Books of Eden

Blessed is the glory of the Lord, for He is our king.

VI.

A song of hope and fearlessness and peace.

Happy is the man whose heart is fixed to call upon the name of the Lord;

When he remembereth the name of the Lord, he will be saved.

His ways are made even by the Lord,

And the works of his hands are preserved by the Lord his God.

At what he sees in his bad dreams, his soul shall not be troubled;

When he passes through rivers and the tossing of the seas, he shall not be dismayed.

He ariseth from his sleep, and blesseth the name of the Lord:

When his heart is at peace, he singeth to the name of his God,

And he entreateth the Lord for all his house.

And the Lord heareth the prayer of every one that feareth God,

And every request of the soul that hopes for Him doth the Lord accomplish.

Blessed is the Lord, who showeth mercy to those who love Him in sincerity.

VII.

The fine old doctrine—"Thou art our Shield!"

Make not Thy dwelling afar from us, O God;

Lest they assail us that hate us without cause.

For Thou hast rejected them, O God;

Let not their foot trample upon Thy holy inheritance.

Chasten us Thyself in Thy good pleasure;

But give us not up to the nations;

For, if Thou sendest pestilence,

Thou Thyself givest it charge concerning us;

For Thou art merciful,

And wilt not be angry to the point of consuming us.

While Thy name dwelleth in our midst, we shall find mercy;

And the nations shall not prevail against us.

The Forgotten Books of Eden

For Thou art our shield,

   And when we call upon Thee, Thou hearkenest to us;

For Thou wilt pity the seed of Israel for ever

   And Thou wilt not reject them:

But we shall, be under Thy yoke for ever,

   And under the rod of Thy chastening.

Thou wilt establish us in the time that Thou helpest us,

   Showing mercy to the house of Jacob on the day wherein Thou didst promise to help them.

VIII.

Some remarkable similes of war creeping on Jerusalem. A survey of the sins that brought all this trouble.

Distress and the sound of war hath my ear heard,

   The sound of a trumpet announcing slaughter and calamity,

The sound of much people as of an exceeding high wind,

   As a tempest with mighty fire sweeping through the Negeb.

And I said in my heart, Surely God judgeth us;

   A sound I hear moving towards Jerusalem, the holy city

My loins were broken at what I heard, my knees tottered;

   My heart was afraid, my bones were dismayed like flax.

I said: They establish their ways in righteousness.

I thought upon the judgments of God since the creation of heaven and earth;

   I held God righteous in His judgements which have been from of old.

God bare their sins in the full light of day;

   All the earth came to know the righteous judgements of God.

In secret places underground their iniquities were committed to provoke Him to anger;

   They wrought confusion, son with mother and father with daughter;

   They committed adultery, every man with his neighhour's wife.

They concluded covenants with one another with an oath touching these things;

   They plundered the sanctuary of God, as though there was no avenger.

The Forgotten Books of Eden

They trode the altar of the Lord, coming straight from all manner of uncleanness;

And with menstrual blood they defiled the sacrifices, as though these were common flesh.

They left no sin undone, wherein they surpassed not the heathen.

Therefore God mingled for them a spirit of wandering;

And gave them to drink a cup of undiluted wine, that they might become drunken.

He brought him that is from the end of the earth, that smiteth mightily;

He decreed war against Jerusalem, and against her land.

The princes of the land went to meet him with joy: they said unto him:

Blessed be thy way! Come ye, enter ye in with peace.

They made the rough ways even, before his entering in;

They opened the gates to Jerusalem, they crowned its walls.

As a father entereth the house of his sons, so he entered Jerusalem in peace;

He established his feet there in great safety.

He captured her fortresses and the wall of Jerusalem;

For God Himself led him in safety, while they wandered.

He destroyed their princes and every one wise in counsel;

He poured out the blood of the inhabitants of Jerusalem, like the water of uncleanness.

He led away their sons and daughters, whom they had begotten in defilement.

They did according to their uncleanness, even as their fathers had done:

They defiled Jerusalem and the things that had been hallowed to the name of God.

But God hath shown Himself righteous in His judgements upon the nations of the earth;

And the pious servants of God are like innocent lambs in their midst.

Worthy to be praised is the Lord that judgeth the whole earth in His righteousness.

Behold, now, O God, Thou hast shown us Thy judgement in Thy righteousness;

Our eyes have seen Thy judgements, O God.

We have justified Thy name that is honoured for ever;

For Thou are the God of righteousness, judsing Israel with chastening.

The Forgotten Books of Eden

Turn, O God, Thy mercy upon us, and have pity upon us;

Gather together the dispersed of Israel, with mercy and goodness;

For Thy faithfulness is with us,

And though we have stiffened our neck, yet Thou art our chastener;

Overlook us not, O our God, lest the nations swallow us up, as though there were none to deliver.

But Thou art our God from the besinning,

And upon Thee is our hope set, O Lord;

And we will not depart from Thee,

For good are Thy judgements upon us.

Ours and our children's be Thy good pleasure for ever;

O Lord, our Saviour, we shall never more be moved.

The Lord is worthy to be praised for His judgements with the mouth of His pious ones;

And blessed be Israel of the Lord for ever.

IX.

The exile of the tribes of Israel. A reference to the covenant which God made with Adam. (See the First Book of Adam and Eve, CHAPTER III, Verse 7).

When Israel was led away captive into a strange land,

When they fell away from the Lord who redeemed them,

They were cast away from the inheritance, which the Lord had given them.

Among every nation were the dispersed of Israel according to the word of God,

That Thou mightest be justified, O God, in Thy righteousness by reason of our transgressions:

For Thou art a just judge over all the peoples of the earth.

For from Thy knowledge none that doeth unjustly is hidden,

And the righteous deeds of Thy pious ones are before Thee, O Lord;

Where, then, can a man hide himself from Thy knowledge, O God?

Our works are subject to our own choice and power

To do right or wrong in the works of our hands;

And in Thy righteousness Thou visitest the sons of men.

The Forgotten Books of Eden

He that doeth righteousness layeth up life for himself with the Lord;

And he that doeth wrongly forfeits his life to destruction;

For the judgements of the Lord are given in righteousness to every man and his house.

Unto whom art Thou good, O God, except to them that call upon the Lord?

He cleanseth from sins a soul when it maketh confession, when it maketh acknowledgement;

For shame is upon us and u on our faces on account of all these things.

And to whom doth He forgive sins, except to them that have sinned?

Thou blessest the righteous, and dost not reprove them for the sins that they have committed;

And Thy goodness is upon them that sin, when they repent.

And, now, Thou art our God, and we the people whom Thou hast loved:

Behold and show pity, O God of Israel, for we are Thine;

And remove not Thy mercy from us, lest they assail us.

For Thou didst choose the seed of Abraham before all the nations,

And didst set Thy name upon us, O Lord,

And Thou wilt not reject us for ever.

Thou madest a covenant with our fathers concerning us;

And we hope in Thee, when our soul turneth unto Thee.

The mercy of the Lord be upon the house of Israel for ever and ever.

X.

A glorious hymn. Further reference to the eternal covenant between God and Man.

Happy is the man whom the Lord remembereth with reproving,

And whom He restraineth from the way of evil with strokes

That he may be cleansed from sin, that it may not be multiplied.

He that maketh ready his back for strokes shall be cleansed,

For the Lord is good to them that endure chastening.

For He maketh straight the ways of the righteous,

And doth not pervert them by His chastening.

The Forgotten Books of Eden

And the mercy of the Lord is upon them that love Him in truth,

And the Lord remembereth His servants in mercy.

For the testimony is in the law of the eternal covenant,

The testimony of the Lord is on the ways of men in His visitation.

Just and kind is our Lord in His judgements for ever,

And Israel shall praise the name of the Lord in gladness.

And the pious shall give thanks in the assembly of the people;

And on the poor shall God have mercy in the gladness of Israel;

For good and merciful is God for ever,

And the assemblies of Israel shall glorify the name of the Lord.

The salvation of the Lord be upon the house of Israel unto everlasting gladness!

XI.

Jerusalem hears a trumpet and stands on tiptoe to see her children returning from the North, East and West.

Blow ye in Zion on the trumpet to summon the saints,

Cause ye to be heard in Jerusalem the voice of him that bringeth good tidings;

For God hath had pity on Israel in visiting them.

Stand on the height, O Jerusalem, and behold thy children,

From the East and the West, gathered together by the Lord;

From the North they come in the gladness of their God,

From the isles afar off God hath gathered them.

High mountains hath He abased into a plain for them;

The hills fled at their entrance.

The woods gave them shelter as they passed by;

Every sweet-smelling tree God caused to spring up for them,

That Israel might pass by in the visitation of the glory of their God.

Put on, O Jerusalem, thy glorious garments;

Make ready thy holy robe;

For God hath spoken good concerning Israel, for ever and ever.

Let the Lord do what He hath spoken concerning Israel and Jerusalem;

The Forgotten Books of Eden

Let the Lord raise up Israel by His glorious name.

The mercy of the Lord be upon Israel for ever and ever.

XII.

An appeal for family tranquility and peace and quiet at home.

O Lord, deliver my soul from the lawless and wicked man,

From the tongue that is lawless and slanderous, and speaketh lies and deceit.

Manifoldly twisted are the words of the tongue of the wicked man,

Even as among a people a fire that burneth up their beauty.

So he delights to fill houses with a lying tongue,

To cut down the trees of gladness which setteth on fire transgressors,

To involve households in warfare by means of slanderous lips.

May God remove far from the innocent the lips of transgressors by brinsing them to want

And may the bones of slanderers be scattered far away from them that fear the Lord!

In flaming fire perish the slanderous tongue far away from the pious!

May the Lord preserve the quiet soul that hateth the unrighteous;

And may the Lord establish the man that followeth peace at home.

The salvation of the Lord be upon Israel His servant for ever;

And let the sinners perish together at the presence of the Lord;

But let the Lord's pious ones inherit the promises of the Lord.

XIII.

Of Solomon. A Psalm. Comfort for the righteous.

The right hand of the Lord hath covered me;

The right hand of the Lord hath spared us.

The arm of the Lord hath saved us from the sword that passed through,

From famine and the death of sinners.

Noisome beasts ran upon them:

With their teeth they tore their flesh,

And with their molars crushed their bones.

But from all these things the Lord delivered us.

The Forgotten Books of Eden

The righteous was troubled on account of his errors,

  Lest he should be taken away along with the sinners;

For terrible is the overthrow of the sinner;

  But not one of all these things toucheth the righteous.

For not alike are the chastening of the righteous for sins done in ignorance,

  And the overthrow of the sinners.

Secretly is the righteous chastened,

  Lest the sinner rejoice over the righteous.

For He correcteth the righteous as a beloved son.

  And his chastisement is as that of a first-born.

For the Lord spareth His pious ones,

  And blotteth out their errors by His chastening.

For the life of the righteous shall be for ever;

  But sinners shall be taken away into destruction,,

  And their memorial shall be found no more.

But upon the pious is the mercy of the Lord,

  And upon them that fear Him His mercy.

XIV.

Sinners "love the brief day spent in companionship with their sin." Profound wisdom, beautifully expressed.

Faithful is the Lord to them that love Him in truth,

  To them that endure His chastening,

To them that walk in the righteousness of His commandments,

  In the law which He commanded us that we might live.

The pious of the Lord shall live by it for ever;

  The Paradise of the Lord, the trees of life, are His pious ones.

Their planting is rooted for ever;

  They shall not be plucked up all the days of heaven:

For the portion and the inheritance of God is Israel.

But not so are the sinners and transgressors,

The Forgotten Books of Eden

Who love the brief day spent in companionship with their sin;

Their delight is in fleeting corruption,

   And they remember not God.

For the ways of men are known before Him at all times,

   And He knoweth the secrets of the heart before they come to pass.

Therefore their inheritance is Sheol and darkness and destruction

   And they shall not be found in the day when the righteous obtain mercy;

But the pious of the Lord shall inherit life in gladness.

XV.

The psalmist restates the great philosophy of Right and Wrong.

When I was in distress I called upon the name of the Lord,

   I hoped for the help of the God of Jacob and was saved;

   For the hope and refuge of the poor art Thou, O God.

For who, O God, is strong except to give thanks unto Thee in truth?

   And wherein is a man powerful except in giving thanks to Thy name?

A new psalm with song in gladness of heart,

   The fruit of the lips with the well-tuned instrument of the tongue,

   The first fruits of the lips from a pious and righteous heart—

He that offereth these things shall never be shaken by evil;

   The flame of fire and the wrath against the unrighteous shall not touch him,

When it goeth forth from the face of the Lord against sinners,

   To destroy all the substance of sinners,

For the mark of God is upon the righteous that they may be saved.

Famine and sword and pestilence shall be far from the righteous,

   For they shall flee away from the pious as men pursued in war;

But they shall pursue sinners and overtake them,

   And they that do lawlessness shall not escape the judgement of God;

As by enemies experienced in war shall they be overtaken,

   For the mark of destruction is upon their forehead.

And the inheritance of sinners is destruction and darkness,

The Forgotten Books of Eden

And their iniquities shall pursue them unto Sheol beneath.

Their inheritance shall not be found of their children,

    For sins shall lay waste the houses of sinners.

And sinners shall perish for ever in the day of the Lord's judgement,

    When God visiteth the earth with His judgement.

But they that fear the Lord shall find mercy therein,

    And shall live by the compassion of their God;

But sinners shall perish for ever.

XVI.

The psalmist again expresses profound truth—"For if Thou givest not strength, who can endure chastisement?"

When my soul slumbered being afar from the Lord, I had all but slipped down to the pit,

    When I was far from God, my soul had been well-nigh poured out unto death,

I had been nigh unto the gates of Sheol with the sinner,

    When my soul departed from the Lord God of Israel—

Had not the Lord helped me with His everlasting mercy.

He pricked me, as a horse is pricked, that I might serve Him,

    My saviour and helper at all times saved me.

I will give thanks unto Thee, O God, for Thou hast helped me to my salvation;

    And hast not counted me with sinners to my destruction.

Remove not Thy mercy from me, O God,

    Nor Thy memorial from my heart until I die.

Rule me, O God, keeping me back from wicked sin,

    And from every wicked woman that causeth the simple to stumble.

And let not the beauty of a lawless woman beguile me,

    Nor any one that is subject to unprofitable sin.

Establish the works of my hands before Thee,

    And preserve my goings in the remembrance of Thee.

Protect my tongue and my lips with words of truth;

    Anger and unreasoning wrath put far from me.

The Forgotten Books of Eden

Murmuring, and impatience in affliction, remove far from me

When, if I sin, Thou chastenest me that I may return unto Thee.

But with goodwill and cheerfulness support my soul;

When Thou strengthenest my soul, what is given to me will be sufficient for me.

For if Thou givest not strength,

Who can endure chastisement with poverty?

When a man is rebuked by means of his corruption,

Thy testing of him is in his flesh and in the affliction of poverty.

If the righteous endureth in all these trials, he shall receive mercy from the Lord.

XVII.

"They set a worldly monarchy . . . . they lay waste the Throne of David!' A poetic narrative about the utter disintegration of a great nation.

O Lord, Thou art our King for ever and ever,

For in Thee, O God, doth our soul glory.

How long are the days of man's life upon the earth?

As are his days, so is the hope set upon him.

But we hope in God, our deliverer;

For the might of our God is for ever with mercy,

And the kingdom of our God is for ever over the nations in judgement.

Thou, O Lord, didst choose David to be king over Israel,

And swaredst to him touching his seed that never should his kingdom fail before Thee.

But, for our sins, sinners rose up against us;

They assailed us and thrust us out;

What Thou hadst not promised to them, they took away from us with violence.

They in no wise glorified Thy honourable name;

They set a worldly monarchy in place of that which was their excellency;

They laid waste the throne of David in tumultuous arrogance.

But Thou, O God, didst cast them down, and remove their seed from the earth,

In that there rose up against them a man that was alien to our race.

According to their sins didst Thou recompense them, O God;

The Forgotten Books of Eden

So that it befell them according to their deeds.

God showed them no pity;

He sought out their seed and let not one of them go free.

Faithful is the Lord in all His judgements

Which He doeth upon the earth.

The lawless one laid waste our land so that none inhabited it,

They destroyed young and old and their children together.

In the heat of His anger He sent them away even unto the west,

And He exposed the rulers of the land unsparingly to derision.

Being an alien the enemy acted proudly,

And his heart was alien from Our God.

And all things whatsoever he did in Jerusalem,

As also the nations in the cities to their gods.

And the children of the covenant in the midst of the mingled peoples surpassed them in evil.

There was not among them one that wrought in the midst of Jerusalem mercy and truth.

They that loved the synagogues of the pious fled from them,

As sparrows that fly from their nest.

They wandered in deserts that their lives might be saved from harm,

And precious in the eyes of them that lived abroad was any that escaped alive from them.

Over the whole earth were they scattered by lawless men.

For the heavens withheld the rain from dropping upon the earth,

Springs were stopped that sprang perennially out of the deeps, that ran down from lofty mountains.

For there was none among them that wrought righteousness and justice;

From the chief of them to the least of them all were sinful;

The king was a transgressor, and the judge disobedient, and the people sinful.

Behold, O Lord, and raise up unto them their king, the son of David,

At the time in the which Thou seest, O God, that he may reign over Israel Thy servant.

The Forgotten Books of Eden

And gird him with strength, that he may shatter unrighteous rulers,

And that he may purge Jerusalem from nations that trample her down to destruction.

Wisely, righteously he shall thrust out sinners from the inheritance,

He shall destroy the pride of the sinner as a potter's vessel.

With a rod of iron he shall break in pieces all their substance,

He shall destroy the godless nations with the word of his mouth;

At his rebuke nations shall flee before him,

And he shall reprove sinners for the thoughts of their heart.

And he shall gather together a holy people, whom he shall lead in righteousness,

And he shall judge the tribes of the people that has been sanctified by the Lord his God.

And he shall not suffer unrighteousness to lodge any more in their midst,

Nor shall there dwell with them any man that knoweth wickedness,

For he shall know them, that they are all sons of their God.

And he shall divide them according to their tribes upon the land,

And neither sojourner nor alien shall sojourn with them any more.

He shall judge peoples and nations in the wisdom of his righteousness. Selah.

And he shall have the heathen nations to serve him under his yoke;

And he shall glorify the Lord in a place to be seen of all the earth;

And he shall purge Jerusalem, making it holy as of old:

So that nations shall come from the ends of the earth to see his glory,

Brinsing as gifts her sons who had fainted.

And to see the glory of the Lord, wherewith God hath glorified her.

And he shall be a righteous king, taught of God, over them,

And there shall be no unrighteousness in his days in their midst,

For all shall be holy and their king the anointed of the Lord.

For he shall not put his trust in horse and rider and bow,

Nor shall he multiply for himself gold and silver for war,

Nor shall he gather confidence from a multitude for the day of battle.

The Lord Himself is his king, the hope of him that is mighty through his hope in

The Forgotten Books of Eden

God.

All nations shall be in fear before him,

For he will smite the earth with the word of his mouth for ever.

He will bless the people of the Lord with wisdom and gladness,

And he himself will be pure from sin, so that he may rule a great people.

He will rebuke rulers, and remove sinners by the might of his word;

And relying upon his God, throughout his days he will not stumble;

For God will make him mighty by means of His holy spirit,

And wise by means of the spirit of understanding, with strength and righteousness.

And the blessing of the Lord will be with him: he will be strong and stumble not;

His hope will be in the Lord: who then can prevail against him?

He will, be mighty in his works, and strong in the fear of God,

He will be shepherding the flock of the Lord faithfully and righteously,

And will suffer none among them to stumble in their pasture.

He will lead them all aright,

And there will be no pride among them that any among them should be oppressed.

This will be the majesty of the king of Israel whom God knoweth;

He will raise him up over the house of Israel to correct him.

His words shall be more refined than costly gold, the choicest;

In the assemblies he will judge the peoples, the tribes of the sanctified.

His words shall be like the words of the holy ones in the midst of sanctified peoples.

Blessed be they that shall be in those days,

In that they shall see the good fortune of Israel which God shall bring to pass in the gathering together of the tribes.

May the Lord hasten His mercy upon Israel!

May He deliver us from the uncleanness of unholy enemies!

The Lord Himself is our king for ever and ever.

XVIII.

With this psalm end the warlike Songs of Solomon.

The Forgotten Books of Eden

Lord, Thy mercy is over the works of Thy hands for ever;

   Thy goodness is over Israel with a rich gift.

Thine eyes look upon them, so that none of them suffers want;

   Thine ears listen to the hopeful prayer of the poor.

Thy judgements are executed upon the whole earth in mercy;

   And Thy love is toward the seed of Abraham, the children of Israel.

Thy chastisement is upon us as upon a first-born, only-begotten son,

   To turn back the obedient soul from folly that is wrought in ignorance.

May God cleanse Israel against the day of mercy and blessing,

   Against the day of choice when

Blessed shall they be that shall be in those days,

   He bringeth back His anointed.

In that they shall see the goodness of the Lord which He shall perform for the generation that is to come,

   Under the rod of chastening of the Lord's anointed in the fear of his God,

   In the spirit of wisdom and righteousness and strength;

That he may direct every man in the works of righteousness by the fear of God,

   That he may establish them all before the Lord,

   A good generation living in the fear of God in the days of mercy. Selah.

Great is our God and glorious, dwelling in the highest.

It is He who hath established in their courses the lights of heaven for determining seasons from year to year,

   And they have not turned aside from the way which He appointed them.

In the fear of God they pursue their path every day,

   From the day God created them and for evermore.

And they have erred not since the day He created them.

   Since the generations of old they have not withdrawn from their path,

   Unless God commanded them so to do by the command of His servants.

THE ODES OF SOLOMON.

HERE are some of the most beautiful songs of peace and joy that the world possesses. Yet their orisin, the date of their writing, and the exact meaning of many of the

The Forgotten Books of Eden

verses remain one of the great literary mysteries.

They have come down to us in a single and very ancient document in Syriac language. Evidently that document is a translation from the orisinal Greek. Critical debate has raged around these Odes; one of the most plausible explanations is that they are songs of newly baptized Christians of the First Century.

They are strangely lacking in historical allusions. Their radiance is no reflection of other days. They do not borrow from either the Old Testament or the Gospels. The inspiration of these verses is first-hand. They remind you of Aristides' remark, "A new people with whom something Divine is mingled." Here is vigor and insight to which we can find parallels only in the most exalted parts of the Scriptures.

For these dazzling mystery odes, we owe our translation to J. Rendel Harris, MA., Hon. Fellow of Clare College, Cambridge. He says about them: "There does not seem to be anything about which everyone seem agreed unless it be that the Odes are of singular beauty and high spiritual value."

ODE 1.

The Lord is on my head like a crown, and I shall not be without Him.

They wove for me a crown of truth, and it caused thy branches to bud in me.

For it is not like a withered crown which buddeth not: but thou livest upon my head, and thou hast blossomed upon my head.

Thy fruits are full-grown and perfect, they are full of thy salvation.

ODE 2.

(No part of this Ode has ever been identified.)

ODE 3.

The first words of this Ode have disappeared.

. . . I put on:

And his members are with him. And on them do I stand, and He loves me:

For I should not have known how to love the Lord, if He had not loved me.

For who is able to distinguish love, except the one that is loved?

I love the Beloved, and my soul loves Him:

And where His rest is, there also am I;

And I shall be no stranger, for with the Lord Most High and Merciful there is no grudsing.

I have been united to I-run, for the Lover has found the Beloved,

And because I shall love Him that, is the Son, I shall become a son;

The Forgotten Books of Eden

For he that is joined to Him that is immortal, will also himself become immortal;

And he who has pleasure in the Living One, will become living.

This is the Spirit of the Lord, which doth not lie, which teacheth the sons of men to know His ways.

Be wise and understanding and vigilant. Hallelujah.

ODE 4.

This Ode is important because of the historical allusion with which it commences. This may refer to the closing of the temple at Leontopolis in Egypt which would date this writing about 73 A. D.

No man, O my God, changeth thy holy place;

And it is not (possible) that he should change it and put it in another place: because he hath no power over it:

For thy sanctuary thou hast designed before thou didst make (other) places:

That which is the older shall not be altered by those that are younger than itself.

Thou has given thy heart, O Lord, to thy believers: never wilt thou fail, nor be without fruits:

For one hour of thy Faith is more precious than all days and years.

For who is there that shall put on thy grace, and be hurt?

For thy seal is known: and thy creatures know it: and thy (heavenly) hosts possess it: and the elect archangels are clad with it.

Thou hast given us thy fellowship: it was not that thou wast in need of us: but that we are in need of thee:

Distill thy dews upon us and open thy rich fountains that pour forth to us milk and honey:

For there is no repentance with thee that thou shouldest repent of anything that thou hast promised:

And the end was revealed before thee: for what thou gavest, thou gavest freely:

So that thou mayest, not draw them back and take them again:

For all was revealed before thee as God, and ordered from the besinning before thee: and thou, O God, hast made all things. Hallelujah.

ODE 5.

This Ode has strangely appeared in a speech by Salome in another ancient work called the Pistis Sophia.

I will give thanks unto thee, O Lord, because I love thee;

The Forgotten Books of Eden

O Most High, thou wilt not forsake me, for thou art my hope:

Freely I have received thy grace, I shall live thereby:

My persecutors will come and not see me:

A cloud of darkness shall fall on their eyes; and an air of thick gloom shall darken them:

And they shall have no light to see: they may not take hold upon me.

Let their counsel become thick darkness, and what I have cunningly devised, let it return upon their own heads:

For they have devised a counsel, and it did not succeed:

For my hope is upon the Lord, and I will not fear, and because the Lord is my salvation, I will not fear:

And He is as a garland on my head and I shall not be moved; even if everything should be shaken, I stand firm;

And if all things visible should perish, I shall not die; because the Lord is with me and I am with Him. Hallelujah.

ODE 6.

First century universalism is revealed in an interesting way in verse 10.

As the hand moves over the harp, and the strings speak.

So speaks in my members the Spirit of the Lord, and I speak by His love.

For it destroys what is foreign, and everything that is bitter:

For thus it was from the besinning and will be to the end, that nothing should be His adversary, and nothing should stand up against Him.

The Lord has multiplied the knowledge of Himself, and is zealous that these things should be known, which by His grace have been given to us.

And the praise of His name He gave us: our spirits praise His holy Spirit.

For there went forth a stream and became a river great and broad;

For it flooded and broke up everything and it brought (water) to the Temple:

And the restrainers of the children of men were not able to restrain it, nor the arts of those whose business it is to restrain waters;

For it spread over the face of the whole earth, and filled everything: and all the thirsty upon earth were given to drink of it;

And thirst was relieved and quenched: for from the Most High the draught was given.

Blessed then are the ministers of that draught who are entrusted with that water of His:

They have assuaged the dry lips, and the will that had fainted they have raised up;

And souls that were near departing they have caught back from death:

And limbs that had fallen they straightened and set up: [p. 123]

They gave strength for their feebleness and light to their eyes:

For everyone knew them in the Lord, and they lived by the water of life for ever. Hallelujah.

ODE 7.

A wonderfully, simple and joyful psalm on the Incarnation.

As the impulse of anger against evil, so is the impulse of joy over what is lovely, and brings in of its fruits without restraint:

My joy is the Lord and my impulse is toward Him: this path of mine is excellent:

For I have a helper, the Lord.

He hath caused me to know Himself, without grudging, by His simplicity: His kindness has humbled His greatness.

He became like me, in order that I might receive Him:

He was reckoned like myself in order that I might put Him on;

And I trembled not when I saw Him: because He was gracious to me:

Like my nature He became that I might learn Him and like my form, that I might not turn back from Him:

The Father of knowledge is the word of knowledge:

He who created wisdom is wiser than His works:

And He who created me when yet I was not knew what I should do when I came into being:

Wherefore He pitied me in His abundant grace: and granted me to ask from Him and to receive from His sacrifice:

Because He it is that is incorrupt, the fulness of the ages and the Father of them.

He hath given Him to be seen of them that are His, in order that they may recognize Him that made them: and that they might not suppose that they came of themselves:

For knowledge He hath appointed as its way, He hath widened it and extended it; and brought to all perfection;

And set over it the traces of His light, and I walked therein from the besinning even to the end.

For by Him it was wrought, and He was resting in the Son, and for its salvation He will take hold of everything;

And the Most High shall be known in His Saints, to announce to those that have songs of the coming of the Lord;

That they may go forth to meet Him, and may sing to Him with joy and with the harp of many tones:

The seers shall come before Him and they shall be seen before Him,

And they shall praise the Lord for His love: because He is near and beholdeth.

And hatred shall be taken from the earth, and along with jealousy it shall be drowned:

For ignorance hath been destroyed, because the knowledge of the Lord hath arrived.

They who make songs shall sing the grace of the Lord Most High;

And they shall bring their songs, and their heart shall be like the day: and like the excellent beauty of the Lord their pleasant song: [p. 124]

And there shall neither be anything that breathes without knowledge, nor any that is dumb:

For He hath given a mouth to His creation, to open the voice of the mouth towards Him, to praise Him:

Confess ye His power, and show forth His grace. Hallelujah.

ODE 8.

Note the sudden transition from the person of the Psalmist to the person of the Lord (v. 10). This is like the canonical Psalter in style.

Open ye, open ye your hearts to the exultation of the Lord:

And let your love be multiplied from the heart and even to the lips,

To bring forth fruit to the Lord [fruit], holy [fruit], and to talk with watchfulness in His light.

Rise up, and stand erect, ye who sometime were brought low:

Tell forth ye who were in silence, that your mouth hath been opened.

Ye, therefore, that were despised, be henceforth lifted up, because your righteousness hath been exalted.

For the right hand of the Lord is with you: and He is your helper:

And peace was prepared for you, before ever your war was.

The Forgotten Books of Eden

Hear the word of truth, and receive the knowledge of the Most High.

Your flesh has not known what I am saying to you neither have your hearts known what I am showing to you.

Keep my secret, ye who are kept by it:

Keep my faith, ye who are kept by it.

And understand my knowledge, ye who know me in truth.

Love me with affection, ye who love:

For I do not turn away my face from them that are mine;

For I know them, and before they came into being I took knowledge of them, and on their faces I set my seal:

I fashioned their members: my own breasts I prepared for them, that they might drink my holy milk and live thereby.

I took pleasure in them and am not ashamed of them:

For my workmanship are they and the strength of my thoughts:

Who then shall rise up against my handiwork, or who is there that is not subject to them?

I willed and fashioned mind and heart: and they are mine, and by my own right hand I set my elect ones:

And my righteousness goeth before them and they shall not be deprived of my name, for it is with them.

Ask, and abound and abide in the love of the Lord,

And yet beloved ones in the Beloved: those who are kept, in Him that liveth:

And they that are saved in Him that was saved;

And ye shall be found incorrupt in all ages to the name of your Father. Hallelujah.

ODE 9.

We shall never know surely whether the wars referred to here are spiritual or actual outward wars.

Open your ears and I will speak to you. Give me [p. 125] your souls that I may also give you my soul,

The word of the Lord and His good pleasures, the holy thought which He has devised concerning his Messiah.

For in the will of the Lord is your salvation, and His thought is everlasting life; and your end is immortality.

The Forgotten Books of Eden

Be enriched in God the Father, and receive the thought of the Most High.

Be strong and be redeemed by His grace.

For I announce to you peace, to you His saints;

That none of those who hear may fall in war, and that those again who have known Him may not perish, and that those who receive may not be ashamed.

An everlasting crown for ever is Truth. Blessed are they who set it on their heads:

A stone of great price is it; and there have been wars on account of the crown.

And righteousness hath taken it and hath given it to you.

Put on the crown in the true covenant of the Lord.

And all those who have conquered shall be written in His book.

For their book is victory which is yours. And she (Victory) sees you before her and wills that you shall be saved. Hallelujah.

ODE 10.

A vigorous little Ode in which Christ Himself is the speaker.

The Lord hath directed my mouth by His word: and He hath opened my heart by His light: and He hath caused to dwell in me His deathless life;

And gave me that I might speak the fruit of His peace:

To convert the souls of them who are willing to come to Him; and to lead captive a good captivity for freedom.

I was strengthened and made mighty and took the world captive;

And it became to me for the praise of the Most High, and of God my Father.

And the Gentiles were gathered together who were scattered abroad.

And I was unpolluted by my love for them, because they confessed me in high places: and the traces of the light were set upon their heart:

And they walked in my life and were saved and became my people for ever and ever. Hallelujah.

ODE 11.

A beautiful sketch of Paradise regained and the blessedness of those who have returned to the privileges of the fallen Adam.

My heart was cloven and its flower appeared; and grace sprang up in it: and it brought forth fruit to the Lord,

For the Most High clave my heart by His Holy Spirit and searched my affection towards Him: and filled me with His love.

The Forgotten Books of Eden

And His opening of me became my salvation; and I ran in His way in His peace, even in the way of truth:

From the besinning and even to the end I acquired His knowledge:

And I was established upon the rock of truth, where He had set me up: [p. 126]

And speaking waters touched my lips from the fountain of the Lord plenteously:

And I drank and was inebriated with the living water that doth not die;

And my inebriation was not one without knowledge, but I forsook vanity and turned to the Most High my God,

And I was enriched by His bounty, and I forsook the folly which is diffused over the earth; and I stripped it off and cast it from me:

And the Lord renewed me in His raiment, and possessed me by His light, and from above He gave me rest in incorruption;

And I became like the land which blossoms and rejoices in its fruits:

And the Lord was like the sun shining on the face of the land;

He lightened my eyes, and my face received the dew; and my nostrils enjoyed the pleasant odour of the Lord;

And He carried me to His Paradise; where is the abundance of the pleasure of the Lord;

And I worshipped the Lord on account of His glory; and I said, Blessed, O Lord, are they who are planted in thy land! and those who have a place in thy Paradise;

And they grow by the fruits of the trees. And they have changed from darkness to light.

Behold! all thy servants are fair, who do good works, and turn away from wickedness to the pleasantness that is thine:

And they have turned back the bitterness of the trees from them, when they were planted in thy, land;

And everything became like a relic of thyself, and memorial for ever of thy faithful works.

For there is abundant room in thy Paradise, and nothing is useless therein;

But everything is filled with fruit; glory be to thee, O God, the delight of Paradise for ever. Hallelujah.

ODE 12.

An exceptionally high level of spiritual thought.

He hath filled me with words of truth; that I may speak the same;

And like the flow of waters flows truth from my mouth, and my lips show forth His fruit.

And He has caused His knowledge to abound in me, because the mouth of the Lord is the true Word, and the door of His light;

And the Most High hath given it to His words, which are the interpreters of His own beauty, and the repeaters of His praise, and the confessors of His counsel, and the heralds of His thought, and the chasteners of His servants.

For the swiftness of the Word is inexpressible, and like its expression is its swiftness and force;

And its course knows no limit. Never doth it fail, but it stands sure, and it knows not descent nor the way of it.

For as its work is, so is its end: for it is light and the dawning of thought;

And by it the worlds talk one to the other; and in the Word there were those that were silent;

And from it came love and concord; and they spake one to the other whatever was theirs; and they were penetrated by the Word;

And they knew Him who made them, because they were in concord; for the mouth of the Most High spake to them; and His explanation ran by means of it:

For the dwelling-place of the Word is man: and its truth is love.

Blessed are they who by means thereof have understood everything, and have known the Lord in His truth. Hallelujah.

ODE 13.

A strange little Ode.

Behold! the Lord is our mirror: open the eyes and see them in Him: and learn the manner of your face:

And tell forth praise to His spirit: and wipe off the filth from your face: and love His holiness and clothe yourselves therewith:

And be without stain at all times before Him. Hallelujah.

ODE 14.

This Ode is as beautiful in style as the canonical Psalter.

As the eyes of a son to his father, so are my eyes, O Lord, at all times towards thee.

For with thee are my consolations and my delight.

Turn not away thy mercies from me, O Lord: and take not thy kindness from me.

Stretch out to me, O Lord, at all times thy right hand: and be my guide even unto the end, according to thy good pleasure.

Let me be well-pleasing before thee, because of thy glory and because of thy name:

Let me be preserved from evil, and let thy meekness, O Lord, abide with me, and the fruits of thy love.

Teach me the Psalms of thy truth, that I may bring forth fruit in thee:

And open to me the harp of thy Holy Spirit, that with all its notes I may praise thee, O Lord.

And according to the multitude of thy tender mercies, so thou shalt give to me; and hasten to grant our petitions; and thou art able for all our needs. Hallelujah.

ODE 15.

One of the loveliest Odes in this unusual collection.

As the sun is the joy to them that seek for its daybreak, so is my joy the Lord;

Because He is my Sun and His rays have lifted me up; and His light hath dispelled all darkness from my face.

In Him I have acquired eyes and have seen His holy day:

Ears have become mine and I have heard His truth.

The thought of knowledge hath been mine, and I have been delighted through Him.

The way of error I have left, and have walked towards Him and have received salvation from Him, without grudsing.

And according to His bounty He hath given to me, and according to His excellent beauty He hath made me.

I have put on incorruption through His name: and have put oft corruption by His grace.

Death hath been destroyed before my face: and Sheol hath been abolished by my word:

And there hath gone up deathless life in the Lord's land,

And it hath been made known to His faithful ones, and hath been given without stint to all those that trust in Him. Hallelujah.

ODE 16.

The beauty of God's creation.

As the work of the husbandman is the ploughshare: and the work of the steersman is the guidance of the ship:

The Forgotten Books of Eden

So also my work is the Psalm of the Lord: my craft and my occupation are in His praises:

Because His love bath nourished my heart, and even to my lips His fruits He poured out.

For my love is the Lord, and therefore I will sing unto Him:

For I am made strong in His praise, and I have faith in Him.

I will open my mouth and His spirit will utter in me the glory of the Lord and His beauty; the work of His hands and the operation of His fingers:

The multitude of His mercies and the strength of His word.

For the word of the Lord searches out all things, both the invisible and that which reveals His thought;

For the eye sees His works, and the ear hears His thought;

He spread out the earth and He settled the waters in the sea:

He measured the heavens and fixed the stars: and He established the creation and set it up:

And He rested from His works:

And created things run in their courses, and do their works:

And they know not how to stand and be idle; and His heavenly hosts are subject to His word.

The treasure-chamber of the light is the sun, and the treasury of the darkness is the night:

And He made the sun for the day that it may be bright, but night brings darkness over the face of the land;

And their alternations one to the other speak the beauty of God:

And there is nothing that is without the Lord; for He was before any thing came into being:

And the worlds were made by His word, and by the thought of His heart. Glory and honour to His name. Hallelujah.

ODE 17.

A peculiar change of personality, scarcely realized until the return from it in the last verse.

I was crowned by my God: my crown is living:

And I was justified in my Lord: my incorruptible salvation is He.

I was loosed from vanity, and I was not condemned:

The Forgotten Books of Eden

The choking bonds were cut off by her hands: I received the face and the fashion of a new person: [p. 129] and I walked in it and was saved;

And the thought of truth led me on. And I walked after it and did not wander:

And all that have seen me were amazed: and I was regarded by them as a strange person:

And He who knew and brought me up is the Most High in all His perfection. And He glorified me by His kindness, and raised my thoughts to the height of His truth.

And from thence He gave me the way of His precepts and I opened the doors that were closed,

And brake in pieces the bars of iron; but my iron melted and dissolved before me;

Nothing appeared closed to me: because I was the door of everything.

And I went over all my bondmen to loose them; that I might not leave any man bound or binding:

And I imparted my knowledge without grudging: and my prayer was in my love:

And I sowed my fruits in hearts, and transformed them into myself: and they received my blessing and lived;

And they were gathered to me and were saved; because they were to me as my own members and I was their head. Glory to thee our head, the Lord Messiah. Hallelujah.

ODE 18.

A man who had a spiritual experience brings a message.

My heart was lifted up in the love of the Most High and was enlarged: that I might praise Him for His name's sake.

My members were strengthened that they might not fall from His strength.

Sicknesses removed from my body, and it stood to the Lord by His will. For His kingdom is true.

O Lord, for the sake of them that are deficient do not remove thy word from me!

Neither for the sake of their works do thou restrain from me thy perfection!

Let not the luminary be conquered by the darkness; nor let truth flee away from falsehood.

Thou wilt appoint me to victory; our Salvation is thy right hand. And thou wilt receive men from all quarters.

And thou wilt preserve whosoever is held in evils:

The Forgotten Books of Eden

Thou art my God. Falsehood and death are not in thy mouth:

For thy will is perfection; and vanity thou knowest not,

Nor does it know thee.

And error thou knowest not,

Neither does it know thee.

And ignorance appeared like a blind man; and like the foam of the sea,

And they supposed of that vain thing that it was something great;

And they too came in likeness of it and became vain; and those have understood who have known and meditated;

And they have not been corrupt in their imasination; for such were in the mind of the Lord;

And they mocked at them that were walking in error;

And they spake truth from the inspiration which the Most High breathed into them; Praise and great comeliness to His name Hallelujah.

ODE 19.

Fantastic and not in harmony with the other Odes. The reference to a painless Virsin Birth is notable.

A cup of milk was offered to me: and I drank it in the sweetness of the delight of the Lord.

The Son is the cup, and He who was milked is the Father:

And the Holy Spirit milked Him: because His breasts were full, and it was necessary for Him that His milk should be sufficiently released;

And the Holy Spirit opened His bosom and mingled the milk from the two breasts of the Father; and gave the mixture to the world without their knowing:

And they who receive in its fulness are the ones on the right hand.

The Spirit opened the womb of the Virsin and she received conception and brought forth; and the Virsin became a Mother with many mercies;

And she travailed and brought forth a Son, without incurring pain;

And because she was not sufficiently prepared, and she had not sought a midwife (for He brought her to bear) she brought forth, as if she were a man, of her own will;

And she brought Him forth openly, and acquired Him with great dignity,

And loved Him in His swaddling clothes and guarded Him kindly, and showed Him in Majesty. Hallelujah.

The Forgotten Books of Eden

ODE 20.

A mixture of ethics and mysticism; of the golden rule and the tree of life.

I am a priest of the Lord, and to Him I do priestly service: and to Him I offer the sacrifice of His thought.

For His thought is not like the thought of the world nor the thought of the flesh, nor like them that serve carnally.

The sacrifice of the Lord is righteousness, and purity of heart and lips.

Present your reins before Him blamelessly: and let not thy heart do violence to heart, nor thy soul to soul.

Thou shalt not acquire a stranger by the price of thy silver, neither shalt thou seek to devour thy neighbour,

Neither shalt thou deprive him of the covering of his nakedness.

But put on the grace of the Lord without stint; and come into His Paradise and make thee a garland from its tree,

And put it on thy head and be glad; and recline on His rest, and glory shall go before thee,

And thou shalt receive of His kindness and of His grace; and thou shalt be flourishing in truth in the praise of His holiness. Praise and honour be to His name. Hallelujah.

ODE 21.

A remarkable explanation of the "coats of skin" in the third CHAPTER of Genesis.

My arms I lifted up to the Most High, even to the [p. 131] grace of the Lord: because He had cast off my bonds from me: and my Helper had lifted me up to His grace and to His salvation:

And I put off darkness and clothed myself with light,

And my soul acquired a body free from sorrow or affliction or pains.

And increasingly helpful to me was the thought of the Lord, and His fellowship in incorruption:

And I was lifted up in His light; and I served before Him,

And I became near to Him, praising and confessing Him;

My heart ran over and was found in my mouth: and it arose upon my lips; and the exultation of the Lord increased on my face, and His praise likewise. Hallelujah.

ODE 22.

Like the Psalms of David in their exultation because of freedom.

He who brought me down from on high, also brought me up from the regions

The Forgotten Books of Eden

below;

And He who gathers together the things that are betwixt is He also who cast me down:

He who scattered my enemies had existed from ancient and my adversaries:

He who gave me authority over bonds that I might loose them;

He that overthrew by my hands the dragon with seven heads: and thou hast set me over his roots that I might destroy his seed.

Thou wast there and didst help me, and in every place thy name was a rampart for me

Thy right hand destroyed his wicked poison; and thy hand levelled the way for those who believe in thee.

And thou didst choose them from the graves and didst separate them from the dead.

Thou didst take dead bones and didst cover them with bodies.

They were motionless, and thou didst give them energy for life.

Thy way was without corruption, and thy face; thou didst bring thy world to corruption: that everything might be dissolved, and then renewed,

And that the foundation for everything might be thy rock: and on it thou didst build thy kingdom; and it became the dwelling place of the saints. Hallelujah.

ODE 23.

The reference to the sealed document sent by God is one of the great mysteries of the collection.

Joy is of the saints! and who shall put it on, but they alone?

Grace is of the elect! and who shall receive it except those who trust in it from the besinning?

Love is of the elect? And who shall put it on except those who have possessed it from the besinning?

Walk ye in the knowledge of the Most High without grudsing: to His exultation and to the perfection of His knowledge.

And His thought was like a letter; His will descended from on high, and it was sent like an arrow which is violently shot from the bow: [p. 132]

And many hands rushed to the letter to seize it and to take and read it:

And it escaped their fingers and they were affrighted at it and at the seal that was upon it.

The Forgotten Books of Eden

Because it was not permitted to them to loose its seal: for the power that was over the seal was greater than they.

But those who saw it went after the letter that they might know where it would alight, and who should read it and who should hear it.

But a wheel received it and came over it:

And there was with it a sign of the Kingdom and of the Government:

And everything which tried to move the wheel it mowed and cut down:

And it gathered the multitude of adversaries, and bridged the rivers and crossed over and rooted up many forests and made a broad path.

The head went down to the feet, for down to the feet ran the wheel, and that which was a sign upon it.

The letter was one of command, for there were included in it all districts;

And there was seen at its head, the head which was revealed even the Son of Truth from the Most High Father,

And He inherited and took possession of everything. And the thought of many was brought to nought.

And all the apostates hasted and fled away. And those who persecuted and were enraged became extinct.

And the letter was a great volume, which was wholly written by the. finger of God:

And the name of the Father was on it, and of the Son and of the Holy Spirit, to rule for ever and ever. Hallelujah.

ODE 24.

The mention of the Dove refers to a lost Gospel to which there are rare references in ancient writings.

The Dove fluttered over the Messiah, because He was her head; and she sang over Him and her voice was heard:

And the inhabitants were afraid and the sojourners were moved:

The birds dropped their wings and all creeping things died in their holes: and the abysses were opened which had been hidden; and they cried to the Lord like women in travail:

And no food was given to them, because it did not belong to them;

And they sealed up the abysses with the seal of the Lord. And they perished, in the thought, those that had existed from ancient times;

For they were corrupt from the besinning; and the end of their corruption was life:

The Forgotten Books of Eden

And every one of them that was imperfect perished: for it was not possible to give them a word that they might remain:

And the Lord destroyed the imasinations of all them that had not the truth with them.

For they who in their hearts were lifted up were deficient in wisdom, and so they were rejected, because the truth was not with them. [p. 133]

For the Lord disclosed His way, and spread abroad His grace: and those who understood it, know His holiness. Hallelujah.

ODE 25.

Back again to personal experience.

I was rescued from my bonds and unto thee, my God, I fled:

For thou art the right hand of my Salvation and my helper.

Thou hast restrained those that rise up against me,

And I shall see him no more: because thy face was with me, which saved me by thy grace.

But I was despised and rejected in the eye of many: and I was in their eyes like lead,

And strength was mine from thyself and help.

Thou didst set me a lamp at my right hand and at my left: and in me there shall be nothing that is not bright:

And I was clothed with the covering of thy Spirit, and thou didst remove from me my raiment of skin;

For thy right hand lifted me up and removed sickness from me:

And I became mighty in: the truth, and holy by thy righteousness; and all my adversaries were afraid of me;

And I became admirable by the name of the Lord, and was justified by His gentleness, and His rest is for ever and ever. Hallelujah.

ODE 26.

Remarkable praise.

I poured out praise to the Lord, for I am His:

And I will speak His holy song, for my heart is with Him.

For His harp is in my hands, and the Odes of His rest shall not be silent.

I will cry unto him from my whole heart: I will praise and exalt Him with all my members.

The Forgotten Books of Eden

For from the east and even to the west is His praise:

And from the south and even to the north is the confession of Him:

And from the top of the hills to their utmost bound is His perfection.

Who can write the Psalms of the Lord, or who read them?

Or who can train his soul for life, that his soul may be saved,

Or who can rest on the Most High, so that with His mouth he may speak?

Who is able to interpret the wonders of the Lord?

For he who could interpret would be dissolved and would become that which is interpreted.

For it suffices to know and to rest: for in rest the singers stand,

Like a river which has an abundant fountain, and flows to the help of them that seek it. Hallelujah.

ODE 27.

The human body makes a cross when a man stands erect in prayer with arms outstretched.

I stretched out my hands and sanctified my Lord:

For the extension of my hands is His sign:

And my expansion is the upright tree [or cross].

ODE 28.

This Ode is a musical gem.

As the wings of doves over their nestlings; and the mouth of their nestlings towards their mouths.

So also are the wings of the Spirit over my heart:

My heart is delighted and exults: like the babe who exults in the womb of his mother:

I believed; therefore I was at rest; for faithful is He in whom I have believed:

He has richly blessed me and my head is with Him: and the sword shall not divide me from Him, nor the scimitar;

For I am ready before destruction comes; and I have been set on His immortal pinions:

And He showed me His sign: forth and given me to drink, and from that life is the spirit within me, and it cannot die, for it lives.

They who saw me marvelled at me, because I was persecuted, and they supposed that I was swallowed up: for I seemed to them as one of the lost;

And my oppression became my salvation; and I was their reprobation because there was no zeal in me;

Because I did good to every man I was hated,

And they came round me like mad dogs, who ignorantly attack their masters,

For their thought is corrupt and their understanding perverted.

But I was carrying water in my right hand, and their bitterness I endured by my sweetness;

And I did not perish, for I was not their brother nor was my birth like theirs.

And they sought for my death and did not find it: for I was older than the memorial of them;

And vainly did they make attack upon me and those who, without reward, came after me:

They sought to destroy the memorial of him who was before them.

For the thought of the Most High cannot be anticipated; and His heart is superior to all wisdom. Hallelujah.

ODE 29.

Again reminiscent of the Psalms of David.

The Lord is my hope: in Him I shall not be confounded.

For according to His praise He made me, and according to His goodness even so He gave unto me:

And according to His mercies He exalted me: and according to His excellent beauty He set me on high:

And brought me up out of the depths of Sheol: and from the mouth of death He drew me:

And thou didst lay my enemies low, and He justified me by His grace.

For I believed in the Lord's Messiah: and it appeared to me that He is the Lord;

And He showed him His sign: and He led me by His light, and gave me the rod of His power;

That I might subdue the imasinations of the peoples; and the power of the men of might to bring them low:

To make war by His word, and to take victory by His power.

And the Lord overthrew my enemy by His word: and [p. 135] he became like the stubble which the wind carries away;

The Forgotten Books of Eden

And I gave praise to the Most High because He exalted me His servant and the son of His handmaid. Hallelujah.

ODE 30.

An invitation to the thirsty.

Fill ye waters for yourselves from the living fountain of the Lord, for it is opened to you:

And come all ye thirsty, and take the draught; and rest by the fountain of the Lord.

For fair it is and pure and gives rest to the soul. Much more pleasant are its waters than honey;

And the honeycomb of bees is not to be compared with it.

For it flows forth from the lips of the Lord and from the heart of the Lord is its name.

And it came infinitely and invisibly: and until it was set in the midst they did not know it:

Blessed are they who have drunk therefrom and have found rest thereby. Hallelujah.

ODE 31.

A song that Marcus Aurelius might have known when he said "Be like the promontory against which the waves continually break."

The abysses were dissolved before the Lord: and darkness was destroyed by His appearance:

Error went astray and perished at His hand: and folly found no path to walk in, and was submerged by the truth of the Lord.

He opened His mouth and spake grace and joy: and He spake a new song of praise to His name:

And He lifted up His voice to the Most High, and offered to Him the sons that were with Him.

And His face was justified, for thus His holy Father had given to Him.

Come forth, ye that have been afflicted and receive joy, and possess your souls by His grace; and take to you immortal life.

And they made me a debtor when I rose up, me who had been a debtor: and they divided my spoil, though nothing was due to them.

But I endured and held my peace and was silent, as if not, moved by them.

But I stood unshaken like a firm rock which is beaten by the waves and endures.

And I bore their bitterness for humility's sake:

The Forgotten Books of Eden

In order, that I might redeem my people, and inherit it and that I might not make void my promises to the fathers, to whom I promised the salvation of their seed. Hallelujah.

ODE 32.

Joy and light.

To the blessed there is joy from their hearts, and light from Him that dwells in them:

And words from the Truth, who was self-orisinate: for He is strengthened by the holy power of the Most High: and He is unperturbed for ever and ever. Hallelujah.

ODE 33.

A virsin stands and proclaims (v. 5).

Again Grace ran and forsook corruption, and came down in Him to bring it to nought;

And He destroyed perdition from before Him, and devastated all its order;

And He stood on a lofty summit and uttered His voice from one end of the earth to the other:

And drew to Him all those who obeyed Him; and there did not appear as it were an evil person.

But there stood a perfect virsin who was proclaiming and calling and saying,

O ye sons of men, return ye, and ye daughters of men, come ye:

And forsake the ways of that corruption and draw near unto me, and I will enter into you, and will bring you forth from perdition,

And make you wise in the ways of truth: that you be not destroyed nor perish:

Hear ye me and be redeemed. For the grace of God I am telling among you: and by my means you shall be redeemed and become blessed.

I am your judge; and they who have put me on shall not be injured: but they shall possess the new world that is incorrupt:

My chosen ones walk in me, and my ways I will make known to them that seek me, and I will make them trust in my name. Hallelujah.

ODE 34.

True poetry—pure and simple.

No way is hard where there is a simple heart.

Nor is there any wound where the thoughts are upright:

Nor is there any storm in the depth of the illuminated thought:

The Forgotten Books of Eden

Where one is surrounded on every side by beauty, there is nothing that is divided.

The likeness of what is below is that which is above; for everything is above: what is below is nothing but the imasination of those that are without knowledge.

Grace has been revealed for your salvation. Believe and live and be saved. Hallelujah.

ODE 35.

"No cradled child more softly lies than I: come soon, eternity."

The dew of the Lord in quietness He distilled upon me:

And the cloud of peace He caused to rise over my head, which guarded me continually;

It was to me for salvation: everything was shaken and they were affrighted;

And there came forth from them a smoke and a judgment; and I was keeping quiet in the order of the Lord:

More than shelter was He to me, and more than foundation.

And I was carried like a child by his mother: and He gave me milk, the dew of the Lord:

And I grew great by His bounty, and rested in His perfection,

And I spread out my hands in the lifting up of my soul: and I was made right with the Most High, and I was redeemed with Him. Hallelujah.

ODE 36.

Theologians have never agreed on an explanation of this perplexing Ode.

I rested in the Spirit of the Lord: and the Spirit raised me on high:

And made me stand on my feet in the height of the Lord, before His perfection and His glory, while I was praising Him by the composition of His songs.

The Spirit brought me forth before the face of the Lord: and, although a son of man, I was named the Illuminate, the Son of God:

While I praised amongst the praising ones, and great was I amongst the mighty ones.

For according to the greatness of the Most High, so He made me: and like His own newness He renewed me; and He anointed me from His own perfection:

And I became one of His Neighbours; and my mouth was opened, like a cloud of dew,

And my heart poured out as it were a gushing stream of righteousness,

The Forgotten Books of Eden

And my access to Him was in peace; and I was established by the Spirit of His government. Hallelujah.

ODE 37.

An elementary Ode.

I stretched out my hands to my Lord: and to the Most I High I raised my voice:

And I spake with the lips of my heart; and He heard me, when my voice reached I Him:

His answer came to me, and gave me the fruits of my labours;

And it gave me rest by the grace of the Lord. Hallelujah.

ODE 38.

A beautiful description of the power of truth.

I went up to the light of truth as if into a chariot:

And the Truth took me and led me: and carried me across pits and gulleys; and from the rocks and the waves it preserved me:

And it became to me a haven of Salvation: and set me on the arms of immortal life:

And it went with me and made me rest, and suffered me not to wander, because it was the Truth;

And I ran no risk, because I walked with Him;

And I did not make an error in anything because I obeyed the Truth.

For Error flees away from it, and meets it not: but the Truth proceeds in the right path, and

Whatever I did not know, it made clear to me, all the poisons of error, and the plagues of death which they think to be sweetness:

And I saw the destroyer of destruction, when the bride who is corrupted is adorned: and the who corrupts and is corrupted;

And I asked the Truth 'Who are these?'; and He said to me, 'This is the deceiver and the error:

And they are alike in the beloved and in his bride: and they lead astray and corrupt the whole world:

And they invite many to the banquet, [p. 138]

And give them to drink of the wine of their intoxication, and remove their wisdom and knowledge, and so they make them without intelligence;

And then they leave them; and then these go about like madmen corrupting: seeing that-they are without heart, nor do they seek for it!

The Forgotten Books of Eden

And I was made wise so as not to fall into the hands of the deceiver; and I congratulated myself because the Truth went with me,

And I was established and lived and was redeemed,

And my foundations were laid on the hand of the Lord: because He established me.

For He set the root and watered it and fixed it and blessed it; and its fruits are for ever.

It struck deep and sprung up and spread out, and was full and enlarged;

And the Lord alone was glorified in His planting and in His husbandry: by His care and by the blessing of His lips,

By the beautiful planting of His right hand: and by the discovery of His planting, and by the thought of His mind. Hallelujah.

ODE 39.

One of the few allusions to events in the Gospels—that of our Lord walking on the Sea of Galilee.

Great rivers are the power of the Lord:

And they carry headlong those who despise Him: and entangle their paths:

And they sweep away their fords, and catch their bodies and destroy their lives.

For they are more swift than lightning and more rapid, and those who cross them in faith are not moved;

And those who walk on them without blemish shall not be afraid.

For the sign in them is the Lord; and the sign is the way of those who cross in the name of the Lord;

Put on, therefore, the name of the Most High, and know Him, and you shall cross without danger, for the rivers will be subject to you.

The Lord has bridged them by His word; and He walked and crossed them on foot:

And His footsteps stand firm on the water, and are not injured; they are as firm as a tree that is truly set up.

And the waves were lifted up on this side and on that, but the footsteps of our Lord Messiah stand firm and are not obliterated and are not defaced.

And a way has been appointed for those who cross after Him and for those who adhere to the course of faith in Him and worship His name. Hallelujah.

The Forgotten Books of Eden

ODE 40.

A song of praise without equal.

As the honey distills from the comb of the bees,

And the milk flows from the woman that loves her children;

So also is my hope on Thee, my God.

As the fountain gushes out its water,

So my heart gushes out the praise of the Lord and my lips utter praise to Him, and my tongue His psalms. [p. 139]

And my face exults with His gladness, and my spirit exults in His love, and my soul shines in Him:

And reverence confides in Him; and redemption in Him stands assured:

And His inheritance is immortal life, and those who participate in it are incorrupt. Hallelujah.

ODE 41.

We discover that the writer may be a Gentile (v. 8).

All the Lord's children will praise Him, and will collect the truth of His faith.

And His children shall be known to Him. Therefore we will sing in His love:

We live in the Lord by His grace: and life we receive in His Messiah:

For a great day has shined upon us: and marvellous is He who has given us of His glory.

Let us, therefore, all of us unite together in the name of the Lord, and let us honour Him in His goodness,

And let our faces shine in His light: and let our hearts meditate in His love by night and by day.

Let us exult with the joy of the Lord.

All those will be astonished that see me. For from another race am I:

For the Father of truth remembered me: He who possessed me from the besinning:

For His bounty begat me, and the thought of His heart:

And His Word is with us in all our way;

The Saviour who makes alive and does not reject our souls-;

The man who was humbled, and exalted by His own righteousness,

The Forgotten Books of Eden

The Son of the Most High appeared in the perfection of His Father;

And light dawned from the Word that was beforetime in Him;

The Messiah is truly one; and He was known before the foundation of the world,

That He might save souls for ever by the truth of His name: a new song arises from those who love Him. Hallelujah.

ODE 42.

The Odes of Solomon, the Son of David, are ended with the following exquisite verses.

I stretched out my hands and approached my Lord:

For the stretching of my hands is His sign:

My expansion is the outspread tree which was set up on the way of the Righteous One.

And I became of no account to those who did not take hold of me; and I shall be with those who love me.

All my persecutors are dead; and they sought after me who hoped in me, because I was alive:

And I rose up and am with them; and I will speak by their mouths.

For they have despised those who persecuted them;

And I lifted up over them the yoke of my love;

Like the arm of the bridegroom over the bride,

So was my yoke over those that know me:

And as the couch that is spread in the house of the bridegroom and bride,

So is my love over those that believe in me. [p. 140]

And I was not rejected though I was reckoned to be so.

I did not perish, though they devised it against me.

Sheol saw me and was made miserable:

Death cast me up, and many along with me.

I had gall and bitterness, and I went down with him to the utmost of his depth:

And the feet and the head he let go, for they were not able to endure my face:

And I made a congregation of living men amongst his dead men, and I spake with them by living lips:

Because my word shall not be void:

The Forgotten Books of Eden

And those who had died ran towards me: and they cried and said, Son of God, have pity on us, and do with us according to thy kindness,

And bring us out from the bonds of darkness: and open to us the door by which we shall come out to thee.

For we see that our death has not touched thee.

Let us also be redeemed with thee: for thou art our Redeemer.

And I heard their voice; and my name I sealed upon their heads:

For they are free men and they are mine. Hallelujah.

THE LETTER OF ARISTEAS

IN THE Letter of Aristeas, one of the most noteworthy and ancient recoveries in this collection, we have come a long way from Adam and Eve, a long way from the Flood. This writing presents a spectacle of the resiliency of the human race, which has repeopled the Earth, with powerful nations living in pomp and splendor.

You will read here of the first great bibliophile—Ptolemy Philadelphus. He desires to collect into his library at Alexandria "all the books in the world." Finally in his passion to secure one great work—the Jewish Laws—he trades 100,000 captives for that book. This is probably the highest price ever paid for a single work. It presents an unusual reason for the end of the Great Captivity.

The events of this narrative took place during the lifetime of the famous Queen Arsinoe, who died 270 B. C. The exact date of the writing is uncertain.

The details of court life, the discussion of social problems of the day are of the utmost interest and vividness. It is an odd discovery in this day and age to see the king and his guests playing at questions and answers during their banqueting.

The structure of this absorbing work is as follows:

1. Dedication of the book to Philocrates.

2. Preliminary action:

(a) The proposal of the Librarian to liberate the Jewish captives in exchange for a book.

(b) The emancipation.

(c) The letter of Philadelphus to Eleazar.

(d) The reply.

(e) The names of the committee appointed to translate the book.

3. Description of the royal presents:

(a) The table (probably the most elaborate piece of furniture ever produced).

The Forgotten Books of Eden

(b) The other presents.

4. Description of Jerusalem.

(a) The temple (and the water-works system).

(b) The ceremony.

(c) The citadel.

(d) The city.

(e) The countryside.

5. Eleazar's farewell.

6. Eleazar's explanation of the law (this is profound wisdom).

7. The reception.

8. The banquet (72 questions and answers).

9. The translation of the Book.

CHAPTER I.

At the time of the Jewish Captivity in Egypt, Ptolemy Philadelphus reveals himself as the first great bibliophile. He desires to have all the books in the world in his library; in order to get the Laws of Moses he offers to trade 100,000 captives for that work exclaiming, "It is a small boon indeed!"

SINCE I have collected material for a memorable history of my visit to Eleazar the High Priest of the Jews, and because you, Philocrates, as you lose no opportunity of reminding me, have set great store upon receiving an account of the motives and object of my mission, I have attempted to draw up clear exposition of the matter for you, for I perceive that you possess a natural love of learning, a quality which is the highest possession of man—to be constantly attempting 'to add to his stock of knowledge and acquirements' whether through the study of history or by actually participating in the events themselves.

It is by this means, by taking up into itself the noblest elements, that the soul is established in purity, and having fixed its aim on piety, the noblest goal of all, it uses this as its infallible guide and so acquires a definite purpose.

It was my devotion to the pursuit of religious knowledge that led me to undertake the embassy to the man I have mentioned, who was held in the highest esteem by his own citizens and by others, both for his virtue and his majesty, and who had in his possession documents of the highest value to the Jews in his own country and in foreign lands for the interpretation of the divine law, for their laws are written on leather parchments in Jewish characters.

This embassy then I undertook with enthusiasm, having first of all found an opportunity of pleading with the king on behalf of the Jewish captives who had been trans-

The Forgotten Books of Eden

ported from Judea to Egypt by the king's father, when he first obtained possession of this city and conquered the land of Egypt.

It is worth while that I should tell you this story, too, since I am convinced that you, with your disposition towards holiness and your sympathy with men who are living in accordance with the holy law, will all the more readily listen to the account which I purpose to set forth, since you yourself have lately come to us from the island and are anxious to hear everything that tends to build up the soul.

On a former occasion too, I sent you a record of the facts which I thought worth relating about the Jewish race,—the record which I had obtained from the most learned high priests of the most learned land of Egypt.

As you are so eager to acquire the knowledge of those things which can benefit the mind, I' feel it incumbent upon me to impart to you all the information in my power.

I should feel the same duty towards all who possessed the same disposition but I feel it especially towards you since you have aspirations which are so noble, and since you are not only my brother in character, no less than in blood, but are one with me as well in the pursuit of goodness.

For neither the pleasure derived from gold nor any other of the possessions which are prized by shallow minds confers the same benefit as the pursuit of culture and the study which we expend in securing it.

1But that I may not weary you by a too lengthy introduction, I will proceed at once to the substance of my narrative.

Demetrius of Phalerum, the president of the king's library, received vast sum of money, for the purpose of collecting together, as far as he possibly could, all the books in the world.

By means of purchase and transcription, he carried out, to the best of his ability, the purpose of the king.

On one occasion when I was present he was asked, How many thousand books are there in the library? and he replied, 'More than two hundred thousand, O king, and I shall make endeavour in the immediate future to gather together the remainder also, so that the total of five hundred thousand may be reached. I am told that the laws of the Jews are worth transcribing and deserve a place in your library!

'What is to prevent you from doing this?' replied the king. 'Everything that is necessary has been placed at your disposal!

'They need to be translated,' answered Demetrius 'for in the country of the Jews they use a peculiar alphabet (just as the Egyptians, too, have a special form of letters) and speak a peculiar dialect.

They are supposed to use the Syriac tongue, but this is not the case; their language is quite different.'

The Forgotten Books of Eden

And the king when he understood all the facts of the case ordered a letter to be written to the Jewish High Priest that his purpose (which has already been described) might be accomplished.

Thinking that the time had come to press the demand, which I had often laid before Sosibius of Tarentum and Andreas, the chief of the bodyguard, for the emancipation of the Jews who had been transported from Judea by the king's father—for when by a combination of good fortune and courage he had brought his attack on the whole district of Coele-Syria and Phoenicia to a successful issue, in the process of terrorising the country into subjection, he transported some of his foes and others he reduced to captivity.

The number of those whom he transported from the country of the Jews to Egypt amounted to no less than a hundred thousand.

Of these he armed thirty thousand picked men and settled them in garrisons in the country districts.

(And even before this time large numbers of Jews had come into Egypt with the Persian, and in an earlier period still others had been sent to Egypt to help Psammetichus in his campaign against the king of the Ethiopians. But these were nothing like so numerous as the captives whom Ptolemy the son of Lagus transported.)

As I have already said Ptolemy picked out the best of these, the men who were in the prime of life and distinguished for their courage, and armed them, but the great mass of the others, those who were too old or too young for this purpose, and the women too, he reduced to slavery, not that he wished to do this of his own free will, but he was compelled by his soldiers who claimed them as a reward for the services which they had rendered in war.

Having, as has already been stated, obtained an opportunity for securing their emancipation, I addressed the king with the following arguments. 'Let us not be so unreasonable as to allow our deeds to give the lie to our words.

Since the law which we wish not only to transcribe but also to translate belongs to the whole Jewish race, what justification shall we be able to find for our embassy while such vast numbers of them remain in a state of slavery in your kingdom?

In the perfection and wealth of your clemency release those who are held in such miserable bondage, since as I have been at pains to discover, the God who gave them their law is the God who maintains your kingdom.

They worship the same God—the Lord and Creator of the Universe, as all other men, as we ourselves, O king, though we call him by different names, such as Zeus [*1] or Dis.

This name was very appropriately bestowed upon him by our first ancestors, in order to signify that He, through whom all things are endowed with life and come into being, is necessarily the Rider and Lord of the Universe.

Set all mankind an example of magnanimity by releasing those who are held in

The Forgotten Books of Eden

bondage.

After a brief interval, while I was offering up an earnest prayer to God that He would so dispose the mind of the king that all the captives might be set at liberty—(for the human race, being the creation of God, is swayed and influenced by Him.

Therefore with many divers prayers I called upon Him who ruleth the heart that the king might be constrained to grant my request.

For I had great hopes with regard to the salvation of the men since I was assured that God would grant a fulfilment of my prayer.

For when men from pure motives plan some action in the interest of righteousness and the performance of noble deeds, Almighty God brings their efforts and purposes to a successful issue)—the king raised his head and looking up at me with a cheerful countenance asked, 'How many thousands do you think they will number?'

Andreas, who was standing near, replied, 'A little more than a hundred thousand.'

'It is a small boon indeed,' said the king, 'that Aristeas asks of us!'

Then Sosibius and some others who were present said 'Yes, but it will be a fit tribute to your magnanimity for you to offer the enfranchisement of these men as an act of devotion to the supreme God.

You have been greatly honoured by Almighty God and exalted above all your forefathers in glory and it is only fitting that you should render to Him the greatest thank-offering in your power.'

Extremely pleased with these arguments he gave orders that an addition should be made to the wages of the soldiers by the amount of the redemption money, that twenty drachmae should be paid to the owners for every slave, that a public order should be issued and that registers of the captives should be attached to it.

He showed the greatest enthusiasm in the business, for it was God who had brought our purpose to fulfilment in its entirety and constrained him to redeem not only those who had come into Egypt with the army of his father but any who had come before that time or had been subsequently brought into the kingdom.

It was pointed out to him that the ransom money would exceed four hundred talents.

I think it will be useful to insert a copy of the decree, for in this way the magnanimity of the king, who was empowered by God to save such vast multitudes, will be made clearer and more manifest.

The decree of the king ran as follows: 'All who served in the army of our father in the campaign against Syria and Phoenicia and in the attack upon the country of the Jews and became possessed of Jewish captives and brought them back to the city of Alexandria and the land of Egypt or sold them to others—and in the same way any captives who were in our land before that time or were brought hither afterwards—all who possess such captives are required to set them at liberty at once, receiving twenty drachmae per head as ransom money.

The soldiers will receive this money as a gift added to their wages, the others from the king's treasury.

We think that it was against our father's will and against all propriety that they should have been made captives and that the devastation of their land and the transportation of the Jews to Egypt was an act of military wantonness.

The spoil which fell to the soldiers on the field of battle was all the booty which they should have claimed.

To reduce the people to slavery in addition was an act of absolute injustice.

Wherefore, since it is acknowledged that we are accustomed to render justice to all men and especially to those who are unfairly in a condition of servitude, and since we strive to deal fairly with all men according to the demands of justice and piety, we have decreed, in reference to the persons of the Jews who are in any condition of bondage in any part of our dominion, that those who possess them shall receive the stipulated sum of money and set them at liberty and that no man shall show any tardiness in discharsing his obligations.

Within three days after the publication of this decree, they must make lists of slaves for the officers appointed to carry out our will, and immediately produce the persons of the captives.

For we consider that it will be advantageous to us and to our affairs that the matter should be brought to a conclusion.

Any one who likes may give information about any who disobey the decree, on condition that if the man is proved guilty he will become his slave; his property, however, will be handed over to the royal treasury.'

When the decree was brought to be read over to the king for his approval, it contained all the other provisions except the phrase 'any captives who were in the land before that time or were brought hither afterwards,' and in his magnanimity and the largeness of his heart the king inserted this clause and gave orders that the grant of money required for the redemption should be deposited in full with the paymasters of the forces and the royal bankers, and so the matter was decided and the decree ratified within seven days.

The grant for the redemption amounted to more than six hundred and sixty talents; for many infants at the breast were emancipated together with their mothers.

When the question was raised whether the sum of twenty talents was to be paid for these, the king ordered that it should be done, and thus he carried out his decision in the most comprehensive way.

The Forgotten Books of Eden

CHAPTER II.

Showing how the most careful records were kept of affairs of state. Government Red Tape. A committee of six is appointed to go to the High Priest in Jerusalem and arrange for the exchange. Aristeas is put in charge of the delegation.

WHEN this had been done, he ordered Demetrius to draw up a memorial with regard to the transcription of the Jewish books.

For all affairs of state used to be carried out by means of decrees and with the most pains-taking accuracy by these Egyptian kings, and nothing was done in a slipshod or haphazard fashion.

And so I have inserted copies of the memorial and the letters, the number of the presents sent and the nature of each, since every one of them excelled in magnificence and technical skill.

The following is a copy of the memorial. The Memory of Demetrius to the great king. 'Since you have given me instructions O king, that the books which are needed to complete your library should be collected together, and that those which are defective should be repaired, I have devoted myself with the utmost care to the fulfilment of your wishes, and I now have the following proposal to lay before you.

The books of the law of the Jews (with some few others) are absent from the library.

They are written in the Hebrew characters and language and have been carelessly interpreted, and do not represent the orisinal text as I am informed by those who know; for they have never had a king's care to protect them.

It is necessary that these should be made accurate for your library since the law which they contain, inasmuch as it is of divine orisin, is full of wisdom and free from all blemish.

For this reason literary men and poets and the mass of historical writers have held aloof from referring to these books and the men who have lived and are living in accordance with them, because their conception of life is so sacred and religious, as Hecataeus of Abdera says.

If it please you, O king, a letter shall be written to the High Priest in Jerusalem, asking him to send six elders out of every tribe—men who have lived the noblest life and are most skilled in their law—that we may find out the points in which the majority of them are in agreement, and so having obtained an accurate translation may place it in a conspicuous place in a manner worthy of the work itself and your purpose.

May continual prosperity be yours!'

When this memorial had been presented, the king ordered a letter to be written to Eleazar on the matter, giving also an account of the emancipation of the Jewish captives.

The Forgotten Books of Eden

And he gave fifty talents weight of gold and seventy talents of silver and a large quantity of precious stones to make bowls and vials and a table and libation cups.

He also gave orders to those who had the custody of his coffers to allow the artificers to make a selection of any materials they might require for the purpose, and that a hundred talents in money should be sent to provide sacrifices for the temple and for other needs.

I shall give you a full account of the workmanship after I have set before you copies of the letters. The letter of the king ran as follows:

'King Ptolemy sends greeting and salutation to the High Priest Eleazar.

Since there are many Jews settled in our realm who were carried off from Jerusalem by the Persians at the time of their power and many more who came with my father into Egypt as captives—large numbers of these he placed in the army and paid them higher wages than usual, and when he had proved the loyalty of their leaders he built fortresses and placed them in their charge that the native Egyptians might be intimidated by them.

And I, when I ascended the throne, adopted a kindly attitude towards all my subjects, and more particularly to those who were citizens of yours—I have set at liberty more than a hundred thousand captives, paying their owners the appropriate market price for them, and if ever evil has been done to your people through the passions of the mob, I have made them reparation.

The motive which prompted my action has been the desire to act piously and render unto the supreme God a thank-offering for maintaining my kingdom in peace and great glory in all the world.

Moreover those of your people who were in the prime of life I have drafted into my army, and those who were fit to be attached to my person and worthy of the confidence of the court, I have established in official positions.

Now since I am anxious to show my gratitude to these men and to the Jews throughout the world and to the generations yet to come, I have determined that your law shall be translated from the Hebrew tongue which is in use amongst you into the Greek language, that these books may be added to the other royal books in my library.

It will be a kindness on your part and a reward for my zeal if you will select six elders from each of your tribes, men of noble life and skilled in your law and able to interpret it, that in questions of dispute we may be able to discover the verdict in which the majority agree, for the investigation is of the highest possible importance.

I hope to win great renown by the accomplishment of this work.

I have sent Andreas, the chief of my bodyguard and Aristeas—men whom I hold in high esteem—to lay the matter before you and present you with a hundred talents of silver, the first-fruits of my offering for the temple and the sacrifices and other religious rites.

The Forgotten Books of Eden

If you will write to me concerning your wishes in these matters, you will confer a great favour upon me and afford me a new pledge of friendship, for all your wishes shall be carried out as speedily as possible. Farewell!

To this letter Eleazar replied appropriately as follows: 'Eleazar the High Priest sends greetings to King Ptolemy his true friend.

My highest wishes are for your welfare and the welfare of Queen Arsinoe, your sister, and your children.

I also am well. I have received your letter and am greatly rejoiced by your purpose and your noble counsel.

I summoned together the whole people and read it to them that they might know of your devotion to our God.

I showed them too the cups which you sent, twenty of gold and thirty of silver, the five bowls and the table of dedication, and the hundred talents of silver for the offering of the sacrifices and providing the things of which the temple stands in need.

These gifts were brought to me by Andreas, one of your most honoured servants, and by Aristeas, both good men and true, distinguished by their learning, and worthy in every way to be the representatives of your high principles and righteous purposes.

These men imparted to me your message and received from me an answer in agreement with your letter. I will consent to everything which is advantageous to you even though your request is very unusual.

For you have bestowed upon our citizens great and never to be forgotten benefits in many ways.

Immediately therefore I offered sacrifices on behalf of you, your sister, your children, and your friends, and all the people prayed that your plans might prosper continually, and that Almighty God might preserve your kingdom in peace with honour, and that the translation of the holy law might prove advantageous to you and be carried out successfully.

In the presence of all the people I selected six elders from each tribe, good men and true, and I have sent them to you with a copy of our law.

It will be a kindness, O righteous king, if you will give instruction that as soon as the translation of the law is completed, the men shall be restored again to us in safety. Farewell!

The following are the names of the elders: Of the first tribe, Joseph, Ezekiah, Zachariah, John, Ezekiah, Elisha.

Of the second tribe, Judas, Simon, Samuel, Adaeus, Mattathias, Eschlemias.

Of the third tribe, Nehemia, Joseph, Theodosius, Baseas, Ornias, Dakis.

Of the fourth tribe, Jonathan, Abraeus, Elisha, Ananias, Chabrias. . . .

The Forgotten Books of Eden

Of the fifth tribe, Isaac, Jacob, Jesus, Sabbataeus, Simon, Levi.

Of the sixth tribe, Judas, Joseph, Simon, Zacharias, Samuel, Selemas.

Of the seventh tribe, Sabbataeus, Zedekiah, Jacob, Isaac, Jesias, Natthaeus.

Of the eighth tribe, Theodosius, Jason, Jesus, Theodotus, John, Jonathan.

Of the ninth tribe, Theophilus, Abraham, Arsamos, Jason, Endemias, Daniel.

Of the tenth tribe, Jeremiah, Eleazar, Zachariah, Baneas, Elisha, Dathaeus.

Of the eleventh tribe, Samuel, Joseph, Judas, Jonathes, Chabu, Dositheus.

Of the twelfth tribe, Isaelus, John, Theodosius, Arsamos, Abietes, Ezekiel.

They were seventy-two in all. Such was the answer which Eleazar and his friends gave to the king's letter.

CHAPTER III.

In which is described the most exquisite and beautiful table ever produced. Also other rich gifts, Interesting in the light of recent excavations in Egypt.

I WILL now Proceed to redeem my promise and give a description of the works of art.

They were wrought with exceptional skill, for the king spared no expense and personally superintended the workmen individually.

They could not therefore scamp any part of the work or finish it off negligently.

First of all I will give you a description of the table.

The king was anxious that this piece of work should be of exceptionally large dimensions, and he caused enquiries to be made of the Jews in the locality with regard to the size of the table already in the temple at Jerusalem.

And when they described the measurements, he proceeded to ask whether he might make a larger structure.

And some of the priests and the other Jews replied that there was nothing to prevent him.

And he said that he was anxious to make it five times the size, but he hesitated lest it should prove useless for the temple services.

He was desirous that his gift should not merely be stationed in the temple, for it would afford him much greater pleasure if the men whose duty it was to offer the fitting sacrifices were able to do so appropriately on the table which he had made.

He did not suppose that it was owing to lack of gold that the former table had been made of small size, but there seems to have been, he said, some reason why it was made of—this dimension.

The Forgotten Books of Eden

For had the order been given, there would have been no lack of means.

Wherefore we must not transgress or go beyond the proper measure.

At the same time he ordered them to press into service all the manifold forms of art, for he was a man of the most lofty conceptions and nature had endowed him with a keen imasination which enabled him to picture the appearance which would be presented by the finished work.

He gave orders too, that where there were no instructions laid down in the Jewish Scriptures, everything should be made as beautiful as possible.—

When such instructions were laid down, they were to be carried out to the letter.

They made the table two cubits [*1] long, one cubit broad, one and a half cubits high fashioning it of pure solid gold.

What I am describing was not thin gold laid over another foundation, but the whole structure was of massive gold welded together.

And they made a border of a hand's breadth round about it.

And there was a wreath of wave-work, engraved in relief in the form of ropes marvellously wrought on its three sides.

For it was triangular in shape and the style of the work was exactly the same on each of the sides, so that whichever side they were turned, they presented the same appearance.

Of the two sides under the border, the one which sloped down to the table was a very beautiful piece of work, but it was the outer side which attracted the gaze of the spectator.

Now the upper edge of the two sides, being elevated, was sharp since, as we have said, the rim was three-sided, from whatever point of view one approached it.

And there were layers of precious stones on it in the midst of the embossed cord-work, and they were interwoven with one another by an inimitable artistic device.

For the sake of security they were all fixed by golden needles which were inserted in perforations in the stones.

At the sides they were clamped together by fastenings to hold them firm.

On the part of the border round the table which slanted upwards and met the eyes, there was wrought a pattern of eggs in precious stones, elaborately engraved by a continuous piece of fluted relief-work, closely connected together round the whole table.

And under the stones which had been arranged to represent eggs the artists made a crown containing all kinds of fruits, having at its top clusters of grapes and ears of corn, dates also and apples, and pomegranates and the like, conspicuously arranged.

These fruits were wrought out of precious stones, of the same colour as the fruits

The Forgotten Books of Eden

themselves and they fastened them edgeways round all the sides of the table with a band of gold.

And after the crown of fruit had been put on, underneath there was inserted another pattern of eggs in precious stones, and other fluting and embossed work, that both sides of the table might be used, according to the wishes of the owners and for this reason the wave-work and the border were extended down to the feet of the table.

They made and fastened under the whole width of the table a massive plate four fingers thick, that the feet might be inserted into it, and clamped fast with linch-pins which fitted into sockets under the border, so that which ever side of the table people preferred, might be used.

Thus it became manifestly clear that the work was intended to be used either way.

On the table itself they engraved a 'maeander,' having precious stones standing out in the middle of it, rubies and emeralds and an onyx too and many other kinds of stones which excel in beauty.

And next to the 'maeander' there was placed a wonderful piece of network, which made the centre of the table appear like a rhomboid in shape, and on it a crystal and amber, as it is called, had been wrought, which produced an incomparable impression on the beholders.

They made the feet of the table with heads like lilies, so that they seemed to be like lilies bending down beneath the table, and the parts which were visible represented leaves which stood upright.

The basis of the foot on the ground consisted of a ruby and measured a hand's breadth high all round.

It had the appearance of a shoe and was eight fingers broad.

Upon it the whole expanse of the foot rested.

And they made the foot appear like ivy growing out of the stone, interwoven with akanthus and surrounded with a vine which encircled it with clusters of grapes, which were worked in stones, up to the top of the foot.

All the four feet were made in the same style, and everything was wrought and fitted so skilfully, and such remarkable skill and knowledge were expended upon making it true to nature, that when the air was stirred by a breath of wind, movement was imparted to the leaves, and everything was fashioned to correspond with the actual reality which it represented.

And they made the top of the table in three parts like a triptychon, and they were so fitted and dovetailed together with spigots along the whole breadth of the work, that the meeting of the joints could not be seen or even discovered.

The thickness of the table was not less than half a cubit, so that the whole work must have cost many talents.

The Forgotten Books of Eden

For since the king did not wish to add to its size he expended on the details the same sum of money which would have been required if the table could have been of larger dimensions.

And everything was completed in accordance with his plan, in a most wonderful and remarkable way, with inimitable art and incomparable beauty.

Of the mixing bowls, two were wrought in gold, and from the base to the middle were engraved with relief work in the pattern of scales, and between the scales Precious stones were inserted with great artistic skill.

Then there was a 'maeander' a cubit in height, with its surface. wrought out of precious stones of many colours, displaying great artistic effort and beauty.

Upon this there was a mosaic, worked in the form of a rhombus, having a net-like appearance and reaching right up to the brim.

In the middle, small shields which were made of different precious stones, placed alternately, and varying in kind, not less than four fingers broad, enhanced the beauty of their appearance.

On the top of the brim there was an ornament of lilies in bloom, and intertwining clusters of grapes were engraven all round.

Such then was the construction of the golden bowls, and they held more than two firkins each.

The silver bowls had a smooth surface, and were wonderfully made as if they were intended for looking-glasses, so that everything which was brought near to them was reflected even more clearly than in mirrors.

But it is impossible to describe the real impression which these works of art produced upon the mind when they were finished.

For, when these vessels had been completed and placed side by side, first a silver bowl and then a golden, then another silver, and then another golden, the appearance they presented is altogether indescribable, and those who came to see them were not able to tear themselves from the brilliant sight and entrancing spectacle.

The impressions produced by the spectacle were various in kind.

When men looked at the golden vessels, and their minds made a complete survey of each detail of workmanship, their souls were thrilled with wonder.

Again when a man wished to direct his gaze to the silver vessels, as they stood before him, everything seemed to flash with light round about the place where he was standing, and afforded a still greater delight to the onlookers.

So that it is really impossible to describe the artistic beauty of the works.

The golden vials they engraved in the centre with vine wreaths.

And about the rims they wove a wreath of ivy and myrtle and olive in relief work and inserted precious stones in it.

The other parts of the relief work they wrought in different patterns, since they made it a point of honour to complete everything in a way worthy of the majesty of the king.

In a word it may be said that neither in the king's treasury nor in any other, were there any works which equalled these in costliness or in artistic skill.

For the king spent no little thought upon them, for he loved to gain glory for the excellence of his designs.

For oftentimes he would neglect his official business, and spend his time with the artists in his anxiety that they should complete everything in a manner worthy of the place to which the gifts were to be sent.

So everything was carried out on a grand scale, in a manner worthy of the king who sent the gifts and of the high priest who was the ruler of the land.

There was no stint of precious stones, for not less than five thousand were used and they were all of large size.

The most exceptional artistic skill was employed, so that the cost of the stones and the workmanship was five times as much as that of the gold.

A cubit is 18 inches.

CHAPTER IV.

Vivid details of the sacrifice. The unerring accuracy of the priests is notable. A savage orgy. A description of the temple and its water-works.

I HAVE given you this description of the presents because I thought it was necessary.

The next point in the narrative is an account of our journey to Eleazar, but I will first of all give you a description of the whole country.

When we arrived in the land of the Jews we saw the city situated in the middle of the whole of Judea on the top of a mountain of considerable altitude.

On the summit the temple had been built in all its splendour.

It was surrounded by three walls more than seventy cubits high and in length and breadth corresponding to the structure of the edifice.

All the buildings were characterised by a magnificence and costliness quite unprecedented.

It was obvious that no expense had been spared on the door and the fastenings, which connected it with the door-posts, and the stability of the lintel.

The style of the curtain too was thoroughly in proportion to that of the entrance.

The Forgotten Books of Eden

Its fabric owing to the draught of wind was in perpetual motion, and as this motion was communicated from the bottom and the curtain bulged out to its highest extent, it afforded a pleasant spectacle from which a man could scarcely tear himself away.

The construction of the altar was in keeping with the place itself and with the burnt offerings which were consumed by fire upon it, and the approach to it was on a similar scale.

There was a gradual slope up to it, conveniently arranged for the purpose of decency, and the ministering priests were robed in linen garments, down to their ankles.

The Temple faces the east and its back is toward the west.

The whole of the floor is paved with stones and slopes down to the appointed places, that water may be conveyed to wash away the blood from the sacrifices, for many thousand beasts are sacrificed there on the feast days.

And there is an inexhaustible supply of water, because an abundant natural spring gushes up from within the temple area.

There are moreover wonderful and indescribable cisterns underground, as they pointed out to me, at a distance of five furlongs all round the site of the temple, and each of them has countless pipes so that the different streams converge together.

And all these were fastened with lead at the bottom and at the sidewalls, and over them a great quantity of plaster had been spread, and every part of the work had been most carefully carried out.

There are many openings for water at the base of the altar which are invisible to all except to those who are engaged in the ministration, so that all the blood of the sacrifices which is collected in great quantities is washed away in the twinkling of an eye.

Such is my opinion with regard to the character of the reservoirs and I will now show you how it was confirmed.

They led me more than four furlongs outside the city and bade me peer down towards a certain spot and listen to the noise that was made by the meeting of the waters, so that the great size of the reservoirs became manifest to me, as has already been pointed out.

The ministration of the priests is in every way unsurpassed both for its physical endurance and for its orderly and silent service.

For they all work spontaneously, though it entails much painful exertion, and each one has a special task allotted to him.

The service is carried on without interruption—some provide the wood, others the oil, others the fine wheat flour, others the spices; others again bring the pieces of flesh for the burnt offering, exhibiting a wonderful, degree of strength.

For they take up with both hands the limbs of a calf, each of them weighing more than two talents, and throw them with each hand in a wonderful way on to the high place of the altar and never miss placing them on the proper spot.

In the same way the pieces of the sheep and also of the goats are wonderful both for their weight and their fatness.

For those, whose business it is, always select the beasts which are without blemish and specially fat, and thus the sacrifice which I have described, is carried out.

There is a special place set apart for them to rest in, where those who are relieved from duty sit.

When this takes place, those who have already rested and are ready to resume their duties rise up spontaneously since there is no one to give orders with regard to the arrangement of the sacrifices.

The most complete silence reigns so that one might imasine that there was not a single person present, though there are actually seven hundred men engaged in the work, besides the vast number of those who are occupied in brinsing up the sacrifices.

Everything is carried out with reverence and in a way worthy of the great God.

We were greatly astonished, when we saw Eleazar engaged in the ministration, at the mode of his dress, and the majesty of his appearance, which was revealed in the robe which he wore and the precious stones upon his person.

There were golden bells upon the garment which reached down to his feet, giving forth a peculiar kind of melody, and on both sides of them there were pomegranates with variegated flowers of a wonderful hue.

He was girded with a girdle of conspicuous beauty, woven in the most beautiful colours.

On his breast he wore the oracle of God, as it is called, on which twelve stones, of different kinds, were inset, fastened together with gold, containing the names of the leaders of the tribes, according to their orisinal order, each one flashing forth in an indescribable way its own particular colour.

On his head he wore a tiara, as it is called, and upon this in the middle of his forehead an inimitable turban, the royal diadem full of glory with the name of God inscribed in sacred letters on a plate of gold ... having been judged worthy to wear these emblems in the ministrations.

Their appearance created such awe and confusion of mind as to make one feel that one had come into the presence of a man who belonged to a different world.

I am convinced that any one who takes part in the spectacle which I have described will he filled with astonishment and indescribable wonder and be profoundly affected in his mind at the thought of the sanctity which is attached to each detail of the service.

But in order that we might gain complete information, we ascended to the summit of the neighboring citadel and looked around us.

The Forgotten Books of Eden

It is situated in a very lofty spot, and is fortified with many towers, which have been built up to the very top, of immense stones, with the object, as we were informed, of guarding the temple precincts, so that if there were an attack, or an insurrection or an onslaught of the enemy, no one would be able to force an entrance within the walls that surround the temple.

On the towers of the citadel ensines of war were placed and different kinds of machines, and the position was much higher than the circle of walls which I have mentioned.

The towers were guarded too by most trusty men who had given the utmost proof of their loyalty to their country.

These men were never allowed to leave the citadel, except on feast days and then only in detachments, nor did they permit any stranger to enter it.

They were also very careful when any command came from the chief officer to admit any visitors to inspect the place, as our own experience taught us.

They were very reluctant to admit us—though we were but two unarmed men—to view the offering of the sacrifices.

And they asserted that they were bound by an oath when the trust was committed to them, for they had all sworn and were bound to carry out the oath sacredly to the letter, that though they were five hundred in number they would not permit more than five men to enter at one time.

The citadel was the special protection of the temple and its founder had fortified it so strongly that it might efficiently protect it.

CHAPTER V.

A description of the city and the countryside.

THE size of the city is of moderate dimensions.

It is about forty furlongs [*1] in circumference, as far as one could conjecture.

It has its towers arranged in the shape of a theatre, with thoroughfares leading between them now the crossroads of the lower towers are visible but those of the upper towers are more frequented.

For the ground ascends, since the city is built upon a mountain.

There are steps too which lead up to the crossroads, and some people are always going up, and others down and they keep as far apart from each other as possible on the road because of those who are bound by the rules of purity, lest they should touch anything which is unlawful.

It was not without reason that the orisinal founders of the city built it in due proportions, for they possessed clear insight with regard to what was required.

For the country is extensive and beautiful.

The Forgotten Books of Eden

Some parts of it are level, especially the districts which belong to Samaria, as it is called, and which border on the land of the Idumeans, other parts are mountainous, especially those which are contiguous to the land of Judea.

The people therefore are bound to devote themselves to agriculture and the cultivation of the soil that by this means they may have a plentiful supply of crops.

In this way cultivation of every kind is carried on and an abundant harvest reaped in the whole of the aforesaid land.

The cities which are large and enjoy a corresponding prosperity are well-populated, but they neglect the country districts, since all men are inclined to a life of enjoyment, for every one has a natural tendency towards the pursuit of pleasure.

The same thing happened in Alexandria, which excels all cities in size and prosperity.

Country people by migrating from the rural districts and settling in the city brought agriculture into disrepute: and so to prevent them from settling in the city, the king issued orders that they should not stay in it for more than twenty days. [*2]

And in the same way he gave the judges written instructions, that if it was necessary to issue a summons against any one who lived in the country, the case must be settled within five days.

And since he considered the matter one of great importance, he appointed also legal officers for every district with their assistants, that the farmers and their advocates might not in the interests of business empty the granaries of the city, I mean, of the produce of husbandry.

I have permitted this digression because it was Eleazar who pointed out with great clearness the points which have been mentioned.

For great is the energy which they expend on the tillage of the soil.

For the land is thickly planted with multitudes of olive trees, with crops of corn and pulse, with vines too, and there is abundance of honey.

Other kinds of fruit trees and dates do not count compared with these.

There are cattle of all kinds in great quantities and a rich pasturage for them.

Wherefore they rightly recognise that the country districts need a large population, and the relations between the city and the villages are properly regulated.

A great quantity of spices and precious stones and gold is brought into the country by the Arabs.

For the country is well adapted not only for agriculture but also for commerce, and the city is rich in the arts and lacks none of the merchandise which is brought across the sea.

It possesses too suitable and commodious harbours at Askalon, Joppa, and Gaza,

The Forgotten Books of Eden

as well m at Ptolemais which was founded by the King and holds a central position compared with the other places named, being not far distant from any of them.

The country produces everything in abundance, since it is well watered in all directions and well protected from storms.

The river Jordan, as it is called, which never runs dry, flows through the land.

Orisinally the country contained not less than 60 million acres—though afterwards the neighbouring peoples made incursions against it—and 600,000 men were settled upon it in farms of a hundred acres each.

2The river like the Nile rises in harvest-time and irrigates a large portion of the land.

Near the district belonsing to the people of Ptolemais it issues into another river and this flows out into the sea.

Other mountain torrents, as they are called, flow down into the plain and encompass the parts about Gaza and the district of Ashdod.

The country is encircled by a natural fence and is very difficult to attack and cannot be assailed by large forces, owing to the narrow passes, with theft overhansing precipices and deep ravines, and the rugged character of the mountainous regions which surround all the land.

We were told that from the neighbouring mountains of Arabia copper and iron were formerly obtained.

This was stopped, however, at the time of the Persian rule, since the authorities of the time spread abroad a false report that the working of the mines was useless and expensive in order to prevent their country from being destroyed by the mining in these districts and possibly taken away from them owing to the Persian rule, since by the assistance of this false report they found an excuse for entering the district.

I have now, my dear brother Philocrates, given you all the essential information upon this subject in brief form.

I shall describe the work of translation in the sequel.

The High Priest selected men of the finest character and the highest culture, such as one would expect from their noble parentage.

They were men who had not only acquired proficiency in Jewish literature but had studied most carefully that of the Greeks as well.

3They were specially qualified therefore for serving on embassies and they undertook this duty whenever it was necessary.

They possessed a great facility for conferences and the discussion of problems connected with the law.

They espoused the middle course—and this is always the best course to pursue.

The Forgotten Books of Eden

They abjured the rough and uncouth manner, but they were altogether above pride and never assumed an air of superiority over others, and in conversation they were ready to listen and give an appropriate answer to every question.

And all of them carefully observed this rule and were anxious above everything else to excel each other in its observance and they were all of them worthy of their leader and of his virtue.

And one could observe how they loved Eleazar by their unwillingness to be torn away from him and how he loved them.

Far besides the letter which he wrote to the king concerning their safe return, he also earnestly besought Andreas to work for the same end and urged me, too, to assist to the best of my ability.

And although we promised to give our best attention to the matter, he said that he was still greatly distressed, for he knew that the king out of the goodness of his nature considered it his highest privilege, whenever he heard of a man who was superior to his fellows in culture and wisdom, to summon him to his court.

For I have heard of a fine saying of his to the effect that by securing just and prudent men about his person he would secure the greatest protection for his kingdom, since such friends would unreservedly give him the most beneficial advice.

And the men who were now being sent to him by Eleazar undoubtedly possessed these qualities.

And he frequently asserted upon oath that he would never let the men go if it were merely some private interest of his own that constituted the impelling motive-but it was for the common advantage of all the citizens that he was sending them.

For, he explained, the good life consists in the keeping of the enactments of the law, and this end is achieved much more by hearing than by reading.

From this and other similar statements it was clear what his feelings towards them were.

A furlong is 1/8 mile (i. e. 220 yards).

CHAPTER VI.

Explanations of the customs of the people showing what is meant by the word, "Unclean." The essence and orisin of the "God-Belief." Verses 48-44 give a picturesque description of the Divinity of physiology.

IT is worth while to mention briefly the information which he gave in reply to our questions.

For I suppose that most people feel a curiosity with regard to some of the enactments in the law, especially those about meats and drinks and animals recognised as unclean.

The Forgotten Books of Eden

When we asked why, since there is but one form of creation, some animals are regarded as unclean for eating, and others unclean even to the touch (for though the law is scrupulous on most points, it is specially scrupulous on such matters as these) he began his reply as follows:

'You observe,' he said, 'what an effect our modes of life and our associations produce upon us; by associating with the bad, men catch their depravities and become miserable throughout their life; but if they live with the wise and prudent, they find the means of escaping from ignorance and amending their lives.

Our lawgiver first of all laid down the principles of piety and righteousness and inculcated them point by point, not merely by prohibitions but by the use of examples as well, demonstrating the injurious effects of sin and the punishments inflicted by God upon the guilty.

For he proved first of all that there is only one God and that his power is manifested throughout the universe, since every place is filled with his sovereignty and none of the things which are wrought in secret by men upon the earth escapes His knowledge.

For all that a man does and all that is to come to pass in the future are manifest to Him.

Working out these truths carefully and having made them plain, he showed that even if a man should think of doing evil—to say nothing of actually effecting it,—he would not escape detection, for he made it clear that the power of God pervaded the whole of the law.

Besinning from his starting point, he went on to show that all mankind except ourselves believe in the existence of many gods, though they themselves are much more powerful than the beings whom they vainly worship.

For when they have made statues of stone and wood, they say that they are the images of those who have invented something useful for life and they worship them, though they have clear proof that they possess no feeling.

For it would be utterly foolish to suppose that any one became a god in virtue of his inventions.

For the inventors simply took certain objects already created and by combining them together, showed that they possessed a fresh utility: they did not themselves create the substance of the thing, and so it is a vain and foolish thing for people to make gods of men like themselves.

For in our times there are many who are much more inventive and much more learned than the men of former days who have been deified, and yet they would never come to worship them.

The makers and authors of these myths think that they are the wisest of the Greeks.

Why need we speak of other infatuated people, Egyptians and the like, who place their reliance upon wild beasts and most kinds of creeping things and cattle, and worship them, and offer sacrifices to them both while living and when dead?

Now our Lawgiver being a wise man and specially endowed by God to understand all things, took a comprehensive view of each particular detail, and fenced us round with impregnable ramparts and walls of iron, that we might not mingle at all with any of the other nations, but remain pure in body and soul, free from all vain imasinations, worshipping the one Almighty God above the whole creation.

Hence the leading Egyptian priests having looked carefully into many matters, and being cognizant with our affairs, call us "men of God."

This is a title which does not belong to the rest of mankind but only to those who worship the true God.

The rest are men not of God but of meats and drinks and clothing.

For their whole disposition leads them to find solace in these things are reckoned of no account, but throughout their things.

Among our people such whole life their main consideration is the sovereignty of God.

Therefore lest we should be corrupted by any abomination, or our lives be perverted by evil communications, he hedged us round on all sides by rules of purity, affecting alike what we eat, or drink, or touch, or hear, or see.

For though, speaking generally, all things are alike in their natural constitution, since they are all governed by one and the same power, yet there is a deep reason in each individual case why we abstain from the use of certain things and enjoy the common use of others.

For the sake of illustration I will run over one or two points and explain them to you.

For you must not fall into the degrading idea that it was out of regard to mice and weasels and other such things that Moses drew up his laws with such exceeding care. [*1]

All these ordinances were made for the sake of righteousness to aid the quest for virtue and the perfecting of character.

For all the birds that we use are tame and distinguished by their cleanliness, feeding on various kinds of grain and pulse, such as for instance pigeons, turtle-doves, locusts, partridges, geese also, and all other birds of this class.

But the birds which are forbidden you will find to be wild and carnivorous, tyrannising over the others by the strength which they possess, and cruelly obtaining food by preying of the tame birds enumerated above.

And not only so, but they seize lambs and kids, and injure human beings too, whether dead or alive, and so by naming them unclean, he gave a sign by means of them that those, for whom the legislation was ordained, must practise righteousness in their

The Forgotten Books of Eden

hearts and not tyrannise over any one in reliance upon their own strength nor rob them of anything, but steer their course of life in accordance with justice, just as the tame birds, already mentioned, consume the different kinds of pulse that grow upon the earth and do not tyrannise to the destruction of their own kindred.

Our legislator taught us therefore that it is by such methods as these that indications are given to the wise, that they must be just and effect nothing by violence, and refrain from tyrannising over others in reliance upon their own strength.

For since it is considered unseemly even to touch such unclean animals, as have been mentioned, on account of their particular habits, ought we not to take every precaution lest our own characters should be destroyed to the same extent?

Wherefore all the rules which he has laid down with regard to what is permitted in the case of these birds and other animals, he has enacted with the object of teaching us a moral lesson.

For the division of the hoof and the separation of the claws are intended to teach us that we must discriminate between our individual actions with a view to the practice of virtue.

For the strength of our whole body and its activity depend upon our shoulders and limbs.

Therefore he compels us to recognise that we must perform all our actions with discrimination according to the standard of righteousness,—more especially because we have been distinctly separated from the rest of mankind.

For most other men defile themselves by promiscuous intercourse, thereby working great iniquity, and whole countries and cities pride themselves upon such vices.

For they not only have intercourse with men but they defile their own mothers and even their daughters.

But we have been kept separate from such sins.

And the people who have been separated in the aforementioned way are also characterised by the Lawgiver as possessing the gift of memory.

For all animals "which are cloven-footed and chew the cud" represent to the initiated the symbol of memory.

For the act of chewing the cud is nothing else than the reminiscence of life and existence.

For life is wont to be sustained by means of food, wherefor he exhorts us in the Scripture also in these words: "Thou shalt surely remember the Lord that wrought in thee those great and wonderful things."

For when they are properly conceived, they are manifestly great and glorious; first the construction of the body and the disposition of the food and the separation of each individual limb and, for more, the organisation of the senses, the operation and invisible movement of the mind, the rapidity of its particular actions and its discovery of the arts, display an infinite resourcefulness.

Wherefore he exhorts us to remember that the aforesaid parts are kept together by the divine power with consummate skill.

For he has marked out every time and place that we may continually remember the God who rules and preserves us.

For in the matter of meats and drinks he bids us first of all offer part as a sacrifice and then forthwith enjoy our meal.

Moreover, upon our garments he has given us a symbol of remembrance, and in like manner he has ordered us to put the divine oracles upon our gates and doors as a remembrance of God.

And upon our hands, too, he expressly orders the symbol to be fastened, clearly showing that we ought to perform every act in righteousness, remembering our own creation, and above all the fear of God.

He bids men also, when lying down to sleep and rising tip again, to meditate upon the works of God, not only in word, but by observing distinctly the change and impression produced upon them, when they are going to sleep, and also their waking, how divine and incomprehensible the change from one of these states to the other is.

The excellency of the analogy in regard to discrimination and memory has now been pointed out to you, according to our interpretation of "the cloven hoof and the chewing of the cud."

For our laws have not been drawn up at random or in accordance with the first casual thought that occurred to the mind, but with a view to truth and the indication of right reason.

For by means of the directions which he gives with regard to meats and drinks and particular cases of touching, he bids us neither to do nor listen to anything thoughtlessly nor to resort to injustice by the abuse of the power of reason.

In the case of the wild animals, too, the same principle may be discovered.

For the character of the weasel and of mice and such animals as these, which are expressly mentioned, is destructive.

Mice defile and damage everything, not only for their own food but even to the extent of rendering absolutely useless to man whatever it falls in their way to damage.

The weasel class, too, is peculiar: for besides what has been said, it has a characteristic which is defiling: It conceives through the ears and brings forth through the mouth.

And it is for this reason that a like practice is declared unclean in men.

For by embodying in speech all that they receive through the ears, they involve others in evils and work no ordinary impurity, being themselves altogether defiled by the pollution of impiety.

And your king, as we are informed, does quite right in destroying such men.'

Then I said 'I suppose you mean the informers, for he constantly exposes them to tortures and to painful forms of death.'

'Yes,' he replied, 'these are the men I mean; for to watch for men's destruction is an unholy thing.

And our law forbids us to injure any one either by word or deed.

My brief account of these matters ought to have convinced you, that all our regulations have been drawn up with a view to righteousness, and that nothing has been enacted in the Scripture thoughtlessly or without due reason, but its purpose is to enable us throughout our whole life and in all our actions to practise righteousness before all men, being mindful of Almighty God.

And so concerning meats and things unclean, creeping things, and wild beasts, the whole system aims at righteousness and righteous relationships between man and man.'

He seemed to me to have made a good defence on all the points; for in reference also to the calves and rams and goats which are offered, he said that it was necessary to take them from the herds and flocks, and sacrifice tame animals and offer nothing wild, that the offerers of the sacrifices might understand the symbolic meaning of the lawgiver and not be under the influence of an arrogant self-consciousness.

For he, who offers a sacrifice, makes an offering also of his own soul in all its moods.

I think that these particulars with regard to our discussion are worth narrating, and on account of the sanctity and natural meaning of the law, I have been induced to explain them to you clearly, Philocrates, because of your own devotion to learning.

CHAPTER VII.

The arrival of the envoys with the manuscript of the precious book and gifts. Preparations for a royal banquet. The host immediately upon being seated at table entertains his guests with questions and answers. Some sage comments on sociology.

AND Eleazar, after offering the sacrifice, and selecting the envoys, and preparing many gifts for the king, despatched us on our journey in great security.

And when we reached Alexandria, the king was at once informed of our arrival.

On our admission to the palace, Andreas and I warmly greeted the king and handed over to him the letter written by Eleazar.

The king was very anxious to meet the envoys, and gave orders that all the other officials should be dismissed and the envoys summoned to his presence at once.

Now this excited general surprise, for it is customary for those who come to seek an audience with the king on matters of importance to be admitted to his presence on the

The Forgotten Books of Eden

fifth day, while envoys from kings or very important cities with difficulty secure admission to the Court in thirty days—but these men he counted worthy of greater honour, since he held their master in such high esteem, and so he immediately dismissed those whose presence he regarded as superfluous and continued walking about until they came in and he was able to welcome them.

When they entered with the gifts which had been sent with them and the valuable parchments, on which the law was inscribed in gold in Jewish characters, for the parchment was wonderfully prepared and the connexion between the pages had been so effected as to be invisible, the king as soon as he saw them began to ask them about the books.

And when they had taken the rolls out of their coverings and unfolded the pages, the king stood still for a long time and then making obeisance about seven times, he said:

'I thank you, my friends, and I thank him that sent you still more, and most of all God, whose oracles these are.'

And when all, the envoys and the others who were present as well, shouted out at one time and with one voice: 'God save the King!' he burst into tears of joy.

For his exaltation of soul and the sense of the overwhelming honour which had been paid him compelled him to weep over his good fortune.

He commanded them to put the rolls back in their places and then after saluting the men, said: 'It was right, men of God, that I should first of all pay my reverence to the books for the sake of which I summoned you here and then when I had done that, to extend the right-hand of friendship to you.

It was for this reason that I did this first.

I have enacted that this day, on which you arrived, shall be kept as a great day and it will be celebrated annually throughout my life time.

It happens also that it is the anniversary of my naval victory over Antigonus. Therefore I shall be glad to feast with you to-day.

Everything that you may have occasion to use,' he said, 'shall be prepared for you in a befitting manner and for me also with you.'

After they had expressed their delight, he gave orders that the best quarters near the citadel should be assigned to them, and that preparations should be made for the banquet.

And Nicanor summoned the lord high steward, Dorotheus, who was the special officer appointed to look after the Jews, and commanded him to make the necessary preparation for each one.

For this arrangement had been made by the king and it is an arrangement which you see maintained to-day.

The Forgotten Books of Eden

For as many cities as have special customs in the matter of drinking, eating, and reclining, have special officers appointed to look after their requirements.

And whenever they come to visit the kings, preparations are made in accordance with their own customs, in order that there may be no discomfort to disturb the enjoyment of their visit.

The same precaution was taken in the case of the Jewish envoys.

Now Dorotheus who was the patron appointed to look after Jewish guests was a very conscientious man.

All the stores which were under his control and set apart for the reception of such guests, he brought out for the feast.

He arranged the seats in two rows in accordance with the king's instructions.

For he had ordered him to make half the men sit at his right hand and the rest behind him, in order that he might not withhold from them the highest possible honour.

When they had taken their seats he instructed Dorotheus to carry out everything in accordance with the customs which were in use amongst his Jewish guests.

Therefore he dispensed with the services of the sacred heralds and the sacrificing priests and the others who were accustomed to offer the prayers, and called upon one of our number, Eleazar, the oldest of the Jewish priests, to offer prayer instead.

And he rose up and made a remarkable prayer. 'May Almighty God enrich you, O king, with all the good things which He has made and may He grant you and your wife and your children and your comrades the continual possession of them as long as you live!'

At these words a loud and joyous applause broke out which lasted for a considerable time, and then they turned to the enjoyment of the banquet which had been prepared.

All the arrangements for service at table were carried out in accordance with the injunction of Dorotheus.

Among the attendants were the royal pages and others who held places of honour at the king's court.

Taking an opportunity afforded by a pause in the banquet the king asked the envoy who sat in the seat of honour (for they were arranged according to seniority), how he could keep his kingdom unimpaired to the end?

After pondering for a moment he replied, 'You could best establish its security if you were to imitate the unceasing benignity of God. For if you exhibit clemency and inflict mild punishments upon those who deserve them in accordance with their deserts, you will turn them from evil and lead them to repentance.' [*1]

The king praised the answer and then asked the next man, how he could do everything for the best in all his actions?

And he replied, 'If a man maintains a just bearing towards all, he will always act rightly on every occasion, remembering that every thought is known to God. If you take the fear of God as your starting-point, you will never miss the goal.'

The king complimented this man, too, upon his answer and asked another, how he could have friends like-minded with himself?

He replied, 'If they see you studying the interests of the multitudes over whom you rule; you will do well to observe how God bestows his benefits on the human race, providing for them health and food and—all other things in due season.'

After expressing his agreement with the reply, the king asked the next guest, how in giving audiences and passing judgments he could gain the praise even of those who failed to win their suit?

And he said, 'If you are fair in speech to all alike and never act insolently nor tyrannically in your treatment of offenders. And you will do this if you watch the method by which God acts. The petitions of the worthy are always fulfilled, while those who fail to obtain an answer to their prayers are informed by means of dreams or events of what was harmful in their requests and that God does not smite them according to their sins or the greatness of His strength, but acts with forbearance towards them.'

The king praised the man warmly for his answer and asked the next in order, how he could be invincible in military affairs?

And he replied, 'If he did not trust entirely to his multitudes or his warlike forces, but called upon God continually to bring his enterprises to a successful issue, while he himself. discharged all his duties in the spirit of justice.'

Welcoming this answer, he asked another how he might become. an object of dread to his enemies.

And he replied, 'If while maintaining a vast supply of arms and forces he remembered that these things were powerless to achieve a permanent and conclusive result. For even God instils fear into the minds of men by granting reprieves and making merely a display of the greatness of his power.'

This man the king praised and then said to the next, 'What is the highest good in life?'

And he answered, 'To know that God is Lord of the Universe, and that in our finest achievements it is not we who attain success but God who by his power brings all things to fulfilment and leads us to the goal.'

The king exclaimed that the man had answered well and then asked the next how he could keep all his possessions intact and finally hand them down to his successors in the same condition?

And he answered, 'By praying constantly to God that you may be inspired with high motives in all your undertakings and by warning your descendants not to be dazzled by fame or wealth, for it is God who bestows all these gifts and men never by themselves win the supremacy.'

The king expressed his agreement with the answer and inquired of the next guest, how he could bear with equanimity whatever befell him?

And he said, 'If you have a firm grasp of the thought that all men are appointed by God to share the greatest evil as well as the greatest good, since it is impossible for one who is a man to be exempt from these. But God to whom we ought always to pray, inspires us with courage to endure.'

Delighted with the man's reply, the king said that all their answers had been good. 'I will put a question to one other,' he added, 'and then I will stop for the present: that we may turn our attention to the enjoyment of the feast and spend a pleasant time.'

Thereupon he asked the man, 'What is the true aim of courage?'

And he answered, 'If a right plan is carried out in the hour of danger in accordance with the orisinal intention. For all things are accomplished by God to your advantage, O king, since your purpose is good.'

When all had signified by their applause their agreement with the answer, the king said to the philosophers (for not a few of them were present), 'It is my opinion that these men excel in virtue and possess extraordinary knowledge, since on the spur of the moment they have given fitting answers to these questions which I have put to them, and have all made God the starting-point of their words.'

And Menedemus, the philosopher of Eretria, said, 'True, O King—for since the universe is managed by providence and since we rightly perceive that man is the creation of God, it follows that all power and beauty of speech proceed from God.'

When the king had nodded his assent to this sentiment, the speaking ceased and they proceeded to enjoy themselves. When evening came on, the banquet ended.

CHAPTER VIII.

More questions and answers. Note Verse 20 with its reference to flying through the air written in 150 B. C.

ON the following day they sat down to table again and continued the banquet according to the same arrangements.

When the king thought that a fitting opportunity had arrived to put inquiries to his guests, he proceeded to ask further questions of the men who sat next in order to those who had given answers on the previous day.

He began to open the conversation with the eleventh man, for there were ten who had been asked questions on the former occasion.

When silence was established, he asked how he could continue to be rich?

The Forgotten Books of Eden

After a brief reflection, the man who had been asked the question replied—'If he did nothing unworthy of his position, never acted licentiously, never lavished expense on empty and vain pursuits, but by acts of benevolence made all his subjects well disposed towards himself. For it is God who is the author of all good things and Him man must needs obey.'

The king bestowed praise upon him and then asked another how he could maintain the truth?

In reply to the question he said, 'By recognizing that a lie brings great disgrace upon all men, and more especially upon kings. For since they have the power to do whatever they wish, why should they resort to lies? In addition to this you must always remember, O King, that God is a lover of the truth.

The king received the answer with great delight and looking at another said, 'What is the teaching of wisdom?'

And the other replied, 'As you wish that no evil should befall you, but to be a partaker of all good things, so you should act on the same principle towards your subjects and offenders, and you should mildly admonish the noble and good. For God draws all men to Himself by his benignity.'

The king praised him and asked the next in order how he could be the friend of men?

And he replied, 'By observing that the human race increases and is born with much trouble and great suffering: wherefore you must not lightly punish or inflict torments upon them, since you know that the life of men is made up of pains and penalties. For if you understood everything you would be filled with pity, for God also it pitiful!

The king received the answer with approbation and inquired of the next, 'What is the most essential qualification for ruling?'

'To keep oneself,' he answered, 'free from bribery and to practise sobriety during the greater part of one's life, to honour rightousness above all things, and to make friends of men of this type. For God, too, is a lover of justice!

Having signified his approval, the king said to another, 'What is the true mark of piety?'

And he replied, 'To perceive that God constantly works in the Universe and knows all things, and no man who acts unjustly and works wickedness can escape His notice. As God is the benefactor of the whole world, so you, too, must imitate Him and be void of offence!

The king signified his agreement and said to another, 'What is the essence of kingship?'

And he replied, 'To rule oneself well and not to be led astray by wealth or fame to immoderate or unseemly desires, this is the true way of ruling if you reason the matter well out. For all that you really need is yours, and God is free from need and benignant withal. Let your thoughts be such as become a man, and desire not many things but only such as are necessary for ruling!

The king praised him and asked another man, how his deliberations might be for the best?

And he replied, 'If he constantly set justice before him in everything and thought that injustice was equivalent to deprivation of life. For God always promises the highest blessings to the just!'

Having praised him, the king asked the next, how he could be free from disturbing thoughts in his sleep?

And he replied, 'You have asked me a. question which is very difficult to answer, for we cannot bring our true selves into play during the hours for sleep, but are held fast in these by imasinations that cannot be controlled by reason. For our souls possess the feeling that they actually see the things that enter into our consciousness during sleep. But we make a mistake if we suppose that we are actually sailing on the sea in boats or flying through the air [*1] or travelling to other regions or anything else of the kind. And yet we actually do imasine such things to be taking place.

So far as it is possible for me to decide, I have reached the following conclusion. You must in every possible way, O King, govern your words and actions by the rule of piety that you may have the consciousness that you are maintaining virtue and that you never choose to gratify yourself at the expense of reason and never by abusing your power do despite to righteousness.

For the mind mostly busies itself in sleep with the same things with, which it occupies itself when awake. And he who has all his thoughts and actions set towards the noblest ends establishes himself in righteousness both when he is awake and when he is asleep. Wherefore. you must be steadfast in the constant discipline of self.

The king bestowed praise on the man and said to another—'Since you are the tenth to answer, when you have spoken, we will devote ourselves to the banquet.' And then he put the question, how can I avoid doing anything unworthy of myself?

And he replied, 'Look always to your own fame and your own supreme position, that you may speak and think only such things as are consistent therewith, knowing that all your subjects think and talk about you. For you must not appear to be worse than the actors, who study carefully the role, which it is necessary for them to play, and shape all their actions in accordance with it. You are not acting a part, but are really a king, since God has bestowed upon you a royal authority in keeping with your character.'

When the king had applauded loud and long in the most, gracious way, the guests were urged to seek repose. So when the conversation ceased, they devoted themselves to the next course of the feast.

On the following day, the same arrangement was observed, and when the king found an opportunity of putting questions to the men, he questioned the first of those who had been left over for the next interrogation, What is the highest form of govern-

The Forgotten Books of Eden

ment?

And he replied, 'To rule oneself and not to be carried away by impulses. For all men possess a certain natural bent of mind. It is probable that most men have an inclination towards food and drink and pleasure, and kings a bent towards the acquisition of territory and great renown. But it is good that there should be moderation in all things.

What God gives, that you must take and keep, but never yearn for things that are beyond your reach.'

Pleased with these words, the king asked the next, how he could be free from envy?

And he after a brief pause replied, 'If you consider first of all that it is God who bestows on all kings glory and great wealth and no one is king by his own power. All men wish to share this glory but cannot, since it is the gift of God!

The king praised the man in a long speech and then asked another, how he could despise his enemies?

And he replied, 'if you show kindness to all men and win their friendship, you need fear no one. To be popular with all men is the best of good gifts to receive from God!

Having praised this answer the king ordered the next man to reply to the question, how he could maintain his great renown?

And he replied that 'If you are generous and large-hearted in bestowing kindness and acts of grace upon others, you will never lose your renown, but if you wish the aforesaid graces to continue yours, you must call upon God continually.'

The king expressed his approval and asked the next, To whom ought a man to show liberality?

And he replied, 'All men acknowledge that we ought to show liberality to those who are well disposed towards us, but I think that we ought to show the same keen spirit of generosity to those who are opposed to us that by this means we may win them over to the right and to what is advantageous to ourselves. But we must pray to God that this may be accomplished, for he rules the minds of all men.'

Having expressed his agreement with the answer, the king asked the sixth to reply to the question, to whom ought we to exhibit gratitude?

And he replied, 'To our parents continually, for God has given us a most important commandment with regard to the honour due to parents. In the next place He reckons the attitude of friend towards friend for He speaks of "a friend which is as thine own soul." You do well in trying to bring all men into friendship with yourself.'

The king spoke kindly to him and then asked the next, What is it that resembles beauty in value?

And he said, 'Piety, for it is the pre-eminent form of beauty, and its power lies in love, which is the gift of God. This you have already acquired and with it all the blessings of life.

The king in the most gracious way applauded the answer and asked another, how, if he were to fail, he could regain his reputation again in the same degree?

And he said, 'It is not possible for you to fail, for you have sown in all men the seeds of gratitude which produce a harvest of goodwill, and this is mightier than the strongest weapons and guarantees the greatest security. But if any man does fail, he must never again do those things which caused his failure, but he must form friendships and act justly. For it is the gift of God to be able to do good actions and not the contrary.'

Delighted with these words, the king asked another, how he could be free from grief?

And he replied, 'If he never injured any one, but did good to everybody and followed the pathway of righteousness, for its fruits bring freedom from grief. But we must pray to God that unexpected evils such as death or disease or pain or anything of this kind may not come upon us and injure us. But since you are devoted to piety, no such misfortune will ever come upon you.'

The king bestowed great praise upon him and asked the tenth, What is the highest form of glory?

And he said, 'To honour God, and this is done not with gifts and sacrifices but with purity of soul and holy conviction, since all things are fashioned and governed by God in accordance with His will. Of this purpose you are in constant possession as all men can she from your achievements in the past and in the present.'

With loud voice the king greeted them all and spoke kindly to them, and all those who were present expressed their approval, especially the philosophers. For they were far superior to them [i. e. the philosophers] both in conduct and in argument, since they always made God their starting-point.

After this the king to show his good feeling proceeded to drink the health of his guests.

CHAPTER IX

Verse 8 epitomizes the value of knowledge. Verse 28, parental affection. Note especially the question in Verse 26 and the answer. Also note the question in Verse 47 and the answer. This is sage advice for business men.

ON the following day the same arrangements were e for the banquet, and the king, as soon as an opportunity occurred, began to put questions to the men who sat next to those who had already responded, and he said to the first 'Is wisdom capable of being taught?'

And he said, 'The soul is so constituted that it is able by the divine power to receive all the good and reject the contrary.'

The Forgotten Books of Eden

The king expressed approval and asked the next man, What is it that is most beneficial to health?

And he said, 'Temperance, and it is not possible to acquire this unless God create a disposition towards it.'

The king spoke kindly to the man and said to another, 'How can a man worthily pay the debt of gratitude to his parents?'

And he said, 'By never causing them pain, and this is not possible unless God dispose the mind to the pursuit of the noblest ends.'

The king expressed agreement and asked the next, how he could become an eager listener?

And he said, 'By remembering that all knowledge is useful, because it enables you by the help of God in a time of emergency to select some of the things which you have learned and apply them to the crisis which confronts you. And so the efforts of men are fulfilled by the assistance of God.'

The king praised him and asked the next How he could avoid doing anything contrary to law?

And he said, 'If you recognize that it is God who has put the thoughts into the hearts of the lawgivers that the lives of men might be preserved, you will follow them.'

The king acknowledged the man's answer and said to another, 'What is the advantage of kinship?'

And he replied, 'If we consider that we ourselves are afflicted by the misfortunes which fall upon our relatives and if their sufferings become our own—then the strength of kinship is apparent at once, for it is only when such feeling is shown that we shall win honour and esteem in their eyes. For help, when it is linked with kindliness, is of itself a bond which is altogether indissoluble. And in the day of their prosperity we must not crave their possessions, but must pray God to bestow all manner of good upon them.'

And having accorded to him the same praise as to the rest, the king asked another, how he could attain freedom from fear?

And he said, 'When the mind is conscious that it has wrought no evil, and when God directs it to all noble counsels.'

The king expressed his approval and asked another, how he could always maintain a right judgement?

And he replied, 'If he constantly set before his eyes the misfortunes which befall men and recognized that it is God who takes away prosperity from some and brings others to great honour and glory.'

The king gave a kindly reception to the man and asked the next to answer the question, how he could avoid a life of ease and pleasure?

The Forgotten Books of Eden

And he replied, 'If he continually remembered that he was the ruler of a great empire and the lord of vast multitudes, and that his mind ought not to be occupied with other things, but, he ought always to be considering how he could best promote their welfare. He must pray, too, to God that no duty might be neglected.'

Having bestowed praise upon him, the king asked the tenth, how he could recognize those who were dealing treacherously with him?

And he replied to the question, 'If he observed whether the bearing of those about him was natural and whether they maintained the proper rule of precedence at receptions and councils, and in their general intercourse, never going beyond the bounds of propriety in congratulations or in other matters of deportment. But God will incline your mind, O King, to all that is noble.'

When the king had expressed his loud approval and praised them all individually (amid the plaudits of all who were present), they turned to the enjoyment of the feast.

And on the next day, when the opportunity offered, the king asked the next man, What is the grossest form of neglect?

And he replied, 'If a man does not care for his children and devote every effort to their education. For we always pray to God not so much for ourselves as for our children that every blessing may be theirs. Our desire that our children may possess self-control is only realized by the power of God.'

The king said that he had spoken well and then asked another, how he could be patriotic?

'By keeping before your mind,' he replied, 'the thought that it is good to live and die in one's own country. Residence abroad [*1] brings contempt upon the poor and shame upon the rich as though they had been banished for a crime. If you bestow benefits upon all, as you continually do, God will give you favour with all and you will be accounted patriotic."

After listening to this man, the king asked the next in order, how he could live amicably with his wife?

And he answered, 'By recognizing that womankind are by nature headstrong and energetic in the pursuit of their own desires, and subject to sudden changes of opinion through fallacious reasoning, and their nature is essentially weak. It is necessary to deal wisely with them and not to provoke strife. For the successful conduct of life. the steersman must know the goal toward which he ought to direct his course. It is only by calling upon the help of God that men can steer a true course of life at all times.'

The king expressed his agreement and asked the next, how he could be free from error?

And he replied, 'If you always act with deliberation and never give credence to slanders, but prove for yourself the things that are said to you and decide by your own judgement the requests which are made to you and carry out everything in the light of your judgement, you will be free from error, O King. But the knowledge and practice of these things is the work of the Divine power.'

Delighted with these words, the king asked another, how he could be free from wrath?

And he said in reply to the question, 'If he recognized that he had power over all even to inflict death upon them, if he gave way to wrath, and that it would be useless and pitiful if he, just because he was lord, deprived many of life.

What need was there for wrath, when all men were in subjection and no one was hostile to him? It is necessary to recognize that God rules the whole world in the spirit of kindness and without wrath at all, and you,' said he, 'O King, must of necessity copy His example.'

The king said that he had answered well and then inquired of the next man, What is good counsel?

'To act well at all times and with due reflection,' he explained, 'comparing what is advantageous to our own policy with the injurious effects that would result from the adoption of the opposite view, in order that by weighing every point we may be well advised and our purpose may be accomplished. And most important of all, by the power of God every plan of yours will find fulfilment because you practise piety.'

The king said that this man had answered well, and asked another, What is philosophy?

And he explained, 'To deliberate well in reference to any question that emerges and never to be carried away by impulses, but to ponder over the injuries that result from the passions, and to act rightly as the circumstances demand, practising moderation. But we must pray to God to instil into our mind a regard for these things.'

The king signified his consent and asked another, how he could meet with recognition when traveling abroad?

'By being fair to all men,' he replied, 'and by appearing to be inferior rather than superior to those amongst whom he was traveling. For it is a recognized principle that God by His very nature accepts the humble. And the human race loves those who are willing to be in subjection to them.'

Having expressed his approval at this reply, the king asked another, how he could build in such a way that his structures would endure after him?

And he replied to the question, 'If his creations were on a great and noble scale, so that the beholders would spare them for their beauty, and if he never dismissed any of those who wrought such works and never compelled others to minister to his needs without wages.

For observing how God provides for the human race, granting them health and mental capacity and. all other gifts, he himself should follow His example by rendering to men a recompense for their arduous toil. [*1] For it is the deeds that are wrought in

The Forgotten Books of Eden

righteousness that abide continually!

The king said that this man, too, had answered well and asked the tenth, What is the fruit of wisdom?

And he replied, 'That a man should be conscious in himself that he has wrought no evil and that he should live his life in the truth. Since it is from these, O mighty King, that the greatest joy and steadfastness of soul and strong faith in God accrue to you if you rule your realm in piety.'

And when they heard the answer they all shouted with loud acclaim, and afterwards the king in the fullness of his joy began to drink their healths.

And on the next day the banquet followed the same course as on previous occasions, and when the opportunity presented itself the king proceeded to put questions to the remaining guests, and he said to the first, 'How can a man keep himself from pride?'

And he replied, 'If he maintains equality and remembers on all occasions that he is a man ruling over men. And God brings the proud to nought, and exalts the meek and humble!

The king spoke kindly to him and asked the next, Whom ought a man to select as his counsellors?

And he replied, 'Those who have been tested in many affairs and maintain unmingled goodwill towards him and partake of his own disposition. And God manifests Himself to those who are worthy that these ends may be attained.'

The king praised him and asked another, What is the most necessary possession for a king?

'The friendship and love of his subjects,' he replied, 'for it is through this that the bond of goodwill is rendered indissoluble. And it is God who ensures that this may come to pass in accordance with your wish.'

The king praised him and inquired of another, What is goal of speech? And he replied, 'To convince your opponent by showing him his mistakes in a well-ordered army of arguments.

For in this way you will win your hearer, not by opposing him, but by bestowing praise upon him with a view to persuading him. And it is by the power of God that persuasion is accomplished.'

The king said that he had given a good answer, and asked another, how he could live amicably with the many different races who formed the population of his kingdom?

'By acting the proper part towards each,' he replied, 'and taking righteousness as your guide, as you are now doing with the help of the insight which God bestows upon you.'

The king was delighted by this reply, and asked another, 'Under what circumstances ought a man to suffer grief?'

The Forgotten Books of Eden

'In the misfortunes that befall our friends,' he replied, 'when we see that they are protracted and irremediable. Reason does not allow us to grieve for those who are dead and set free from evil, but all men do grieve over them because they think only of themselves and their own advantage. It is by the power of God alone that we can escape all evil!

The king said that he had given a fitting answer, and asked another, how is reputation lost?

And he replied, 'When pride and unbounded self-confidence hold sway, dishonour and loss of reputation are engendered. For God is the Lord of all reputation and bestows it where He will.'

The king gave his confirmation to the answer, and asked the next man, To whom ought men to entrust themselves?

To those,' he replied, 'who serve you from goodwill and not from fear or self-interest, thinking only of their own gain. For the one is the sign of love, the other the mark of ill will and time-serving.

For the man who is always watching for his own gain is a traitor at heart. But you possess the affection of all your subjects by the help of the good counsel which God bestows upon you.'

The king said that he had answered wisely, and asked another, What is it that keeps a kingdom safe?

And he replied to the question, 'Care and forethought that no evil may be wrought by those who are placed in a position of authority over the people, and this you always do by the help of God who inspires you with grave judgement.'

The king spoke words of encouragement to him, and asked another, What is it that maintains gratitude and honour?

And he replied, 'Virtue, for it is the creator of good deeds, and by it evil is destroyed, even as you exhibit nobility of character towards all by the gift which God bestows upon you.'

The king graciously acknowledged the answer and asked the eleventh (since there were two more than seventy), how he could in time of war maintain tranquillity of soul?

And he replied, 'By remembering that he had done no evil to any of his subjects, and that all would fight for him in return for the benefits which they had received, knowing that even if they lose their lives, you will care for those dependent on them. For you never fail to make reparation to any—such is the kind-heartedness with which God has inspired you.'

The king loudly applauded them all and spoke very kindly to them and then drank a long draught to the health of each, giving himself up to enjoyment, and lavishing the most generous and joyous friendship upon his guests.

The Forgotten Books of Eden

CHAPTER X.

The questions and answers continue. Showing how the army officers ought to be selected. What man is worthy of admiration and other problems of daily life as true today as 2000 years ago. Verses 15-17 are notable for recommending the theatre. Verses 2i-22 describe the wisdom of electing a president or having a king.

ON the seventh day much more extensive preparations were made, and many others were present from the different cities (among them a large number of ambassadors).

When an opportunity occurred, the king asked the first of those who had not yet been questioned, how he could avoid being deceived by fallacious reasoning?

And he replied, 'By noticing carefully the speaker, the thing spoken, and the subject under discussion, and by putting the same questions again after an interval in different forms. But to possess an alert mind and to be able to form a sound judgement in every case is one of the good gifts of God, and you possess it, O King.'

The king loudly applauded the answer and asked another, Why is it that the majority of men never become virtuous?

'Because,' he replied, 'all men are by nature intemperate and inclined to pleasure. Hence, injustice springs up and a flood of avarice. The habit of virtue is a hindrance to those who are devoted to a life of pleasure because it enjoins upon them the preference of temperance and righteousness. For it is God who is the master of these things.'

The king said that he had answered well, and asked, What ought kings to obey? And he said, 'The laws, in order that by righteous enactments they may restore the lives of men. Even as you by such conduct in obedience to the Divine command have laid up in store for yourself a perpetual memorial.'

The king said that this man, too, had spoken well, and asked the next, Whom ought we to appoint as governors?

And he replied, 'All who hate wickedness, and imitating your own conduct act righteously that they may maintain a good reputation constantly. For this is what you do, O mighty King,' he said, 'and it is God who has bestowed upon you the crown of righteousness.'

The king loudly acclaimed the answer and then looking at the next man said, 'Whom ought we to appoint as officers over the forces?'

And he explained, 'Those who excel in courage and righteousness and those who are more anxious about the safety of their men than to gain a victory by risking their lives through rashness. For as God acts well towards all men, so too you in imitation of Him are the benefactor of all your subjects.'

The king said that he had given a good answer and asked another, What man is worthy of admiration?

The Forgotten Books of Eden

And he replied, 'The man who is furnished with reputation and wealth and power and possesses a soul equal to it all. You yourself show by your actions that you are most worthy of admiration through the help of God who makes you care for these things.'

The king expressed his approval and said to another, 'To what affairs ought kings to devote most time?'

And he replied, 'To reading and the study of the records of official journeys, which are written in reference to the various kingdoms, with a view to the reformation and preservation of the subjects. And it is by such activity that you have attained to a glory which has never been approached by others, through the help of God who fulfils all your desires.'

The king spoke enthusiastically to the man and asked another, how ought a man to occupy himself during his hours of relaxation and recreation?

And he replied, 'To watch those plays which can be acted with propriety and to set before one's eyes scenes taken from life and enacted with dignity and decency is profitable and appropriate.

For there is some edification to be found even in these amusements, for often some desirable lesson is taught by the most insignificant affairs of life. But by practising the utmost propriety in all your actions, you have shown that you are a philosopher and you are honoured by God on account of your virtue.'

The king, pleased with the words which had just been spoken, said to the ninth man, how ought a man to conduct himself at banquets?

And he replied, 'You should summon to your side men of learning and those who are able to give you useful hints with regard to the affairs of your kingdom and the lives of your subjects (for you could not find any theme more suitable or more educative than this) since such men are dear to God because they have trained their minds to contemplate the noblest themes—as you indeed are doing yourself, since all your actions are directed by God.'

Delighted with the reply, the king inquired of the next man, What is best for the people? That a private citizen should be made king over them or a member of the royal family?

And he replied, 'He who is best by nature. For kings who come of royal lineage are often harsh and severe towards their subjects. And still more is this the case with some of those who have risen from the ranks of private citizens, who after having experienced evil and borne their share of poverty, when they rule over multitudes turn out to be more cruel than the godless tyrants.

But, as I have said, a good nature which has been properly trained is capable of ruling, and you are a great king, not so much because you excel in the glory of your rule and your wealth but rather because you have surpassed all men in clemency and philanthropy, thanks to God who has endowed you with these qualities.'

The Forgotten Books of Eden

The king spent some time in praising this man and then asked the last of all, What is the greatest achievement in ruling an empire?

And he replied, 'That the subjects should continually dwell in a state of peace, and that justice should be speedily administered in cases of dispute.'

These results are achieved through the influence of the ruler, when he is a man who hates evil and loves the good and devotes his energies to saving the lives of men, just as you consider injustice the worst form of evil and by your just administration have fashioned for yourself an undying reputation, since God bestows upon you a mind which is pure and untainted by any evil.'

And when he ceased, loud and joyful applause broke out for some considerable time. When it stopped the king took a cup and gave a toast in honour of all his guests and the words which they had uttered.

Then in conclusion he said, I have derived the greatest benefit from your presence. I have profited much by the wise caching which you have given me in reference to the art of ruling.'

Then he ordered that three talents of silver should be presented to each of them, and appointed one of his slaves to deliver over the money.

All at once shouted their approval, and the banquet became a scene of joy, while the king gave himself up to a continuous round of festivity.

CHAPTER XI.

For a comment on ancient stenography, see Verse 7. The translation is submitted for approval and accepted as read, and (Verse 23) a rising vote of approval is taken and unanimously carried.

I HAVE written at length and must crave your pardon, Philocrates.

I was astonished beyond measure at the men and the way in which on the spur of the moment they gave answers which really needed a long time to devise.

For though the questioner had given great thought to each particular question, those who replied one after the other had their answers to the questions ready at once and so they seemed to me and to all who were present and especially to the philosophers to be worthy of admiration.

And I suppose that the thing will seem incredible to those who will read my narrative in the future.

But it is unseemly to misrepresent facts which are recorded in the public archives.

And it would not be right for me to transgress in such a matter as this. I tell the story just as it happened, conscientiously avoiding any error.

I was so impressed by the force of their utterances, that I made an effort to consult those whose business it was to make a record of all that happened at the royal audiences

The Forgotten Books of Eden

and banquets.

For it is the custom, as you know, from the moment the king besins to transact business until the time when he retires to rest, for a record to be taken of all his sayings and doings—a most excellent and useful arrangement.

For on the following day the minutes of the doings and sayings of the previous day are read over before business commence, and if there has been any irregularity, the matter is at once set right.

I obtained therefore, as has been said, accurate information from the public records, and I have set forth the facts in proper order since I know how eager you are to obtain useful information.

Three days later Demetrius took the men and passing along the sea-wall, seven stadia long, to the island, crossed the bridge and made for the northern districts of Pharos.

There he assembled them in a house, which had been built upon the sea-shore, of great beauty and in a secluded situation, and invited them to carry out the work of translation, since everything that they needed for the purpose was placed at their disposal.

So they set to work comparing their several results and making them agree, and whatever they agreed upon was suitably copied out under the direction of Demetrius.

And the session lasted until the ninth hour; after this they were set free to minister to their physical needs.

Everything they wanted was furnished for them on a lavish scale. In addition to this Dorotheus made the same preparations for them daily as were made for the king himself—for thus he had been commanded by the king.

In the early morning they appeared daily at the Court, and after saluting the king went back to their own place.

And as is the custom of all the Jews, they washed their hands in the sea and prayed to God and then devoted themselves to reading and translating the particular passage upon which they were engaged, and I put the question to them, Why it was that they washed their hands before they prayed?

And they explained that it was a token that they had done no evil (for every form of activity is wrought by means of the hands) since in their noble and holy way they regard everything as a symbol of righteousness and truth.

As I have already said, they met together daily in the place which was delightful for its quiet and its brightness and applied themselves to their task.

And it so chanced that the work of translation was completed in seventy-two days, just as if this had been arranged of set purpose.

When the work was completed, Demetrius collected together the Jewish population in the place where the translation had been made, and read it over to all, in the presence of the translators, who met with a great reception also from the people, be-

The Forgotten Books of Eden

cause of the great benefits which they had conferred upon them.

They bestowed warm praise upon Demetrius, too, and urged him to have the whole law transcribed and present a copy to their leaders.

After the books had been read, the priests and the elders of the translators and the Jewish community and the leaders of the people stood up and said, that since so excellent and sacred and accurate a translation had been made, it was only right that it should remain as it was and no alteration should be made in it

And when the whole company expressed their approval, they bade them pronounce a curse in accordance with their custom upon anyone who should make any alteration either by adding anything or chansing in any way whatever any of the words which had been written or making any omission.

This was a very wise precaution to ensure that the book might be preserved for all the future time unchanged.

When the matter was reported to the king, he rejoiced greatly, for he felt that the design which he had formed had been safely carried out.

The whole book was read over to him and he was greatly astonished at the spirit of the lawgiver.

And he said to Demetrius, 'How is it that none of the historians or 'the poets have ever thought it worth their while to allude to such a wonderful achievement?'

And he replied, 'Because the law is sacred and of divine orisin. And some of those who formed the intention of dealing with it have been smitten by God and therefore desisted from their purpose.'

He said that he had heard from Theopompus that he had been driven out of his mind for more than thirty days because he intended to insert in his history some of the incidents from the earlier and somewhat unreliable translations of the law.

When he had recovered a little, he besought God to make it clear to him why the misfortune had befallen him.

And it was revealed to him in a dream, that from idle curiosity he was wishing to communicate sacred truths to common men, and that if he desisted he would recover his health.

I have heard, too, from the lips of Theodektes, one of the tragic poets, that when he was about to adapt some of the incidents recorded in the book for one of his plays, he was affected with cataract in both his eyes.

And when he perceived the reason why the misfortune had befallen him, he prayed to God for many days and was afterwards restored.

And after, the king, as I have already said, had received the explanation of Demetrius on this point, he did homage and ordered that great care should be taken of the books, and that they should be sacredly guarded.

The Forgotten Books of Eden

And he urged the translators to visit him frequently after their return to Judea, for it was only right, he said, that he should now send them home.

But when they came back, he would treat them as friends, as was right, and they would receive rich presents from him.

He ordered preparations to be made for them to return home, and treated them most munificently.

He presented each one of them with three robes of the finest sort, two talents of gold, a sideboard weighing one talent, all the furniture for three couches.

And with the escort he sent Eleazar ten couches with silver legs and all the necessary equipment, a sideboard worth thirty talents, ten robes, purple, and a magnificent crown, and a hundred pieces of the finest woven linen, also bowls and dishes, and two golden beakers to be dedicated to God.

He urged him also in a letter that if any of the men preferred to come back to him, not to hinder them.

For he counted it a great privilege to enjoy the society of such learned men, and he would rather lavish his wealth upon them than upon vanities.

And now Philocrates, you have the complete story in accordance with my promise.

I think that you find greater pleasure in these matters than in the writings of the mythologists.

For you are devoted to the study of those things which can benefit the soul, and spend much time upon it. I shall attempt to narrate whatever other events are worth recording, that by perusing them you may secure the highest reward for your zeal.

FOURTH BOOK OF MACCABEES

THIS book is like a fearful peal of thunder echoing out of the dim horrors of ancient tyranny. It is a CHAPTER based on persecution by Antiochus, the tyrant of Syria, whom some called Epiphanes, The Madman. Roman history of the first centuries records two such tyrants—the other, Caligula, the Second Brilliant Madman.

The form of this writing is that of an oration. So carefully timed are the risings and fallings of the speech; so devastating are its arguments; so unfaltering is its logic; so deep its thrusts; so cool its reasoning—that it takes its place as a sample of the sheerest eloquence.

The keynote is—Courage. The writer besins with an impassioned statement of the Philosophy of Inspired Reason. We like to think of this twentieth Century as the Age of Reason and contrast it with the Age of Myths—yet a writing such as this is a challenge to such an assumption. We find a writer who probably belonged to the first century before the Christian Era stating a clear-cut philosophy of Reason that is just as potent today as it was two thousand years ago.

The Forgotten Books of Eden

The setting of the observations in the torture chambers is unrelenting. On our modern ears attuned to gentler things it strikes appallingly. The detail's of the successive tortures (suggesting the instruments of the Spanish Inquisition centuries later) are elaborated in a way shocking to our taste. Even the emergence of the stoical characters of the Old man, the Seven Brothers, and the Mother, does nothing to soften the ferocity with which this orator conjures Courage.

The ancient Fathers of the Christian Church carefully preserved this book (we have it from a Syrian translation) as a work of high moral value and teaching, and it was undoubtedly familiar to many of the early Christian martyrs, who were aroused to the pitch of martyrdom by reading it.

CHAPTER I.

An outline of philosophy from ancient times concerning Inspired Reason. Civilization has never achieved higher thought. A discussion of "Repressions." Verse 48 sums up the whole Philosophy of mankind.

PHILOSOPHICAL in the highest degree is the question I propose to discuss, namely whether the Inspired Reason is supreme ruler over the passions; and to the philosophy of it I would seriously entreat your earnest attention.

For not only is the subject generally necessary as a branch of knowledge, but it includes the praise of the greatest of virtues, whereby I mean self-control.

That is to say, if Reason is proved to control the passions adverse to temperance, gluttony and lust, it is also clearly shown to be lord over the passions, like malevolence, opposed to justice, and over those opposed to manliness, namely rage and pain and fear.

But, some may ask, if the Reason is master of the passions, why does it not control forgetfulness and ignorance? their object being to cast ridicule.

The answer is that Reason is not master over defects inhering in the mind itself, but over the passions or moral defects that are adverse to justice and manliness and temperance and judgement; and its action in their case is not to extirpate the passions, but to enable us to resist them successfully.

I could bring before you many examples, drawn from various sources, where Reason has proved itself master over the passions, but the best instance by far that I can give is the noble conduct of those who died for the sake of virtue, Eleazar, and the Seven Brethren and the Mother.

For these all by their contempt of pains, yea, even unto death, proved that Reason rises superior to the passions.

I might enlarge here in praise of their virtues, they, the men with the Mother, dying on this day we celebrate for the love of moral beauty and goodness, but rather would I felicitate them on the honours they have attained.

For the admiration felt for their courage and endurance, not only by the world at large but by their very executioners, made them the authors of the downfall of the tyranny under which our nation lay, they defeating the tyrant by their endurance, so that through them was their country purified.

But I shall presently take opportunity to discuss this, after we have begun with the general theory, as I am in the habit of doing, and I will then proceed to their story, giving glory to the all-wise God.

Our enquiry, then, is whether the Reason is supreme master over the passions.

But we must define just what the Reason is and what passion is, and how many forms of passion there are, and whether the Reason is supreme over all of them.

Reason I take to be the mind preferring with clear deliberation the life of wisdom.

Wisdom I take to be the knowledge of things, divine and human, and of their causes.

This I take to be the culture acquired under the Law, through which we learn with due reverence the things of God and for our worldly profit the things of man.

Now wisdom is manifested under the forms of judgement and justice, and courage, and temperance.

But judgement or self-control is the one that dominates them all, for through it, in truth, Reason asserts its authority over the passions.

But of the passions there are two comprehensive sources, namely, pleasure and pain, and either belongs essentially also to the soul as well as to the body.

And with respect both to pleasure and pain there are many cases where the passions have certain sequences.

Thus while desire goes before pleasure, satisfaction follows after, and while fear goes before pain, after pain comes sorrow.

Anger, again, if a man will retrace the course of his feelings, is a passion in which are blended both pleasure and pain.

Under pleasure, also, comes that moral debasement which exhibits the widest variety of the passions.

It manifests itself in the soul as ostentation, and covetousness, and vain-glory, and contentiousness, and backbiting, and in the body as eating of strange meat, and gluttony, and gormandizing in secret.

Now pleasure and pain being as it were two trees, growing from body and soul, many offshoots of these passions sprout up; and each man's Reason as master-gardener, weeding and pruning and binding up, and turning on the water and directing it hither and thither, brings the thicket of dispositions and passions under domestication.

For while Reason is the guide of the virtues it is master of the passions.

Observe, now, in the first place, that Reason becomes supreme over the passions in virtue of the inhibitory action of temperance.

Temperance, I take it, is the repression of the desires; but of the desires some are mental and some physical, and both kinds are clearly controlled by Reason; when we are tempted towards forbidden meats, how do we come to relinquish the pleasures to be derived from them?

Is it not that Reason has power to repress the appetites? In my opinion it is so.

Accordingly when we feel a desire to eat water-animals and birds and beasts and meats of every description forbidden to us under the Law, we abstain through the predominance of Reason.

For the propensions of our appetites are checked and inhibited by the temperate mind, and all the movements of the body obey the bridle of Reason.

And what is there to be surprised at if the natural desire of the soul to enjoy the fruition of beauty is quenched?

This, certainly, is why we praise the virtuous Joseph, because by his Reason, with a mental effort, he checked the carnal impulse. [*1] For he, a young man at the age when physical desire is strong, by his Reason quenched the impulse of his passions.

And Reason is proved to subdue the impulse not only of sexual desire, but of all sorts of covetings.

For the Law says, 'Thou shalt not covet thy neighbour's wife, nor anything that is thy neighbour's.'

Verily, when the Law orders us not to covet, it should, I think, confirm strongly the argument that the Reason is capable of controlling covetous desires, even as it does the passions that militate against justice.

How else, can a man, naturally gormandizing and greedy and drunken, be taught to change his nature, if the Reason be not manifestly the master of the passions?

Certainly, as soon as a man orders his life according to the Law, if he is miserly he acts contrary to his nature, and lends money to the needy without interest, and at the seventh-year periods cancels the debt.

And if he is parsimonious, he is overruled by the Law through the action of Reason, and refrains from gleaning his stubbles or picking the last grapes from his vineyards.

And with regard to all the rest we can recognize that Reason is in the position of master over the passions or affections.

For the Law ranks above affection for parents, so that a man may not for their sakes surrender his virtue, and it overrides love for a wife, so that if she transgress a man should rebuke her, and it governs love for children, so that if they are naughty a man should punish them, and it controls the claims of friendship, so that a man should reprove his friends if they do evil.

The Forgotten Books of Eden

And do not think it a paradoxical thing when Reason through the Law is able to overcome even hatred, so that a man refrains from cutting down the enemy's orchards, and protects the property of the enemy from the spoilers, and gathers up their goods that have been scattered.

And the rule of Reason is likewise proved to extend through the more aggressive passions or vices, ambition, vanity, ostentation, pride, and backbiting.

For the temperate mind repels all these debased passions, even as it does anger, for it conquers even this.

Yea, Moses when he was angered against Dathan and Abiram did not give free course to his wrath, but governed his anger by his Reason.

For the temperate mind is able, as I said, to win the victory over the passions, modifying some, while crushing others absolutely.

Why else did our wise father Jacob blame the houses of Simeon and Levi for their unreasoning slaughter of the tribe of the Shechemites, saying, 'Accursed be their anger!'

For had not Reason possessed the power to restrain their anger he would not have spoken thus.

For in the day when God created man, he implanted in him his passions and inclinations, and also, at the very same time, set the mind on a throne amidst the senses to be his sacred guide in all things; and to the mind he gave the Law, by the which if a man order himself, he shall reign over a kingdom that is temperate, and just, and virtuous, and brave.

CHAPTER II.

The ruling of Desire and Anger. The story of David's thirst. Stirring CHAPTERs of ancient history. Savage attempts to make the Jews eat swine. Interesting references to an ancient bank (Verse 21.)

WELL then, someone may ask, if Reason is master of the passions why is it not master of forgetfulness and ignorance?

But the argument is supremely ridiculous. For Reason is not shown to be master over passions or defects in itself, but over those of the body.

For example, none of you is able to extirpate our natural desire, but the Reason can enable him to escape being made a slave by desire.

None of you is able to extirpate anger from the soul, but it is possible for the Reason to come to his aid against anger.

None of you can extirpate a malevolent disposition, but Reason can be his powerful ally against being swayed by malevolence.

Reason is not the extirpate of the passions, but their antagonist.

The Forgotten Books of Eden

The case of the thirst of King David may serve at least to make this clearer.

For when David had fought the live-long day against the Philistines, and by the help of our country's warriors had slain many of them, he came at eventide, all fordone with sweat and toil, to the royal tent, around which was encamped the whole army of our ancestors.

So all the host fell to their evening meal; but the king, being consumed with an intense thirst, though he had abundance of water, was unable to slake it.

Instead, an irrational desire for the water that was in the possession of the enemy with growing intensity burned him up and unmanned and consumed him.

Then when his body-guard murmured against the craving of the king, two youths, mighty warriors, ashamed that their king should lack his desire, put on all their armour, and took a water-vessel, and scaled the enemy's ramparts; and stealing undetected past the guards at the gate, they searched through all the enemy's camp.

And they bravely found the spring, and drew from it a draught for the king.

But David, though still burning with the thirst, considered that such a draught, reckoned as equivalent to blood, was a grievous danger to his soul.

Therefore, opposing his Reason to his desire, he poured out the water as an offering to God.

For the temperate mind is able to conquer the dictates of the passions, and to quench the fires of desire, and to wrestle victoriously with the pangs of our bodies though they be exceeding strong, and by the moral beauty and goodness of Reason to defy with scorn all the domination of the passions.

And now the occasion calls us to set forth the story of the self-controlled Reason.

At a time when our fathers enjoyed great peace through the due observance of the Law, and were in happy case, so that Seleucus Nicanor, the king of Asia, sanctioned the tax for the temple-service, and recognized our polity, precisely then, certain men, acting factiously against the general concord, involved us in many and various calamities.

Onias, a man of the highest character, being then high priest and having the office for his life, a certain Simon raised a faction against him, but since despite every kind of slander he failed to injure him on account of the people, he fled abroad with intent to betray his country.

So he came to Apollonius, the governor of Syria and Phoenicia and Cilicia, and said, 'Being loyal to the king, I am here to inform you that in the treasuries of Jerusalem are stored many thousands of private deposits, not belonging to the temple account, and rightfully the property of King Seleucus.'

Apollonius having made inquiry into the details of the matter, praised Simon for his loyal service to the king, and hastening to the court of Seleucus, disclosed to him the

The Forgotten Books of Eden

valuable treasure; then, after receiving authority to deal with the matter, he promptly marched into our country, accompanied by the accursed Simon and a very powerful army, and announced that he was there by the king's command to take possession of the private deposits in the treasury.

Our people were deeply angered by this announcement, and protested strongly, considering it, an outrageous thing for those who had entrusted their deposits to the temple treasury to be robbed of them, and they threw all possible obstacles in his way.

Apollonius, however, with threats, made his way into the temple.

Then the priests in the temple and the women and children besought God to come to the rescue of his Holy Place that was being violated; and when Apollonius with his armed host marched in to seize the moneys, there appeared from heaven angels, riding upon horses, with lightning flashing from their arms, and cast great fear and trembling upon them.

And Apollonius fell down half-dead in the Court of the Gentiles, and stretched out his hands to heaven, and with tears he entreated the Hebrews that they would make intercession for him and stay the wrath of the heavenly host.

For he said that he had sinned and was worthy even of death, and that if he were given his life he would laud to all men the blessedness of the Holy Place.

Moved by these words, Onias, the high-priest, although most scrupulous in other cases, made intercession for him lest king Seleucus should possibly think that Apollonius had been overthrown by a human device and not by divine justice.

Apollonius, accordingly, after his astonishing deliverance departed to report to the king the things that had befallen him.

But Seleucus dying, his successor on the throne was his son Antiochus Epiphanes, an overweening terrible man; who dismissed Onias from his sacred office, and made his brother Jason high-priest instead, the condition being that in return for the appointment Jason should pay him three thousand six hundred and sixty talents yearly.

So he appointed Jason high-priest and made him chief ruler over the people.

And he (Jason) introduced to our people a new way of life and a new constitution in utter defiance of the Law; so that not only did he lay out a gymnasium on the Mount of our fathers, but he actually abolished the service of the temple.

Wherefore the divine justice was kindled to anger and brought Antiochus himself as an enemy against us.

For when. be was carrying on war with Ptolemy in Egypt and heard that the people of Jerusalem had rejoiced exceedingly over a report of his death, he immediately marched back against them.

And when he had plundered the city he made a decree denouncing the penalty of death upon any who should be seen to live after the law of our fathers.

The Forgotten Books of Eden

But he found all his decrees of no avail to break down the constancy of our people to the Law, and he beheld all his threats and penalties utterly despised, so that even women for circumcising their sons, though they knew beforehand what would be their fate, were flung, together with their offspring, headlong from the rocks.

When therefore his decrees continued to be contemned by the mass of the people, he personally tried to force by tortures each man separately to eat unclean meats and thus abjure the Jewish religion.

Accordingly, the tyrant Antiochus, accompanied by his councillors, sat in judgement on a certain high place with his troops drawn up around him in full armour, and he ordered his guards to drag there every single man of the Hebrews and compel them to eat swine's flesh and things offered to idols; but if any should refuse to defile themselves with the unclean things, they were to he tortured and put to death.

And when many had been taken by force, one man first from among the company was brought before Antiochus, a Hebrew whose name was Eleazar, a priest by birth, trained in knowledge of the law, a man advanced in years and well known to many of the tyrant's court for his philosophy.

And Antiochus, looking on him, said: 'Before I allow the tortures to besin for you, O venerable man, I would give you this counsel, that you should eat of the flesh of the swine and save your life; for I respect your age and your grey hairs, although to have worn them so long a time, and still to cling to the Jewish religion, makes me think you no philosopher.

For most excellent is the meat of this animal which Nature has graciously bestowed upon us, and why should you abominate it? Truly it is folly not to enjoy innocent pleasures, and it is wrong to reject Nature's favours.

But it will be still greater folly, I think, on your part if with idle vapouring about truth you shall proceed to defy even me to your own punishment.

Will you not awake from your preposterous philosophy? Will you not fling aside the nonsense of your calculations and, adopting another frame of mind befitting your mature years, learn the true philosophy of expediency, and how to my charitable counsel, and have pity on your own venerable age?

For consider this, too, that even if there be some Power whose eye is upon this religion of yours, he will always pardon you for a transgression done under compulsion.'

Thus urged by the tyrant to the unlawful eating of unclean meat, Eleazar asked permission to speak; and receiving it, he began his speech before the court as follows:

'We, O Antiochus, having accepted the Divine Law as the Law of our country, do not believe any stronger necessity is laid upon us than that of our obedience to the Law.

Therefore we do surely deem it right not. in any way whatsoever to transgress the Law.

And yet, were our Law, as you suggest, not truly divine, while we vainly believed

The Forgotten Books of Eden

it to be divine, not even so would it be right for us to destroy our reputation for piety.

Think it not, then, a small sin for us to eat the unclean thing, for the transgression of the Law, be it in small things or in great, is equally heinous; for in either case equally the Law is despised.

And you scoff at our philosophy, as if under it we were living in a manner contrary to reason.

Not so, for the Law teaches us self-control, so that we are masters of all our pleasures and desires and are thoroughly trained in manliness so as to endure all pain with readiness; and it teaches justice, so that with all our various dispositions we act fairly, and it teaches righteousness, so that with due reverence we worship only the God who is.

Therefore do we eat no unclean meat; for believing our Law to be given by God, we know also that the Creator of the world, as a Lawgiver, feels for us according to our nature.

He has commanded us to eat the things that will be convenient for our souls, and he has forbidden us to eat meats that would be the contrary.

But it is the act of a tyrant that you should compel us not only to transgress the Law, but should also make us eat in such manner that you may mock at' this defilement so utterly abominable to us.

But you shall not mock at me thus, neither will I break the sacred oaths of my ancestors to keep the Law, not even though you tear out mine eyes and bum out mine entrails.

I am not so unmanned by old age but that when righteousness is at stake the strength of youth returns to my Reason.

So twist hard your racks and blow your furnace hotter. I do not so pity mine old age as to break the Law of my fathers in mine own person.

I will not belie thee, O Law that wast my teacher; I will not desert thee, O beloved self-control; I will not put thee to shame, O wisdom-loving Reason, nor will I deny ye, O venerated priesthood and knowledge of the Law.

Neither shalt thou sully the pure mouth of mine old age and my lifelong constancy to the Law. Clean shall my fathers receive me, unafraid of thy torments even to the death.

For thou indeed mayest be tyrant over unrighteous men, but thou shalt not lord it over my resolution in the matter of righteousness either by thy words or through thy deeds.'

CHAPTER III.

Eleazar, the gentle spirited old man, shows such fortitude that even as we read these words 2000 years later, they seem like an inextinguishable fire.

The Forgotten Books of Eden

BUT when Eleazar replied thus eloquently to the exhortations of the tyrants, the guards around him dragged him roughly to the torturing place.

And first they unclothed the old man, who was adorned with the beauty of holiness.

Then binding his arms on either side they scourged him, a herald standing and shouting out over against him, 'Obey the orders of the king!'

But the great-souled and noble man, an Eleazar in very truth, was no more moved in his mind than if he were being tormented in a dream; yea, the old man keeping his eyes steadfastly raised to heaven suffered his flesh to be torn by the scourges till he was bathed in blood and his sides became a mass of wounds; and even when he fell to the ground because his body could no longer support the pain he still kept his Reason erect and inflexible.

With his foot then one of the cruel guards as he fell kicked him savagely in the side to make him get up.

But he endured the anguish, and despised the compulsion, and bore up under the torments, and like a brave athlete taking punishment, the old man outwore his tormentors.

The sweat stood on his brow, and he drew his breath in hard gasps, till his nobility of soul extorted the admiration of his tormentors themselves.

Hereupon, partly in pity for his old age, partly in sympathy for their friend, partly in admiration of his courage, some of the courtiers of the king went up to him and said:

'Why, O Eleazar, dost thou madly destroy thyself in this misery? We will bring to thee of the seethed meats, but do thou feign only to partake of the swine's flesh, and so save thyself.'

And Eleazar, as if their counsel did but add to his tortures, cried loudly: 'No. May we sons of Abraham never have so evil a thought as with faint heart to counterfeit a part unseemly to us.

Contrary to Reason, indeed, were it for us, after living unto the truth till old age, and guarding in lawful guise the repute of so living, now to change and become in our own persons a pattern to the young of impiety, to the end that we should encourage them to eat unclean meat.

Shame were it if we should live on a little longer, during that little being mocked of all men for cowardice, and while despised by the tyrant as unmanly should fail to defend the Divine Law unto the death.

Therefore, O sons of Abraham, do ye die nobly for righteousness' sake; but as for you, O minions of the tyrant, why pause ye in your work?'

So they, seeing him thus triumphant over the tortures and unmoved even by the pity of his executioners, dragged him to the fire.

The Forgotten Books of Eden

There they cast him on it, burning him with cruelly cunning devices, and they poured broth of evil odour into his nostrils.

But when the fire already reached to his bones and he was about to give up the ghost, he lifted up his eyes to God and said:

'Thou, O God, knowest that though I might save myself I am dying by fiery torments for thy Law. Be merciful unto thy people, and let our punishment be a satisfaction in their behalf. Make my blood their purification, and take my soul to ransom their souls,,

And with these words the holy man nobly yielded up his spirit under the torture I and for the sake of the Law held out by his Reason even against the torments unto death.

Beyond question, then, the Inspired Reason is master over the passions; for if his passions or sufferings had prevailed over his Reason we should have credited them with this evidence of their superior power.

But now his Reason having conquered his passions, we properly attribute to it the power of commanding them.

And it is right that we should admit that the mastery lies with Reason, in cases at least where it conquers pains that come from outside ourselves; for it were ridiculous to deny it.

And my proof covers not only the superiority of Reason to pains, but its superiority to pleasures also; neither does it surrender to them.

CHAPTER IV.

This so called "Age of Reason" may in this CHAPTER read that the Philosophy of Reason is 2000 years old. The story of seven sons and their mother.

FOR the Reason of our father Eleazar, like a fine steersman steering the ship of sanctity on the sea of the passions, though buffeted by the threats of the tyrant and swept by the swelling waves of the tortures, never shifted for one moment the helm of sanctity until he sailed into the haven of victory over death.

No city besieged with many and cunning ensines ever defended itself so well as did that holy man when his sacred soul was attacked with scourge and rack and flame, and he moved them who were laying siege to his soul through his Reason that was the shield of sanctity.

For our father Eleazar, setting his mind film as a beetling sea-cliff, broke the mad onset of the surges of the passions.

O priest worthy of thy priesthood, thou didst not defile thy holy teeth, nor didst thou befoul with unclean meat thy belly that had room only for piety and purity.

O confessor of the Law and philosopher of the Divine life! Such should those be whose office is to serve the Law and defend it with their own blood and honourable sweat in the face of sufferings to the death.

The Forgotten Books of Eden

Thou, O father, didst fortify our fidelity to the Law through thy steadfastness unto glory; and having spoken in honour of holiness thou didst not belie thy speech, and didst confirm the words of divine philosophy by thy deeds, O aged man that wast more forceful than the tortures.

O reverend elder that wast tenser-strung than the flame, thou great king over the passions, Eleazar.

For as our father Aaron, armed with the censer, ran through the massed congregation against the fiery angel and overcame him, so the son of Aaron, Eleazar, being consumed by the melting heat of the fire, remained unshaken in his Reason.

And yet most wonderful of all, he, being an old man, with the sinews of his body unstrung and his muscles relaxed and his nerves weakened, grew a young man again in the spirit of his Reason and with Isaac-like Reason turned the hydra-headed torture to impotence.

O blessed age, O reverend grey head, O life faithful to the Law and perfected by the seal of death!

Assuredly, then, if an old man despised the torments unto death for righteousness' sake it must be admitted that the Inspired Reason is able to guide the passions.

But some perhaps may answer that not all men are masters of the passions because not all men have their Reason enlightened.

But as many as with their whole heart make righteousness their first thought, these alone are able to master the weakness of the flesh, believing that unto God they die not, as our patriarchs, Abraham and Isaac and Jacob, died not, but that they live unto God.

Therefore there is nothing contradictory in certain persons appearing to be slaves to passion in consequence of the weakness of their Reason.

For who is there that being a philosopher following righteously the whole rule of philosophy, and having put his trust in God, and knowing that it is a blessed thing to endure all hardness for the sake of virtue, would not conquer his passions for the sake of righteousness?

For the wise and self-controlled man alone is the brave ruler of the passions.

Yea, by this means even young boys, being philosophers by virtue of the Reason which is according to righteousness, have triumphed over yet more grievous tortures.

For when the tyrant found himself notably defeated in his first attempt, and impotent to compel an old man to eat unclean meat, then truly in violent rage he ordered the guards to bring others of the young men of the Hebrews, and if they would eat unclean meat to release them after eating it, but if they refused, to torture them yet more savagely.

And under these orders of the tyrant seven brethren together with their aged mother were brought prisoners before him, all handsome, and modest, and well-born,—

The Forgotten Books of Eden

and generally attractive.

And when the tyrant saw them there, standing as if they were a festal choir with their mother in the midst, he took notice of them, and struck by their noble and distinguished bearing he smiled at them, and calling them nearer said:

'O young men, I wish well to each one of you, and admire your beauty, and honour highly so large a band of brothers; so not only do I advise you not to persist in the madness of that old man who has already suffered, but I even entreat of you to yield to me and become partakers in my friendship.

For, as I am able to punish those who disobey my orders, so am I able to advance those who do obey me.

Be assured then that you shall be given positions of importance and authority in my service if you will reject the ancestral law of your polity.

Share in the Hellenic life, and walk in a new way, and take some pleasure in your youth; for if you drive me to anger with your disobedience you will compel me to resort to terrible penalties and put every single one of you to death by torture.

Have pity then on yourselves, whom even I, your opponent, pity for your youth and your beauty.

Will you not consider with yourselves this thing, that if you disobey me there is nothing before you but death in torments?'

With these words he ordered the instruments of torture to be brought forward in order to persuade them by fear to eat unclean meat.

But when the guards had produced wheels, and joint-dislocators, and racks, and bone-crushers, and catapults, and cauldrons, and braziers, and thumb-screws, and iron claws, and wedges, and branding irons, the tyrant spoke again and said:

'You had better feel fear, my lads, and the justice you worship will pardon your unwilling transgression.'

But they, hearing his persuasions, and seeing his dreadful ensines, not only showed no fear but actually arrayed their philosophy in opposition to the tyrant, and by their right Reason did abase his tyranny.

And yet consider; supposing some amongst them to have been faint-hearted and cowardly, what sort of language would they have used? would it not have been to this effect?

'Alas! miserable creatures that we are and foolish above measure! When the king invites us and appeals to us on terms of kind treatment shall we not obey him?

Why do we encourage ourselves with vain desires and dare a disobedience that is to cost us our lives? Shall we not, O men my brothers, fear the dread instruments and weigh well his threats of the tortures, and abandon these empty vaunts and this fatal bragging?

The Forgotten Books of Eden

Let us take pity on our own youth and have compassion on our mother's age; and let us lay to heart that if we disobey we shall die.

And even the divine justice will have mercy on us, if compelled by necessity we yield to the king in fear. Why should we cast away from us this dear life and rob ourselves of this sweet world?

Let us not strive against necessity nor with vain confidence invite our torture.

Even the Law itself does not willingly condemn us to death, we being in terror of the instruments of torture.

Why does such contentiousness inflame us and a fatal obstinacy find favour with us, when we might have a peaceful life by obeying the king?'

But no such words escaped these young men at the prospect of the torture, nor did such thoughts enter into their minds.

For they were despisers of the passions and masters over pain.

CHAPTER V.

A CHAPTER of horror and torture revealing ancient tyranny at its utmost savagery. Verse 26 is profound truth.

AND thus no sooner did the tyrant conclude his ursing of them to eat unclean meat than all with one voice together, and as with one soul, said to him:

'Why dost thou delay, O tyrant? We are ready to die rather than transgress the commandments of our fathers.

For we should be putting our ancestors also to shame, if we did not walk in obedience to the Law and take Moses as our counsellor.

O tyrant that counsellest us to transgress the Law, do not, hating us, pity us beyond ourselves.

For we esteem thy mercy, giving. us our life in return for a breach of the Law, a thing harder to bear than death itself.

Thou wouldst terrify us with thy threats of death under torture, as if a little while ago thou hadst learned nothing from Eleazar.

But if the old men of the Hebrews endured the tortures for righteousness' sake, yea, until they died, more befittingly will we young men die despising the torments of thy compulsion, over which he our aged teacher also triumphed.

Make trial therefore, O tyrant. And if thou takest our lives for the sake of righteousness, think not that thou hurtest us with thy tortures.

For we through this our evil entreatment and our endurance of it shall win the prize of virtue; but thou for our cruel murder shalt suffer at the hands of divine justice sufficient torment by fire for ever.'

The Forgotten Books of Eden

These words of the youths redoubled the wrath of the tyrant, not at their disobedience only but at what he considered their ingratitude.

So by his orders the scourgers brought forward the eldest of them and stripped him of his garment and bound his hands and arms on either side with thongs.

But when they had scourged him till they were weary, and gained nothing thereby, they cast him upon the wheel.

And on it the noble youth was racked till his bones were out of joint. And as joint after joint gave way, he denounced the tyrant in these words:

'O thou most abominable tyrant, thou enemy of the justice of heaven and bloody-minded, thou dost torment me in this fashion not for manslaying nor for impiety but for defending the Law of God.'

And when the guards said to him, 'Consent to eat, that so you may be released from your tortures,' he said to them, 'Your method, O miserable minions, is not strong enough to lead captive my Reason. Cut off my limbs, and burn my flesh, and twist my joints; through all the torments I will show you that in behalf of virtue the sons of the Hebrews alone are unconquerable.'

As he thus spake they set hot coals upon him besides, and intensifying the torture strained him yet tighter on the wheel.

And all the wheel was besmeared with his blood, and the heaped coals were quenched by the humours of his body dropping down, and the rent flesh ran round the axles of the machine.

And with his bodily frame already in dissolution this great-souled youth, like a true son of Abraham, groaned not at all; but as if he were suffering a change by fire to incorruption, he nobly endured the torment, saying:

'Follow my example, O brothers. Do not for ever desert me, and forswear not our brotherhood in nobility of soul.

War a holy and honourable warfare on behalf of righteousness, through which may the just Providence that watched over our fathers become merciful unto his people and take vengeance on the accursed tyrant.'

And with these words the holy youth yielded up the ghost.

But while all were wondering at his constancy of soul, the guards brought forward the second in age of the. sons, and grappling him with sharp-clawed hands of iron they fastened him to the ensines and the catapult.

But when they heard his noble resolve in answer to their question, 'Would he eat rather than he tortured?' these panther-like beasts tore at his sinews with claws of iron, and rent away all the flesh from his cheeks, and tore off the skin from his head.

But he steadfastly enduring this agony said, 'How sweet is every form of death for the sake of the righteousness of our fathers!'

The Forgotten Books of Eden

And to the tyrant he said, 'O most ruthless of tyrants, doth not it seem to thee that at this moment thou thyself sufferest tortures worse than mine in seeing thy tyranny's arrogant intention overcome by my endurance for righteousness' sake?

For I am supported under pain by the joys that come through virtue, whereas thou art in torment whilst glorying in thy impiety; neither shalt thou escape, O most abominable tyrant, the penalties of the divine wrath.'

And when he had bravely met his glorious death, the third son was brought forward and was earnestly entreated by many to taste and so to save himself.

But he answered in a loud voice, 'Are ye ignorant that the same father begat me and my brothers that are dead, and the same mother gave us birth, and in the same doctrines was I brought up?

I do not forswear the noble bond of brotherhood.

Therefore if ye have any ensine of torment, apply it to this body of mine; for my soul ye cannot reach, not if ye would.'

But they were greatly angered at the bold speech of the man, and they dislocated his hands and his feet with their dislocating ensines, and wrenched his limbs out of their sockets, and unstrung them; and they twisted round his fingers, and his arms, and his legs, and his elbow-joints.

And in no wise being able to strangle his spirit they stripped off his skin, taking the points of the fingers with it, and tore in Scythian fashion the scalp from his head, and straightway brought him to the wheel.

And on this they twisted his spine till he saw his own flesh hansing in strips and great gouts of blood pouring down from his entrails.

And at the point of death he said, 'We, O most abominable tyrant, suffer thus for our upbrinsing and our virtue that are of God; but thou for thy impiety and thy cruelty shall endure torments without end.'

And when' this man had died worthily of his brothers, they brought up the fourth, and said to him, 'Be not thou also mad with the same madness as thy brethren, but obey the king and save thyself.'

But he said unto them, 'For me ye have no fire so exceeding hot as to make me a coward.

By the blessed death of my brethren, by the eternal doom of the tyrant, and by the glorious life of the righteous, I will not deny my noble brotherhood.

Invent tortures, O tyrant, in order that thou mayest learn thereby that I am brother of those who have been already tortured.'

When he heard this the bloodthirsty, murderous, and utterly abominable Antiochus bade them cut out his tongue.

But he said, 'Even if thou dost remove my organ of speech, God is a hearer also of the speechless.

Lo, I put out my tongue ready: cut it out, for thou shalt not thereby silence my Reason.

Gladly do we give our bodily members to be mutilated for the cause of God.

But God will speedily pursue after thee; for thou cuttest out the tongue that sang songs of praise unto him.'

But when this man also was put to a death of agony with the tortures, the fifth sprang forward saying, 'I shrink not, O tyrant, from demanding the torture for virtue's sake.

Yea, of myself I come forward, in order that, slaying me also, thou mayest by yet more misdeeds increase the penalty thou owest to the justice of Heaven.

O enemy of virtue and enemy of man, for what crime dost thou destroy us in this way?

Doth it seem evil to thee that we worship the Creator of all and live according to his virtuous Law?

But these things are worthy of honours not of tortures, if thou didst understand human aspirations and hadst hope of salvation before God.

Lo, now thou art God's enemy and makest war on those that worship God.'

As he spake thus the guards bound him and brought him before the catapult; and they tied him thereto on his knees, and, fastening them there with iron clamps, they wrenched his loins over the rolling 'wedge' so that he was completely curled back like a scorpion and every joint was disjointed.

And thus in grievous strait for breath and anguish of body he exclaimed, 'Glorious, O tyrant, glorious against thy will are the boons that thou bestowest on me, enabling me to show my fidelity to the Law through yet more honourable tortures.'

And when this man also was dead, the sixth was brought, a mere boy, who in answer to the tyrant's inquiry whether he was willing to eat and be released, said:

'I am not so old in years as my brethren, but I am as old in mind. For we were born and reared for the same purpose and are equally bound also to die for the same cause; so if thou chooseth to torture us for not eating unclean meat, torture.'

As he spake these words they brought him to the wheel, and with care they stretched him out and dislocated the bones of his back and set fire under him.

And they made sharp skewers red-hot and ran them into his back, and piercing through his sides they burned away his entrails also.

But he in the midst of his tortures exclaimed, 'O contest worthy of saints, wherein so many of us brethren, in the cause of righteousness, have been entered for a competition in torments, and have not been conquered!

The Forgotten Books of Eden

For the righteous understanding, O tyrant, is unconquerable.

In the armour of virtue I go to join my brothers in death, and to add in myself one strong avenger more to punish thee, O deviser of the tortures and enemy of the truly righteous.

We six youths have overthrown thy tyranny. 'For is not thine impotence to alter our Reason or force us to eat unclean meat an overthrow for thee?

Thy fire is cool for us, thy ensines of torture torment not, and thy violence is impotent.

For the guards have been officers for us, not of a tyrant, but of the Divine Law; and therefore have we our Reason yet unconquered.'

CHAPTER VI.

Brotherly bonds and a mother's love.

AND when this one also died a blessed death, being cast into the cauldron, the seventh son, the youngest of them all, came forward.

But the tyrant, although fiercely exasperated by his brethren, felt pity for the boy, and seeing him there already bound he had him brought near, and sought to persuade him, saying: 'Thou seest the end of the folly of thy brethren; for through their disobedience they have been racked to death. Thou, too, if thou dost not obey, wilt thyself also be miserably tortured and put to death before thy time; but if thou dost obey thou shalt be my friend, and thou shalt be advanced to high office in the business of the kingdom.'

And while thus appealing to him he sent for the boy's mother, in order that in her sorrow for the loss of so many sons she might urge the survivor to obey and be saved.

But the mother, speaking in the Hebrew tongue, as I shall tell later on, encouraged the boy, and he said to the guards, 'Loose me, that I may speak to the king and to all his friends with him.'

And they, rejoicing at the boy's request, made haste to loose him.

And running up to the red-hot brazier, 'O impious tyrant,' he cried, 'and most ungodly of all sinners, art thou not ashamed to take thy blessings and thy kingship at the hands of God, and to slay his servants and torture the followers of righteousness?

For which things the divine justice delivers thee unto a more rapid and an eternal fire and torments which shall not leave hold on thee to all eternity.

Art thou not ashamed, being a man, O wretch with the heart of a wild beast, to take men of like feelings with thyself, made from the same elements, and tear out their tongues, and scourge and torture them in this manner?

But while they have fulfilled their righteousness towards God in their noble deaths, thou shalt miserably cry "Woe is met" for thy unjust slaying of the champions of virtue.'

And then standing on the brink of death he said, 'I am no renegade to the witness

The Forgotten Books of Eden

borne by my brethren.

And I call upon the God of my fathers to be merciful unto my nation.

And thee will he Punish both in this present life and after that thou art dead.'

And with this prayer he cast himself into the red-hot brazier, and so gave up the ghost.

If therefore the seven brethren despised the tortures even to the death, it is universally proved that the Inspired Reason is supreme lord over the passions.

For if they had yielded to their passions or sufferings and eaten unclean meat we should have said that they had been conquered thereby.

But in this cam it was not so; on the contrary by their Reason, which was commended in the sight of God, they rose superior to their passions.

And it is impossible to deny the supremacy of the mind; for they won the victory over their passions and their pains.

How can we do otherwise than admit right Reason's mastery over passion with these men who shrank not before the agonies of burning?

For even as towers on harbour-moles repulse the assaults of the waves and offer a calm entrance to those entering the haven, so the seven-towered right Reason of the youths defended the haven of righteousness and repulsed the tempestuousness of the passions.

They formed a holy choir of righteousness as they cheered one another on, saying:

'Let us die like brothers, O brethren, for the Law.

Let us imitate the Three Children at the Assyrian court who despised this same ordeal of the furnace.

Let us not turn cravens before the proof of righteousness.'

And one said, 'Brother, be of good cheer,' and another, 'Bear it out nobly'; and another recalling the past, 'Remember of what stock ye are, and at whose fatherly hand Isaac for righteousness' sake yielded himself to be a sacrifice.'

And each and all of them together, looking at each other brightly and very boldly, said, 'With a whole heart will we consecrate ourselves unto God who gave us our souls, and let us lend our bodies to the keeping of the Law.

Let us not fear him who thinketh he kills; for a great struggle and peril of the soul awaits in eternal torment those who transgress the ordinance of God.

Let us then arm ourselves with divine Reason's mastery of the passions.

After this our passion, Abraham, Isaac, and Jacob shall receive us, and all our forefathers shall praise us.'

The Forgotten Books of Eden

And to each separate one of the brothers, as they were dragged off, those whose turn was yet to come said, 'Do not disgrace us, brother, nor be false to our brethren already dead.'

You are not ignorant of the love of brethren, whereof the divine and all-wise Providence has given an inheritance to those who are begotten though their fathers, implanting it in them even through the mother's womb; wherein brethren do dwell the like period, and take their form during the same time, and are nourished from the same blood, and are quickened with the same soul, and are brought into the world after the same space, and they draw milk from the same founts, whereby their fraternal souls are nursed together in arms at the breast; and they are knit yet closer through a common nurture and daily companionship and other education, and through our discipline under the Law of God.

The feeling of brotherly love being thus naturally strong, the seven brethren had their mutual concord made yet stronger. For trained in the same Law, and disciplined in the same virtues, and brought up together in the upright life, they loved one another the more abundantly. Their common zeal for moral beauty and goodness heightened their mutual concord, for in conjunction with their piety it rendered their brotherly love more fervent.

But though nature, companionship, and their virtuous disposition increased the ardour of their brotherly love, nevertheless the surviving sons through their religion supported the sight of their brethren, who were on the rack, being tortured to death; nay more, they even encouraged them to face the agony, so as not only to despise their own tortures, but also to conquer their passion of brotherly affection for their brethren.

O Reasoning minds, more kingly than kings, than freemen more free, of the harmony of the seven brethren, holy and well attuned to the keynote of piety!

None of the seven youths turned coward, none shrunk in the face of death, but all hastened to the death by torture as if running the road to immortality.

For as hands and feet move in harmony with the promptings of the soul, so those holy youths, as if prompted by the immortal soul of religion, went in harmony to death for its sake.

O all-holy sevenfold companionship of brethren in harmony!

For as the seven days of the creation of the world do enring religion, so did the youths choir-like enring their sevenfold companionship, and made the terror of the tortures of no account.

We now shudder when we hear of the suffering of those youths; but they, not only seeing it with their eyes, nor merely hearing the spoken, imminent threat, but actually feeling the pang, endured it through; and that in the torture by fire, than which what greater agony can be found?

For sharp and stringent is the power of fire, and swiftly did it bring their bodies to dissolution.

The Forgotten Books of Eden

And think it not wonderful if with those men Reason triumphed over the tortures, when even a woman's soul despised a yet greater diversity of pains; for the mother of the seven youths endured the torments inflicted on each several one of her children.

But consider how manifold are the yearnings of a mother's heart, so that her feeling for her offspring becomes the centre of her whole world; and indeed, here, even the irrational animals have for their young an affection and love similar to men's.

For example, among the birds, the tame ones sheltering under our roofs defend their nestlings; and those that nest upon the mountain tops, and in the rock clefts, and in the holes of trees, and in the branches, and hatch their young there, do also drive away the intruder.

And then, if they be unable to drive him away, they flutter around the nestlings in a passion of love, calling to them in their own speech, and they give succour to their young ones in whatever fashion they can.

And what need have we of examples of the love of offspring among irrational animals, when even the bees, about the season of the making of the comb, fend off intruders, and stab with their sting, as with a sword, those who approach their brood, and do battle against them even to the death?

But she, the mother of those young men, with a soul like Abraham, was not moved from her purpose by her affection for her children.

CHAPTER VII.

A comparison of a mother's and father's affections, in this CHAPTER are some mountain peaks of eloquence.

REASON of the sons, lord over the passions! O religion, that wast dearer to the mother than her children!

The mother, having two choices before her, religion and the present saving alive of her seven sons according to the tyrant's promise, loved rather religion, which saveth unto eternal life according to God.

O how may I express the passionate love of parents for children? We stamp a marvellous likeness of our soul and of our shape on the tender nature of the child, and most of all through the mother's sympathy with her children being deeper than the father's.

For women are softer of soul than men, and the more children they bear the more do they abound in love for them.

But, of all mothers, she of the seven sons abounded in love beyond the rest, seeing that, having in seven child-bearings felt maternal tenderness for the fruit of her womb, and having been constrained because of the many pangs in which she bore each to a close affection, she nevertheless through the fear of God rejected the present safety of her children.

The Forgotten Books of Eden

Ay, and more than that, through the moral beauty and goodness of her sons and their obedience to the Law, her maternal love for them was made stronger.

For they were just, and temperate, and brave and great-souled, and lovers of each other and of their mother in such manner that they obeyed her in the keeping of the Law even unto death.

But nevertheless, though she had so many temptations to yield to her maternal instincts, in no single instance did the dreadful variety of tortures have power to alter her Reason; but the mother urged each son separately, and all together, to die for their religion.

O holy nature, and parental love, and yearning of parents for offspring, and wages of nursing, and unconquerable affection of mothers!

The mother, seeing them one by one racked and burned, remained unshaken in soul for religion's sake.

She saw the flesh of her sons being consumed in the fire, and the extremities of their hands and feet scattered on the ground, and the flesh-covering, torn off from their heads right to their cheeks, strewn about like masks.

O mother, who now knew sharper pangs than the pangs of labour! O woman, alone among women, the fruit of whose womb was perfect religion!

Thy firstborn, giving up the ghost, did not alter thy resolution, nor thy second, looking with eyes of pity on thee under his tortures, nor thy third, breathing out his spirit.

Neither didst thou weep when thou beheldest the eyes of each amid the torments looking boldly on the same anguish, and sawest in their quivering nostrils the signs of approaching death.

When thou sawest the flesh of one son being severed after the flesh of another, and hand after hand being cut off, and head after head being flayed, and corpse cast upon corpse, and the place crowded with spectators on account of the tortures of thy children, thou sheddest not a tear.

Not the melodies of the sirens nor the songs of swans with sweet sound do so charm the hearer's ears, as sounded the voices of the sons, speaking to the mother from amid the torments.

How many and how great were the tortures with which the mother was tormented while her sons were being tortured with torments of rack and fire!

But Inspired Reason lent her heart a man's strength under her passion of suffering, and exalted her to make no account of the present yearnings of mother-love.

And although she saw the destruction of her seven children and the many and varied forms of their torments, the noble mother willingly surrendered them through faith in God.

For she beheld in her own mind, even as it had been cunning advocates in a council-chamber, nature, and parenthood, and mother-love, and her children on the rack, and it was as if she, the mother, having the choice between two votes in the case of her children, one for their death and one to save them alive, thereupon regarded not the saving of her seven sons for a little time, but, as a true daughter of Abraham, called to mind his God-fearing courage.

O mother of the race, vindicator of our Law, defender of our religion, and winner of the prize in the struggle within thyself!

O woman, nobler to resist than men, and braver than warriors to endure!

For as the Ark of Noah, with the whole living world for her burden in the world-whelming Deluge, did withstand the mighty surges, so thou, the keeper of the Law, beaten upon every side by the sursing waves of the passions, and strained as with strong blasts by the tortures of thy sons, didst nobly weather the storms that assailed thee for religion's sake.

Thus then, if one both a woman and advanced in years, and the mother of seven sons, endured the sight of her children being tortured to death, the Inspired Reason must confessedly be supreme ruler over the passions.

I have proved, accordingly, that not only have men triumphed over their sufferings, but that a woman also has despised the most dreadful tortures.

And not so fierce were the lions around Daniel, not so hot was the burning fiery furnace of Mishael, as burned in her the instinct of motherhood at the sight of her seven sons being tortured.

But by her religion-guided Reason the mother quenched her passions, many and strong as they were.

For there is this also to consider, that had the woman been weak of spirit, despite her motherhood, she might have wept over them, and perchance spoken thus:

'Ah, thrice wretched me, and more than thrice wretched! Seven children have I borne and am left childless!

In vain was I seven times with child, and to no profit was my ten months' burden seven times borne, and fruitless have been my nursings, and sorrowful my sucklings.

In vain for you, O my sons, did I endure the many pangs of labour, and the more difficult cares of your upbrinsing.

Alas, for my sons, that some were yet unwed, and those that were wedded had begotten no children; I shall never see children of yours, nor shall I be called by the name of grandparent.

Ah me, that had many beautiful children, and am a widow and desolate in my woe! Neither will there be any son to bury me when I am dead!'

But the holy and God-fearing mother wailed not with this lamentation over any one of them, neither besought she any to escape death, nor lamented over them as dying men; but, as though she had a soul of adamant and were brinsing forth the number of her sons, for a second time, into immortal life, she besought rather and entreated of them that they should die for religion's sake.

O mother, warrior of God in the cause of religion, old and a woman, thou didst both defeat the tyrant by thy endurance, and wast found stronger than a man, in deeds as well as words.

For verily when thou wast put in bonds with thy sons, thou stoodest there seeing Eleazar being tortured, and thou spakest to thy sons in the Hebrew tongue:

'My sons, noble is the fight; and do ye, being called thereto to bear witness for our nation, fight therein zealously on behalf of the Law of our fathers.

For it would be shameful if, while this aged man endured the agony for religion's sake, you that are young men shrank before the pain.

Remember that for the sake of God ye have come into the world, and have enjoyed life, and that therefore ye owe it to God to endure all pain for his sake; for whom also our father Abraham made haste to sacrifice his son Isaac, the ancestor of our nation; and Isaac, seeing his father's hand lifting the knife against him, did not shrink.

And Daniel, the just man, was cast to the lions, and Ananias, Azarias, and Mishael were flung into the furnace of fire, and they endured for God's sake.

And ye also, having the same faith unto God, be not troubled; for it were against Reason that ye, knowing righteousness, should not withstand the pains.'

With these words the mother of the seven encouraged every single one of her sons to die rather than transgress the ordinance of God; they themselves also knowing well that men dying for God live unto God, as live Abraham, and Isaac, and Jacob, and all the patriarchs.

CHAPTER VIII.

The famous "Athletes of Righteousness." Here ends the story of courage called the Fourth Book of Maccabees.

SOME of the guards declared that when she also was about to be seized and put to death, she cast herself on the pyre in order that no man might touch her body.

O mother, that together with thy seven sons didst break the tyrant's force, and bring to nought his evil devices, and gavest an example of the nobleness of faith.

Thou wert nobly set as a roof upon thy sons as pillars, and the earthquake of the torments shook thee not at all.

Rejoice therefore, pure-souled mother, having the hope of thy endurance certain at the hand of God.

Not so majestic stands the moon amid the stars in heaven as thou, having lit the path of thy seven starlike sons unto righteousness, standest in honour with God; and thou art set in heaven with them.

For thy child-bearing was from the son of Abraham.

And had it been lawful for us to paint, as might some artist, the tale of thy piety, would not the spectators have shuddered at the mother of seven sons suffering for righteousness' sake multitudinous tortures even unto death?

And indeed it were fitting to inscribe these words over their resting-place, speaking for a memorial to future generations of our people:

HERE LIE AN AGED PRIEST

AND A WOMAN FULL OF YEARS

AND HER SEVEN SONS

THROUGH THE VIOLENCE OF A TYRANT

DESIRING TO DESTROY THE HEBREW NATION.

THEY VINDICATED THE RIGHTS OF OUR PEOPLE

LOOKING UNTO GOD AND ENDURING

THE TORMENTS EVEN UNTO

DEATH.

For truly it was a holy war which was fought by them. For on that day virtue, proving them through endurance, set before them the prize of victory in incorruption in everlasting life.

But the first in the fight was Eleazar, and the mother of the seven sons played her part, and the brethren fought.

The tyrant was their adversary and the world and the life of man were the spectators.

And righteousness won the victor and gave the crown to her athletes. Who but wondered at the athletes of the true Law?

Who were not amazed at them? The tyrant himself and his whole council admired their endurance, whereby they now do both Stand beside the throne of God and live the blessed age.

For Moses says, 'All also who have sanctified themselves are under thy hands.'

And these men, therefore, having sanctified themselves for God's sake, not only have received this honour, but also the honour that through them the enemy had no more power over our people, and the tyrant suffered punishment, and our country was purified, they having as it were become a ransom for our nation's sin; and through the blood of these righteous men and the propitiation of their death, the divine Providence delivered Israel that before was evil entreated.

The Forgotten Books of Eden

For when the tyrant Antiochus saw the heroism of their virtue, and their endurance under the tortures, he publicly held up their endurance to his soldiers as an example; and he thus inspired his men with a sense of honour and heroism on the field of battle and in the labours of besiesing, so that he plundered and overthrew all his enemies.

O Israelites, children born of the seed of Abraham, obey this Law, and be righteous in all ways, recognizing that Inspired Reason is lord over the passions, and over pains, not only from within, but from without ourselves; by which means those men, delivering up their bodies to the torture for righteousness' sake, not only won the admiration of mankind, but were deemed worthy of a divine inheritance.

And through them the nation obtained peace and restoring the observance of the Law in our country hath captured the city from the enemy.

And vengeance hath pursued the tyrant Antiochus upon earth, and in death he suffers punishment.

For when he failed utterly to constrain the people of Jerusalem to live like Gentiles and abandon the customs of our fathers, he thereupon left Jerusalem and marched away against the Persians.

Now these are the words that the mother of the seven sons, the righteous woman, spake to her children:

'I was a pure maiden, and I strayed not from my father's house, and I kept guard over the rib that was builded into Eve.

No seducer of the desert, no deceiver in the field, corrupted me; nor did the false, beguiling Serpent sully the purity of my maidenhood; I lived with my husband all the days of my youth; but when these my sons were grown up, their father died.

Happy was he; for he lived a life blessed with children, and he never knew the pain of their loss.

Who, while he was yet with us, taught you the Law and the prophets. He read to us of Abel who was slain by Cain, and of Isaac who was offered as a burnt-offering, and of Joseph in the prison.

And he spake to us of Phineas, the zealous priest, and he taught you the song of Ananias, Azarias, and Mishael in the fire.

And he glorified also Daniel in the den of lions, and blessed him; and he called to your minds the saying of Isaiah,

"Yea even though thou pass through the fire, the flame shall not hurt thee."

He sang to us the words of David the psalmist, "Many are the afflictions of the just."

He quoted to us the proverb of Solomon, "He is a tree of life to all them that do his will."

The Forgotten Books of Eden

He confirmed the words of Ezekiel, "Shall these dry bones live?" For he forgat not the song that Moses taught, which teaches, "I will slay and I will make alive. This is your life and the blessedness of your days."'

Ah, cruel was the day, and yet not cruel, when the cruel tyrant of the Greeks set the fire blazing for his barbarous braziers, and with his passions boiling brought to the catapult and back again to his tortures the seven sons of the daughter of Abraham, and blinded the eyeballs of their eyes, and cut out their tongues, and slew them with many kinds of torment.

For which cause the judgement of God pursued, and shall pursue, the accursed wretch.

But the sons of Abraham, with their victorious mother, are gathered together unto the place of their ancestors, having received pure and immortal souls from God, to whom be glory for ever and ever.

THE STORY OF AHIKAR

WE HAVE in The Story of Ahikar one of the most ancient sources of human thought and wisdom. Its influence can be traced through the legends of many people, including the Koran, and the Old and New Testaments.

A mosaic found in Treves, Germany, pictured among the wise men of the world the character of Ahikar. Here is his colorful tale.

The date of this story has been a subject of lively discussion. Scholars finally put it down about the First Century when they were proved in error by the orisinal story turning up in an Aramaic papyrus of 500 B. C. among the ruins of Elephantine.

The story is obviously fiction and not history. In fact the reader can make its acquaintance in the supplementary pages of The Arabian Nights. It is brilliantly written, and the narrative which is full of action, intrigue, and narrow escape holds the attention to the last. The liberty of imasination is the most precious possession of the writer.

The writing divides itself into four phases: (1) The Narrative; (2) The Teaching (a remarkable series of Proverbs); (3) The Journey to Egypt; (4) The Similitudes or Parables (with which Ahikar completes the education of his erring nephew).

CHAPTER I.

Ahikar, Grand Vizier of Assyria, has 60 wives but is fated to have no son. Therefore he adopts his nephew. He crams him full of wisdom and knowledge more than of bread and water.

THE story of Haiqar the Wise, Vizier of Sennacherib the King, and of Nadan, sister's son to Haiqar the Sage.

There was a Vizier in the days of King Sennacherib, son of Sarhadum, King of Assyria and Nineveh, a wise man named Haiqar, and he was Vizier of the king Sennacherib.

The Forgotten Books of Eden

He had a fine, fortune and much goods, and he was skilful, wise, a philosopher, in knowledge, in opinion and in government, and he had married sixty women, and had built a castle for each of them.

But with it all he had no child by any. of these women, who might be his heir.

And he was very sad on account of this, and one day he assembled the astrologers and the learned men and the wizards and explained to them his condition and the matter of his barrenness.

And they said to him, 'Go, sacrifice to the gods and beseech them that perchance they may provide thee with a boy.'

And he did as they told him and offered sacrifices to the idols, and besought them and implored them with request, and entreaty.

And they answered him not one word. And he went away sorrowful and dejected, departing with a pain at his heart.

And he returned, and implored the Most High God, and believed, beseeching Him with a burning in his heart, saying, 'O Most High God, O Creator of the Heavens and of the earth, O Creator of all created things!

I beseech Thee to give me a boy, that I may be consoled by him that he may be present at my heath, that he may close my eyes, and that he may bury me.'

Then there came to him a voice saying, 'Inasmuch as thou hast relied first of all on graven images, and hast offered sacrifices to them, for this reason thou shalt remain childless thy life long.

But take Nadan thy sister's son, and make him thy child and teach him thy learning and thy good breeding, and at thy death he shall bury thee.'

Thereupon he took Nadan his sister's son, who was a little suckling. And he handed him over to eight wet-nurses, that they might suckle him and bring him up.

And they brought him up with good food and gentle training and silken clothing, and purple and crimson. And he was seated upon couches of silk.

And when Nadan grew big and walked, shooting up like a tall cedar, he taught him good manners and writing and science and philosophy.

And after many days King Sennacherib looked at Haiqar and saw that he had grown very old, and moreover he said to him.

'O my honoured friend, the skilful, the trusty, the wise, the governor, my secretary, my vizier, my Chancellor and director; verily thou art grown very old and weighted with years; and thy departure from this world must be near.

Tell me who shall have a place in my service after thee.' And Haiqar said to him, 'O my lord, may thy head live for ever! There is Nadan my sister's son, I have made him my child.

The Forgotten Books of Eden

And I have brought him up and taught him my wisdom and my knowledge.'

And the king said to him, 'O Haiqar! bring him to my presence, that I may see him, and if I find him suitable, put him in thy place; and thou shalt go thy way, to take a rest and to live the remainder of thy life in sweet repose.'

Then Haiqar went and presented Nadan his sister's son. And he did homage and wished him power and honour.

And he looked at him and admired him and rejoiced in him and said to Haiqar: 'Is this thy son, O Haiqar? I pray that God may preserve him. And as thou hast served me and my father Sarhadum so may this boy of thine serve me and fulfil my undertakings, my needs, and my business, so that I may honour him and make him powerful for thy sake.'

And Haiqar did obeisance to the king and said to him, 'May thy head live, O my lord the king, for ever! I seek from thee that thou mayst be patient with my boy Nadan and forgive his mistakes that he may serve thee as it is fitting.'

Then the king swore to him that he would make him the greatest of his favourites, and the most powerful of his friends, and that he should be with him in all honour and respect. And he kissed his hands and bade him farewell.

And he took Nadan. his sister's son with him and seated him in a parlour and set about teaching him night and day till he had crammed him with wisdom and knowledge more than with bread and water.

CHAPTER II.

A "Poor Richard's Almanac" of ancient days. Immortal precepts of human conduct concerning money, women, dress, business, friends. Especially interesting proverbs are found in Verses 12, 17, 23, 37, 45, 47. Compare Verse 63 with some of the cynicism of today.

THUS he taught him, saying: 'O my son! hear my speech and follow my advice and remember what I say.

O my son! if thou hearest a word, let it die in thy heart, and reveal it not to another, lest it become a live coal and burn thy tongue and cause a pain in thy body, and thou gain a reproach, and art shamed before God and man.

O my son! if thou hast heard a report, spread it not; and if thou hast seen something, tell it not.

O my son! make thy eloquence easy to the listener, and be not hasty to return an answer.

O my son! when thou hast heard anything, hide it not.

O my son! loose not a sealed knot, nor untie it, and seal not a loosened knot.

O my son! covet not outward beauty, for it wanes and passes away, but an

The Forgotten Books of Eden

honourable remembrance lasts for aye.

O my son! let not a silly woman deceive thee with her speech, lest thou die the most miserable of deaths, and she entangle thee in the net till thou art ensnared.

O my son! desire not a woman bedizened with dress and with ointments, who is despicable and silly in her soul. Woe o thee if thou bestow on her anything that is thine, or commit to her what is in thine hand and she entice thee into sin, and God be wroth with thee.

O my son! be not like the almond-tree, for it brings forth leaves before all the trees, and edible fruit after them all, but be like the mulberry-tree, which brings forth edible fruit before all the trees, and leaves after them all.

O my son! bend thy head low down, and soften thy voice, and be courteous, and walk in the straight path, and be not foolish. And raise not thy voice when thou laughest for if it were by a loud voice that a house was built, the ass would build many houses every day; and if it were by dint of strength that the plough were driven, the plough would never be removed from under the shoulders of the camels.

O m son! the removing of stones with a wise man is better than the drinking of wine with a sorry man.

O my son! pour out thy wine on the tombs of the just, and drink not with ignorant, contemptible people.

O my son! cleave to wise men who fear God and be like them, and go not near the ignorant, lest thou become like him and learn his ways.

O my son! when thou hast got thee a comrade or a friend, try him, and afterwards make him a comrade and a friend; and do not praise him without a trial; and do not spoil thy speech with a man who lacks wisdom.

O my son! while a shoe stays on thy foot, walk with it on the thorns, and make a road for thy son, and for thy household and thy children, and make thy ship taut before she goes on the sea and its waves and sinks and cannot he saved.

O my son! if the rich man eat a snake, they say,—"It is by his wisdom," and if a poor man eat it, the people say, "From his hunger."

O my son! he content with thy daily bread and thy goods, and covet not what is another's.

O my son! be not neighbour to the fool, and eat not bread with him, and rejoice not in the calamities of thy neighbours. [*1] If thine enemy wrong thee, show him kindness.

O my son! a man who fears God do thou fear him and honour him.

O my son! the ignorant man falls and stumbles, and the wise man, even if he stumbles, he is not shaken, and even if he falls he gets up quickly, and if he is sick, he can take care of his life. But as for the ignorant, stupid man, for his disease there is no drug.

The Forgotten Books of Eden

O my son! if a man approach thee who is inferior to thyself, go forward to meet him, and remain standing, and if he cannot recompense thee, his Lord will recompense thee for him.

O my son! spare not to beat thy son, for the drubbing of thy son is like manure to the garden, and like tying the mouth of a purse, and like the tethering of beasts, and like the bolting of the door.

O my son! restrain thy son from wickedness, and teach him manners before he rebels against thee and brings thee into contempt amongst the people and thou hang thy head in the streets and the assemblies and thou be punished for the evil of his wicked deeds.

O my son! get thee a fat ox with a foreskin, and an ass great with its hoofs, and get not an ox with large horns, nor make friends with a tricky man, nor get a quarrelsome slave, nor a thievish handmaid, for everything which thou committest to them they will ruin.

O my son! let not thy parents curse thee, and the Lord be pleased with them; for it hath been said, "He who despiseth his father or his mother let him die the death (I mean the death of sin); and he who honoureth his parents shall prolong his days and his life and shall see all that is good."

O my son! walk not on the road without weapons, for thou knowest not when the foe may meet thee, so that thou mayst be ready for him.

O my son! be not like a bare, leafless tree that doth not grow, but be like a tree covered with its leaves and its boughs; for the man who has neither wife nor children is disgraced in the world and is hated by them, like a leafless and fruitless tree.

O my son! be like a fruitful tree on the roadside, whose fruit is eaten by all who pass by, and the beasts of the desert rest under its shade and eat of its leaves.

O my son! every sheep that wanders from its path and its companions becomes food for the wolf.

O my son! say not, "My lord is a fool and I am wise," and relate not the speech of ignorance and folly, lest thou be despised by him.

O my son! be not one of those servants, to whom their lords say, "Get away from us," but be one of those to whom they say, "Approach and come near to us."

O my son! caress not thy slave in the presence of his companion, for thou knowest not which of them shall be of most value to thee in the end.

O my son! be not afraid of thy Lord who created thee, lest He be silent to thee.

O my son! make thy speech fair and sweeten thy tongue; and permit not thy companion to tread on thy foot, lest he tread at another time on thy breast.

O my son! if thou beat a wise man with a word of wisdom, it will lurk in his breast like a subtle sense of shame; but if thou drub the ignorant with a stick he will neither

The Forgotten Books of Eden

understand nor hear.

O my son! if thou send a wise man for thy needs, do not give him many orders, for he will do thy business as thou desirest: and if thou send a fool, do not order him, but go thyself and do thy business, for if thou order him, he will not do what thou desirest. If they send thee on business, hasten to fulfil it quickly.

O my son! make not an enemy of a man stronger than thyself, for he will take thy measure, and his revenge on thee.

O my son! make trial of thy son, and of thy servant, before thou committest thy belongings to them, lest they make away with them; for he who hath a full hand is called wise, even if he be stupid and ignorant, and he who hath an empty hand is called poor, ignorant, even if he be the prince of sages.

O my son! I have eaten a colocynth, and swallowed aloes, and I have found nothing more bitter than poverty and scarcity.

O my son! teach thy son frugality and hunger, that he may do well in the management of his household.

O my son! teach not to the ignorant the language of wise men, for it will be burdensome to him.

O my son! display not thy condition to thy friend, lest thou be despised by him.

O my son! the blindness of the heart is more grievous than the blindness of the eyes, for the blindness of the eyes may be guided little by little, but the blindness of the heart is not guided, and it leaves the straight path, and goes in a crooked way.

O my son! the stumbling of a man with his foot is better than the stumbling of a n with his tongue.

O my son! a friend who is near is better than a more excellent brother who is far away.

O my son! beauty fades but learning lasts, and the world wanes and becomes vain, but a good name neither becomes vain nor wanes.

O my son! the man who hath no rest, his death were better than his life; and the sound of weeping is better than the sound of sinsing; for sorrow and weeping, if the fear of God be in them, are better than the sound of sinsing and rejoicing.

O my child! the thigh of a frog in thy hand is better than a goose in the pot of thy neighbour; and a sheep near thee is better than an ox far away; and a sparrow in thy hand is better than a thousand sparrows flying; [*1] and poverty which gathers is better than the scattering of much provision; and a living fox is better than a dead lion; and a pound of wool is better than a pound of wealth, I mean of gold and silver; for the gold and the silver are hidden and covered up in the earth, and are not seen; but the wool stays in the markets and it is seen, and it is a beauty to him who wears it.

O my son! a small fortune is better than a scattered fortune.

The Forgotten Books of Eden

O my son! a living dog is better than a dead poor man.

O my son! a poor man who does right is better than a rich man who is dead in sins.

O my son! keep a word in thy heart, and it shall be much to thee, and beware lost thou reveal the secret of thy friend.

O my son! let not a word issue from thy mouth till thou hast taken counsel with thy heart. And stand not betwixt persons quarrelling, because from a bad word there comes a quarrel, and from a quarrel there comes war, and from war there comes fighting, and thou wilt be forced to bear witness; but run from thence and rest thyself.

O my son! withstand not a man stronger than thyself, but get thee a patient spirit, and endurance and an upright conduct, for there is nothing more excellent than that.

O my son! hate not thy first friend, for the second one may not last.

O my son! visit the poor in his affliction, and speak of him in the Sultan's presence, and do thy diligence to save him from the mouth of the lion. [*2]

O my son! rejoice not in the death of thine enemy, for after a little while thou shalt be his neighbour, and him who mocks thee do thou respect and honour and be beforehand with him in greeting.

O my son! if water would stand still in heaven, and a black crow become white, and myrrh grow sweet as honey, then ignorant men and fools might understand and become wise.

O my son! if thou desire to be wise, restrain thy tongue from lying, and thy hand from stealing, and thine eyes from beholding evil; then thou wilt be called wise.

O my son! let the wise man beat thee with a rod, but let not the fool anoint thee with sweet salve. Be humble in thy youth and thou shalt be honoured in thine old age.

O my son! withstand not a man in the days of his power, nor a river in the days of its flood.

O my son! be not hasty in the wedding of a wife, for if it turns out well, she will say, 'My lord, make provision for me'; and if it turns out ill, she will rate at him who was the cause of it.

O my son! whosoever is elegant in his dress, he is the same in his speech; and he who has a mean appearance in his dress, he also is the same in his speech.

O my son! if thou hast committed a theft, make it known to the Sultan, and give him a share of it, that thou mayst be delivered from him, for otherwise thou wilt endure bitterness.

O my son! make a friend of the man whose hand is satisfied and filled, and make no friend of the man whose hand is closed and hungry.

There are four things in which neither the king nor his army can be secure: oppression by the vizier, and bad government, and perversion of the will, and tyranny over the subject; and four things which cannot be hidden: the prudent, and the foolish, and the rich, and the poor.'

CHAPTER III.

Ahikar retires from active participation in affairs of state. He turns over his possessions to his treacherous nephew. Here is the amazing story of how a thankless profligate turns forger. A clever plot to entangle Ahikar results in his being condemned to death. Apparently the end of Ahikar.

THUS spake Haiqar, and when he had finished these injunctions and proverbs to Nadan, his sister's son, he imasined that he would keep them all, and he knew not that instead of that he was displaying to him weariness and contempt and mockery.

Thereafter Haiqar sat still in his house and delivered over to Nadan all his goods, and the slaves, and the handmaidens, and the horses, and the cattle, and everything else that he had possessed and gained; and the power of bidding and of forbidding remained in the hand of Nadan.

And Haiqar sat at rest in his house, and every now and then Haiqar went and paid his respects to the king, and returned home.

Now when Nadan perceived that the power of bidding and of forbidding was in his own hand, he despised the position of Haiqar and scoffed at him, and set about blaming him whenever he appeared, saying, 'My uncle Haiqar is in his dotage, and he knows nothing now.'

And he began to beat the slaves and the handmaidens, and to sell the horses and the camels and be spendthrift with all that his uncle Haiqar had owned.

And when Haiqar saw that he had no compassion on his servants nor on his household, he arose and chased him from his house, and sent to inform the king that he had scattered his possessions and his provision.

And the king arose and called Nadan and said to him: 'Whilst Haiqar remains in health, no one shall rule over his goods, nor over his household, nor over his possessions.'

And the hand of Nadan was lifted off from his uncle Haiqar and from all his goods, and in the meantime he went neither in nor out, nor did he greet him.

Thereupon Haiqar repented him of his toil with Nadan his sister's son, and he continued to be very sorrowful.

And Nadan had a younger brother named Benuzardan, so Haiqar took him to himself in place of Nadan, and brought up and honoured him with the utmost honour. And he delivered over to him all that he possessed, and made him governor of his house.

Now when Nadan perceived what had happened he was seized with envy and jealousy, and he began to complain to every one who questioned him, and to mock his, uncle Haiqar, saying: 'My uncle has chased me from his house, and has preferred my brother to me, but if the Most High God give me the power, I shall bring upon him the misfortune of being killed.'

And Nadan continued to meditate as to the stumbling-block he might contrive for him. And after a while Nadan turned it over in his mind, and wrote a letter to Achish, son of Shah the Wise, king of Persia, saying thus:

'Peace and health and might and honour from Sennacherib king of Assyria and Nineveh, and from his vizier and his secretary Haiqar unto thee, O great king! Let there be pence between thee and me.

And when this letter reaches thee, if thou wilt arise and go quickly to the plain of Nisrin, and to Assyria, and Nineveh, I will deliver up the kingdom to thee without war and without battle-array.'

And he wrote also another letter in the name of Haiqar to Pharaoh king of Egypt. 'Let there be peace between thee and me, O mighty king!

If at the time of this letter reaching thee thou wilt arise and go to Assyria and Nineveh to the plain of Nisrin, I will deliver up to thee the kingdom without war and without fighting.'

And the writing of Nadan was like to the writing of his uncle Haiqar.

Then he folded the two letters, and sealed them with the seal of his uncle Haiqar; they were nevertheless in the king's palace.

Then he went and wrote a letter likewise from the king to his uncle Haiqar: 'Peace and health to my Vizier, my Secretary, my Chancellor, Haiqar.

O Haiqar, when this letter reaches thee, assemble all the soldiers who are with thee, and let them be perfect in clothing and in numbers, and bring them to me on the fifth day in the plain of Nisrin.

And when thou shalt see me there coming towards thee, haste and make the army move against me as an enemy who would fight with me, for I have with me the ambassadors of Pharaoh king of Egypt, that they may see the strength of our army and may fear us, for they are our enemies and they hate us.'

Then he sealed the letter and sent it to Haiqar by one of the king's servants. And he took the other letter which he had written and spread it before the king and read it to him and showed him the seal.

And when the king heard what was in the letter he was perplexed with a great perplexity and was wroth with a great and fierce wrath, and said, 'Ah, I have shown my wisdom! what have I done to Haiqar that he has written these letters to my enemies? Is this my recompense from him for my benefits to him?'

And Nadan said to him, 'Be not grieved, O king! nor be wroth, but let us go to the plain of Nisrin and see if the tale be true or not.'

Then Nadan arose on the fifth day and took the king and the soldiers and the vizier, and they went to the desert to the plain of Nisrin. And the king looked, and lo! Haiqar and the army were set in array.

And when Haiqar saw that the king was there, he approached and signalled to the army to move as in war and to fight in array against the king as it had been found in the letter, he not knowing what a pit Nadan had digged for him.

And when the king saw the act of Haiqar he was seized with anxiety and terror and perplexity, and was wroth with a great wrath.

And Nadan said to him, 'Hast thou seen, O my lord the king! what this wretch has done? but be not thou wroth and be not grieved nor pained, but go to thy house and sit on thy throne, and I will bring Haiqar to thee bound and chained with chains, and I will chase away thine enemy from thee without toil.'

And the king returned to his throne, being provoked about Haiqar, and did nothing concerning him. And Nadan went to Haiqar and said to him, 'W'allah, O my uncle! The king verily rejoiceth in thee with great joy and thanks thee for having done what he commanded thee.

And now he hath sent me to thee that thou mayst dismiss the soldiers to their duties and come thyself to him with thy hands bound behind thee, and thy feet chained, that the ambassadors of Pharaoh may see this, and that the king may be feared by them and by their king.'

Then answered Haiqar and said, 'To hear is to obey.' And he arose straightway and bound his hands behind him, and chained his feet.

And Nadan took him and went with him to the king. And when Haiqar entered the king's presence he did obeisance before him on the ground, and wished for power and perpetual life to the king.

Then said the king, 'O Haiqar, my Secretary, the Governor of my affairs, my Chancellor, the ruler of my State, tell me what evil have I done to thee that thou hast rewarded me by this ugly deed.'

Then they showed him the letters in his writing and with his seal. And when Haiqar saw this, his limbs trembled and his tongue was tied at once, and he was unable to speak a word from fear; but he hung his head towards the earth and was dumb.

And when the king saw this, he felt certain that the thing was from him, and he straightway arose and commanded them to kill Haiqar, and to strike his neck with the sword outside of the city.

Then Nadan screamed and said, 'O Haiqar, O blackface! what avails thee thy meditation or thy power in the doing of this deed to the king?'

Thus says the story-teller. And the name of the swordsman was Abu Samik. And the king said to him, 'O swordsman! arise, go, cleave the neck of Haiqar at the door of his house, and cast away his head from his body a hundred cubits.'

The Forgotten Books of Eden

Then Haiqar knelt before the king, and said, 'Let my lord the king live for ever! and if thou desire to slay me, let thy wish be fulfilled; and I know that I am not guilty, but the wicked man bas to give an account of his wickedness; nevertheless, O my lord the king! I beg of thee and of thy friendship, permit the swordsman to give my body to my slaves, that they may bury me, and let thy slave be thy sacrifice.'

The king arose and commanded the swordsman to do with him according to his desire.

And he straightway commanded his servants to take Haiqar and the swordsman and go with him naked that they might slay him.

And when Haiqar knew for certain that he was to be slain he sent to his wife, and said to her, 'Come out and meet me, and let there be with thee a thousand young virsins, and dress them in gowns of purple and silk that they may weep for me before my death.

And prepare a table for the swordsman and for his servants. And mingle plenty of wine, that they may drink.'

And she did all that he commanded her. And she was very wise, clever, and prudent. And she united all possible courtesy and learning.

And when the army of the king and the swordsman arrived the found the table set in order, and the wine and the luxurious viands, and they began eating and drinking till they were gorged and drunken.

Then Haiqar took the swordsman aside apart from the company and said, 'O Abu Samik, dost thou not know that when Sarhadum the king, the father of Sennacherib, wanted to kill thee, I took thee and hid thee in a certain place till the king's anger subsided and he asked for thee?

And when I brought thee into his presence he rejoiced in thee: and now remember the kindness I did thee.

And I know that the king will repent him about me and will be wroth with a great wrath about my execution.

For I am not guilty, and it shall be when thou shalt present me before him in his palace, thou shalt meet with great good fortune, and know that Nadan my sister's son has deceived me and has done this bad deed to me, and the king will repent of having slain me; and now I have a cellar in the garden of my house, and no one knows of it.

Hide me in it with the knowledge of my wife. And I have a slave in prison who deserves to be killed.

Bring him out and dress him in my clothes, and command the servants when they are drunk to slay him. They will not know who it is they are killing.

And cast away his head a hundred cubits from his body, and give his body to my slaves that they may bury it. And thou shalt have laid up a great treasure with me.

And then the swordsman did as Haiqar had commanded him, and he went to the king and said to him, 'May thy head live for ever!'

Then Haiqar's wife let down to him in the hiding-place every week what sufficed for him, and no one knew of it but herself.

And the story was reported and repeated and spread abroad in every place of how Haiqar the Sage had been slain and was dead, and all the people of that city mourned for him.

And they wept and said: 'Alas for thee, O Haiqar! and for thy learning and thy courtesy! How sad about thee and about thy knowledge! Where can another like thee be found? and where can there be a man so intelligent, so learned, so skilled in ruling as to resemble thee that he may fill thy place?'

But the king was repenting about Haiqar, and his repentance availed him naught.

Then he called for Nadan and said to him, 'Go and take thy friends with thee and make a mourning and a weeping for thy uncle Haiqar, and lament for him as the custom is, doing honour to his memory.'

But when Nadan, the foolish, the ignorant, the hardhearted, went to the house of his uncle, he neither wept nor sorrowed nor wailed, but assembled heartless and dissolute people and set about eating and drinking. [*1]

And Nadan began to seize the maidservants and the slaves belonging to Haiqar, and bound them and tortured them and drubbed them with a sore drubbing.

And he did not respect the wife of his uncle, she who had brought him up like her own boy, but wanted her to fall into sin with him.

But Haiqar had been cut into the hiding-place, and he heard the weeping of his slaves and his neighbours, and he praised the Most High God, the Merciful One, and gave thanks, and he always prayed and besought the Most High God.

And the swordsman came from time to time to Haiqar whilst he was in the midst of the hiding-place: and Haiqar came and entreated him. And he comforted him and wished him deliverance.

And when the story was reported in other countries that Haiqar the Sage had been slain, all the kings were grieved and despised king Sennacherib, and they lamented over Haiqar the solver of riddles.

CHAPTER IV.

"The Riddles of the Sphinx." What really happened to Ahikar. His return.

AND when the king of Egypt had made sure that Haiqar was slain, he arose straightway and wrote a letter to king Sennacherib, reminding him in it 'of the peace and the health and the might and the honour which we wish specially for thee, my beloved brother, king Sennacherib.

I have been desiring to build a castle between the heaven and the earth, and I

The Forgotten Books of Eden

want thee to send me a wise, clever man from thyself to build it for me, and to answer me all my questions, and that I may have the taxes and the custom duties of Assyria for three years.'

Then he sealed the letter and sent it to Sennacherib.

He took it and read it and gave it to his viziers and to the nobles of his kingdom, and they were perplexed and ashamed, and he was wroth with a great wrath, and was puzzled about how he should act.

Then he assembled the old men and the learned men and the wise men and the philosophers, and the diviners and the astrologers, and every one who was in his country, and read them the letter and said to them, 'Who amongst you will go to Pharaoh king of Egypt and answer him his questions?'

And they said to him, 'O our lord the king! know thou that there is none in thy kingdom who is acquainted with these questions except Haiqar, thy vizier and secretary.

But as for us, we have no skill in this, unless it be Nadan, his sister's son, for he taught him all his wisdom and learning and knowledge. Call him to thee, perchance he may untie this hard knot.'

Then the king called Nadan and said to him, 'Look at this letter and understand what is in it.' And when Nadan read it, he said, 'O my lord! who is able to build a castle between the heaven and the earth?'

And when the king heard the speech of Nadan he sorrowed with a great and sore sorrow, and stepped down from his throne and sat in the ashes, and began to weep and wail over Haiqar.

Saying, 'O my grief! O Haiqar, who didst know the secrets and the riddles! woe is me for thee, O Haiqar! O teacher of my country and ruler of my kingdom, where shall I find thy like? O Haiqar, O teacher of my country, where shall I turn for thee? woe is me for thee! how did I destroy thee! and I listened to the talk of a stupid, ignorant boy without knowledge, without religion, without manliness.

Ah! and again Ah for myself! who can give thee to me just for once, or bring me word that Haiqar is alive? and I would give him the half of my kingdom.

Whence is this to me? Ah, Haiqar! that I might see thee just for once, that I might take my fill of gazing at thee, and delighting in thee.

Ah! O my grief for thee to all time! O Haiqar, how have I killed thee! and I tarried not in thy case till I had seen the end of the matter.'

And the king went on weeping night and day. Now when the swordsman saw the wrath of the king and his sorrow for Haiqar, his heart was softened towards him,, and he approached into his presence and said to him:

'O my lord! command thy servants to cut off my head.' Then said the king to him: 'Woe to thee, Abu Samik, what is thy fault?'

The Forgotten Books of Eden

And the swordsman said unto him, 'O my master! every slave who acts contrary to the word of his master is killed, and I have acted contrary to thy command.'

Then the king said unto him. 'Woe unto thee, O Abu Samik, in what hast thou acted contrary to my command?'

And the swordsman said unto him, 'O my lord! thou didst command me to kill Haiqar, and I knew that thou wouldst repent thee concerning him, and that he had been wronged, and I hid him in a certain place, and I killed one of his slaves, and he is now safe in the cistern, and if thou command me I will bring him to thee.'

And the king said unto him. 'Woe to thee, O Abu Samik! thou hast mocked me and I am thy lord.'

And the swordsman said unto him, 'Nay, but by the life of thy head, O my lord! Haiqar is safe and alive.'

And when the king heard that saying, he felt sure of the matter, and his head swam, and he fainted from joy, and he commanded them to bring Haiqar.

And he said to the swordsman, 'O trusty servant! if thy speech be true, I would fain enrich thee, and exalt thy dignity above that of all thy friends.'

And the swordsman went along rejoicing till he came to Haiqar's house. And he opened the door of the hiding-place, and went down and found Haiqar sitting, praising God, and thanking Him.

And he shouted to him, saying, 'O Haiqar, I bring the greatest of joy, and happiness, and delight!'

And Haiqar said to him, 'What is the news, O Abu Samik?' And he told him all about Pharaoh from the besinning to the end. Then he took him and went to the king.

And when the king looked at him, he saw him in a state of want, and that his hair had grown long like the wild beasts' and his nails like the claws of an eagle, and that his body was dirty with dust, and the colour of his face had changed and faded and was now like ashes.

And when the king saw him he sorrowed over him and rose at once and embraced him and kissed him, and wept over him and said: 'Praise be to God! who hath brought thee back to me.'

Then he consoled him and comforted him. And he stripped off his robe, and put it on the swordsman, and was very gracious to him, and gave him great wealth, and made Haiqar rest.

Then said Haiqar to the king, 'Let my lord the king live for ever! These be the deeds of the children of the world. I have reared me a palm-tree that I might lean on it, and it bent sideways, and threw me down.

But, O my Lord! since I have appeared fore thee, let not care oppress thee! And the king said to him: 'Blessed be God, who showed thee mercy, and knew that thou wast wronged, and saved thee and delivered thee from being slain.

But go to the warm bath, and shave thy head, and cut thy nails, and change thy clothes, and amuse thyself for the space of forty days, that thou mayst do good to thyself and improve thy condition and the colour of thy face may come back to thee.'

Then the king stripped off his costly robe, and put it on Haiqar, and Haiqar thanked God and did obeisance to the king, and departed to his dwelling glad and happy, praising the Most High God.

And the people of his household rejoiced with him, and his friends and every one who heard that he was alive rejoiced also.

CHAPTER V.

The letter of the "riddles" is shown to Ahikar. The boys on the eagles. The first "airplane" ride. Off to Egypt. Ahikar, being a man of wisdom also has a sense of humor. (Verse 27).

AND he did as the king commanded him, and took rest for forty days.

Then he dressed himself his gayest dress, and went riding to the king, with his slaves behind him and before him, rejoicing and delighted.

But when Nadan his sister's son perceived what was happening, fear took hold of him and terror, and he was perplexed, not knowing what to do.

And when Haiqar saw it he entered into the king's presence and greeted him, and he returned the greeting, and made him sit down at his side, saying to him, 'O my darling Haiqar! look at these letters which the, king of Egypt sent to us, after he had heard that thou wast slain.

They have provoked us and overcome us, and many of the people of our country have fled to Egypt for fear of the taxes that the king of Egypt has sent to demand from us.

Then Haiqar took the letter and read it and understood its contents.

Then he said to the king. 'Be not wroth, O my lord! I will go to Egypt, and I will return the answers to Pharaoh, and I will display this letter to him, and I will reply to him about the taxes, and I will send back all those who have run away; and I will put thy enemies to shame with the help of the Most High God, and for the Happiness of thy kingdom.'

And when the king heard this speech from Haiqar he rejoiced with a great joy, and his heart was expanded and he showed him favour.

And Haiqar said to the king: 'Grant me a delay of forty days that I may consider this question and manage it.' And the king permitted this.

And Haiqar went to his dwelling, and he commanded the huntsmen to capture two young eaglets for him, and they captured them and brought them to him: and he commanded the weavers of ropes to weave two cables of cotton for him, each of them two thousand cubits long, and he had the carpenters brought and ordered them to make two great boxes, and they did this.

Then he took two little lads, and spent every day sacrificing lambs and feeding the eagles and the boys, and making the boys ride on the backs of the eagles, and he bound them with a firm knot, and tied the cable to the feet of the eagles, and let them soar upwards little by little every day, to a distance of ten cubits, till they grew accustomed and were educated to it; and they rose all the length of the rope till they reached the sky; the boys being on their backs. Then he drew them to himself.

And when Haiqar saw that his desire was fulfilled he charged the boys that when they were borne aloft to the sky they were to shout, saying:

'Bring us clay and stone, that we may build a castle for king Pharaoh, for we are idle.'

And Haiqar was never done training them and exercising them till they had reached the utmost possible point (of skill).

Then leaving them he went to the king and said to him, 'O my lord! the work is finished according to thy desire. Arise with me that I may show thee the wonder.'

So the king sprang up and sat with Haiqar and went to a wide place and sent to bring the eagles and the boys, and Haiqar tied them and let them off into the air all the length of the ropes, and they began to shout as he had taught them. Then he drew them to himself and put them in their places.

And the king and those who were with him wondered with a great wonder: and the king kissed Haiqar between his eyes and said to him, 'Go in peace, O my beloved! O pride of my kingdom! to Egypt and answer the questions of Pharaoh and overcome him by the strength of the Most High God.'

Then he bade him farewell, and took his troops and his army and the young men and the eagles, and went towards the dwellings of Egypt; and when he had arrived, he turned towards the country of the king.

And when the people of Egypt knew that Sennacherib had sent a man of his Privy Council to talk with Pharaoh and to answer his questions, they carried the news to king Pharaoh, and he sent a party of his Privy Councillors to bring him before him.

And he came and entered into the presence of Pharaoh, and did obeisance to him as it is fitting to do to kings.

And he said to him: 'O my lord the king! Sennacherib the king hails thee with abundance of peace and might, and honour.

And he has sent me, who am one of his slaves, that I may answer thee thy questions, and may fulfil all thy desire: for thou hast sent to seek from my lord the king a man who will build thee a castle between the heaven and the earth.

And I by the help of the Most High God and thy noble favour and the power of my

The Forgotten Books of Eden

lord the king will build it for thee as thou desirest.

But, O my lord the king! what thou hast said in it about the taxes of Egypt for three years—now the stability of a kingdom is strict justice, and if thou winnest and my hand hath no skill in replying to thee, then my lord the king will send thee the taxes which thou hast mentioned.

And if I shall have answered thee in thy questions, it shall remain for thee to send whatever thou hast mentioned to my lord the king.'

And when Pharaoh heard that speech, he wondered and was perplexed by the freedom of his tongue and the pleasantness of his speech.

And king Pharaoh said to him, 'O man! what is thy name?' And he said, 'Thy servant is Abiqam, and I a little ant of the ants of king Sennacherib.'

And Pharaoh said to him, 'Had thy lord no one of higher dignity than thee, that he has sent me a little ant to reply to me, and to converse with me?'

And Haiqar said to him, 'O my lord the king! I would to God Most High that I may fulfil what is on thy mind, for God is with the weak that He may confound the strong.'

Then Pharaoh commanded that they should prepare a dwelling for Abiqam and supply him with provender, meat, and drink, and all that he needed.

And when it was finished, three days afterwards Pharaoh clothed himself in purple and red and sat on his throne, and all his viziers and the magnates of his kingdom were standing with their hands crossed, their feet close together, and their heads bowed.

And Pharaoh sent to fetch Abiqam, and when he was presented to him, he did obeisance before him, and kissed the ground in front of him.

And king Pharaoh said to him, 'O Abiqam, whom am I like? and the nobles of my kingdom, to whom are they like?'

And Haiqar said to him, 'O my lord the kin I thou art like the idol Bel, and the nobles of thy kingdom are like his servants.'

He said to him, 'Go, and come back hither to-morrow.' So Haiqar went as king Pharaoh had commanded him.

And on the morrow Haiqar went into the presence of Pharaoh, and did obeisance, and stood before the king. And Pharaoh was dressed in a red colour, and the nobles were dressed in white.

And Pharaoh said to him 'O Abiqam, whom am I like? and the nobles of my kingdom, to whom are they like?'

And Abiqam said to him, 'O my lord! thou art like the sun, and thy servants are like its beams.' And Pharaoh said to him, 'Go to thy dwelling, and come hither to-morrow.'

Then Pharaoh commanded his Court to wear pure white, and Pharaoh was dressed

The Forgotten Books of Eden

like them and sat upon his throne, and he commanded them to fetch Haiqar. And he entered and sat down before him.

And Pharaoh said to him, 'O Abiqam, whom am I like? and my nobles, to whom are they like?'

And Abiqam said to him, 'O my lord! thou art like the moon, and thy nobles are like the planets and the stars.' And Pharaoh said to him, 'Go, and to-morrow be thou here.'

Then Pharaoh commanded his servants to wear robes of various colours, and Pharaoh wore a red velvet dress, and sat on his throne, and commanded them to fetch Abiqam. And he entered and did obeisance before him.

And he said, 'O Abiqam, whom am I like? and my armies, to whom are they like?' And he said, 'O my lord! thou art like the month of April, and thy armies are like its flowers.'

And when the king heard it he rejoiced with a great joy and said, 'O Abiqam! the first time thou didst compare me to the idol Bel, and my nobles to his servants.

And the second time thou didst compare me to the sun, and my nobles to the sunbeams.

And the third time thou didst compare me to the moon, and my nobles to the planets and the stars.

And the fourth time thou didst compare me to the month of April, and my nobles to its flowers. But now, O Abiqam! tell me, thy lord, king Sennacherib, whom is he like? and his nobles, to whom are they like?'

And Haiqar shouted with a loud voice and said: 'Be it far from me to make mention of my lord the king and thou seated on thy throne. But get up on thy feet that I may tell thee whom my lord the king is like and to whom his nobles are like.'

And Pharaoh was perplexed by the freedom of his tongue and his boldness in answering. Then Pharaoh arose from his throne, and stood before Haiqar, and said to him, 'Tell me now, that I may perceive whom thy lord the king is like, and his nobles, to whom they are like.'

And Haiqar said to him: 'My lord is the God of heaven, and his nobles are the lightnings and the thunder, and when he wills the winds blow and the rain falls.

And he commands the thunder, and it lightens and rains, and he holds the sun, and it gives not its light, and the moon and the stars, and they circle not.

And he commands the tempest, and it blows and the rain falls and it tramples on April and destroys its flowers and its houses.'

And when Pharaoh heard this speech, he was greatly perplexed and was wroth with a great wrath, and said to him: 'O man! tell me the truth, and let me know who thou really art.'

And he told him the truth. 'I am Haiqar the scribe, greatest of the Privy Councillors of king Sennacherib, and I am his vizier and the Governor of his kingdom, and his Chancellor.'

And he said to him, 'Thou hast told the truth in this saying. But we have heard of Haiqar, that king Sennacherib has slain him, yet thou dost seem to be alive and well.'

And Haiqar said to him, 'Yes, so it was, but praise be to God, who knoweth what is hidden, for my lord the king commanded me to be killed, and he believed the word of profligate men, but the Lord delivered me, and blessed is he who trusteth in Him.'

And Pharaoh said to Haiqar, 'Go, and to-morrow be thou here, and tell me a word that I have never heard from my nobles nor from the people of my kingdom and my country.'

CHAPTER VI.

The ruse succeeds. Ahikar answers every question of Pharaoh. The boys on the eagles are the climax of the day. Wit, so rarely found in the ancient Scriptures, is revealed in Verses 34-45.

AND Haiqar went to his dwelling, and wrote a letter, saying in it on this wise:

From Sennacherib king of Assyria. and Nineveh to Pharaoh king of Egypt.

'Peace be to thee, O my brother! and what we make known to thee by this is that a brother has need of his brother, and kings of each other, and my hope from thee is that thou wouldst lend me nine hundred talents of gold, for I need it for the victualling of some of the soldiers, that, I may spend it upon them. And after a little while I will send it thee.'

Then he folded the letter, and presented it on the morrow to Pharaoh.

And when he saw it, he was perplexed and said to him, 'Verily I have never heard anything like this language from any one.'

Then Haiqar said to him, 'Truly this is a debt which thou owest to my lord the king.'

And Pharaoh accepted this, saying, 'O Haiqar, it is the like of thee who are honest in the service of kings.

Blessed be God who hath made thee perfect in wisdom and hath adorned thee with philosophy and knowledge.

And now, O Haiqar, there remains what we desire from thee, that thou shouldst build as a castle between heaven and earth.'

Then said Haiqar, 'To hear is to obey. I will build thee a castle according to thy wish and choice; but, O my lord I prepare us lime and stone and clay and workmen, and I have skilled builders who will build for thee as thou desirest.'

And the king prepared all that for him, and they went to a wide place; and Haiqar and his boys came to it, and he took the eagles and the young men with him; and the king

The Forgotten Books of Eden

and all his nobles went and the whole city assembled, that they might see what Haiqar would do.

Then Haiqar let the eagles out of the boxes, and tied the young men on their backs, and tied the ropes to the eagles' feet, and let them go in the air. And they soared upwards, till they remained between heaven and earth.

And the boys began to shout, saying, 'Bring bricks, bring clay, that we may build the king's castle, for we are standing idle!'

And the crowd were astonished and perplexed, and they wondered. And the king and his nobles wondered.

And Haiqar and his servants began to beat the workmen, and they shouted for the king's troops, saying to them, 'Bring to the skilled workmen what they want and do not hinder them from their work.'

And the king said to him, 'Thou art mad; who can bring anything up to that distance?'

And Haiqar said to him, 'O my lord! how shall we build a castle in the air? and if my lord the king were here, he would have built several castles in a single day.'

And Pharaoh said to him, 'Go, O Haiqar, to thy dwelling, and rest, for we have given up building the castle, and to-morrow come to me.'

Then Haiqar went to his dwelling and on the morrow he appeared before Pharaoh. And Pharaoh said, 'O Haiqar, what news is there of the horse of thy lord? for when he neighs in the country of Assyria and Nineveh, and our mares hear his voice, they cast their young.'

And when Haiqar heard this speech he went and took a cat, and bound her and began to flog her with a violent flogsing till the Egyptians heard it, and they went and told the king about it.

And Pharaoh sent to fetch Haiqar, and said to him, 'O Haiqar, wherefore dost thou flog thus and beat that dumb beast?'

And Haiqar said to him, my lord the king! verily she has done an ugly deed to me, and has deserved this drubbing and flogsing, for my lord king Sennacherib had given me a fine cock, and he had a strong true voice and knew the hours of the day and the night.

And the cat got up this very night and cut off its head and went away, and because of this deed I have treated her to this drubbing.'

And Pharaoh said to him, 'O Haiqar, I see from all this that thou art growing old and art in thy dotage, for between Egypt and Nineveh there are sixty-eight parasangs, and how did she go this very night and cut off the head of thy cock and come back?'

And Haiqar said to him, 'O my lord! if there were such a distance between Egypt and Nineveh how could thy mares hear when my lord the king's horse neighs and cast their young? and how could the voice of the horse reach to Egypt?'

And when Pharaoh heard that, he knew that Haiqar had answered his questions.

And Pharaoh said, 'O Haiqar, I want thee to make me ropes of the sea-sand.'

28 And Haiqar said to him, "O my lord the king! order them to bring me a rope out of the treasury that I may make one like it.'

Then Haiqar went to the back of the house, and bored holes in the rough shore of the sea, and took a handful of sand in his hand, sea-sand, and when the sun rose, and penetrated into the holes, he spread the sand in the sun till it became as if woven like ropes.

And Haiqar said, 'Command thy servants to take these ropes, and whenever thou desirest it, I will weave thee some like them.'

And Pharaoh said, 'O Haiqar, we have a millstone here and it has been broken and I want thee to sew it up.'

Then Haiqar looked at it, and found another stone.

And he said to 'O my lord! I am a foreigner: and I have no tool for sewing.

But I want thee to command thy faithful shoemakers to cut awls from this stone, that I may sew that millstone.'

Then Pharaoh and all his nobles laughed. And he said, 'Blessed be the Most High God, who gave thee this wit and knowledge.'

And when Pharaoh saw that Haiqar had overcome him, and returned him his answers, he at once became excited, and commanded them to collect for him three years' taxes, and to bring them to Haiqar.

And he stripped off his robes and put them upon Haiqar, and his soldiers, and his servants, and gave him the expenses of his journey.

And he said to him, 'Go in peace, O strength of his lord and pride of his Doctors! have any of the Sultans thy like? give my greetings to thy lord king Sennacherib, and say to him how we have sent him gifts, for kings are content with little.'

Then Haiqar arose, and kissed king Pharaoh's hands and kissed the ground in front of him, and wished him strength and continuance, and abundance in his treasury, and said to him, 'O my lord! I desire from thee that not one of our countrymen may remain in Egypt.'

And Pharaoh arose and sent heralds to proclaim in the streets of Egypt that not one of the people of Assyria or Nineveh should remain in the land of Egypt, but that they should go with Haiqar.

Then Haiqar went and took leave of king Pharaoh, and journeyed, seeking the land of Assyria and Nineveh; and he had some treasures and a great deal of wealth.

The Forgotten Books of Eden

And when the news reached king Sennacherib that Haiqar was coming, he went out to meet him and rejoiced over him exceedingly with great joy and embraced him and kissed him and said to him, 'Welcome home: O kinsman! my brother Haiqar, the strength of my kingdom, and pride of my realm.

Ask what thou would'st have from me, even if thou desirest the half of my kingdom and of my possessions.'

Then said Haiqar unto him, 'O my lord the king, live for ever! Show favour, O my lord the king! to Abu Samik in my stead, for my life was in the hands of God and in his.'

Then said Sennacherib the king, 'Honour be to thee, O my beloved Haiqar! I will make the station of Abu Samik the swordsman higher than all my Privy Councillors and my favourites.'

Then the king began to ask him how he had got on with Pharaoh from his first arrival until he had come away from his presence, and how he had answered all his questions, and how he had received the taxes from him, and the changes of raiment and the presents.

And Sennacherib the king rejoiced with a great joy, and said to Haiqar, 'Take what thou wouldst fain have of this tribute, for it is all within the grasp of thy hand.'

And Haiqar mid: 'Let the king live for ever! I desire naught but the safety of my lord the king and the continuance of his greatness.

O my lord! what can I do with wealth and its like? but if thou wilt show me favour, give me Nadan, my sister's son, that I may recompense him for what he has done to me, and grant me his blood and hold me guiltless of it.'

And Sennacherib the king said, 'Take him, I have given him to thee.' And Haiqar took Nadan, his sister's son, and bound his hands with chains of iron, and took him to his dwelling, and put a heavy fetter on his feet, and tied it with a tight knot, and after binding him thus he cast him into a dark room, beside the retiring-place, and appointed Nebu-hal as sentinel over him to give him a loaf of bread and a little water every day.

CHAPTER VII.

The parables of Ahikar in which he completes his nephews education. Striking similes. Ahikar calls the boy picturesque names. Here ends the story of Ahikar.

And whenever Haiqar went in or out he scolded Nadan, his sister's son, saying to him wisely:

O Nadan, my boy! I have done to thee all that is good and kind and thou hast rewarded me for it with what is ugly and bad and with killing.

'O my son! it is said in the proverbs: He who listeneth not with his ear, they will make him listen with the scruff of his neck.'

And Nadan said, 'For what cause art thou wroth with me?'

The Forgotten Books of Eden

And Haiqar said to him, 'Because I brought thee up, and taught thee, and gave thee honour and respect and made thee great, and reared thee with the best of breeding, and seated thee in my place that thou mightest be my heir in the world, and thou didst treat me with killing and didst repay me with my ruin.

But the Lord knew that I was wronged, and He saved me from the ware which thou hadst set for me, for the Lord healeth the broken hearts and hindereth the envious and the haughty.

O my boy! thou hast been to me like the scorpion which when it strikes on brass, pierces it.

O my boy! thou art like the gazelle who was eating the roots of the madder, and it add me to-day and to-morrow they will tan they hide in my roots."

O my boy! thou hast been to who saw his comrade naked in the chilly time of winter; and he took cold water and poured it on him.

O my boy! thou hast been to me like a man who took a stone, and threw it up to heaven to stone his Lord with it. And the stone did not hit, and did not reach high enough, but it became the cause of guilt and sin.

O my boy! if thou hadst honoured me and respected me and hadst listened to my words thou wouldst have been my heir and wouldst have reigned over my dominions.

O my son! know thou that if the tail of the dog or the pig were ten cubits long it would not approach to the worth of the horse's even if it were like silk.

O my boy! I thought that thou wouldst have been my heir at my death; and thou through thy envy and thy insolence didst desire to kill me. But the Lord delivered me from thy cunning.

O my son! thou hast been to me like a trap which was set up on the dunghill, and there came a sparrow and found the trap set up. And the sparrow said to the trap, "What doest thou here?" Said the trap, "I am praying here to God."

And the lark asked it also, "What is the piece of wood that thou holdest?" Said the trap, "That is a young oak-tree on which I lean at the time of prayer."

Said the lark: "And what is that thing in thy mouth?" Said the trap: "That is bread and victuals which I carry for all the hungry and the poor who come near to me."

Said the lark: "Now then may I come forward and eat, for I am hungry?" And the trap said to him, "Come forward." And the lark approached that it, might eat.

But the trap sprang up and seized the lark by its neck.

And the lark answered and said to the trap, "If that is thy bread for the hungry God accepteth not thine alms and thy kind deeds.

And if that is thy fasting and thy prayers, God accepteth from thee neither thy fast nor thy prayer, and God will not perfect what is good concerning thee."

The Forgotten Books of Eden

O my boy! thou hast been to me (as) a lion who made friends with an ass, and the ass kept walking before the lion for a time; and one day the lion sprang upon the ass and ate it up.

O my boy! thou hast been to me like a weevil in the wheat, for it does no good to anything, but spoils the wheat and gnaws it.

O my boy! thou hast been like a man who sowed ten measures of wheat, and when it was harvest time, he arose and reaped it, and garnered it, and threshed it, and toiled over it to the very utmost, and it turned out to be ten measures, and its master said to it: "O thou lazy thing! thou hast not grown and thou hast not shrunk."

O my boy! thou hast been to me like the partridge that had been thrown into the net, and she could not save herself, but she called out to the partridges, that she might cast them with herself into the net.

O my son! thou hast been to me like the dog that was cold and it went into the potter's house to get warm. And when it had got warm, it began to bark at them, and they chased it out and beat it, that it might not bite them.

O my son! thou hast been to me like the pig who went into the hot bath with people of quality, and when it came out of the hot bath, it saw a filthy hole and it went down and wallowed in it.

O my son! thou hast been to me like the goat which joined its comrades on their way to the sacrifice, and it was unable to save itself.

O my boy! the dog which is not fed from its hunting becomes food for flies.

O my son! the hand which does not labour and plough and (which) is greedy and cunning shall be cut away from its shoulder.

O my son! the eye in which light is not seen, the ravens shall pick at it and pluck it out.

O my boy! thou hast been to me like a tree whose branches they were cutting, and it said to them, "If something of me were not in your hands, verily you would be unable to cut me."

O my boy! thou art like the cat to whom they said: "Leave off thieving till we make for thee a chain of gold and feed thee with sugar and almonds."

And she said, "I am not forgetful of the craft of my father and my mother."

O my son! thou hast been like the serpent riding on a thorn-bush when he was in the midst of a river, and a wolf saw them and said, "Mischief upon mischief, and let him who is more mischievous than they direct both of them."

And the serpent said to the wolf, "The lambs and the goats and the sheep which thou hast eaten all thy life, wilt thou return them to their fathers and to their parents or no?"

The Forgotten Books of Eden

37 Said the wolf, "No." And the serpent said to him, "I think that after myself thou art the worst of us."

O my boy! I fed thee with good food and thou didst not feed me with dry bread.

O my boy! I gave thee sugared water to drink and good syrup, and thou didst not give me water from the well to drink.

O my boy! I taught thee, and brought thee up, and thou didst dig a hiding-place for me and didst conceal me.

O my boy! I brought thee up with the best upbrinsing and trained thee like a tall cedar; and thou hast twisted and bent me.

O my boy! it was my hope concerning thee that thou wouldst build me a fortified castle, that I might be concealed from my enemies in it, and thou didst become to me like one burying in the depth of the earth; but the Lord took pity on me and delivered me from thy cunning.

O my boy! I wished thee well, and thou didst reward me with evil and hatefulness, and now I would fain tear out thine eyes, and make thee food for dogs, and cut out thy tongue, and take off thy head with the edge of the sword, and recompense thee for thine abominable deeds.'

And when Nadan heard this speech from his uncle Haiqar, he said: 'O my uncle! deal with me according to thy knowledge, and forgive me my sins, for who is there who hath sinned like me, or who is there who forgives like thee?

Accept me, O my uncle! Now I will serve in thy house, and groom thy horses and sweep up the dung of thy cattle, and feed thy sheep, for I am the wicked and thou art the righteous: I the guilty and thou the forgiving.' [*1]

And Haiqar said to him, 'O my boy! thou art like the tree which was fruitless beside the water, and its master was fain to cut it down, and it said to him, "Remove me to another place, and if I do not bear fruit, cut me down."

And its master said to it, "Thou being beside the water hast not borne fruit, how shalt thou bear fruit when thou art in another place?"

O my boy! the old age of the eagle is better than the youth of the crow.

O my boy! they said to the wolf, "Keep away from the sheep lest their dust should harm thee." And the wolf said, "The dregs of the sheep's milk are good for my eyes."

O my boy! they made the wolf go to school that he might learn to read and they said to him, "Say A, B." He said, "Lamb and goat in my bell"

O my boy! they set the ass down at the table and he fell, and began to roll himself in the dust and one said, "Let him roll himself, for it is his nature, he will not change.

O my boy! the saying has been confirmed which runs: "If thou begettest a boy, call him thy son, and if thou rearest a boy, call him thy slave."

The Forgotten Books of Eden

O my boy! he who doeth good shall meet with good; and he who doeth evil shall meet with evil, for the Lord requiteth a man according to the measure of his work.

O my boy! what shall I say more to thee than these sayings? for the Lord knoweth what is hidden, and is acquainted with the mysteries and the secrets.

And He will requite thee and will judge, betwixt me and thee, and will recompense thee according to thy desert.',

And when Nadan heard that speech from his uncle Haiqar, he swelled up immediately and became like a blown-out bladder.

And his limbs swelled and his legs and his feet and his side, and he was torn and his belly burst asunder and his entrails were scattered, and he perished, and died.

And his latter end was destruction, and he went to hell. For he who digs a pit for his brother shall fall into it; and he who sets up traps shall be caught in them.

This is what happened and (what) we found about the tale of Haiqar, and praise be to God for ever. Amen, and peace.

This chronicle is finished with the help of God, may He be exalted! Amen, Amen, Amen.

THE TESTAMENTS OF THE TWELVE PATRIARCHS

THE following twelve books are biographies written between 107 and 137 B.C. They are a forceful exposition, showing how a Pharisee with a rare gift of writing secured publicity by using the names of the greatest men of ancient times. "There were intellectual giants in those days" and the Twelve Patriarchs were the Intellectual Giants!

Each is here made to tell his life story. When he is on his deathbed he calls all his children and grandchildren and great-grandchildren about him, and proceeds without reservation to lay bare his experiences for the moral guidance of his hearers. If he fell into sin he tells all about it and then counsels them not to err as he did. If he was virtuous, he shows what rewards were his.

When you look beyond the unvarnished—almost brutally frank—passages of the text, you will discern a remarkable attestation of the expectations of the Messiah which existed a hundred years before Christ. And there is another element of rare value in this strange series. As Dr. R. H. Charles says in his scholarly work on the Pseudepigrapha: its ethical teaching "has achieved a real immortality by influencing the thought and diction of the writers of the New Testament, and even those of our Lord. This ethical teaching, which is very much higher and purer than that of the Old Testament, is yet its true spiritual child and helps to bridge the chasm that divides the ethics of the Old and New Testaments."

The instances of the influence of these writings on the New Testament are notable in the Sermon on the Mount which reflects the spirit and even uses phrases from these Testaments. St. Paul appears to have borrowed so freely that it seems as though he must have carried a copy of the Testaments with him on his travels.

The Forgotten Books of Eden

Thus, the reader has before him in these pages what is at once striking for its blunt primitive style and valuable as some of the actual source books of the Bible.

TESTAMENT OF REUBEN

The First-Born Son of Jacob and Leah.

CHAPTER I.

Reuben, the first-born son of Jacob and Leah. The man of experience counsels against fornication and points out the ways in. which men are most apt to fall into error.

THE Copy of the Testament of Reuben, even the commands which he gave his sons before he died in the hundred and twenty-fifth year of his life.

Two years after the death of Joseph his brother, when Reuben fell ill, his sons and his sons' sons were gathered together to visit him. And he said to them: My children, behold I am dying, and go the way of my fathers.

And seeing there Judah, and Gad, and Asher, his brethren, he said to them: Raise me up that I may tell to my brethren and to my children what things I have hidden in my heart, for behold now at length I am passing away.

And he arose and kissed them, and said unto them: Hear, my brethren, and do ye my children, give ear to Reuben your father, in the commands which I give unto you.

And behold I call to witness against you this day the God of heaven, that ye walk not in the sins of youth and fornication, wherein I was poured out, and defiled the bed of my father Jacob.

And I tell you that he smote me with a sore plague in my loins for seven months; and had not my father Jamb prayed for me to the Lord, the Lord would have destroyed me.

For I was thirty years old when I wrought the evil thing before the Lord, and for seven months I was sick unto death.

And after this I repented with set purpose of my soul for seven years before the Lord.

And wine and strong drink I drank not, and flesh entered not into my mouth, and I ate no pleasant food; but I mourned over my sin, for it was great, such as had not been in Israel.

And now hear me, my children, what things I saw concerning the seven spirits of deceit, when I repented.

Seven spirits therefore are appointed against man, and they are the leaders in the works of youth.

And seven other spirits are given to him at his creation, that through them should

The Forgotten Books of Eden

be done every work of man.

The first is the spirit of life, with which the constitution of man is created.

The second is the sense of sight, with which ariseth desire.

The third is the sense of hearing, with which cometh teaching.

The fourth is the sense of smell, with which tastes are given to draw air and breath.

The fifth is the power of speech, with which cometh knowledge.

The sixth is the sense of taste, with which cometh the eating of meats and drinks; and by it strength is produced, for in food is the foundation of strength.

The seventh is the power of procreation and sexual intercourse, with which through love of pleasure sins enter in.

Wherefore it is the last in order of creation, and the first in that of youth, because it is filled with ignorance, and leadeth the youth as a blind man to a pit, and as a beast to a precipice.

Besides all these there is an eighth spirit of sleep, with which is brought about the trance of nature and the of death.

With these spirits are mingled the spirits of error.

First, the spirit of fornication is seated in the nature and in the senses;

The second, the spirit of insatiableness in the belly;

The third, the spirit of fighting, in the liver and gall.

The fourth is the spirit of obsequiousness and chicanery, that through officious attention one may be fair in seeming.

The fifth is the spirit of pride, that one may be boastful and arrogant.

The sixth is the spirit of lying, in perdition and jealousy to practise deceits, and concealments from kindred and friends.

The seventh is the spirit of injustice, with which are thefts and acts of rapacity, that a man may fulfil the desire of his heart; for injustice worketh together with the other spirits by the taking of gifts.

And with all these the spirit of sleep is joined which is that of error and fantasy.

And so perisheth every young man, darkening his mind from the truth, and not understanding the law of God, nor obeying the admonitions of his fathers, as befell me also in my youth.

And now, my children, love the truth, and it will preserve you: hear ye the words of Reuben your father.

Pay no heed to the face of a woman,

The Forgotten Books of Eden

Nor associate with another man's wife,

Nor meddle with affairs of womankind.

For had I not seen Bilhah bathing in a covered place, I had not fallen into this great iniquity.

For my mind taking in the thought of the woman's nakedness, suffered me not to sleep until I had wrought the abominable thing.

For while Jacob our father had gone to Isaac his father, when we were in Eder, near to Ephrath in Bethlehem, Bilhah became drunk and was asleep uncovered in her chamber.

Having therefore gone in and beheld her nakedness, I wrought the impiety without her perceiving it, and leaving her sleeping departed.

And forthwith an angel of God revealed to my father concerning my impiety, and he came and mourned over me, and touched her no more.

CHAPTER II.

Reuben continues with his experiences and his good advice.

PAY no heed, therefore, my children, to the beauty of women, nor set your mind— on their affairs; but walk in singleness of heart in the fear of the Lord, and expend labour on good works, and on study and on your flocks, until the Lord give you a wife, whom He will, that ye suffer not as I did.

For until my father's death I had not boldness to look in his face, or to speak to any of my brethren, because of the reproach.

Even until now my conscience causeth me anguish on account of my impiety.

And yet my father comforted me much, and prayed for me unto the Lord, that the anger of the Lord might pass from me, even as the Lord showed.

And thenceforth until now I have been on my guard and sinned not.

Therefore, my children, I say unto you, observe all things whatsoever I command you, and ye shall not sin.

For a pit unto the soul is the sin of fornication, separating it from God, and brinsing it near to idols, because it deceiveth the mind and understanding, and leadeth down young men into Hades before their time.

For many hath fornication destroyed; because, though a man be old or noble, or rich or poor, he bringeth reproach upon himself with the sons of men and derision with Beliar.

For ye heard regarding Joseph how he guarded himself from a woman, and purged his thoughts from all fornication, and found favour in the sight of God and men.

For the Egyptian woman did many things unto him, and summoned magicians,

The Forgotten Books of Eden

and offered him love potions, but the purpose of his soul admitted no evil desire.

Therefore the God of your fathers delivered him from every evil and hidden death.

For if fornication overcomes not your mind, neither can Beliar overcome you.

For evil are women, my children; and since they have no power or strength over man, they use wiles by outward attractions, that they may draw him to themselves.

And whom they cannot bewitch by outward attractions, him they overcome by craft.

For moreover, concerning them, the angel of the Lord told me, and taught me, that women are overcome by the spirit of fornication more than men, and in their heart they plot against men; and by means of their adornment they deceive first their minds, and by the glance of the eye instil the poison, and then through the accomplished act they take them captive.

For a woman cannot force a man openly, but by a harlot's bearing she beguiles him.

Flee, therefore, fornication, my children, and command your wives and your daughters, that they adorn not their heads and faces to deceive the mind: because every woman who useth these wiles bath been reserved for eternal punishment.

For thus they allured the Watchers [*1] who were before the flood; for as these continually beheld them, they lusted after them, and they conceived the act in their mind; for they changed themselves into the shape of men, and appeared to them when they were with their husbands.

And the women lusting in their minds after their forms, gave birth to giants, for the Watchers appeared to them as reaching even unto heaven.

Beware, therefore, of fornication; and if you wish to be pure in mind, guard your senses from every woman.

And command the women likewise not to associate with men, that they also may be pure in mind.

For constant meetings, even though the ungodly deed be not wrought, are to them an irremediable disease, and to us a destruction of Beliar and an eternal reproach.

For in fornication there is neither understanding nor godliness, and all jealousy dwelleth in the lust thereof.

Therefore, then I say unto you, ye will be jealous against the sons of Levi, and will seek to be exalted over them; but ye shall not be able.

For God will avenge them, and ye shall die by an evil death. For to Levi God gave the sovereignty and to Judah with him and to me also, and to Dan and Joseph, that we should be for rulers.

Therefore I command you to hearken to Levi, because he shall know the law of the

Lord, and shall give ordinances for judgement and shall sacrifice for all Israel until the consummation of the times, as the anointed High Priest, of whom the Lord spake.

I adjure you by the God of heaven to do truth each one unto his neighbour and to entertain love each one for his brother.

And draw ye near to Levi in humbleness, of heart, that ye may receive a blessing from his mouth.

For he shall bless Israel and Judah, because him hath the Lord chosen to be king over all the nation.

And bow down before his seed, for on our behalf it will die in wars visible and invisible, and will be among you an eternal king.

And Reuben died, having given these commands to his sons. And they placed him in a coffin until they carried him up from Egypt, and buried him in Hebron in the cave where his father was.

TESTAMENT OF SIMEON

The Second Son of Jacob and Leah.

CHAPTER I.

Simeon, the second son of Jacob and Leah. The strong man. He becomes jealous of Joseph and is an instigator of the plot against Joseph.

THE copy of the words of Simeon, the things which he spake to his sons before he died, in the hundred and twentieth year of his life, at which time Joseph, his brother, died.

For when Simeon was sick, his sons came to visit him. and he strengthened himself and sat up and kissed them, and said:—

Hearken, my children, to Simeon your father and I will declare unto you what things I have in my heart.

I was born of Jacob as my father's second son; and my mother Leah called me Simeon, because the Lord had heard her prayer.

Moreover, I became strong exceedingly; I shrank from no achievement nor was I afraid of ought. For my heart was hard, and my liver was immovable, and my bowels without compassion.

Because valour also has been given from the Most High to men in soul and body.

For in the time of my youth I was jealous in many things of Joseph, because my father loved him beyond all.

And I set my mind against him to destroy him because the prince of deceit sent forth the spirit of jealousy and blinded my mind, so that I regarded him not as a brother, nor did I spare even Jacob my father.

The Forgotten Books of Eden

But his God and the God of his fathers sent forth His angel, and delivered him out of my hands.

For when I went to Shechem to bring ointment for the flocks, and Reuben to Dothan, where were our necessaries and all our stores, Judah my brother sold him to the Ishmaelites.

And when Reuben heard these things he was grieved, for he wished to restore him to his father.

But on hearing this I was exceedingly wroth against Judah in that he let him go away alive, and for five months I continued wrathful against him.

But the Lord restrained me, and withheld from me the power of my hands; for my right hand was half withered for seven days.

And I knew, my children, that because of Joseph this had befallen me, and I repented and wept; and I besought the Lord God that my hand might be restored and that I might hold aloof from all pollution and envy and from all folly.

For I knew that I had devised an evil thing before the Lord and Jacob my father, on account of Joseph my brother, in that I envied him.

And now, my children, hearken unto me and beware of the spirit of deceit and envy.

For envy ruleth over the whole mind of a man, and suffereth him neither to eat nor to drink, nor to do any good thing. But it ever suggesteth to him to destroy him that he envieth; and so long as he that is envied flourisheth, he that envieth fadeth away.

Two years therefore I afflicted my soul with fasting in the fear of the Lord, and I learnt that deliverance from envy cometh by the fear of God.

For if a man flee to the Lord, the evil spirit runneth away from him and his mind is lightened.

And henceforward he sympathiseth with him whom he envied and forgiveth those who are hostile to him, and so ceaseth from his envy.

CHAPTER II.

Reuben counsels his hearers against envy.

AND my father asked concerning me, because he saw that I was sad; and I said unto him, I am pained in my liver.

For I mourned more than they all, because I was guilty of the selling of Joseph.

And when we went down into Egypt, and he bound me as a spy, I knew that I was suffering justly, and I grieved not.

Now Joseph was a good man, and had the Spirit of God within him: being compassionate and pitiful, he bore no malice against me; but loved me even as the rest of his brethren.

Beware, therefore, my children, of all jealousy and envy, and walk in singleness of heart, that God may give you also grace and glory, and blessing upon your heads, even as ye saw in Joseph's case.

All his days he reproached us not concerning this thing, but loved us as his own soul, and beyond his own sons glorified us, and gave us riches, and cattle and fruits.

Do ye also, my children, love each one his brother with a good heart, and the spirit of envy will withdraw from you.

For this maketh savage the soul and destroyeth the body; it causeth anger and war in the mind, and stirreth up unto deeds of blood, and leadeth the mind into frenzy, and causeth tumult to the soul and trembling to the body.

For even in sleep malicious jealousy gnaweth, and with wicked spirits disturbeth the soul, and causeth the body to be troubled, and waketh the mind from sleep in confusion; and as a wicked and poisonous spirit, so appeareth it to men.

Therefore was Joseph comely in appearance, and goodly to look upon, because no wickedness dwelt in him; for some of the trouble of the spirit the face manifesteth.

1And now, my children, make your hearts good before the Lord, and your ways straight before men, and ye shall find grace before the Lord and men.

Beware, therefore, of fornication, for fornication is mother of all evils, separating from God, and brinsing near to Beliar.

For I have seen it inscribed in the writing of Enoch that your sons shall be corrupted in fornication, and shall do harm to the sons of Levi with the sword.

But they shall not be able to withstand Levi; for he shall wage the war of the Lord, and shall conquer all your hosts.

And they shall be few in number, divided in Levi and Judah, and there shall be none of you for sovereignty, even as also our father prophesied in his blessings.

CHAPTER III.

A prophecy of the coming of the Messiah.

BEHOLD I have told you all things, that I may be acquitted of your sin.

Now, if ye remove from you your envy and all stiff-neckedness, is a rose shall my bones flourish in Israel, and as a lily my flesh in Jacob, and my odour shall be as the odour of Libanus; and as cedars shall holy ones be multiplied from me for ever, and their branches shall stretch afar off.

Then shall perish the seed of Canaan, and a remnant shall not be unto Amalek, and all the Cappadocians shall perish, and all Hittites shall be utterly destroyed.

Then shall fail the land of Ham, and all the people shall perish.

The Forgotten Books of Eden

Then shall all the earth rest from trouble, and all the world under heaven from war.

Then the Mighty One of Israel shall glorify Shem.

For the Lord God shall appear on earth, and Himself save men,

Then shall all the spirits of deceit be given to be trodden under foot, and men shall, rule over wicked spirits.

Then shall I arise in Joy and will bless the Most High because of his marvellous works, because God hath taken a body and eaten with men and saved men.

And now, my children,, and Judah, and obey Levi and Judah, and be not lifted up against these two tribes, for from them shall arise unto you the salvation of God.

For the Lord shall raise up from Levi as it were a High Priest, and from Judah as it were a King, God and man, He shall save all the Gentiles and the race of Israel.

Therefore I give you these commands that ye also may command your children, that they may observe them throughout their generations.

And when Simeon had made an end of commanding his sons, he slept with fathers, an hundred and twenty years old.

And they laid him in a wooden coffin, to take up his bones to Hebron. And they took them up secretly during a war of the Egyptians. For the bones of Joseph the Egyptians guarded in the tombs of the kings.

For the sorcerers told them, that on the departure of the bones of Joseph there should be throughout all the land darkness and gloom, and an exceeding great plague to the Egyptians, so that even with a lamp a man should not recognize his brother.

And the sons of Simeon bewailed their father.

And they were in Egypt until the day of their departure by the hand of Moses.

TESTAMENT OF LEVI

The Third Son of Jacob and Leah.

CHAPTER I.

Levi, the third son of Jacob and Leah. A mystic and dreamer of dreams, a prophet.

THE copy of the words of Levi, the things which he ordained unto his sons, according to all that they should do, and what things should befall them until the day of judgement.

He was sound in health when he called them to him; for it had been revealed to him that he should die.

3 And when they were gathered together he said to them:

I, Levi, was born in Haran, and I came with my father to Shechem.

The Forgotten Books of Eden

And I was young, about twenty years of age, when, with Simeon, I wrought vengeance on Hamor for our sister Dinah.

And when I was feeding the flocks in Abel-Maul, the spirit of understand of the Lord came upon me, and I saw all men corrupting their way, and that unrighteousness had built for itself walls, and lawlessness sat upon towers.

And I was grieving for the race of the sons of men, and I prayed to the Lord that I might be saved.

Then there fell upon me a sleep, and I beheld a high mountain, and I was upon it.

And behold the heavens were opened, and an angel of God said to me, Levi, enter.

And I entered from the first heaven, and I saw there a great sea hansing.

And further I saw a second heaven far brighter and more brilliant, for there was a boundless light also therein,

And I said to the angel, Why is this so? And the angel said to me, Marvel not at this, for thou shalt see another heaven more brilliant and incomparable.

And when thou hast ascended thither, Thou shalt stand near the Lord, and shalt be His minister, and shalt, declare His mysteries to men, and shalt proclaim concerning Him that shall redeem Israel.

And by thee and Judah shall the Lord appear among men, saving every race of men.

And from the Lord's portion shall be thy life, and He shall be thy field and vineyard, and fruits, gold, and silver.

Hear, therefore, regarding the heavens which have been shown to thee.

The lowest is for this cause gloomy unto thee, in that it beholds all the unrighteous deeds of men.

And it has fire, snow, and ice made ready for the day of judgement, in the righteous judgement of God; for in it are all the spirits of the retributions for vengeance on men.

And in the second are the hosts Of the armies which are ordained for the day of judgement, to work vengeance on the spirits of deceit and of Beliar.

And above them are the holy ones.

And in the highest of all dwelleth the Great Glory, far above all holiness.

In the heaven next to it are the archangels, who minister and make propitiation to the Lord for all the sins of ignorance of the righteous;

Offering to the Lord a sweet smelling savour, a reasonable and a bloodless offering.

The Forgotten Books of Eden

And in the heaven below this are the angels who bear answers to the angels of the presence of the Lord.

And in the heaven next to this are thrones and dominions, in which always they offer praise to God.

When, therefore, the Lord looketh upon us, all of us are shaken; yea, the heavens, and the earth, and the abysses are shaken at the presence of His majesty.

But the sons of men, having no perception of these things, sin and provoke the Most High.

CHAPTER II.

Levi urges piety and education.

NOW, therefore, know that the Lord shall execute judgement upon the sons of men.

Because when the rocks are being rent, and the sun quenched, and the waters dried up, and the fire cowering, and all creation troubled, and the invisible spirits melting away, and Hades taketh spoils through the visitations of the Most High, men will be unbelieving and persist in their iniquity.

On this account with punishment shall they be judged.

Therefore the Most High hath heard thy prayer, to separate thee from iniquity, and that thou shouldst become to Him a son, and a servant, and a minister of His presence.

The light of knowledge shalt thou light up in Jacob, and as the sun shalt thou be to all the seed of Israel.

And there shall be given to thee a blessing, and to all thy seed until the Lord shall visit all the Gentiles in His tender mercies for ever.

And therefore there have been given to thee counsel and understanding, that thou mightest instruct thy sons concerning this;

Because they that bless Him shall be blessed, and they that curse Him shall perish.

And thereupon the angel opened to me the gates of heaven, and I saw the holy temple, and upon a throne of glory the Most High.

And He said to me: Levi, I have given thee the blessing of the priesthood until I come and sojourn in the midst of Israel.

Then the angel brought me down to the earth, and gave me a shield and a sword, and said to me: Execute vengeance on Shechem because of Dinah, thy sister, and I will be with thee because the Lord hath sent me.

And I destroyed at that time the sons of Hamor, as it is written in the heavenly

The Forgotten Books of Eden

tables.

And I said to him: I pray thee, O Lord, tell me Thy name, that I may call upon Thee in a day of tribulation.

And he said: I am the angel who intercedeth for the nation of Israel that they may not be smitten utterly, for every evil spirit attacketh it.

And after these things I awaked, and blessed the Most High, and the angel who intercedeth for the nation of Israel and for all the righteous.

CHAPTER III.

Levi has visions and shows what rewards are in store for the righteous.

AND when I was going to my father, I found a brazen shield; wherefore also the name of the mountain is Aspis, which is near Gebal, to the south of Abila.

And I kept these words in my heart. And after this I counselled my father, and Reuben my brother, to bid the sons of Hamor not to be circumcised; for I was zealous because of the abomination which they had wrought on my sister.

And I slew Shechem first, and Simeon slew Hamor. And after this my brothers came and smote that city with the edge of the sword.

And my father heard these things and was wroth, and he was grieved in that they had received the circumcision, and after that had been put to death, and in his blessings he looked amiss upon us.

For we sinned because we had done this thing against his will, and he was sick on that day.

But I saw that the sentence of God was for evil upon Shechem; for they sought to do to Sarah and Rebecca as they had done to Dinah our sister, but the Lord prevented them.

And they persecuted Abraham our father when he was a stranger, and they vexed his flocks when they were big with young; and Eblaen, who was born in his house, they most shamefully handled.

And thus they did to all strangers, taking away their wives by force, and they banished them.

But the wrath of the Lord came upon them to the uttermost.

And I said to my father Jacob: By thee will the Lord despoil the Canaanites, and will give their land to thee and to thy seed after thee.

For from this day forward shall Shechem be called a city of imbeciles; for as a man mocketh a fool, so did we mock them.

Because also they had wrought folly in Israel by defiling my sister. And we departed and came to Bethel.

The Forgotten Books of Eden

And there again I saw a vision as the former, after we had spent there seventy days.

And I saw seven men in white raiment saying unto me: Arise, put on the robe of the priesthood, and the crown of righteousness, and the breastplate of understanding, and the garment of truth, and the late of faith, and the turban of the head, and the ephod of prophecy.

And they severally carried these things and put them on me, and said unto me: From henceforth become a priest of the Lord, thou and thy seed for ever.

And the first anointed me with holy oil, and gave to me the staff of judgement.

The second washed me with pure. water, and fed me with bread and wine even the most holy things, and clad me with a holy and glorious robe.

The third clothed me with a linen vestment like an ephod.

The fourth put round me a girdle like unto purple.

The fifth gave me a branch of rich olive.

The sixth placed a crown on my head.

The seventh placed on my head a diadem of priesthood, and filled my hands with incense, that I might serve as priest to the Lord God.

And they said to me: Levi, thy seed shall be divided into three offices, for a sign of the glory of the Lord who is to come.

And the first portion shall be great; yea, greater than it shall none be.

The second shall be in the priesthood.

And the third shall be called by a new name, because a king shall arise in Judah, and shall establish a new priesthood, after the fashion of the Gentiles.

And His presence is beloved, as a prophet of the Most High, of the seed of Abraham our father.

Therefore, every desirable thing in Israel shall be for thee and for thy seed, and ye shall eat everything fair to look upon, and the table of the Lord shall thy seed apportion.

And some of them shall be high priests, and judges, and scribes; for by their mouth shall the holy place be guarded.

And when I awoke, I understood that this dream was like the first dream. And I hid this also in my heart, and told it not to any man upon the earth.

And after two days I and Judah went up with our father Jacob to Isaac our father's father.

And my father's father blessed me according to all the words of the visions which

The Forgotten Books of Eden

I had seen. And he would not come with us to Bethel.

And when we came to Bethel, my father saw a vision concerning me, that I should be their priest unto God.

And he rose up early in the morning, and paid tithes of all to the Lord through me. And so we came to Hebron to dwell there.

And Isaac called me continually to put me in remembrance of the law of the Lord, even as the angel of the Lord showed unto me.

And he taught me the law of the priesthood of sacrifices, whole burnt-offerings, first-fruits, freewill-offerings, peace-offerings.

And each day he was instructing me, and was busied on my behalf before the Lord, and said to me: Beware of the spirit of fornication; for this shall continue and shall by thy seed pollute the holy place.

Take, therefore, to thyself a wife without blemish or pollution, while yet thou are young, and not of the race of strange nations.

And before entering into the holy place, bathe; and when thou offerest the sacrifice, wash; and again, when thou finishest the sacrifice, wash.

Of twelve trees having leaves offer to the Lord, as Abraham taught me also.

And of every clean beast and bird offer a sacrifice to the Lord.

And of all thy first-fruits and of wine offer the first, as a sacrifice to the Lord God; and every sacrifice thou shalt salt with salt.

Now, therefore, observe whatsoever I command you, children; for whatsoever things I have heard from my fathers I have declared unto you.

And behold I am clear from your ungodliness and transgression, which ye shall commit in the end of the ages against the Saviour of the world, Christ, acting godlessly, deceiving Israel, and stirring up against it great evils from the Lord.

And ye shall deal lawlessly together with Israel, so He shall not bear with Jerusalem because of your wickedness; but the veil of the temple shall be rent, so as not to cover your shame.

And ye shall be scattered as captives among the Gentiles, and shall be for a reproach and for a curse there.

For the house which the Lord shall choose shall be called Jerusalem, as is contained in the book of Enoch the righteous.

Therefore when I took a wife I was twenty-eight years old, and her name was Melcha.

And she conceived and bare a son, and I called his name Gersam, for we were sojourners in our land.

The Forgotten Books of Eden

And I saw concerning him, that he would not be in the first rank.

And Kohath was born in the thirty-fifth year of my life, towards sunrise.

And I saw in a vision that he was standing on high in the midst of all the congregation.

Therefore I called his name Kohath which is, besinning of majesty and instruction.

And she bare me a third son, in the fortieth year of my life; and since his mother bare him with difficulty, I called him Merari, that is, 'my bitterness,' because he also was like to die.

And Jochebed was born. in Egypt, in my sixty-fourth year, for I was renowned then in the midst of my brethren.

And Gersam took a wife, and she bare to him Lomni and Semei. And the sons of Kohath, Ambram, Issachar, Hebron, and Ozeel. And the sons of Merari, Mooli, and Mouses.

And in the ninety-fourth year Ambram took Jochebed my daughter to him to wife, for they were born in one day, he and my daughter.

Eight years old was I when I went into the land of Canaan, and eighteen years when I slew Shechem, and at nineteen years I became priest, and at twenty-eight years I took a wife, and at forty-eight I went into Egypt.

And behold, my children, ye are a third generation. In my hundred and eighteenth year Joseph died.

CHAPTER IV.

Levi shows how wisdom survives destruction. He has no use for scornful people.

AND now, my children, I command you: Fear the Lord your God with your whole heart, and walk in simplicity according to all His law.

And do ye also teach your children letters, that they may have understanding all their life, reading unceasingly the law of God.

For every one that knoweth the law of the Lord shall be honoured, and shall not be a stranger whithersoever he goeth.

Yea, many friends shall he gain more than his parents, and many men shall desire to serve him, and to hear the law from his mouth.

Work righteousness, therefore, my children, upon the earth, that ye may have it as a treasure in heaven.

And sow good things in your souls, that ye may find them in your life.

But if ye sow evil things, ye shall reap every trouble and affliction.

Get wisdom in the fear of God with diligence; for though there be a leading into captivity, and cities and lands be destroyed, and gold and silver and every possession

The Forgotten Books of Eden

perish, the wisdom of the wise nought can take away, save the blindness of ungodliness, and the callousness that comes of sin.

For if one keep oneself from these evil things, then even among his enemies shall wisdom be a glory to him, and in a strange country a fatherland, and in the midst of foes shall prove a friend.

Whosoever teaches noble things and does them, shall be enthroned with kings, as was also Joseph my brother.

Therefore, my children, I have learnt that at the end of the ages ye will transgress against the Lord, stretching out hands to wickedness against Him; and to all the Gentiles shall ye become a scorn.

For our father Israel is pure from the transgressions of the chief priests [who shall lay their hands upon the Saviour of the world].

For as the heaven is purer in the Lord's sight than the earth, so also be ye, the lights of Israel, purer than all the Gentiles.

But if ye be darkened through transgressions, what, therefore, will all the Gentiles do living in blindness?

Yea, ye shall bring a curse upon our race, because the light of the law which was given for to lighten every man this ye desire to destroy by teaching commandments contrary to the ordinances of God.

The offerings of the Lord ye shall rob, and from His portion shall ye steal choice portions, eating them contemptuously with harlots.

And out of covetousness ye shall teach the commandments of the Lord, wedded women shall ye pollute, and the virsins of Jerusalem shall ye defile; and with harlots and adulteresses shall ye be joined, and the daughters of the Gentiles shall ye take to wife, purifying them with an unlawful purification; and your union shall be like unto Sodom and Gomorrah,

And ye shall be puffed up because of your priesthood, lifting yourselves up against men, and not only so, but also against the commands of God.

For ye shall contemn the holy things with jests and laughter.

Therefore the temple, which the Lord shall choose, shall be laid waste through your uncleanness, and ye shall be captives throughout all nations.

And ye shall be an abomination unto them, and ye shall receive reproach and everlasting shame from the righteous judgement of God.

And all who hate you shall rejoice at your destruction.

And if you were not to receive mercy through Abraham, Isaac, and Jacob, our fathers, not one of our seed should be left upon the earth.

And now I have learnt that for seventy weeks ye shall go astray, and profane the priesthood, and pollute the sacrifices.

And ye shall make void the law, and set at nought the words of the prophets by evil perverseness.

And ye shall persecute righteous men, and hate the godly; the words of the faithful shall ye abhor.

And a man who reneweth the law in the power of the Most High, ye shall call a deceiver; and at last ye shall rush upon him to slay him, not knowing his dignity, taking innocent blood through wickedness upon your heads.

And your holy places shall be laid waste even to the ground because of him.

And ye shall have no place that is clean; but ye shall be among the Gentiles a curse and a dispersion until He shall again visit you, and in pity shall receive you through faith and water.

CHAPTER V.

He prophesies the coming of the Messiah. This was written 100 years before Christ.

AND whereas ye have heard concerning the seventy weeks, hear also concerning the priesthood. For in each jubilee there shall be a priesthood.

And in the first jubilee, the first who is anointed to the priesthood shall be great, and shall speak to God as to a father.

And his priesthood shall be perfect with the Lord, and in the day of his gladness shall he arise for the salvation of the world.

In the second jubilee, he that is anointed shall be conceived in the sorrow of beloved ones; and his priesthood shall be honoured and shall be glorified by all.

And the third priest shall he taken hold of by sorrow.

And the fourth shall be in pain, because unrighteousness shall gather itself against him exceedingly, and all Israel shall hate each one his neighbour.

The fifth shall be taken hold of by darkness. Likewise also the sixth and the seventh.

And in the seventh shall, be such pollution as I cannot express before men, for they shall know it who do these things.

Therefore shall they be taken captive and become a prey, and their land and their substance shall be destroyed.

And in the fifth week they shall return to their desolate country, and shall renew the house of the Lord.

And in the seventh week shall become priests, who are idolaters, adulterers, lovers of money, proud, lawless, lascivious, abusers of children and beasts.

The Forgotten Books of Eden

And after their punishment shall have come from the Lord, the priesthood shall fail.

Then shall the Lord raise up a new priest.

And to him all the words of the Lord shall be revealed; and he shall execute a righteous judgement upon the earth for a multitude of days.

And his star shall arise in heaven as of a king.

Lighting up the light of knowledge as the sun the day, and he shall be magnified in the world.

He shall shine forth as the sun on the earth, and shall remove all darkness from under heaven, and there shall be peace in all the earth.

The heavens shall exult in his days, and the earth shall be glad, and the clouds shall rejoice;

And the knowledge of the Lord shall be poured forth upon the earth, as the water of the seas;

And the angels of the glory of the presence of the Lord shall be glad in him.

The heavens shall be opened, and from the temple of glory shall come upon him sanctification, with the Father's voice as from Abraham to Isaac.

And the glory of the Most High shall be uttered over him, and the spirit of understanding and sanctification shall rest upon him in the water.

For he shall give the majesty of the Lord to His sons in truth for evermore;

And there shall none succeed him for all generations for ever.

And in his priesthood the Gentiles shall be multiplied in knowledge upon the earth, and enlightened through the grace of the Lord. In his priesthood shall sin come to an end, and the lawless shall cease to do evil.

And he shall open the gates of paradise, and shall remove the threatening sword against Adam, and he shall give to the saints to eat from the tree of life, and the spirit of holiness shall be on them.

And Beliar shall be bound by him, and he shall give power to His children to tread upon the evil spirits.

And the Lord shall rejoice in His children, and be well pleased in His beloved ones for ever.

Then shall Abraham and Isaac and Jacob exult, and I will be glad, and all the saints shall clothe themselves with joy.

And now, my children, ye have heard all; choose, therefore, for yourselves either the light or the darkness, either the law of the Lord or the works of Beliar.

The Forgotten Books of Eden

And his sons answered him., saying, Before the Lord we will walk according to His law.

And their father said unto them, The Lord is witness, and His angels are witnesses, and ye are witnesses, and I am witness, concerning the word of your mouth.

And his sons said unto him: We are witnesses.

And thus Levi ceased commanding his sons; and he stretched out his feet on the bed, and was gathered to his fathers, after he had lived a hundred and thirty-seven years.

And they laid him in a coffin, and afterwards they buried him in Hebron, with Abraham, Isaac, and Jacob.

THE TESTAMENT OF JUDAH

The Fourth Son of Jacob and Leah.

CHAPTER I.

Judah, the fourth son of Jacob and Leah. He is the giant, athlete, warrior; he recounts heroic deeds. He runs so fast that he can outstrip a hind.

THE copy of the words of Judah, what things he spake to his sons before he died.

They gathered themselves together, therefore, and came to him, and he said to them: Hearken, my children, to Judah your father.

I was the fourth son born to my father Jacob; and Leah my mother named me Judah, saying, I give thanks to the Lord, because He hath given me a fourth son also.

I was swift in my youth, and obedient to my father in everything.

And I honoured my mother and my mother's sister.

And it came to pass, when I became a man, that my father blessed me, saying, Thou shalt be a king, prospering in all things.

And the Lord showed me favour in all my works both in the field and in the house.

I know that I raced a hind, and caught it, and prepared the meat for my father, and he did eat.

And the roes I used to master in the chase, and overtake all that was in the plains.

A wild mare I overtook, and caught it and tamed it.

I slew a lion and plucked a kid out of its mouth.

I took a bear by its paw and hurled it down the cliff, and it was crushed.

I outran the wild boar, and seizing it as I ran, I tore it in sunder.

A leopard in Hebron leaped upon my dog, and I caught it by the tail, and hurled it on the rocks, and it was broken in twain

284

The Forgotten Books of Eden

I found a wild ox feeding in the fields, and seizing it by the horns, and whirling it round and stunning it, I cast it from me and slew it.

And when the two kings of the Canaanites came sheathed, in armour against our flocks, and much people with them, single handed I rushed upon the king of Hazor, and smote him on the greives and dragged him down, and so I slew him.

And the other, the king of Tappuah, as he sat upon his horse, I slew, and so I scattered all his people.

Achor, the king, a man of giant stature, I found, hurling javelins before and behind as he sat on horseback, and I took up a stone of sixty pounds weight, and hurled it and smote his horse, and killed it.

And I fought with this other for two hours; and I clave his shield in twain, and I chopped off his feet, and killed him.

And as I was stripping off his breastplate, behold nine men his companions began to fight with me,

And I wound my garment on my hand; and I slung stones at them, and killed four of them, and the rest fled.

And Jacob my father slew Beelesath, king of all the kings, a giant in strength, twelve cubits high.

And fear fell upon them, and they ceased warring against us.

Therefore my father was free from anxiety in the wars when I was with my brethren.

For he saw in a vision concerning me that an angel of might followed me everywhere, that I should not be overcome.

And in the south there came upon us a greater war than that in Shechem; and I joined in battle array with my brethren, and pursued a thousand men, and slew of them two hundred men and four kings.

And I went up upon the wall, and I slew four mighty men.

And so we captured Hazor, and took all the spoil.

And the next day we departed to Aretan, a city strong and walled and inaccessible, threatening us with death.

But I and Gad approached on the east side of the city, and Reuben and Levi on the west.

And they that were upon the wall, thinking that we were alone, were drawn down against us.

And so my brothers secretly climbed up the wall on both sides by stakes, and entered the city, while the men knew it not.

The Forgotten Books of Eden

And we took it with the edge of the sword.

And as for those who had taken refuge in the tower, we set fire to the tower and took both it and, them.

And as we were departing the men of Tappuah seized our spoil, and seeing this we fought with them.

And we slew them all and recovered our spoil.

And when I was at the waters of Kozeba, the men of Jobel came against us to battle.

And we fought with them and routed them; and their allies from Shiloh we slew, and we did not leave them power to come in against us.

And the men of Makir came upon us the fifth day, to seize our spoil; and we attacked them and overcame them in fierce battle: for there was a host of mighty men amongst them, and we slew them before they had gone up the ascent.

And when we came to their city their women rolled upon us stones from the brow of the hill on which the city stood.

And I and Simeon had ourselves behind the town, and seized upon the heights, and destroyed this city also.

And the next day it was told us that the king of the city of Gaash with. a mighty host was coming against us.

I, therefore, and Dan feigned ourselves to be Amorites, and as allies went into their city.

And in the depth of night our brethren came and we opened to them the gates; and we destroyed all the men and their substance, and we took for a prey all that was theirs, and their three walls we cast down.

And we drew near to Thamna, where was all the substance of the hostile kings.

Then being insulted by them, I was therefore wroth, and rushed against them to the summit; and they kept slinsing against me stones and darts.

And had not Dan my brother aided me, they would have slain me.

We came upon them, therefore, with wrath, and they all fled; and passing by another way, they fought my father, and he made peace with them.

And we did to them no hurt, and they became tributary to us, and we restored to them their spoil.

And I built Thamna, and my father built Pabael.

I was twenty years old when this war befell. And the Canaanites feared me and my brethren.

And I had much cattle, and I had for chief herdsman Iram the Adullamite.

The Forgotten Books of Eden

And when I went to him I saw Parsaba, king of Adullam; and he spake unto us, and he made us a feast; and when I was heated he gave me his daughter Bathshua to wife.

She bare me Er, and Onan and Shelah; and two of them the Lord smote: for Shelah lived, and his children are ye.

CHAPTER II.

Judah describes some findings, a city with walls of Iron and gates of brass. He has an encounter with an adventuress.

AND eighteen years my father abode in peace with his brother Esau, and his sons with us, after that we came from Mesopotamia, from Laban.

And when eighteen years were fulfilled, in the fortieth year of my life, Esau, the brother of my father, came upon us with a mighty and strong people.

And Jacob smote Esau with an arrow, and he was taken up wounded on Mount Seir, and as he went he died at Anoniram.

And we pursued after the sons of Esau.

Now they had a city with walls of iron and gates of brass; and we could not enter into it, and we encamped around, and besieged it.

And when they opened not to us in twenty days, I set up a ladder in the sight of all and with my shield upon my head I went up, sustaining the assault of stones, upwards of three talents weight; and I slew four of their mighty men.

And Reuben and Gad slew six others.

Then they asked from us terms of peace; and having taken counsel with our father, we received them as tributaries.

And they gave us five hundred cors of wheat, five hundred baths of oil, five hundred measures of wine, until the famine, when we went down into Egypt.

And after these things my son Er took to wife Tamar, from Mesopotamia, a daughter of Aram.

Now Er was wicked, and he was in need concerning Tamar, because she was not of the land of Canaan.

And on the third night an angel of the Lord smote him.

And he had not known her according to the evil craftiness of his mother, for he did not wish to have children by her.

In the days of the wedding feast I gave Onan to her in marriage; and he also in wickedness knew her not, though he spent with her a year.

And when I threatened him he went in unto her, but he spilled the seed on the ground, according to the command of his mother, and he also died through wickedness.

The Forgotten Books of Eden

And I wished to give Shelah also to her, but his mother did not permit it; for she wrought evil against Tamar, because she was not the daughters of Canaan, as she also herself was.

And I knew that the race of the Canaanites was wicked, but the impulse of youth blinded my mind.

And when I saw her pouring out wine, owing to the intoxication of wine I was deceived, and took her although my father had not counselled it.

And while I was away she went and took for Shelah a wife from Canaan.

And when I knew what she had done, I cursed her in the anguish of my soul.

And she also died through her wickedness together with her sons.

And after these things, while Tamar was a widow, she heard after two years that I was going up, to shear my sheep, and adorned herself in bridal array, and sat in the city Enaim by the gate.

For it was a law of the Amorites, that she who was about to marry should sit in fornication seven days by the gate.

Therefore being drunk with wine, I did not recognize her; and her beauty deceived me, through the fashion of her adorning.

And I turned aside to her, and said: Let me go in unto thee.

And she said: What wilt thou give me? And I gave her my staff, and my girdle, and the diadem of my kingdom in pledge.

And I went in unto her, and she conceived.

And not knowing what I had done, I wished to slay her; but she privily sent my pledges, and put me to shame.

And when I called her, I heard also the secret words which I spoke when lying with her in my drunkenness; and I could not slay her, because it was from the Lord.

For I said, Lest haply she did it in subtlety, having received the pledge from another woman.

But I came not again near her while I lived, because I had done this abomination in all Israel.

Moreover, they who were in the city said there was no harlot in the gate, because she came from another place, and sat for a while in the gate.

And I thought that no one knew that I had gone in to her.

And after this we came into Egypt to Joseph, because of the famine.

And I was forty and six years old, and seventy and three years lived I in Egypt.

The Forgotten Books of Eden

CHAPTER III.

He counsels against wine and lust as twin evils. "For he who is drunken reverenceth no man." (Verse 13).

AND now I command you, my children, hearken to Judah your father, and keep my sayings to perform all the ordinances of the Lord, and to obey the commands of God.

And walk not after your lusts, nor in the imasinations of your thoughts in haughtiness of heart; and glory not in the deeds and strength of your youth, for this also is evil in the eyes of the Lord.

Since I also gloried that in wars no comely woman's face ever enticed me, and reproved Reuben my brother concerning Bilhah, the wife of my father, the spirits of jealousy and of fornication arrayed themselves against me, until I lay with Bathshua the Canaanite, and Tamar, who was espoused to my sons.

For I said to my father-in-law: I will take counsel with my father, and so will I take thy daughter.

And he was unwilling but he showed me a boundless store of gold in his daughter's behalf; for be was a king.

And he adorned her with gold and pearls, and caused her to pour out wine for us at the feast with the beauty of women.

And the wine turned aside my eyes, and pleasure blinded my heart.

And I became enamoured of and I lay with her, and transgressed the commandment of the Lord and the commandment of my fathers, and I took her to wife.

And the Lord rewarded me according to the imasination of my heart, inasmuch as I had no joy in her children.

And now, my children, I say unto you, be not drunk with wine; for wine turneth the mind away from, the truth, and inspires the passion of lust, and leadeth the eyes into error.

For the spirit of fornication hath wine as a minister to give pleasure to the mind; for these two also take away the mind of man.

For if a man drink wine to drunkenness, it disturbeth the mind with filthy thoughts leading to fornication, and heateth the body to carnal union; and if the occasion of the lust be present, he worketh the sin, and is not ashamed.

Such is the inebriated man, my children; for he who is drunken reverenceth no man.

For, lo, it made me also to err, so that I was not ashamed of the multitude in the city, in that before the eyes of all I turned aside unto Tamar, and I wrought a great sin, and I uncovered the covering of my sons' shame.

After I had drunk wine I reverenced not the commandment of God, and I took a woman of Canaan to wife.

For much discretion needeth the man who drinketh wine, my children; and herein is discretion in drinking wine, a man may drink so long as he preserveth modesty.

But if he go beyond this limit the spirit of deceit attacketh his mind, and it maketh the drunkard to talk filthily, and to transgress and not to be ashamed, but even to glory in his shame, and to account himself honourable.

He that committeth fornication is not aware when he suffers loss, and is not ashamed when put to dishonour.

For even though a man be a king and commit fornication, he is stripped of his kingship by becoming the slave of fornication, as I myself also suffered.

For I gave my staff, that is, the stay of my tribe; and my girdle, that is, my power; and my diadem, that is, the glory of my kingdom.

And indeed I repented of these things; wine and flesh I eat not until my old age, nor did I behold any joy.

And the angel of God showed me that for ever do women bear rule over king and beggar alike.

And from the king they take away his glory, and from the valiant man his might, and from the beggar even that little which is the stay of his poverty.

Observe, therefore, my children, the right limit in wine; for there are in it four evil spirits—of lust, of hot desire, of profligacy, of filthy lucre.

If ye drink wine in gladness, be ye modest in the fear of God.

For if in your gladness the fear of God departeth, then drunkenness ariseth and shamelessness stealeth in.

But if ye would live soberly do not touch wine at all, lest ye sin in words of outrage, and in fightings and slanders, and transgressions of the commandments of God, and ye perish before your time.

Moreover, wine revealeth the mysteries of God and men, even as I also revealed the commandments of God and the mysteries of Jacob my father to the Canaanitish woman Bathshua, which God bade me not to reveal.

And wine is a cause both of war and confusion.

And now, I command you, my children, not to love money, nor to gaze upon the beauty of women; because for the sake of money and beauty I was led astray to Bathshua the Canaanite.

For I know that because of these two things shall my race fall into wickedness.

For even wise men among my sons shall they mar, and shall cause the kingdom of Judah to be diminished, which the Lord gave me because of my obedience to my father.

The Forgotten Books of Eden

For I never caused grief to Jacob, my father; for all things whatsoever he commanded I did.

And Isaac, the father of my father, blessed me to be king in Israel, and Jacob further blessed me in like manner.

And I know that from me shall the kingdom be established.

And I know what evils ye will do in the last days.

Beware, therefore, my children, of fornication, and the love of money, and hearken to Judah your father.

For these things withdraw au from the law of God, and blind the inclination of the soul, and teach arrogance, and suffer not a man to have compassion upon his neighbour.

They rob his soul of all goodness, and oppress him with toils and troubles, and drive away sleep from him, and devour his flesh.

And he hindereth the sacrifices of God; and he remembereth not the blessing of God, he hearkeneth not to a prophet when he speaketh, and resenteth the words of godliness.

For he is a slave to two contrary passions, and cannot obey God, because they have blinded his soul, and he walketh in the day as in the night.

My children, the love of money leadeth to idolatry; because, when led astray through money, men name as gods those who are not gods, and it causeth him who hath it to fall into madness.

For the sake of money I lost my children, and had not my repentance, and my humiliation, and the prayers of my father been accepted, I should have died childless.

But the God of my fathers had mercy on me, because I did it in ignorance.

And the prince of deceit blinded me, and I sinned as a man and as flesh, being corrupted through sins; and I learnt my own weakness while thinking myself invincible.

Know, therefore, my children, that two spirits wait upon man-the spirit of truth and the spirit of deceit.

And in the midst is the spirit of understanding of the mind, to which it belongeth to turn whithersoever it will. And the works of truth and the works of deceit are written upon the hearts of men, and each one of them the Lord knoweth.

And there is no time at which the works of men can be hid; for on the heart itself have they been written down before the Lord.

nd the spirit of truth testifieth all things, and accuseth all; and the sinner is burnt up by his own heart, and cannot raise his face to the judge.

CHAPTER IV.

Judah makes a vivid simile concerning tyranny and a dire prophecy concerning the morals of his listeners.

AND now, my children, I command you, love Levi, that ye may abide, and exalt not yourselves against him, lest ye be utterly destroyed.

For to me the Lord gave the kingdom, and to him the priesthood, and He set the kingdom beneath the priesthood.

To me He gave the things upon the earth; to him the things in the heavens.

As the heaven is higher than the earth, so is the priesthood of God higher than the earthly kingdom, unless it falls away through sin from the Lord and is dominated by the earthly kingdom.

For the angel of the Lord said unto me: The Lord chose him rather than thee, to draw near to Him, and to eat of His table and to offer Him the first-fruits of the choice things of the sons of Israel; but thou shalt be king of Jacob.

And thou shalt be amongst them as the sea.

For as, on the sea, just and unjust are tossed about, some taken into captivity while some are enriched, so also shall every race of men be in thee: some shall be impoverished, being taken captive, and others grow rich by plundering the possessions of others.

For the kings shall be as sea-monsters.

They shall swallow men like fishes: the sons and daughters of freemen shall they enslave; houses, lands, flocks, money shall they plunder:

And with the flesh of many shall they wrongfully feed the ravens and the cranes; and they shall advance in evil in covetousness uplifted, and there shall be false prophets like tempest, and they shall persecute all righteous men.

And the Lord shall bring upon them divisions one against another.

And there shall be continual wars in Israel; and among men of another race shall my kingdom be brought to an end, until the salvation of Israel shall come.

Until the appearing of the God of righteousness, that Jacob, and all the Gentiles may rest in peace.

And He shall guard the might of my kingdom for ever; for the Lord aware to me with an oath that He would not destroy the kingdom from my seed for ever.

Now I have much grief, my children, because of your lewdness and witchcrafts, and idolatries which ye shall practise against the kingdom, following them that have familiar spirits, diviners, and demons of error.

Ye shall make your daughters sinsing girls and harlots, and ye shall mingle in the abominations of the Gentiles.

For which things' sake the Lord shall bring upon you famine and pestilence, death

The Forgotten Books of Eden

and the sword, beleaguering by enemies, and revilings of friends, the slaughter of children, the rape of wives, the plundering of possessions, the burning of the temple of God, the laying waste of the land, the enslavement of yourselves among the Gentiles.

And they shall make some of you eunuchs for their wives.

Until the Lord visit you, when with perfect heart ye repent and walk in all His commandments, and He bring you up from captivity among the Gentiles.

And after these things shall a star arise to you from Jacob in peace,

And a man shall arise from my seed, like the sun of righteousness,

Walking with the sons of men in meekness and righteousness;

And no sin shall be found in him.

2And the heavens shall be opened unto him, to pour out the spirit, even the blessing of the Holy Father; and He shall pour out the spirit of grace upon you;

And ye shall be unto Him sons in truth, and ye shall walk in His commandments first and last.

Then shall the sceptre of my kingdom shine forth; and from your root shall arise a stem; and from it shall grow a rod of righteousness to the Gentiles, to judge and to save all that call upon the Lord.

And after these things shall Abraham and Isaac and Jacob arise unto life; and I and my brethren shall be chiefs of the tribes of Israel:

Levi first, I the second, Joseph third, Benjamin fourth, Simeon fifth, Issachar sixth, and so all in order.

And the Lord blessed Levi, and the Angel of the Presence, me; the powers of glory, Simeon; the heaven, Reuben; the earth, Issachar; the sea, Zebulun; the mountains, Joseph; the tabernacle, Benjamin; the luminaries, Dan; Eden, Naphtali; the sun, Gad; the moon, Asher.

And ye shall be the people of the Lord, and have one tongue; and there shall be there no spirit of deceit of Beliar, for he shall be cast into the fire for ever.

And they who have died in grief shall arise in joy, and they who were poor for the Lord's sake shall be made rich, and they who are put to death for the Lord's sake shall awake to life.

And the harts of Jacob shall run in joyfulness, and the eagles of Israel shall fly in gladness; and all the people shall glorify the Lord for ever.

Observe, therefore, my children, all the law of the Lord, for there is hope for all them who hold fast unto, His ways.

And he said to them: Behold, I die before your eyes this day, a hundred and nineteen years old.

The Forgotten Books of Eden

Let no one bury me in costly apparel, nor tear open my bowels, for this shall they who are kings do; and carry me up to Hebron with you.

And Judah, when he had said these things, fell asleep; and his sons did according to all whatsoever he commanded them, and they buried him in Hebron, with his fathers.

THE TESTAMENT OF ISSACHAR

The Fifth Son of Jacob and Leah.

CHAPTER I.

Issachar, the fifth son of Jacob and Leah. The sinless child of hire for mandrakes. He appeals for simplicity.

THE copy of the words of Issachar.

For he called his sons and said to them: Hearken, my children, to Issachar your father; give ear to the words of him who is beloved of the Lord.

I was born the fifth son to Jacob, by way of hire for the mandrakes.

For Reuben my brother brought in mandrakes from the field, and Rachel met him and took them.

And Reuben wept, and at his voice Leah my mother came forth.

Now these mandrakes were sweet-smelling apples which were produced in the land of Haran below a ravine of water.

And Rachel said: I will not give them to thee, but they shall be to me instead of children.

For the Lord hath despised me, and I have not borne children to Jacob.

Now there were two apples; and Leah said to Rachel: Let it suffice thee that thou hast taken my husband: wilt thou take these also?

And Rachel said to her: Thou shalt have Jacob this night for the mandrakes of thy son,

And Leah said to her: Jacob is mine, for I am the wife of his youth.

But Rachel said: Boast not, and vaunt not thyself; for he espoused me before thee, and for my sake he served our father fourteen years.

And had not craft increased on the earth and the wickedness of men prospered, thou wouldst not now see the face of Jacob.

For thou art not his wife, but in craft wert taken to him in my stead.

And my father deceived me, and removed me on that night, and did not suffer Jacob to see me; for had I been there, this had not happened to him.

Nevertheless, for the mandrakes I am hiring Jacob to thee for one night.

The Forgotten Books of Eden

And Jacob knew Leah, and she conceived and bare me, and on account of the hire I was called Issachar.

Then appeared to Jacob an angel of the Lord, saying: Two children shall Rachel bear, inasmuch as she hath refused company with her husband, and hath chosen continency.

And had not Leah my mother paid the two apples for the sake of his company, she would have borne eight sons; for this reason she bare six, and Rachel bare the two: for on account of the mandrakes the Lord visited her.

For He knew that for the sake of children she wished to company with Jacob, and not for lust of pleasure.

For on the morrow also she again gave up Jacob.

Because of the mandrakes, therefore, the Lord hearkened to Rachel.

For though she desired them, she cat them not, but offered them in the house of the Lord, presenting them to the priest of the Most High who was at that time.

When, therefore, I grew up, my children, I walked in uprightness of heart, and I became a husbandman for my father and my brethren, and I brought in fruits from the field according to their season.

And my father blessed me, for he saw that I walked in rectitude before him.

And I was not a busybody in my doings, nor envious and malicious against my neighbour.

I never slandered any one, nor did I censure the life of any man, walking as I did in singleness of eye.

Therefore, when I was thirty-five years old, I took to myself a wife, for my labour wore away my strength, and I never thought upon pleasure with women; but owing to my toil, sleep overcame me.

And my father always rejoiced in my rectitude, because I offered through the priest to the Lord all first-fruits; then to my father also.

And the Lord increased ten thousandfold His benefits in my hands; and also Jacob, my father, knew that God aided my singleness.

For on all the poor and oppressed I bestowed the good things of the earth in the singleness of my heart.

And now, hearken to me, my children, and walk in singleness of your heart, for I have seen in it all that is well-pleasing to the Lord. '

The single-minded man coveteth not gold, he overreacheth not his neighbour, he longeth not after manifold dainties, he delighteth not in varied apparel.

He doth not desire to live a long life, but only waiteth for the will of God.

The Forgotten Books of Eden

And the spirits of deceit have no power against him, for he looketh not on the beauty of women, lest he should pollute his mind with corruption.

There is no envy in his thoughts, no malicious person maketh his soul to pine away, nor worry with insatiable desire in his mind.

For he walketh in singleness of soul, and beholdeth all things in uprightness of heart, shunning eyes made evil through the error of the world, lest he should see the perversion of any of the commandments of the Lord.

Keep, therefore, my children, the law of God, and get singleness, and walk in guilelessness, not playing the busybody with the business of your neighbour, but love the Lord and your neighbour, have compassion on the poor and weak.

Bow down your back unto husbandry, and toil in labours in all manner of husbandry, offering gifts to the Lord with thanksgiving.

For with the first-fruits of the earth will the Lord bless you, even as He blessed all the saints from Abel even until now.

For no other portion is given to you than of the fatness of the earth, whose fruits are raised by toil.

For our father Jacob blessed me with blessings of the earth and of first-fruits.

And Levi and Judah were glorified by the Lord even among the sons of Jacob; for the Lord gave them an inheritance, and to Levi He gave the priesthood, and to Judah the kingdom.

And do ye therefore obey them, and walk in the singleness of your father; for unto Gad hath it been given to destroy the troops that are coming upon Israel.

CHAPTER II.

KNOW ye therefore, my children, that in the last times your sons will forsake singleness, and will cleave unto insatiable desire.

And leaving guilelessness, will draw near to malice; and forsaking the commandments of the Lord, they will cleave unto Beliar.

And leaving husbandry, they will follow after their own wicked devices, and they shall be dispersed among the Gentiles, and shall serve their enemies.

And do you therefore give these commands to your children, that, if they sin, they may the more quickly return to the Lord; For He is merciful, and will deliver them, even to bring them back into their land.

Behold, therefore, as ye see, I am a hundred and twenty-six years old and am not conscious of committing any sin.

Except my wife I have not known any woman. I never committed fornication by the uplifting of my eyes.

The Forgotten Books of Eden

I drank not wine, to be led astray thereby;

I coveted not any desirable thing that was my neighbour's.

Guile arose not in my heart;

A lie passed not through my lips.

If any man were in distress I joined my sighs with his,

1And I shared my bread with the poor.

I wrought godliness, all my days I kept truth.

I loved the Lord; likewise also every man with all my heart.

So do you also these things, my children, and every spirit of Beliar shall flee from you, and no deed of wicked men shall rule over you;

And every wild beast shall ye subdue, since you have with you the God of heaven and earth and walk with men in singleness of heart.

And having said these things, he commanded his sons that they should carry him up to Hebron, and bury him there in the cave with his fathers.

And he stretched out his feet and died, at a good old age; with every limb sound, and with strength unabated, he slept the eternal sleep.

THE TESTAMENT OF ZEBULUN

The Sixth Son of Jacob and Leah.

CHAPTER I.

Zebulun, the sixth son of Jacob and Leah. The inventor and philanthropist., What he learned as a result of the plot against Joseph.

THE copy of the words of Zebulun, which he enjoined on his sons before he died in the hundred and fourteenth year of his life, two years after the death of Joseph.

And he said to them: Hearken to me, ye sons of Zebulun attend to the words of your father.

I, Zebulun, was born a good gift to my parents.

For when I was born my father was increased very exceedingly, both in flocks and herds, when with the straked rods he had his portion.

I am not conscious that I have sinned all my days, save in thought.

Nor yet do I remember that I have done any iniquity, except the sin of ignorance which I committed against Joseph; for I covenanted with my brethren not to tell my father what had been done.

But I wept in secret many days on account of Joseph, for I feared my brethren, because they had all agreed that if any one should declare the secret, he should be slain.

But when they wished to kill him, I adjured them much with tears not to be guilty of this sin.

For Simeon and Gad came against Joseph to kill him, and he said unto them with tears: Pity me, my brethren, have mercy upon the bowels of Jacob our father: lay not upon me your hands to shed innocent blood, for I have not sinned against you.

And if indeed I have sinned, with chastening chastise me, my brethren, but lay not upon me your hand, for the sake of Jacob our father,

And as he spoke these words, wailing as he did so, I was unable to bear his lamentations, and began to weep, and my liver was poured out, and all the substance of my bowels was loosened.

And I wept with Joseph and my heart sounded, and the joints of my body trembled, and I was not able to stand.

And when Joseph saw me weeping with him, and them coming against him to slay him, he fled behind me, beseeching them.

But meanwhile Reuben arose and said: Come, my brethren, let us not slay him, but let us cast him into one of these dry pits, which our fathers digged and found no water.

For for this cause the Lord forbade that water should rise up in them in order that Joseph should be preserved.

And they did so, until they sold him to the Ishmaelites.

For in his price I had no share, my children.

But Simeon and Gad and six other of our brethren took the price of Joseph, and bought sandals for themselves, and their wives, and their children, saying:

We will not eat of it, for it is the price of our brother's blood, but we will assuredly tread it under foot, because he said that he would be king over us, and so let us see what will become of his dreams.

Therefore it is written in the writing of the law of Moses, that whosoever will not raise up seed to his brother, his sandal should be unloosed, and they should spit in his face.

And the brethren of Joseph wished not that their brother should live, and the Lord loosed from them the sandal which they wore against Joseph their brother.

For when they came into Egypt they were unloosed by the servants of Joseph outside the gate, and so they made obeisance to Joseph after the fashion of King Pharaoh.

And not only did they make obeisance to him, but were spit upon also, falling down before him forthwith, and so they were put to shame before. the Egyptians.

For after this the Egyptians heard all the evils that they had done to Joseph.

The Forgotten Books of Eden

And after he was sold my brothers sat down to eat and drink.

But I, through pity for Joseph, did not eat, but watched the pit, since Judah feared lest Simeon, Dan, and Gad should rush off and slay him.

But when they saw that I did not eat, they set me to watch him, till he was sold to the Ishmaelites.

And when Reuben came and heard that while he was away Joseph had been sold, he rent his garments, and mourning, said:

How shall I look on the face of my father Jacob? And he took the money and ran after the merchants but as he failed to find them he returned grieving.

But the merchants had left the broad road and marched through the Troglodytes by a short cut.

But Reuben was grieved, and ate no food that day.

Dan therefore came to him and said: Weep not, neither grieve; for we have found what we can say to our father Jacob.

Let us slay a kid of the goats, and dip in it the coat of Joseph; and let us send it to Jacob, saying: Know, is this the coat of thy son?

And they did so. For they stripped off from Joseph his coat when they were selling him, and put upon him the garment of a slave.

Now Simeon took the coat, and would not give it up, for he wished to rend it with his sword, as he was angry that Joseph lived and that he had not slain him.

Then we all rose up and said unto him: If thou givest not up the coat, we will say to our father that thou alone didst this evil thing in Israel.

And so he gave it unto them, and they did even as Dan had said.

CHAPTER II.

He urges human sympathy and understanding of one's fellow men.

AND now children, I you (sic) to keep the commands of the Lord, and to show mercy to your neighbours, and to have compassion towards all, not towards men only, but also towards beasts.

For all this thing's sake the Lord blessed me, and when all my brethren were sick, I escaped without sickness, for the Lord knoweth the purposes of each.

Have, therefore, compassion in your hearts, my children, because even as a man doeth to his neighbour, even so also will the Lord do to him.

For the sons of my brethren were sickening and were dying on account of Joseph, because they showed not mercy in their hearts; but my sons were preserved without sickness, as ye know.

The Forgotten Books of Eden

And when I was in the land of Canaan, by the sea-coast, I made a catch of fish for Jacob my father; and when many were choked in the sea, I continued unhurt.

I was the first to make a boat to sail upon the sea, for the Lord gave me understanding and wisdom therein.

And I let down a rudder behind it, and I stretched a sail upon another upright piece of wood in the midst.

And I sailed therein along the shores, catching fish for the house of my father until we came to Egypt.

And through compassion I shared my catch with every stranger.

And if a man were a stranger, or sick, or aged, I boiled the fish, and dressed them well, and offered them to all men, as every man had need, grieving with and having compassion upon them.

Wherefore also the Lord satisfied me with abundance of fish when catching fish; for he that shareth with his neighbour receiveth manifold more from the Lord.

For five years I caught fish and gave thereof to every man whom I saw, and sufficed for all the house of my father.

And in the summer I caught fish, and in the winter I kept sheep with my brethren.

Now I will declare unto you what I did.

I saw a man in distress through nakedness in wintertime, and had compassion upon him, and stole away a garment secretly from my father's house, and gave it to him who was in distress.

Do you, therefore, my children, from that which God bestoweth upon you, show compassion and mercy without hesitation to all men, and give to every man with a good heart.

And if ye have not the wherewithal to give to him that needeth, have compassion for him in bowels of mercy.

I know that my hand found not the wherewithal to give to him that needed, and I walked with him weeping for seven furlongs, and my bowels yearned towards him in compassion.

Have, therefore, yourselves also, my children, compassion towards every man with mercy, that the Lord also may have compassion and mercy upon you.

Because also in, the last days God will send His compassion on the earth, and wheresoever He findeth bowels of mercy He dwelleth in him.

For in the degree in which a man hath compassion upon his neighbours, in the same degree hath the Lord also upon him.

And when we went down into Egypt, Joseph bore no malice against us.

The Forgotten Books of Eden

To whom taking heed, do ye also, my children, approve yourselves without malice, and love one another; and do not set down in account, each one of you, evil against his brother.

For this breaketh unity and divideth all kindred, and troubleth the soul, and weareth away the countenance.

Observe, therefore, the waters, and know when they flow together, they sweep along stones, trees, earth, and other things.

But if they are divided into many streams, the earth swalloweth them up, and they vanish away.

So shall ye also be if ye be divided. Be not Ye, therefore, divided into two heads for everything which the Lord made .hath but one head, and two shoulders, two hands, two feet, and all the remaining members.

For I have learnt in the writing of my fathers, that ye shall be divided in Israel, and ye shall follow two kings, and shall work every abomination.

And your enemies shall lead you captive, and ye shall be evil entreated among the Gentiles, with many infirmities and tribulations.

And after these things ye shall remember the Lord and repent, and He shall have mercy upon you, for He is merciful and compassionate.

And He setteth not down in account evil against the sons of men, because they are flesh, and are deceived through their own wicked deeds.

And after these things shall there arise unto you the Lord Himself, the light of righteousness, and ye shall return unto your land.

And ye shall see Him in Jerusalem, for His name's sake.

And again through the wickedness of your works shall ye provoke Him to anger,

And ye shall be cast away by Him unto the time of consummation.

And now, my children, grieve not that I am dying, nor be cast down in that I am coming to my end.

For I shall rise again in the midst of you, as a ruler in the midst of his sons; and I shall rejoice in the midst of my tribe, as many as shall keep the law of the Lord, and the commandments of Zebulun their father.

But upon the ungodly shall the Lord bring eternal fire, and destroy them throughout all generations.

But I am now hastening away to my rest, as did also my fathers.

But do ye fear the Lord our God with all your strength all the days of your life.

And when he had said these things he fell asleep, at a good old age.

The Forgotten Books of Eden

And his sons laid him in a wooden coffin. And afterwards they carried him up and buried him in Hebron, with his fathers.

THE TESTAMENT OF DAN

The Seventh Son of Jacob and Bilhah.

CHAPTER I.

The seventh son of Jacob and Bilhah. The jealous one. He counsels against anger saying that "it giveth peculiar vision." This is a notable thesis on anger.

THE copy of the words of Dan, which he spake to his sons in his last days, in the hundred and twenty-fifth year of his life.

For he called together his I family, and said: Hearken to my words, ye sons of Dan; and give heed to the words of your father.

I have proved in my heart, and in my whole life, that truth with just dealing is good and well pleasing to God, and that lying and anger are evil, because they teach man all wickedness.

I confess, therefore, this day to you, my children, that in my heart I resolved on the death of Joseph my brother, the true and good man. .

And I rejoiced that he was sold, because his father loved him more than us.

For the spirit of jealousy and vainglory said to me: Thou thyself also art his son.

And one of the spirits of Beliar stirred me up, saying: Take this sword, and with it slay Joseph: so shall thy father love thee when he is dead.

Now this is the spirit of anger that persuaded me to crush Joseph as a leopard crusheth a kid.

But the God of my fathers did not suffer him to fall into my hands, so that I should find him alone and slay him, and cause a second tribe to be destroyed in Israel.

And now, my children, behold I am dying, and I tell you of a truth, that unless ye keep yourselves from the spirit of lying and of anger, and love truth and longsuffering, ye shall perish.

For anger is blindness, and does not suffer one to see the face of any man with truth.

For though it be a father or a mother, he behaveth towards them as enemies; though it be a brother, he knoweth him not; though it be a prophet of the Lord, he disobeyeth him; though a righteous man, he regardeth him not; though a friend, he doth not acknowledge him.

For the spirit of anger encompasseth him with the net of deceit, and blindeth his eyes, and through lying darkeneth his mind, and giveth him its own peculiar vision.

And wherewith encompasseth it his eyes? With hatred of heart, so as to be envi-

The Forgotten Books of Eden

ous of his brother.

For anger is an evil thing, my children, for it troubleth even the soul itself.

And the body of the angry man it maketh its own, and over his soul it getteth the mastery, and it bestoweth upon the body power that it may work all iniquity.

And when the body does all these things, the soul justifieth what is done, since it seeth not aright.

Therefore he that is wrathful, if he be a mighty man, hath a threefold power in his anger: one by the help of his servants; and a second by his wealth, whereby he persuadeth and overcometh wrongfully; and thirdly, having his own natural power he worketh thereby the evil.

And though the wrathful man be weak, yet hath he a power twofold of that which is by nature; for wrath ever aideth such in lawlessness.

This spirit goeth always with lying at the right hand of Satan, that with cruelty and lying his works may be wrought.

Understand ye, therefore, the power of wrath, that it is vain.

For it first of all giveth provocation by word; then by deeds it strengtheneth him who is angry, and with sharp losses disturbeth his mind, and so stirreth up with great wrath his soul.

Therefore, when any one. speaketh against you, be not ye moved to anger, and if any man praiseth you as holy men, be not uplifted: be not moved either to delight or to disgust.

For first it pleaseth the hearing, and so maketh the mind keen to perceive the grounds for provocation; and then being enraged, he thinketh that he is justly angry.

If ye fall into any loss or ruin, my children, be not afflicted; for this very spirit maketh a man desire that which is perishable, in order that he may be enraged through the affliction.

And if ye suffer loss voluntarily, or involuntarily, be not vexed; for from vexation ariseth wrath with lying.

Moreover, a twofold mischief is wrath with lying; and they assist one another in order to disturb the heart; and when the soul is continually disturbed, the Lord departeth from it, and Beliar ruleth over it.

CHAPTER II.

A prophecy of the sins, captivity, plagues, and ultimate restitution of the nation. They still talk of Eden (See Verse 18). Verse 23 is remarkable in the light of prophecy.

OBSERVE, therefore, my children, the commandments of the Lord, and keep His law; depart from wrath, and hate lying, that the Lord may dwell among you, and Beliar may flee from you.

The Forgotten Books of Eden

Speak truth each one with his neighbour. So shall ye not fall into wrath and confusion; but ye shall be in peace, having the God of peace, so shall no war prevail over you.

Love the Lord through all your life, and one another with a true heart.

I know that in the last days ye shall depart from the Lord, and ye shall provoke Levi unto anger, and fight against Judah; but ye shall not prevail against them, for an angel of the Lord shall guide them both; for by them shall Israel stand.

And whensoever ye depart from the Lord, ye shall walk in all evil and work the abominations of the Gentiles, going a-whoring after women of the lawless ones, while with all wickedness the spirits of wickedness work in you.

For I have read in the book of Enoch, the righteous, that your prince is Satan, and that all the spirits of wickedness and pride will conspire to attend constantly on the sons of Levi, to cause them to sin before the Lord.

And my sons will draw near to Levi, and sin with them in all things; and the sons of Judah will be covetous, plundering other men's goods like lions.

Therefore shall ye be led away with them into captivity, and there shall ye receive all the plagues of Egypt, and all the evils of the Gentiles.

And so when ye return to the Lord ye shall obtain mercy, and He shall bring you into His sanctuary, and He shall give you peace.

And there shall arise unto you from the tribe of Judah and of Levi the salvation of the Lord; and he shall make war against Beliar.

And execute an everlasting vengeance on our enemies; and the captivity shall he take from Beliar the souls of the saints, and turn disobedient hearts unto the Lord, and give to them that call upon him eternal peace.

And the saints shall rest in Eden, and in the New Jerusalem shall the righteous rejoice, and it shall be unto the glory of God for ever.

And no longer shall Jerusalem endure desolation, nor Israel be led captive; for the Lord shall be in the midst of it [living amongst men], and the Holy One of Israel shall reign over it in humility and in poverty; and he who believeth on Him shall reign amongst men in truth.

And now, fear the Lord, my children, and beware of Satan and his spirits.

Draw near unto God and unto the angel that intercedeth for you, for he is a mediator between God and man, and for the peace of Israel he shall stand up against the kingdom of the enemy.

Therefore is the enemy eager to destroy all that call upon the Lord.

For he knoweth that upon the day on which Israel shall repent, the kingdom of the enemy shall be brought to an end.

For the very angel of peace shall strengthen Israel, that it fall not into the extremity of evil.

And it shall be in the time of the lawlessness of Israel, that the Lord will not depart from them, but will transform them into a nation that doeth His will, for none of the angels will be equal unto him.

And His name shall be in every place in Israel, and among the Gentiles.

Keep, therefore, yourselves, my children, from every evil work, and cast away wrath and all lying, and love truth and long-suffering.

And the things which ye have heard from your father, do ye also impart to your children that the Saviour of the Gentiles may receive you; for he is true and long-suffering, meek and lowly, and teacheth by his works the law of God.

Depart, therefore, from all unrighteousness, and cleave unto the righteousness of God, and your race will be saved for ever.

And bury me near my fathers.

And when he had said these things he kissed them, and fell asleep at a good old age.

And his sons buried him, and after that they carried up his bones, and placed them near Abraham, and Isaac, and Jacob.

Nevertheless, Dan prophesied unto them that they should forget their God, and should be alienated from the land of their inheritance and from the race of Israel, and from the family of their seed.

THE TESTAMENT OF NAPHTALI

The Eighth Son of Jacob and Bilhah.

CHAPTER I.

Naphtali, the eighth son of Jacob and Bilhah. The Runner. A lesson in physiology.

THE copy of, the testament of Naphtali, which he ordained at the time of his death in the hundred and thirtieth year of his life.

When his sons were gathered together in the seventh month, on the first day of the month, while still in good health, he made them a feast of food and wine.

And after he was awake in the morning, he said to them, I am dying; and they believed him not.

And as he glorified the Lord, he grew strong and said that after yesterday's feast he should die.

And he began then to say: Hear, my children, ye sons of Naphtali, hear the words of your father.

I was born from Bilhah, and because Rachel dealt craftly, and gave Bilhah in place

The Forgotten Books of Eden

of herself to Jacob, and she conceived and bare me upon Rachel's knees, therefore she called my name Naphtali.

For Rachel loved me very much because I was born upon her lap; and when I was still young she was wont to kiss me, and say: May I have a brother of thine from mine own womb, like unto thee.

Whence also Joseph was like unto me in all things, according to the prayers of Rachel.

Now my mother was Bilhah, daughter of Rotheus the brother of Deborah, Rebecca's nurse, who was born on one and the self-same day with Rachel.

And Rotheus was of the family of Abraham, a Chaldean, God-fearing, free-born, and noble.

And he was taken captive and was bought by Laban; and he gave him Euna his handmaid to wife, and she bore a daughter, and called her name Zilpah, after the name of the village in which he had been taken captive.

And next she bore Bilhah, saying: My daughter hastens after what is new, for immediately that she was born she seized the breast and hastened to suck it.

And I was swift on my feet like the deer, and my father Jacob appointed me for all messages, and as a deer did he give me his blessing.

For as the potter knoweth the vessel, how much it is to contain, and bringeth clay accordingly, so also doth the Lord make the body after the likeness of the spirit, and according to the capacity of the body doth He implant the spirit.

And the one does not fall short of the other by a third part of a hair; for by weight, and measure, and rule was all the creation made.

And as the potter knoweth the use of each vessel, what it is meet for, so also doth the Lord know the body, how far it will persist in goodness, and when it besinneth in evil.

For there is no inclination or thought which the Lord knoweth not, for He created every man after His own image.

For as a man's strength, so also in his work; as his eye, so also in his sleep; as his soul, so also in his word either in the law of the Lord or in the law of Beliar.

And as there is a division between light and darkness, between seeing and hearing, so also is there a division between man and man, and between woman and woman; and it is not to be said that the one is like the other either in face or in mind.

For God made all things good in their order, the five senses in the head, and He joined on the neck to the head, adding to it the hair also for comeliness and glory, then the heart for understanding, the belly for excrement, and the stomach for grinding, the windpipe for taking in the breath, the liver for wrath, the gall for bitterness, the spleen for laughter, the reins for prudence, the muscles of the loins for power, the lungs for drawing in, the loins for strength, and so forth.

The Forgotten Books of Eden

So then, my children, let all your works be done in order with good intent in the fear of God, and do nothing disorderly in scorn or out of its due season.

For if thou bid the eye to hear, it cannot; so neither while ye are in darkness can ye do the works of light.

Be ye, therefore, not eager to corrupt your doings through covetousness or with vain words to beguile your souls; because if ye keep silence in purity of heart, ye shall understand how to hold fast the will of God, and to cast away the will of Beliar.

Sun and moon and stars, change not their order; so do ye also change not the law of God in the disorderliness of your doings.

The Gentiles went astray, and forsook the Lord, and charged their order, and obeyed stocks and stones, spirits of deceit.

But ye shall not be so, my children, recognizing in the firmament, in the earth, and in the sea, and in all created things, the Lord who made all things, that ye become not as Sodom, which changed the order of nature.

In like manner the Watchers also changed the order of their nature, whom the Lord cursed at the flood, on whose account He made the earth without inhabitants and fruitless.

These things I say unto you, my children, for I have read in the writing of Enoch that ye yourselves also shall depart from the Lord, walking according to all the lawlessness of the Gentiles, and ye shall do according to all the wickedness of Sodom.

And the Lord shall bring captivity upon you, and there shall ye serve your enemies, and ye shall be bowed down with every affliction and tribulation, until the Lord have consumed you all.

And after ye have become diminished and made few, ye return and acknowledge the Lord your God; and He shall bring you back into your land, according to His abundant mercy.

And it shall be, that after that they come into the land of their fathers, they shall again forget the Lord and become ungodly.

And the Lord shall scatter them upon the face of all the earth, until the compassion of the Lord shall come, a man working righteousness and working mercy unto all them that are afar off, and to them that are near.

CHAPTER II.

He makes a plea for orderly living. Notable for their eternal wisdom are Verses 27-40.

FOR in the fortieth year of my life, I saw a vision on the Mount of Olives, on the east of Jerusalem, that the sun and the moon were standing still.

And behold Isaac, the father of my father, said to us; Run and lay hold of them,

The Forgotten Books of Eden

each one according to his strength; and to him that seizeth them will the sun and moon belong.

And we all of us ran together, and Levi laid hold of the sun, and Judah outstripped the others and seized the moon, and they were both of them lifted up with them.

And when Levi became as a sun, lo, a certain young man gave to him twelve branches of palm; and Judah was bright as the moon, and under their feet were twelve rays.

And the two, Levi and Judah, ran, and laid hold of them.

And lo, a bull upon the earth, with two great horns, and an eagle's wings upon its back; and we wished to seize him, but could not.

But Joseph came, and seized him, and ascended up with him on high.

And I saw, for I was there, and behold a holy writing appeared to us, saying: Assyrians, Medes, Persians, Chaldeans, Syrians, shall possess in captivity the twelve tribes of Israel.

And again, after seven days, I saw our father Jacob standing by the sea of Jamnia, and we were with him.

And behold, there came a ship sailing by, without sailors or pilot; and there was written upon the ship, The Ship of Jacob.

And our father said to us: Come, let us embark on our ship.

And when he had gone on board, there arose a vehement storm, and a mighty tempest of wind; and our father, who was holding the helm, departed from us.

And we, being tost with the tempest, were borne along over the sea; and the ship was filled with water, and was pounded by mighty waves, until it was broken up.

And Joseph fled away upon a little boat, and we were all divided upon nine planks, and Levi and Judah were together.

And we were all scattered unto the ends of the earth.

Then Levi, girt about with sackcloth, prayed for us all unto the Lord.

And when the storm ceased, the ship reached the land as it were in peace.

And, lo, our father came, and we all rejoiced with one accord.

These two dreams I told to my father; and he said to me: These things must be fulfilled in their season, after that Israel hath endured many things.

Then my father saith unto me: I believe God that Joseph liveth, for I see always that the Lord numbereth him with you.

And he said, weeping: Ah me, my son Joseph, thou livest, though I behold thee not, and thou seest not Jacob that begat thee.

The Forgotten Books of Eden

He caused me also, therefore, to weep by these words, and I burned in my heart to declare that Joseph had been sold, but I feared my brethren.

And lo! my children, I have shown unto you the last times, how everything shall come to pass in Israel.

Do ye also, therefore, charge your children that they be united to Levi and to Judah; for through them shall salvation arise unto Israel, and in them shall Jacob be blessed.

For through their tribes shall God appear dwelling among men on earth, to save the race of Israel, and to gather together the righteous from amongst the Gentiles.

If ye work that which is good, my children, both men and angels shall bless you; and God shall be glorified among the Gentiles through you, and the devil shall flee from you, and the wild beasts shall fear you, and the Lord shall love you, and the angels shall cleave to you.

As a man who has trained a child well is kept in kindly remembrance; so also for a good work there is a good remembrance before God.

But him that doeth not that which is good, both angels and men shall curse, and God shall be dishonoured among the Gentiles through him, and the devil shall make him as his own peculiar instrument, and every wild beast shall master him, and the Lord shall hate him.

For the commandments of the law are twofold, and through prudence must they be fulfilled.

For there is a season for a man to embrace his wife, and a season to abstain therefrom for his prayer.

So, then, there are two commandments; and, unless they be done in due order, they bring very great sin upon men.

So also is it with the other commandments.

Be ye therefore wise in God, my children, and prudent, understanding the order of His commandments, and the laws of every word, that the Lord may love you,

And when he had charged them with many such words, he exhorted them that they should remove his bones to Hebron, and that they should bury him with his fathers.

And when he had eaten and drunken with a merry heart, he covered his face and died.

And his sons did according to all that Naphtali their Father had commanded them.

THE TESTAMENT OF GAD

The Ninth Son of Jacob and Zilpah.

CHAPTER I.

Gad, the ninth son of Jacob and Zilpah. Shepherd and strong man but a murderer

The Forgotten Books of Eden

at heart.

THE copy of the testament of Gad, what things he spake unto his sons, in the hundred and twenty-fifth year of his life, saying unto them:

Hearken, my children, I was the ninth son born to Jacob, and I was valiant in keeping the flocks.

Accordingly I guarded at night the flock; and whenever the lion came, or the wolf, or any wild beast against the fold, I pursued it, and overtaking it I seized its foot with my hand and hurled it about a stone's throw, and so killed it.

Now Joseph my brother was feeding the flock with us for upwards of thirty days, and being young, he fell sick by reason of the heat.

And he returned to Hebron to our father, who made him lie down near him, because he loved him greatly.

And Joseph told our father that the sons of Zilpah and Bilhah were slaying the best of the flock and eating them against the judgement of Reuben and Judah.

For he saw that I had delivered a lamb out of the mouth of a bear, and put the bear to death; but had slain the lamb, being grieved concerning it that it could not live, and that we had eaten it.

And regarding this matter I was wroth with Joseph until the day that he was sold.

And the spirit of hatred was in me, and I wished not either to hear of Joseph with the ears, or see him with the eyes, because he rebuked us to our faces saying that we were eating of the flock without Judah.

For whatsoever things he told our father, he believed him.

I confess now my sin, my children, that oftentimes I wished to kill him, because I hated him from my heart.

Moreover, I hated him yet more for his dreams; and I wished to lick [*1] him out of the land of the living, even as an ox licketh up the grass of the field.

And Judah sold him secretly to the Ishmaelites.

Thus the God of our fathers delivered him from our hands, that we should not work great lawlessness in Israel.

And now, my children, hearken to the words of truth to work righteousness, and all the law of the Most High, and go not astray through the spirit of hatred, for it is evil in all the doings of men.

Whatsoever a man doeth the hater abominateth him: and though a man worketh the law of the Lord, he praiseth him not; though a man feareth the Lord, and taketh pleasure in that which is righteous, he loveth him not.

He dispraiseth the truth, he envieth him that prospereth, he welcometh evil-speak-

The Forgotten Books of Eden

ing, he loveth arrogance, for hatred blindeth his soul; as I also then looked on Joseph.

Beware, therefore, my children of hatred, for it worketh lawlessness even against the Lord Himself.

For it will not hear the words of His commandments concerning the loving of one's— neighbour, and it sinneth against God.

For if a brother stumble, it delighteth immediately to proclaim it to all men, and is urgent that he should be judged for it, and be punished and be put to death.

And if it be a servant it stirreth him up against his master, and with every affliction it deviseth against him, if possibly he can be put to death.

For hatred worketh with envy also against them that prosper: so long as it heareth of or seeth their success it always languisheth.

For as love would quicken even the dead, and would call back them that are condemned to die, so hatred would slay the living, and those that had sinned venially it would not suffer to live.

For the spirit of hatred worketh together with Satan, through hastiness of spirits, in all things to men's death; but the spirit of love worketh together with the law of God in long-suffering unto the salvation of men.

Hatred, therefore, is evil, for it constantly mateth with lying, speaking against the truth; and it maketh small things to be great, and causeth the light to be darkness, and calleth the sweet bitter, and teacheth slander, and kindleth wrath, and stirreth up war, and violence and all covetousness; it filleth the heart with evils and devilish poison.

These things, therefore, I say to you from experience, my children, that ye may drive forth hatred, which is of the devil, and cleave to the love of God.

Righteousness casteth out hatred, humility destroyeth envy.

For he that is just and humble is ashamed to do what is unjust, being reproved not of another, but of his own heart, because the Lord looketh on his inclination.

He speaketh not against a holy man, because the fear of God overcometh hatred.

For fearing lest he should offend the Lord, he will not do wrong to any man, even in thought.

These things I learnt at last, after I had repented concerning Joseph.

For true repentance after a godly sort destroyeth ignorance, and driveth away the darkness, and enlighteneth the eyes, and giveth knowledge to the soul, and leadeth the mind to salvation.

And those things which it hath not learnt from man, it knoweth through repentance.

For God brought upon me a disease of the liver; and had not the prayers of Jacob my father succoured me, it had hardly failed but my spirit had departed.

For by what things a man transgresseth by the same also is he punished.

Since, therefore, my liver was set mercilessly against Joseph, in my liver too I suffered mercilessly, and was judged for eleven months, for so long a time as I had been angry against Joseph.

CHAPTER II.

Gad exhorts his listeners against hatred showing how it has brought him into so much trouble. Verses 8-11 are memorable.

AND now, my children, I exhort you, love ye each one his brother, and put away hatred from your hearts, love one another in deed, and in word, and in the inclination of the soul.

For in the presence of my father I spake peaceably to Joseph; and when I had gone out, the spirit of hatred darkened my mind, and stirred up my soul to slay him.

Love ye one another from the heart; and if a man sin against thee, speak peaceably to him, and in thy soul hold not guile; and if he repent and confess, forgive him.

But if he deny it, do not get into a passion with him, lest catching the poison from thee he take to swearing and so thou sin doubly.

Let not another man hear thy secrets when engaged in legal strife, lest he come to hate thee and become thy enemy, and commit a great sin against thee; for ofttimes he addresseth thee guilefully or busieth himself about thee with wicked intent.

And though he deny it and yet have a sense of shame when reproved, give over reproving him.

For be who denieth may repent so as not again to wrong thee; yea, he may also honour thee, and fear and be at peace with thee.

And if he be shameless and persist in his wrong-doing, even so forgive him from the heart, and leave to God the avensing.

If a man prospereth more than you, do not be vexed, but pray also for him, that he may have perfect prosperity.

For so it is expedient for you.

And if he be further exalted, be not envious of him, remembering that all flesh shall die; and offer praise to God, who giveth things good and profitable to all men.

Seek out the judgments of the Lord, and thy mind will rest and be at peace.

And though a man become rich by evil means, even as Esau, the brother of my father, be not jealous; but wait for the end of the Lord.

For if he taketh away from a man wealth gotten by evil means He forgiveth him if he repent, but the unrepentant is reserved for eternal punishment.

The Forgotten Books of Eden

For the poor man, if free from envy, he pleaseth the Lord in all things, is blessed beyond all men, because he hath not the travail of vain men.

Put away, therefore, jealousy from your souls, and love one another with uprightness of heart.

Do ye also therefore tell these things to your children, that they honour Judah and Levi, for from them shall the Lord raise up salvation to Israel.

For I know that at the last your children shall depart from Him, and shall walk in O wickedness, and affliction and corruption before the Lord.

And when he had rested for a little while, he said again; My children, obey your father, and bury me near to my fathers.

And he drew up his feet, and fell asleep in peace.

And after five years they carried him up to Hebron, and laid him with his fathers.

THE TESTAMENT OF ASHER

The Tenth Son of Jacob and Zilpah.

CHAPTER I.

Asher, the tenth son of Jacob and Zilpah. An explanation of dual personality. The first Jekyll and Hyde story. For a statement of the Law of Compensation that Emerson would have enjoyed, see Verse 27.

THE copy of the Testament To Asher, what things he spake to his sons in the hundred and twenty-fifth year of his life.

For while he was still in health, he said to them: Hearken, ye children of Asher, to your father, and I will declare to you all that is upright in the sight of the Lord.

Two ways hath God given to the sons of men, and two inclinations, and two kinds of action, and two modes of action, and two issues.

Therefore all things are by twos, one over against the other.

For there are two ways of good and evil, and with these are the two inclinations in our breasts discriminating them.

Therefore if the soul take pleasure in the good inclination, all its actions are in righteousness; and if it sin it straightway repenteth.

For, having its thoughts set upon righteousness, and casting away wickedness, it straightway overthroweth the evil, and uprooteth the sin.

But if it incline to the evil inclination, all its actions are in wickedness, and it driveth away the good, and cleaveth to the evil, and is ruled by Beliar; even though it work what is good, he perverteth it to evil.

For whenever it besinneth to do good, he forceth the issue of the action into evil for him, seeing that the treasure of the inclination is filled with an evil spirit.

A person then may with words help the good for the sake of the evil, yet the issue of the action leadeth to mischief.

There is a man who showeth no compassion upon him who serveth his turn in evil; and this thing bath two aspects, but the whole is evil.

And there is a man that loveth him that worketh evil, because he would prefer even to die in evil for his sake; and concerning this it is clear that it bath two aspects, but the whole is an evil work.

Though indeed he have love, yet is he wicked who concealeth what is evil for the sake of the good name, but the end of the action tendeth unto evil.

Another stealeth, doeth unjustly, plundereth, defraudeth, and withal pitieth the poor: this too bath a twofold aspect, but the whole is evil.

He who defraudeth his neighbour provoketh God, and sweareth falsely against the Most High, and yet pitieth the poor: the Lord who commanded the law he setteth at nought and provoketh, and yet he refresheth the poor.

He defileth the soul, and maketh gay the body; he killeth many, and pitieth a few: this, too, bath a twofold aspect, but the whole is evil.

Another committeth adultery and fornication, and abstaineth from meats, and when he fasteth he doeth evil, and by the power of his wealth overwhelmeth many; and notwithstanding his excessive wickedness he doeth the commandments: this, too, hath a twofold aspect, but the whole is evil.

Such men are hares; clean,—like those that divide the hoof, but in very deed are unclean.

For God in the tables of the commandments hath thus declared.

But do not ye, my children, wear two faces like unto them, of goodness and of wickedness; but cleave unto goodness only, for God hath his habitation therein, and men desire it.

But from wickedness flee away, destroying the evil inclination by your good works; for they that are double-faced serve not God, but their own lusts, so that they may please Beliar and men like unto themselves.

For good men, even they that are of single face, though they be thought by them that are double-faced to sin, are just before God.

For many in killing the wicked do two works, of good and evil; but the whole is good, because he hath uprooted and destroyed that which is evil.

One man hateth the merciful and unjust man, and the man who committeth adultery and fasteth: this, too, hath a twofold aspect, but the whole work is good, because he followeth the Lord's example, in that he accepteth not the seeming good as the genuine

The Forgotten Books of Eden

good.

Another desireth not to see good day with them that not, lest be defile his body and pollute his soul; this, too, is double-faced, but the whole is good.

For such men are like to stags and to hinds, because in the manner of wild animals they seem to be unclean, but they are altogether clean; because they walk in zeal for the Lord and abstain from what God also hateth and forbiddeth by His commandments, warding off the evil from the good.

Ye see, my children, how that there are two in all things, one against the other, and the one is hidden by the other: in wealth is hidden covetousness, in conviviality drunkenness, in laughter grief, in wedlock profligacy.

Death succeedeth to life, dishonour to glory, night to day, and darkness to light; and all things are under the day, just things under life, unjust things under death; wherefore also eternal life awaiteth death.

Nor may it be said that truth is a lie, nor right wrong; for all truth is under the light, even as all things are under God.

All these things, therefore, I proved in my life, and I wandered not from the truth of the Lord, and I searched out the commandments of the Most High, walking according to all my strength with singleness of face unto that which is good.

Take heed, therefore, ye also, my children, to the commandments of the Lord, following the truth with singleness of face.

For they that are double-faced are guilty of a twofold sin; for they both do the evil thing and they have pleasure in them that do it, following the example of the spirits of deceit, and striving against mankind.

Do ye, therefore, my children, keep the law of the Lord, and give not heed unto evil as unto good; but look unto the thing that is really good, and keep it in all commandments of the Lord, having your conversation therein, and resting therein.

For the latter ends of men do show their righteousness or unrighteousness, when they meet the angels of the Lord and of Satan.

For when the soul departs troubled, it is tormented by the evil spirit which also it served in lusts and evil works.

But if he is peaceful with joy he meeteth the angel of peace, and he leadeth him into eternal life.

Become not, my children, as Sodom, which sinned against the angels of the Lord, and perished for ever.

For I know that ye shall sin, and be delivered into the hands of your enemies; and your land shall be made desolate, and your holy places destroyed, and ye shall be scattered unto the four corners of the earth.

The Forgotten Books of Eden

And ye shall be set at nought in the dispersion vanishing away as water.

Until the Most High shall visit the earth, coming Himself as man, with men eating and drinking, and breaking the head of the dragon in the water.

He shall save Israel and all the Gentiles, God speaking in the person of man.

Therefore do ye also, my children, tell these things to your children, that they disobey Him not.

For I have known that ye shall assuredly be disobedient, and assuredly act ungodly, not giving heed to the law of God, but to the commandments of men, being corrupted through wickedness.

And therefore shall ye be scattered as Gad and Dan my brethren, and ye shall know not your lands, tribe, and tongue.

But the Lord will gather you together in faith through His tender mercy, and for the sake of Abraham, Isaac, and Jacob.

And when he had said these things unto them, he commanded them, saying: Bury me in Hebron.

And he fell asleep and died at a good old age.

And his sons did as he had commanded them, and they carried him up to Hebron, and buried him with his fathers.

THE TESTAMENT OF JOSEPH

The Eleventh Son of Jacob and Rachel.

CHAPTER I.

Joseph, the eleventh son of Jacob and Rachel, the beautiful and beloved. His struggle against the Egyptian temptress.

THE copy of the Testament of Joseph.

When he was about to die he called his sons and his brethren together, and said to them:—

My brethren and my children, hearken to Joseph the beloved of Israel; give ear, my sons, unto your father.

I have seen in my life envy and death, yet I went not astray, but persevered in the truth—of the Lord.

These my brethren hated me, but the Lord loved me:

They wished to slay me, but the God of my fathers guarded me:

They let me down into a pit, and the Most High brought me up again.

I was sold into slavery, and the Lord of all made me free:

The Forgotten Books of Eden

I was taken into captivity, and His strong hand succoured me.

I was beset with hunger, and the Lord Himself nourished me.

I was alone, and God comforted me:

I was sick, and the Lord visited me.

I was in prison, and my God showed favour unto me;

In bonds, and He released me;

Slandered, and He pleaded my cause;

Bitterly spoken against by the Egyptians, and He delivered me;

Envied by my fellow-slaves, and He exalted me.

And this chief captain of Pharaoh entrusted to me his house.

And I struggled against a shameless woman, ursing me to transgress with her; but the God of Israel my father delivered me from the burning flame.

I was cast into prison, I was beaten, I was mocked; but the Lord granted me to find mercy, in the sight of the keeper of the prison.

For the Lord doth not forsake them that fear Him, neither in darkness, nor in bonds, nor in tribulations, nor in necessities.

For God is not put to shame as a man, nor as the son of man is he afraid, nor as one that is earth-born is He weak or affrighted.

But in all those things doth He give protection, and in divers ways doth He comfort, though for a little space He departeth to try the inclination of the soul.

In ten temptations He showed me approved, and in all of them I endured; for endurance is a mighty charm, and patience giveth many good things.

How often did the Egyptian woman threaten me with death!

How often did she give me over to punishment, and then call me back and threaten me, and when I was unwilling to company with her, she said to me:

Thou shalt be lord of me, and all that is in my house, if thou wilt give thyself unto me, and thou shalt be as our master.

But I remembered the words of my father, and going into my chamber, I wept and prayed unto the Lord.

And I fasted in those seven years, and I appeared to the Egyptians as one living delicately, for they that fast for God's sake receive beauty of face.

And if my lord were away from home, I drank no wine; nor for three days did I take my food, but I gave it to the poor and sick.

And I sought the Lord early, and I wept for the Egyptian woman of Memphis, for

The Forgotten Books of Eden

very unceasingly did she trouble me, for also at night she came to me under pretence of visiting me.

And because she had no male child she pretended to regard me as a son.

And for a time she embraced me as a son, and I knew it not; but later, she sought to draw me into fornication.

And when I perceived it I sorrowed unto death; and when she had gone out, I came to myself, and lamented for her many days, because I recognized her guile and her deceit.

And I declared unto her the words of the Most High, if haply she would turn from her evil lust.

Often, therefore, did she flatter me with words as a holy man, and guilefully in her talk praise my chastity before her husband, while desiring to ensnare me when we were alone.

For she lauded me openly as chaste, and in secret she said unto me: Fear not my husband; for he is persuaded concerning thy chastity: for even should one tell him concerning us, he would not believe.

Owing to all these things I lay upon the ground, and besought God that the Lord would deliver me from her deceit.

And when she had prevailed nothing thereby, she came again to me under the plea of instruction, that she might learn the word of God.

And she said unto me: If thou willest that I should leave my idols, lie with me, and I will persuade my husband to depart from his idols, and we will walk in the law by thy Lord.

And I said unto her: The Lord willeth not. that those who reverence Him should be in uncleanness, nor doth He take pleasure in them that commit adultery, but in those that approach Him with a pure heart and undefiled lips.

But she heed her peace, lonsing to accomplish her evil desire.

And I gave myself yet more to fasting and prayer, that the Lord might deliver me from her.

And again, at another time she said unto me: If thou wilt not commit adultery, I will kill my husband by poison; and take thee to be my husband.

I therefore, when I heard this, rent my garments, and said unto her:

Woman, reverence God, and do not this evil deed, lest thou be destroyed; for know indeed that I will declare this thy device unto all men.

She therefore, being afraid, besought that I would not declare this device.

And she departed soothing me with gifts, and sending to me every delight of the

The Forgotten Books of Eden

sons of men.

And afterwards she sent me food mingled with enchantments.

And when the eunuch who brought it came, I looked up and beheld a terrible man giving me with the dish a sword, and I perceived that her scheme was to beguile me.

And when he had gone out I wept, nor did I taste that or any other of her food.

So then after one day she came to me and observed the food, and said unto me: Why is it that thou hast not eaten of the food?

And I said unto her: It is because thou hast filled it with deadly enchantments; and how saidst thou: I come not near to idols but to the Lord alone.

Now therefore know that the God of my father hath revealed unto me by His angel thy wickedness, and I have kept it to convict thee, if haply thou mayst see and repent.

But that thou mayst learn that the wickedness of the ungodly hath no power over them that worship God with chastity behold I will take of it and eat before thee.

And having so said, I prayed thus: The God of my fathers and the angel of Abraham, be with me; and ate.

And when she saw this she fell upon her face at my feet, weeping; and I raised her up and admonished her.

And she promised to do this iniquity no more.

But her heart was still set upon evil, and she looked around how to ensnare me, and sighing deeply she became downcast, though she was not sick.

And when her husband saw her, he said unto her: Why is thy countenance fallen?

And she said unto him: I have a pain at my heart, and the groanings of my spirit oppress me; and so he comforted her who was not sick.

Then, accordingly seizing an opportunity, she rushed unto me while her husband was yet without, and said unto me: I will hang myself, or cast myself over a cliff, if thou wilt not lie with me.

And when I saw the spirit of Beliar was troubling her, I prayed unto the Lord, and said unto her:

Why, wretched woman, art thou troubled and disturbed, blinded through sins?

Remember that if thou kill thyself, Asteho, the concubine of thy husband, thy rival, will beat thy children, and thou wilt destroy thy memorial from off the earth.

And she said unto me: Lo, then thou lovest me; let this suffice me: only strive for my life and my children, and I expect that I shall enjoy my desire also.

But she knew not that because of my lord I spake thus, and not because of her.

For if a man hath fallen before the passion of a wicked desire and become en-

The Forgotten Books of Eden

slaved by it, even as she, whatever good thing he may hear with regard to that passion, he receiveth it with a view to his wicked desire.

I declare, therefore, unto you, my children, that it was about the sixth hour when she departed from me; and I knelt before the Lord all day, and all the night; and about dawn I rose up, weeping the while and praying for a release from her.

At last, then, she laid hold of my garments, forcibly dragsing me to have connexion with her.

When, therefore, I saw that in her madness she was holding fast to my garment, I left it behind, and fled away naked.

And holding fast to the garment she falsely accused me, and when her husband came he cast me into prison in his house; and on the morrow he scourged me and sent me into Pharaoh's prison.

And when I was in bonds, the Egyptian woman was oppressed with grief, and she came and heard how I gave thanks unto the Lord and sang praises in the abode of darkness, and with glad voice rejoiced, glorifying my God that I was delivered from the lustful desire of the Egyptian woman.

And often hath she sent unto me saying: Consent to fulfil my desire, and I will release thee from thy bonds, and I will free thee from the darkness.

And not even in thought did I incline unto her.

For God loveth him who in a den of wickedness combines fasting with chastity, rather than the man who in kings' chambers combines luxury with license.

And if a man liveth in chastity, and desireth also glory, and the Most High knoweth that it is expedient for him, He bestoweth this also upon me.

How often, though she were sick, did she come down to me at unlooked for times, and listened to my voice as I prayed!

And when I heard her groanings I held my peace.

For when I was in her house she was wont to bare her arms, and breasts, and legs, that I might lie with her; for she was very beautiful, splendidly adorned in order to beguile me.

And the Lord guarded me from her devices.

CHAPTER II.

Joseph is the victim of many plots by the wicked ingenuity of the Memphian woman. For an interesting prophetic parable, see Verses 73-74.

YE see, therefore, my children, how great things patience worketh, and prayer with fasting.

So ye too, if ye follow after chastity and purity with patience and prayer, with fast-

The Forgotten Books of Eden

ing in humility of heart, the Lord will dwell among you because He loveth chastity.

And wheresoever the Most High dwelleth, even though envy, or slavery, or slander befalleth a man, the Lord who dwelleth in him, for the sake of his chastity not only delivereth him from evil, but also exalteth him even as me.

For in every way the man is lifted up, whether in deed, or in word, or in thought.

My brethren knew how my father loved me, and yet I did not exalt myself in my mind: although I was a child, I had the fear of God in my heart; for I knew that all things would pass away.

And I did not raise myself against them with evil intent, but I honoured my brethren; and out of respect for them, even when I was being sold, I refrained from telling the Ishmaelites that I was a son of Jacob, a great man and a mighty.

Do ye also, my children, have the fear of God in all your works before your eyes, and honour your brethren.

For every one who doeth the law of the Lord shall be loved by Him.

And when I came to the Indocolpitae with the Ishmaelites, they asked me, saying:

Art thou a slave? And I said that I was a home-born slave, that I might not put my brethren to shame.

And the eldest of them said unto me: Thou art not a slave, for even thy appearance doth make it manifest.

But I said that I was their slave.

Now when we came into Egypt they strove concerning me, which of them should buy me and take me.

Therefore it seemed good to all that I should remain in Egypt with the merchant of their trade, until they should return brinsing merchandise.

And the Lord gave me favour in the eyes of the merchant, and he entrusted unto me his house.

And God blessed him by my means, and increased him in gold and silver and in household servants.

And I was with him three months and five days.

And about that time the Memphian woman, the wife of Pentephris came down in a chariot, with great pomp, because she had heard from her eunuchs concerning me.

And she told her husband that the merchant had become rich by means of a young Hebrew, and they say that he had assuredly been stolen out of the land of Canaan.

Now, therefore, render justice unto him, and take away the youth to thy house; so shall the God of the Hebrews bless thee, for grace from heaven is upon him.

The Forgotten Books of Eden

And Pentephris was persuaded by her words, and commanded the merchant to be brought, and said unto him:

What is this that I hear concerning thee, that thou stealest persons out of the land of Canaan, and sellest them for slaves?

But the merchant fell at his feet, and besought him, saying: I beseech thee, my lord, I know not what thou sayest.

And Pentephris said unto him: Whence, then, is the Hebrew slave?

And he said: The Ishmaelites entrusted him unto me until they should return.

But he believed him not, but commanded him to be stripped and beaten.

And when he persisted in this statement, Pentephris said: Let the youth be brought.

And when I was brought in, I did obeisance to Pentephris for he was third in rank of the officers of Pharaoh.

And he took me apart from him, and said unto me: Art thou a slave or free?

And I said: A slave.

And he said: Whose?

And I said: The Ishmaelites'.

And he said: How didst thou become their slave?

And I said: They bought me out of the land of Canaan.

And he said unto me: Truly thou liest; and straightway he commanded me to be stripped and beaten.

Now, the Memphian woman was looking through a window at me while I was being beaten, for her house was near, and she sent unto him saying:

Thy judgement is unjust; for thou dost punish a free man who hath been stolen, as though he were a transgressor.

And when I made no change in my statement, though I was beaten, he ordered me to be imprisoned, until, he said, the owners of the boy should come.

And the woman said unto her husband: Wherefore dost thou detain the captive and wellborn lad in bonds, who ought rather to be set at liberty, and be waited upon?

For she wished to see me out of a desire of sin, but I was ignorant concerning all these things.

And he said to her: It is not the custom of the Egyptians to take that which belongeth to others before proof is given.

This, therefore, he said concerning the merchant; but as for the lad, he must be imprisoned.

The Forgotten Books of Eden

Now after four and twenty days came the Ishmaelites; for they had heard that Jacob my father was mourning much concerning me.

And they came and said unto me: How is it that thou saidst that thou wast a slave? and lo, we have learnt that thou art the son of a mighty man in the land of Canaan, and thy father still mourneth for thee in sackcloth and ashes.

When I heard this my bowels were dissolved and my heart melted, and I desired greatly to weep, but I restrained myself that I should not put my brethren to shame.

And I said unto them, I know not, I am a slave.

Then, therefore, they took counsel to sell me, that I should not be found in their hands.

For they feared my father, lest he should come and execute upon them a grievous vengeance.

For they had heard that he was mighty with God and with men.

Then said the merchant unto them: Release me from the judgement of Pentiphri.

And they came and requested me, saying: Say that thou wast bought by us with money, and he will set us free.

Now the Memphian woman said to her husband: Buy the youth; for I hear, said she, that they are selling him.

And straightway she sent a eunuch to the Ishmaelites, and asked them to sell me.

5But since the eunuch would not agree to buy me at their price he returned, having made trial of them, and he made known to his mistress that they asked a large price for their slave.

And she sent another eunuch, saying: Even though they demand two minas, give them, do not spare the gold; only buy the boy, and bring him to me.

The eunuch therefore went and gave them eighty pieces of gold, and he received me; but to the Egyptian woman he said I have given a hundred.

And though I knew this I held my peace, lest the eunuch should be put to shame.

Ye see, therefore, my children, what great things I endured that I should not put my brethren to shame.

Do ye also, therefore, love one another, and with long-suffering hide ye one another's faults.

For God delighteth in the unity of brethren, and in the purpose of a heart that takes pleasure in love.

And when my brethren came into Egypt they learnt that I had returned their money unto them, and upbraided them not, and comforted them.

The Forgotten Books of Eden

And after the death of Jacob my father I loved them more abundantly, and all things whatsoever he commanded I did very abundantly for them.

And I suffered them not to be afflicted in the smallest matter; and all that was in my hand I gave unto them.

And their children were my children, and my children as their servants; and their life was my life, and all their suffering was my suffering, and all their sickness was my infirmity.

My land was their land, and their counsel my counsel.

And I exalted not myself among them in arrogance because of my worldly glory, but I was among them as one of the least.

If ye also, therefore, walk in the commandments of the Lord, my children, He will exalt you there, and will bless you with good things for ever and ever.

And if any one seeketh to do evil unto you, do well unto him, and pray for him, and ye shall be redeemed of the Lord from all evil.

For, behold, ye see that out of my humility and longsuffering I took unto wife the daughter of the priest of Heliopolis.

And a hundred talents of gold were given me with her, and the Lord made them to serve me.

And He gave me also beauty as a flower beyond the beautiful ones of Israel; and He preserved me unto old age in strength and in beauty, because I was like in all things to Jacob.

And hear ye, my children, also the vision which I saw.

There were twelve harts feeding: and the nine were first dispersed over all the earth, and likewise also the three.

And I saw that from Judah was born a virsin wearing a linen garment, and from her, was born a lamb, without spot; and on his left hand there was as it were a lion; and all the beasts rushed against him, and the lamb overcame them, and destroyed them and trod them under foot.

And because of him the angels and men rejoiced, and all the land.

And these things shall come to pass in their season, in the last days.

Do ye therefore, my children, observe the commandments of the Lord, and honour Levi and Judah; for from them shall arise unto you the Lamb of God, who taketh away the sin of the world, one who saveth all the Gentiles and Israel.

For His kingdom is an everlasting kingdom, which shall not pass away; but my kingdom among you shall come to an end as a watcher's hammock, which after the summer disappeareth.

The Forgotten Books of Eden

For I know that after my death the Egyptians will afflict you, but God will avenge you, and will bring you into that which He promised to your fathers.

But ye shall carry up my bones with you; for when my bones are being taken up thither, the Lord shall be with you in light, and Beliar shall be in darkness with the Egyptians.

And carry ye up Asenath your mother to the Hippodrome, and near Rachel your mother bury her.

And when he had said these things he stretched out his feet, and died at a good old age.

And all Israel mourned for him, and all Egypt, with a great mourning.

And when the children of Israel went out of Egypt, they took with them the bones of Joseph, and they buried him in Hebron with his fathers, and the years of his life were one hundred and ten years.

THE TESTAMENT OF BENJAMIN

The Twelfth Son of Jacob and Rachel.

CHAPTER I.

Benjamin, the twelfth son of Jacob and Rachel, the baby of the family, turns philosopher and philanthropist.

THE copy of the words of Benjamin, which he commanded his sons to observe, after he had lived a hundred and twenty-five years.

And he kissed them, and said: As Isaac was born to Abraham in his old age, so also was I to Jacob.

And since Rachel my mother died in giving me birth, I had no milk; therefore I was suckled by Bilhah her handmaid.

For Rachel remained barren for twelve years after she had borne Joseph; and she prayed the Lord with fasting twelve days, and she conceived and bare Me.

For my father loved Rachel dearly, and prayed that he might see two sons born from her.

Therefore was I called Benjamin, that is, a son of days.

And when I went into Egypt, to Joseph, and my brother recognized me, he said unto me: What did they tell my father when they sold me?

And I said unto him, They dabbled thy coat with blood and sent it, and said: Know whether this be thy son's coat.

And he said unto me: Even so, brother, when they had stripped me of my coat they gave me to the Ishmaelites, and they gave me a loin cloth, and scourged me, and bade me run.

The Forgotten Books of Eden

And as for one of them that had beaten me with a rod, a lion met him and slew him.

And so his associates were affrighted.

Do ye also, therefore, my children, love the Lord God of heaven and earth, and keep His commandments, following the example of the good and holy man Joseph.

And let your mind be unto good, even as ye know me; for he that bath his mind right seeth all things rightly.

Fear ye the Lord, and love your neighbour; and even though the spirits of Beliar claim you to afflict you with every evil, yet shall they not have dominion over you, even as they had not over Joseph my brother.,

How many men wished to slay him, and God shielded him!

For he that feareth God and loveth his neighbour cannot be smitten by the spirit of Beliar, being shielded by the fear of God.

Nor can he be ruled over by the device of men or beasts, for he is helped by the Lord through the love which he hath towards his neighbour.

For Joseph also besought our father that he would pray for his brethren, that the Lord would not impute to them as sin whatever evil they had done unto him.

And thus Jacob cried out: My good child, thou hast prevailed over the bowels of thy father Jacob.

And he embraced him, and kissed him for two hours, saying:

In thee shall be fulfilled the prophecy of heaven concerning the Lamb of God, and Saviour of the world, and that a blameless one shall be delivered up for lawless men, and a sinless one shall die for ungodly men in the blood of the covenant, for the salvation of the Gentiles and of Israel, and shall destroy Beliar and his servants.

See ye, therefore, my children, the end of the good man?

Be followers of his compassion, therefore, with a good mind, that ye also may wear crowns of glory.

For the good man hath not a dark eye; for he showeth mercy to all men, even though they be sinners.

And though they devise with evil intent. concerning him, by doing good he overcometh evil, being shielded by God; and he loveth the righteous as his own soul.

If any one is glorified, he envieth him not; if any one is enriched, he is not jealous; if any one is valiant, he praiseth him; the virtuous man he laudeth; on the poor man he hath mercy; on the weak he hath compassion; unto God he singeth praises.

And him that hath the grace of a good spirit he loveth as his own soul.

If therefore, ye also have a good mind, then will both wicked men be at peace with you, and the profligate will reverence you and turn unto good; and the covetous will

The Forgotten Books of Eden

not only cease from their inordinate desire, but even give the objects of their covetousness to them that are afflicted.

If ye do well, even the unclean spirits will flee from you; and the beasts will dread you.

For where there is reverence for good works and light in the mind, even darkness fleeth away from him.

For if any one does violence to a holy man, he repenteth; for the holy man is merciful to his reviler, and holdeth his peace.

And if any one betrayeth a righteous man, the righteous man prayeth: though for a little he be humbled, yet not long after he appeareth far more glorious, as was Joseph my brother.

The inclination of the good man is not in the power of the deceit of the spirit of Beliar, for the angel of peace guideth his soul.

And he gazeth not passionately upon corruptible things, nor gathereth together riches through a desire of pleasure.

He delighteth not in pleasure, he grieveth not his neighbour, he sateth not himself with luxuries, he erreth not in the uplifting of the eyes, for the Lord is his portion.

The good inclination receiveth not glory nor dishonour from men, and it knoweth not any guile, or lie, or fighting or reviling; for the Lord dwelleth in him and lighteth up his soul, and he rejoiceth towards all men.

The good mind hath not two tongues, of blessing and of cursing, of contumely and of honour, of sorrow and of joy, of quietness and of confusion, of hypocrisy and of truth, of poverty and of wealth; but it hath one disposition, uncorrupt and pure, concerning all men.

It hath no double sight, nor double hearing; for in everything which he doeth, or speaketh, or seeth, he knoweth that the Lord looketh on his soul.

And he cleanseth his mind that he may not be condemned by men as well as by God.

And in like manner the works of Beliar are twofold, and there is no singleness in them.

Therefore, my children, I tell you, flee the malice of Beliar; for he giveth a sword to them that obey him.

And the sword is the mother of seven evils. First the mind conceiveth through Beliar, and first there is bloodshed; secondly ruin; thirdly, tribulation; fourthly, exile; fifthly, dearth; sixthly, panic; seventhly, destruction.

'Therefore was Cain also delivered over to seven vengeances by God, for in every hundred years the Lord brought one plague upon him.

The Forgotten Books of Eden

And when he was two hundred years old he began to suffer, and in the nine-hundredth year he was destroyed.

For on account of Abel, his brother, with -all the evils was he judged, but Lamech with seventy times seven.

Because for ever those, who are like Cain in envy and hatred of brethren, shall be punished with the same judgement.

CHAPTER II.

Contains a striking example of the homeliness—yet vividness of the figures of speech of these ancient patriarchs.

AND do ye, my children, flee evil-doing, envy, and hatred of, and cleave to goodness and love.

He that hath a pure mind in love, looketh not after a woman with a view to fornication; for he hath no defilement in his heart, because the Spirit of God resteth upon him.

For as the sun is not defiled by shining on dung and mire, but rather drieth up both and driveth away the evil smell; so also the pure mind, though encompassed by the defilements of earth, rather cleanseth them and is not itself defiled.

And I believe that there will be also evil-doings among you, from the words of Enoch the righteous: that ye shall commit fornication with the fornication of Sodom, and shall perish, all save a few, and shall renew wanton deeds with women; and the kingdom of the Lord shall not be among you, for straightway He shall take it away.

Nevertheless the temple of God shall be in your portion, and the last temple shall be more glorious than the first.

And the twelve tribes shall be gathered together there, and all the Gentiles, until the Most High shall send forth His salvation in the visitation of an only-begotten prophet.

And He shall enter into the first temple, and there shall the Lord be treated with outrage, and He shall be lifted up upon a tree.

And the veil of the temple shall be rent, and the Spirit of God shall pass on to the Gentiles as fire poured forth.

And He shall ascend from Hades and shall pass from earth into heaven.

And I know how lowly He shall be upon earth, and how glorious in heaven.

Now when Joseph was in Egypt, I longed to see his figure and the form of his countenance; and through the prayers of Jacob my father I saw him, while awake in the daytime, even his entire figure exactly as he was.

And when he had said these things, he said unto them: Know ye, therefore, my children, that I am dying.

Do ye, therefore, truth each one to his neighbour, and keep the law of the Lord

The Forgotten Books of Eden

and His commandments.

For these things do I leave you instead of inheritance.

Do ye also, therefore, give them to your children for an everlasting possession; for so did both Abraham, and Isaac, and Jacob.

For all these things they gave us for an inheritance, saying: Keep the commandments of God, until the Lord shall reveal His salvation to all Gentiles.

And then shall ye see Enoch, Noah, and Shem, and Abraham, and Isaac, and Jacob, rising on the right hand in gladness,

Then shall we also rise, each one over our tribe, worshipping the King of heaven, who appeared upon earth in the form of a man in humility.

And as many as believe on Him on the earth shall rejoice with Him.

Then also all men shall rise, some unto glory and some unto shame.

And the Lord shall judge Israel first, for their unrighteousness; for when He appeared as God in the flesh to deliver them they believed Him not.

And then shall He judge all the Gentiles, as many as believed Him not when He appeared upon earth.

And He shall convict Israel through the chosen ones of the Gentiles, even as He reproved Esau through the Midianites, who deceived their brethren, so that they fell into fornication, and idolatry; and they were alienated from God, becoming therefore children in the portion of them that fear the Lord.

If ye therefore, my children, walk in holiness according to the commandments of the Lord, ye shall again dwell securely with me, and all Israel shall be gathered unto the Lord.

And I shall no longer be called a ravening wolf on account of your ravages, but a worker of the Lord distributing food to them that work what is good.

And there shall arise in the latter days one beloved of the Lord, of the tribe of Judah and Levi, a doer of His good pleasure in his mouth, with new knowledge enlightening the Gentiles.

Until the consummation of the age shall he be in the synagogues of the Gentiles, and among their rulers, as a strain of music in the mouth of all.

And he shall be inscribed in the holy books, both his work and his word, and he shall be a chosen one of God for ever.

And through them he shall go to and fro as Jacob my father, saying: He shall fill up that which lacketh of thy tribe.

And when he had said these things he stretched out his feet.

And died in a beautiful and good sleep.

The Forgotten Books of Eden

And his sons did as he had enjoined them, and they took up his body and buried it in Hebron with his fathers.

And the number of the days of his life was a hundred and twenty-five years.

THUS ENDS THE BOOKS OF EDEN

The Forgotten Books of Eden

HERE ARE THE LATEST MYSTICAL SECRETS FROM FAMED HUNGARIAN BORN PSYCHIC MARIA D'ANDREA, REVEALED IN HER NEW BOOK AND VIDEO DRAMATIZATION

TURN AN ORDINARY GLASS OF DRINKING WATER AND AN INEXPENSIVE CRYSTAL INTO A POWERFUL ELIXIR FOR IMPROVED GOOD HEALTH, ENHANCED PSYCHIC ABILITIES AND THE FORTIFICATION OF INNER STRENGTH

Just about everyone has their favorite crystal or gemstone these days. Anyone who believes in the power of nature's most beautiful "gifts from God" realizes that there is power in them there stones. It has been scientifically proven that they can be used as psychic energizers and to greatly enhance one's life and bring about amazing benefits. **The Old Testament**, for example, is rich in references to crystals and gemstones. The breastplate of Aaron was made up of 12 gemstones, including emerald, beryl, topaz, sapphire, agate, onyx, jasper, amethyst, lapis and turquoise. These stones seemingly embraced all of the colors of the spectrum and were used to absorb or repel the radiation emitted from the Ark of the Covenant which had stored up the energy of an atomic bomb.

But do you know how to get the most out of your favorite crystal or gemstone? You can't just hold it in your hand and say abracadabra – you need to know the proper way to energize and enhance the powers that are stored up inside. Maria D'Andrea, Hungarian born psychic and shaman through the pages of her latest book and a video dramatization will teach you how to unlock the enormous vibrations that you have at your very own fingertips with a simple "trick" that includes just using an ordinary glass of tap water.

Maria's SECRET MAGICKAL ELIXIRS OF LIFE workbook and DVD study guide kit contains everything you need to know to "pump up the power" of what may seem to be ordinary stones that can be found right outside your door, turning them into highly personal talismans. The importance of a stone's shape is also described as well as what the color of a particular stone signifies. You will even find out the necessity of wearing certain crystals and gems during specific times of the week due to their astrological connections, as ruled by the magnetism of the planets.

MAGICAL STONES

Just about every type of stone has relevance in God's order of things. "Special Blessings" and protections can come to the wearer of a crystal or stone, if worn while repeating certain prayers or performing simple rituals.

Such stones can be utilized when business is bad…when you need to take a purification bath…when you need to receive information about another person…when money is needed…when you wish to attract good luck…find a new friend., or a potential lover.

You will be given specific rituals using stones that the author says can bring you great prosperity…can help in meditation…can promote harmony around you…can strengthen the user spiritually, and can grant all your wishes. There are instructions on how to turn an ordinary glass of tap water into the "Fountain of Youth" with one of the formulas given in this book. And best of all, these "Magickal Stones" need NOT be expensive gems like diamonds or rubies. In most cases, they are ordinary stones which have little – or no – monetary value and which you can easily obtain on your own.

PREDICTING THE FUTURE

Fortune tellers and diviners have always been with us. In addition to various forms of crystals, other stones can also be used to peer into the future. Using Maria's proven methods, the reader will learn how to have prophetic dreams with stones, how to pick up psychic vibrations from other people using crystals and gemstones, and how to see into the future in order to guide and shape your own life, as well as the lives of perfect strangers and those closest to you.

BIRTHSTONES AND WEDDING RINGS

Find out which stones are best suited for you according to your individual birthday and what engagement or wedding ring you should give or receive to enhance the relationship. Maria D'Andrea's **SECRET MAGICKAL ELIXIRS OF LIFE** is guaranteed to add great meaning to your life and is of importance to every person who would like to increase their position in the cosmic arrangement of things.

ORDER NOW!

Your copy of **SECRET MAGICKAL ELIXIRS** book and DVD kit awaits you. To order just send $25.00 + $5.00 shipping and handling to:

**TIMOTHY G. BECKLEY, BOX 753
NEW BRUNSWICK, NJ 08903**

AMAZING BENEFITS OF GEMSTONES

MARIA'S SECRET MAGICKAL ELIXIRS OF LIFE WILL TELL YOU HOW TO BE ABLE TO EASILY ASCERTAIN WHICH STONES ARE BEST SUITED FOR...

O Healing Purposes;
O Telepathy;
O Strengthening The Aura;
O Attracting A Lover;
O Obtaining Money And Prosperity;
O Controlling The Weather;
O Magnifying Your Desires;
O Shedding All Worries And Anxieties;
O Protection From Negativity;
O Bringing Courage To The Holder;
O Winning A Court Case;
O Use As An Elixir.

ALSO AVAILABLE — SPECIALLY PREPARED GEMSTONE KIT YOU CAN USE WITH MARIA'S BOOK & DVD

. This kit contains green agate, amethyst, carnelian, citrine, hematite, green jasper, rose quartz, green quartz, clear quartz, sodalite, and tiger's eye, as well as a vial of lavender oil and a blue bag to carry the kit in when you travel.

**MARIA'S BOOK, DVD AND GEMSTONE KIT —
All items this page just
$45.00 + $7.00 S/H**

The Forgotten Books of Eden

OTHER VALUABLE BOOKS BY MARIA D'ANDREA
– ALL LARGE FORMAT WORKBOOKS · EACH INCLUDES A BONUS DVD –

( ) HEAVEN SENT MONEY SPELLS – DIVINELY INSPIRED FOR YOUR WEALTH

Find out why Maria is called "The Money Psychic." Imagine receiving money just by using the powers of your mind. Want a new home? Or pay off an existing mortgage?

Would you like to go on an exotic "dream" vacation with someone who is sexy or your true love? Want to sell the items laying around in your garage or attic for BIG CASH? Interested in picking a large prize lottery ticket, or winning at the tables or slot machines?

Tired of seeing someone else wearing the "Bling?" Diamonds are a girls best friend, but who cares about anyone else when that fabulous stone could be around your finger or neck?

Includes Simple Money Spells DVD— $21.95

Author And Practitioner
Maria D' Andrea

( ) YOUR PERSONAL MEGA POWER SPELLS
Includes Free 60 Minute DVD – "Put A Spell On You 'Cause Your Mine!"

Hundreds of spells that are so powerful their practitioners were once put to death for being witches. Includes spells for protection against unseen forces. Spells for love and romance. Spells for drawing the cornucopia of luck into your life. Spells for creating positive cash flow to enhance your prosperity. Spells for a healthy life. Spells for divining life's purposes with positive magick. Spells for faxing your heart's desires through meditation and visualization. — $24.00

EXPLORE THE SPIRITUAL WORLD WITH MARIA - MINI WORKSHOPS AND SEMINARS NOW ON DVD

Check Off Desired Titles: $10 each
– 3 for $22.00 10 for $79.95
All 16 just $99.95

1. ( ) Rearrange Your Life With Positive Energy
2. ( ) Adventures Of A UFO Tracker With Tim Beckley And Maria
3. ( ) The Amazing Power Of Tesla Energy
4. ( ) 2012 And Beyond – What Can We Expect?
5. ( ) Manifesting A New Reality
6. ( ) Exploring The Healer Within You
7. ( ) Spiritual And Magickal Runes
8. ( ) Soul Mind Dreaming
9. ( ) Gemstones How They Rock
10. ( ) Tap To Manifest
11. ( ) Angels And The Fall
12. ( ) A Shamanic Life
13. ( ) Surrender – Effortless Techniques
14. ( ) The Power Of Planting Positive Seeds
15. ( ) Attracting A Relationship
16. ( ) Gemstones And Your Chakras

Ordering Information: Each Episode Of Exploring The Spiritual World Of Maria is approximately 30 minutes in length and are of broadcast quality. Add $5.00 for S/H.

(Because of their low price these DVDs are shipped in sleeves. Cases not included).

( ) OCCULT GRIMOIRE AND MAGICAL FORMULARY

Cover Art by Carol Ann Rodriguez

Ten books in one! – Over 500 spells! Over 200 oversized pages! With the help of this book you will learn: To manifest your own future destiny. To prevent psychic attack. To use herbal magnets. To apply candle magic to receive individual blessings. To unlock secrets of love potions. To mix the best mystical incense. To draw on the powers of crystals and stones. How prayer really works. The only true application for ritualistic oils. — $25.00

( ) SPECIAL OFFER OF THESE 3 BOOKS/DVDS BY MARIA — $59.95 + $8 P/H

ORDER DIRECTLY FROM:
TIMOTHY G. BECKLEY, BOX 753
NEW BRUNSWICK, NJ 08903

www.ingramcontent.com/pod-product-compliance
Lightning Source LLC
Chambersburg PA
CBHW080357170426
43193CB00016B/2743